THE INTERBRAIN

by the same author

**Autism Spectrum Disorders
Through the Life Span**
Digby Tantam
ISBN 978 1 84310 993 8 (hardback)
ISBN 978 1 84905 344 0 (paperback)
eISBN 978 0 85700 511 3

**Can the World Afford
Autistic Spectrum Disorder?**
**Nonverbal Communication,
Asperger Syndrome and the Interbrain**
Digby Tantam
ISBN 978 1 84310 694 4
eISBN 978 1 84642 936 1

THE
INTERBRAIN

Embodied Connections
Versus Common Knowledge

Digby Tantam

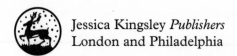

Jessica Kingsley *Publishers*
London and Philadelphia

First published in 2018
by Jessica Kingsley Publishers
73 Collier Street
London N1 9BE, UK
and
400 Market Street, Suite 400
Philadelphia, PA 19106, USA

www.jkp.com

Library of Congress Cataloging in Publication Data
Names: Tantam, Digby, author.
Title: The interbrain : embodied connections versus common knowledge / Digby
    Tantam.
Description: Philadelphia : Jessica Kingsley Publishers, [2018] | Includes
    bibliographical references and index.
Identifiers: LCCN 2017032050 | ISBN 9781849054768 (alk. paper)
Subjects: LCSH: Nonverbal communication. | Social interaction. | Social
    psychology. | Human behavior.
Classification: LCC BF637.N66 T36 2018 | DDC 153--dc23
LC record available at https://lccn.loc.gov/2017032050

British Library Cataloguing in Publication Data
A CIP catalogue record for this book is available from the British Library

ISBN 978 1 84905 476 8
eISBN 978 0 85700 856 5

Printed and bound in Great Britain

To Emmy van Deurzen, always

Acknowledgements

I thank Jessica Kingsley – a publisher of great courage and endless patience, who has gone out on a limb in support of this book. I owe the greatest intellectual and emotional debt to Emmy van Deurzen, my 'Otherbrain'. For which, I give lifelong grateful thanks.

Contents

Preface   13

A note on organization   14

CHAPTER 1. THE INTERBRAIN   17

Thought experiments   24

Connectedness and mirroring   25

Deliberate and involuntary mirroring   26

Real and not-so-real connections   27

Philosophical intuitions about connectedness   29

Nonverbal communication and connectedness   33

Types of nonverbal communication   33

Reflective or top-down nonverbal communication   34

Top-down theories of nonverbal communication   35

Communication central: the orbitofrontal cortex   37

What is theory of mind?   38

Cognitive empathy   41

A mind of one's own   42

Theory of mind and self-awareness   44

Bottom-up nonverbal communication   46

*Why non-awareness leads to denial that bottom-up
nonverbal communication occurs*   47

Bottom-up nonverbal communication that is non-reciprocal   52

Pain   56

Humean sympathy, identification, attachment,
and attribution   57

The insula and emotional flavour   61

Bottom-up nonverbal connections that are apparently innate   62

Bottom-up nonverbal connections based on similarity or
complementarity: the interbrain   63

Establishing interbrain connections   66

Gaze reflexes: orientating to the eyes and gaze following   67

Facial and other imitation   70

The mirror neuron paradigm   72

Emotional contagion   74

Shared attention   76

What makes the interbrain?   78

Notes   80

CHAPTER 2. THE INTERBRAIN IN ACTION   **82**

Introjection   84

Infancy   86

Altruism   90

Giving over to the other   93

Crowds   95

Deindividuation   96

Organismic analogies   99

People enjoy crowd participation   102

Swarms and mobs   105

Equality   108

Equality in spontaneous groups   109

Other animal swarms and interbrain connections   *110*

Are swarm-like crowds stupid?   *111*

Cohesion, crowding, and swarming   113

In- and out-groups   117

In- and out-group mobs   *120*

Religion and crowds   *121*

Two types of leader   124

Families and familiarity   126

Summary so far   127

Why this chapter is about the brain, and not about, say, extended cognition   128

Notes   131

CHAPTER 3. BEING DOMINATED BY THE THEORY-OF-MIND CONNECTION   **133**

Summary so far   133

Inner conflict   134

When does the opposition between the interbrain and the theory of mind begin?   138

Three examples of the impact of both the interbrain and the theory of mind on social interaction   *139*

Play   139

Titus Livius   142

Sympathy or law?   145

The trolley problem   148

Kinship   153

The original theory-of-mind studies   154

Narrative   157

Deceit   162

Further problems with 'mind'   163

Other people   164

Inequality   166

Gramarye   167

Notes   168

CHAPTER 4. CONNECTING TO *FINNEGANS WAKE*   *170*

When narrative truth comes into play   176

Minds and 'theories of mind'   179
   Communicating information   *180*

Perspective taking   181
   Connecting feelings   *183*

Emotional connection through narrative   187

How narratives induce emotions   188

The example of embarrassment or 'cringe'   191

The professor of signs   196

Notes   199

CHAPTER 5. CONNECTING THROUGH COMMON KNOWLEDGE   **200**

Cooperation and coordination   202

The madness of crowds   206

How does knowledge become 'common'?   207

Gaining common knowledge   209

Common knowledge and the interbrain   210

The question arises: in such a world how can people
afford to act cooperatively?   212

The public persona   214

Notes   215

CHAPTER 6. LEADERS 216

Submission 220

Obedience 221

The saving idea 224

The connection between the leader and the group 225

How does a leader gain a more permanent connection with others who become followers? 227

Emotions of obedience 228

Common knowledge 229

Disconnection 234

Disconnecting 235

Disconnecting through negativity 236

Hegemony and hate 238

Morality, demons, and beasts 239

Dehumanization 240

In- and out-groups 243

In-groups 244

Justice, obedience, honour, and duty 245

An example from Lodz 247

Notes 249

CHAPTER 7. CONNECTIONS AND MORALITY 250

War 254

What leads to war? 260

The moral importance of war 263

Terror management theory 264

What leads to terror? 264

How does war end? 267

The interbrain in war 268

What effect does war have? 272

Does the contrast between types of connections provide any guidance about conducting peace? 273

The connections of terrorists   275
    Moral panic: impersonal and disembodied   277
    Moral panic or moral terror   278
    The lone terrorist   283
    The democratization of terror   284
Another story about monsters   285
    The psychopath   289
    Who is a psychopath?   291
    Dangerous, severely abnormal personality disorder   296
    Myths about psychopathy and insights about connection   298
    The othering manoeuvre   299
    If psychopaths existed, what would they be like?   299
    Why do we connect to psychopathy?   300
Internet connections   301
Final conclusions   306
Notes   307

References   **309**

Subject Index   **369**

Author Index   **376**

Preface

When I began to work as a psychiatrist, my interests lay in social or community psychiatry, that is the study and application of the influence of families or social groups on the development, diagnosing, and outcome of psychiatric disorder. It was the alternative to other schools of psychiatry: biological psychiatry, which focused on the brain, and psychotherapy or psychological medicine, which focused on individual vulnerability and strength.

Although I also had training in all of these approaches and became a psychotherapy specialist in my work for the NHS after seven years as a consultant in general psychiatry, I thought that there was a missing dimension, which I called the 'microsocial'. It seemed to me that the interactions of two or more people were likely to be as important in understanding mental illness as the influence of large groups, in which roles and statuses were considered more important than individuals.

Working with people with autism as I have, alongside other roles, for nearly 40 years, provided me with rich opportunities to develop a microsocial theory. The fundamental problem for people with autism, it seemed to me, was not community rejection or, on the other hand, an inability to make relationships, but a disorder of the minutiae of social reaction. This was not one-sided either. It does not do to look at any social interaction as if it is between a disordered person and a fully functioning person. It is the interaction itself that must be considered. This came home to me when I told one of my patients that I was interested in nonverbal communication – 'empathy and suchlike', I said, to try to locate this interest in a contemporary discourse. I meant that I was studying why people with autism do not easily empathize with other people. But he said, 'About time. We need to know why neurotypicals don't empathize with people with autism.' Clearly, the problem was one of interaction implicating both parties, and not just one.

Once I developed these ideas about autism, it was natural to consider whether they had any application to anyone, and not just people with autism. This book is one of the results. It starts not with a focus on the individual person, but with interaction. This is not, of course, a new idea but perhaps my take on it is new: I think that the starting point is the network of interacting brains – the 'interbrain'.

A note on organization

I wanted to write a book that simplified, as much as it could, a complex subject.

I also wanted to write a book that brought together what is, I think, a considerable weight of evidence in support of the interbrain and, as it turned out, a considerable weight of evidence for narrative theories of epistemology that explain how 'facts' have become organizing foci for different and

sometimes opposed or even inimical communities. Books full
of citations inevitably become hard-going and often come to
no very great conclusion. It's much easier to read a popular
science account that provides a digest that the expert author
makes of their topic. Unfortunately, any truths that we can rely
on will always be hedged about by conditions and reservations,
and what the popular scientist provides are well-founded
opinions, more often than not.

Synthesizing these two different types of book – the
monograph and the popular account, one might call them
– is not easy. Perhaps it is even a hopeless endeavour. Even
so, I have attempted it, largely by writing the book in two
voices: a straightforward text that can be read through without
any consultation with the footnotes, and a set of more or less
detailed footnotes that provide much more detailed evidence.

Chapter 1

THE INTERBRAIN

It is hard to combine intuition with science. Not that scientists lack intuition; far from it: it is their intuition that leads them into research areas, and towards particular research questions that pay dividends if their intuitions are good. But the scientist's intuition about fruitful questions is a rather specialist one. Intuition for many non-scientists means almost the opposite of what scientists do. It means knowing things by some other route than demonstrating them.

Fred confided in me that he and Roseanne '...were crazily in love. Even over a room full of people at the office do, I would look towards her and she would look up and fix my eyes at the same time. It was like there was a cord between us, and I could almost feel her pulling me towards her. Afterwards, she said it has been the same for her. It was like telepathy almost, you know. I didn't, like, hear her thoughts but I knew she was thinking how much she wanted me. I didn't really know what it was like to love someone like that before.'

Fred knew, or thought he knew, what Roseanne was feeling. Philosophers might argue that his was not a well-founded epistemological claim. Scientists might argue that Fred's belief met many of the criteria of a delusion except that this particular delusion is so common in the early stages of sexually driven bonding that it should not really be termed a delusion, even though it is thoroughly irrational.

I would agree with both of these viewpoints when applied to much of what we claim we know about our own, or other people's, inner lives. But I think – and I will argue in this first chapter – that we can know directly about other people's emotions and what they are paying attention to. This knowledge is not propositional, like the philosopher's, nor causal, like the scientist's. It is based on a direct connection between our brain* and other people's, and between their brain and ours. For obvious reasons, I will call this the 'interbrain'.

---

* **What is a human brain?** Saying that the human brain is that organ that is contained within the human skull is straightforward anatomically. But if we consider the limits of the functional brain, it becomes less clear whether we should include other body parts, too. Movement planning, for example, does not just require computation in the brain, but also information about balance from the ears and the neck, and about the musculature's current state from muscle spindles. Then there is the strange relationship between the brain and the gut, which has its own nervous system, the myenteric plexus, which uses many of the same transmitters as are used in the brain and derives from the same embryological tissue. Fortunately, for the purpose of the argument in this book, it does not matter which of these definitions apply. It is only necessary to consider that the brain is a living, material object, whose activity can be attributed to interacting cells, neurons (and possibly glial cells), that influence each other chemically and electrically.

Applying the term 'brain' as an explanation is a little more complicated. If I say that 'my brain moves my arm', I am leaving out the agent in that statement that is clearly there if I say, 'I move my arm.' There are many philosophers who argue and have argued that the second statement is directly reducible to the first, although I would not myself agree with them. There must be very few philosophers, and no neuroscientists or psychologists, who would argue that the

I have discussed this in two previous books in relation to autism spectrum disorder (ASD), with a focus on the effects of having little or no interbrain connection. In this book, I will be concentrating on the advantages and disadvantages of having an interbrain connection, and therefore the advantages and disadvantages of what most of us would consider normality. One of its advantages is that the connection exists in the background. We take it for granted unless it is brought to the surface of our minds by passion, as it was in Fred. Being in the background means that we do not talk about it, and when we don't talk about something it hardly exists for us.

---

second statement does not also imply the first, i.e. that if I move my arm, it is only because my brain has effected the correct motor signals to my arm muscles.

If I say, 'my brain moves my arm to swat away the fly', many philosophers and scientists would argue that this is an inappropriate teleology. Brains do not have reasons to do things. Reasons belong to the realm of discourse, of justification. If I say, 'the eyes see a fly – this triggers a guarding reflex in the brain that leads to the brain moving the arm violently towards the fly', then philosophers and the scientists would be likely to be unanimously in support. The brain provides the causal mechanism but not the reason or, to use the term that the influential philosopher Frans Brentano proposed to be a determinant of mind, the intention.

The computational power of the human brain allows for much more complex activities than swatting a fly. Indeed, so complex might they be that the behaviour that they cause may give the appearance of being intentional: hence the philosophical position of monism that rejects the idea that there is a necessary distinction to be made between mind and brain. This is not the assumption that I will be making. Although I will not be setting out to justify my dualist approach, the reasons for it will become obvious as the book progresses.

Tom is rebellious and angry. He has grown up in a broken family and a broken neighbourhood. He has only got as far as he has because he learnt early on that you have to look out for yourself. No-one else would do it for you. Fighting has been one thing that he has used to look out for himself. He likes the idea of fighting wars, especially with superior hardware. He joined the army and tried to cope with basic training as he has coped with other situations, by undermining authority. Drilling seemed an easy target. 'Marching up and down,' he says. 'What a farce. Don't they have anything better to do with us?'

At the end of six weeks, marching in time, presenting arms, turning to the left or right in formation, standing at ease, and standing easy have all become second nature. Curiously, Tom also found himself proud of his training unit, defensive of the army when he goes to the pub, and upset when one of his fellow trainees fails to make the grade.

What do the military know that Tom doesn't? A lot probably, but one particular thing is germane to this example. Marching in step makes men feel that an adversary is less formidable,[1] and other synchronous movement increases altruistic concern between those whose movements are synchronized[2] and cooperation between them.[3] Marching in step also increases obedience to a leader even if that means complying with destructive actions.[4]

Tom scoffed at the drill, but it had a substantial effect on him, even so, although this effect was out of his awareness.

Rachel loved clubbing, and she thought that she would enjoy doing some more dancing, so she joined a line-dancing group. It seemed a bit naff at first, but then she started to look forward to it, finding that she came away from a class feeling more settled, as if she belonged in a way that she did not before.

Line dancing offers the opportunity of synchronous movement, like marching, although it is less clearly leader-centric and more communal. Both engender connectedness.* Rachel, like Tom, experienced a greater degree of togetherness as a result of it.

---

* Some of the experiences that people describe as being most important to them are experiences of connection. Those that occur to me, based on my own experience and on what other people have told me, include: feeling a connection with the natural world or feeling at 'one with nature' as people often say; as a parent, feeling connected to one's own newborn child; feeling connected to a partner during sex; feeling connected to other team members in a match. This is not to say that going to a match, or having sex, always creates this experience. Sometimes it creates the opposite feeling – of being alone or disconnected. When the connection happens, it seems involuntary, sometimes disturbingly so. Adults may find themselves screaming or dancing at a concert, even though they thought that they had long grown out of such adolescent behaviour, because they are swept away by the music and the atmosphere.

That we sense that we are connected to other people does not mean that we are. It may be our imagination. Philosophers often stumble over the same, solipsism, issue. How can we prove that other people exist? We may imagine that they do, but it is hard to prove it on rational grounds.

We act as if other people exist though, and that may be indication enough, as Wittgenstein argued (Wittgenstein, 1958). We phone people, text them, go online with them, meet them, live with them, and cuddle them. But people sometimes feel that they are still alone, despite doing all of these things. They report that they can see other people act, and hear their reports of their experiences, but that there is still a barrier. They argue that they can never know other people at their core, because actions are influenced by social desirability, and words may be deceptive or even self-deceptive. They conclude that each of us is fundamentally alone and separate.

Buber, a theologian and philosopher, termed the latter kind of connection an I-it relationship (Buber, 1958) and contrasted it with an 'I-thou' relationship in which a connection is not made with the other person as an object of scrutiny but with them as another 'subjectivity'. To experience another person's subjectivity is to be conscious of their sensations, experiences, and emotions with the same richness that we are conscious of our own. Schutz, influenced like Buber by Husserl's ideas, wrote: '[Intersubjectivity] is the fundamental ontological category of human existence in the world and therefore of all philosophical anthropology. As long as man is born of woman, intersubjectivity and the we-relationship will be the foundation for all other categories of human existence. The possibility of reflection on the self, discovery of the ego, capacity for performing any epoché, and the possibility of all communication and of establishing a communicative surrounding world as well, are founded on the primal experience of the we-relationship' (Schutz, 1966, p.82).

Some people with a high degree of interpersonal sensitivity and imagination might be able to feel that degree of identification, even with a fictional character. They might be able to nearly convince us that the vividness of their characterization of a person is accurate, but we would still want to be sure that it is unbiased. This would be hard to do unless there was some way of actually seeing into someone's head, to experience the other person's experience directly, perhaps through a physical connection. Imagine two of your friends are having a phone conversation. You are in the same room as one of them, who keeps whispering to you what your other friend is saying. You would get a fair idea of the conversation from this, but if it was an important phone conversation you might suggest that we listened in on an extension. That way you could hear what your distant friend was actually saying, unmediated by your other friend's ideas about what was relevant.

Pinel *et al.* (2006) set out to test their belief that feeling connected to another person is influenced by how much we wish we are connected. Their measure of feeling connected is somewhat complex, and the experimental design even more so. They did succeed in increasing or decreasing the score on their complex measure of 'I sharing' according to how similar the interests or preferences of the participant and a fictional other person were, and they did show that 'I sharing' increased if participants were 'primed' to be in touch with their interpersonal need. This was done by having the participants remember a particularly lonely period of their life (Pinel *et al.*, 2006). The authors concluded that 'I connectedness' was a kind of defence against the reality of 'existential isolation'.

Another experiment led the researchers Cwir *et al.* (2011) to a different conclusion. In this one, social connectedness between the research participant and one of the researchers was induced by a similar method to the one used by Pinel *et al.*, although this time the connection was with a real and not a simulated person. The participants' responses to a number of questions about preferences were surreptitiously passed to the researcher, who was posing as a research participant, and some of the researchers gave the same answers to the questions about preferences in important areas as those given by the participants. In the jargon of the study, these participant researcher pairs were 'connected'. Checks using tests of liking as in the Pinel *et al.* study confirmed that connected participants liked their researcher better than unconnected participants liked theirs. Two experiments were conducted, both with comparable results, but the second one was the more interesting. In this, the researcher (still masquerading as a fellow participant) ran vigorously on the spot, and the heart rate and blood pressure of the real participant, who was sitting on a chair, was measured. The participants did not exercise but observed exercise in the researcher. Researchers and participants who had been connected had a significantly higher heart rate and blood pressure rise after the vicarious exercise than unconnected participants did even though their researcher had exercised as hard.

These results demonstrate that being with someone who has an increase in activity in the sympathetic nervous system, in this case as a consequence of exercise, increases one's own sympathetic arousal without any deliberate effort being made to produce this effect. The same contagion of arousal has also been observed in people watching films of strangers running (Collet *et al.*, 2013).

More direct evidence of connection is provided by the measurement of the activity of interacting brains. One method of doing this is to measure blood flow optically by measuring near-infrared radiation (functional near-infrared spectroscopy or fNIRS). Using fNIRS, it can be shown that pairs of women and men engaged in cooperative tasks show homologous patterns of blood flow, or 'coherence', in the prefrontal cortex (Cheng, Li, and Hu, 2015).

Preparing to play a musical piece with other musicians is associated with synchronization of the neuronal rhythms of each of the players as shown in EEG studies (Dumas *et al.*, 2010; Hennig, 2014; Lindenberger *et al.*, 2009; Müller, Sänger, and Lindenberger, 2013; Sänger, Müller, and Lindenberger, 2012, 2013) and the synchronization is sustained whilst the musicians play together.

More such direct findings of brain-to-brain interaction can be expected as brain activity is recorded simultaneously in two or more interactants (Liu and Pelowski, 2014). Jiang *et al.* (2012) monitored brain activity in two conversation partners standing either back to back or face to face. There was synchronization of the activity in the inferior frontal area of the partners' brains when they were face to face, but not when they were back to back (Jiang *et al.*, 2012).

Thought experiments

At this point, I should come clean. Fred, Roseanne, Tom, and Rachel are not real people. I made them up. Even though I made them up, I believe that readers will recognize them, or someone like them, either in their own experience or in their observations of other people. I could perhaps have quoted from autobiographies to make the same points, and maybe that would be a stronger claim that these effects do occur, but it would only be marginally stronger. The illustrations were appeals to the kind of intuitive knowledge that I referred to at the beginning of this chapter. I will often be asking the reader to test my intuitions against theirs in this and subsequent chapters, but I will not be entirely relying on this. Each chapter, including this one, will include notes on what scientific knowledge, or at least scientific evidence, there is that backs up my intuition.

A great deal of this evidence comes from studies of empathy.*

---

* **Empathy:** One possible explanation of these results is 'empathy': that one feels for the person doing the exercising and this involves, to some degree, actually having the same feelings oneself. One person experiencing the feelings of another has been termed empathy since the English psychologist Edward Titchener hijacked the Greek word (which means something entirely different) in 1909 as a translation of the German 'Einfühlung' (Titchener, 2014/1909). Einfühlung had been used in German aesthetics for at least a century (Nowak, 2011) but was first applied by one of Titchener's fellow graduate students in Leipzig, Theodore Lipps, to what David Hume called 'sympathy' (Montag, Gallinat, and Heinz, 2008). Lipps inspired St Teresa Benedicta del Cruce (Edith Stein) who developed her distinct ideas about empathy as a research assistant to Husserl (Zahavi, 2014), in turn influencing Husserl's ideas and those of her friend, Max Scheler (Scheler, 1954).

   Hume's term 'sympathy' has moved its meaning much closer to its cognate Latinism, 'compassion', since Hume. Empathy has been dragged closer to this, too, and has connotations of caring or concern for others (see, for example, Decety, 2014). In this book, though, I am going to concentrate on what might be considered to be the basis of empathy – knowing the feelings, and on occasions the thoughts, of another person.

Connectedness and mirroring

Not only *my* intuition tells me (and I believe that most if not all of my readers will share this commonplace intuition) that people feel connected when they move together, in synchrony in time or congruently in space;[5] infants of 15 months old also make this judgement.[6] Synchrony and congruent posture are often considered expressions of a more general category of social interaction called, variously, 'mirroring', 'mimicry', 'emulation', 'simulation', 'dissimulation', 'mimesis', 'copying', or 'imitation'.[7] Mirroring* is also expressed by congruent facial expressions such as smiling when someone else smiles, copying another person's gesture, as in shaking hands, or copying their tone of voice. Most people will have come across the idea of 'mirroring' as an expression of closeness. It is a standard element of courses on interviewing technique, where it contributes to what are often called 'listening' or 'listening with attention' skills. Good listeners move in time with interviewees and copy their posture at key points, for example adopting the same leaning forward or backwards postures, or crossing their legs congruently.

Going on an interviewing skills course suggests that synchrony or congruence are skills that must be learnt. But the same behaviours have often been observed in people who are close and getting on well, such as mothers and babies, even without any training. It might be thought that mothers would have learnt how to mirror, but it is hard to see how babies might have learnt to do it, even though they also mirror a carer, just as the carer mirrors them.[8] In fact, the evidence is

---

* This is not quite the same usage as when a novelist of the last century would write something along the lines of 'Jonny was shocked and when turned around he say that Hubert's expression exactly mirrored his own', but clearly it is related, as is the *Looking Glass Self*, a book of lectures by Cooley in which he attributes learning about oneself from seeing the reactions of others to oneself (Cooley, 1902).

that mirroring is innate,* a kind of reflex that does not require any thought.†

Most of us probably feel that there is an innate connection between mothers and their infants, and we apply a name to the process that might usually be found labelling shelves in a DIY store – attachments or, on the adhesives shelf, bonding. Connections do not end in infancy. We might sometimes say that we feel connected, or disconnected, from the world around us.

Deliberate and involuntary mirroring

Training in customer skills might involve training someone to smile when the customer smiles, even if one's back is aching. The instructor would hope that the customer would experience his or her smile being mirrored by the sales person and perhaps

---

* And it is enhanced by another kind of innate reflex, reciprocal gaze (Prinsen *et al.*, 2017).

† Nagy introduces a special issue of *Infant and Child Development* that provides evidence that the tendency to imitate the mother's movements is present in the human infant from birth (Nagy, 2011). Infants also imitate their mothers vocally. A surprising finding about the newborn baby's cries is that they are shaped by the mother's voice prosody, usually dictated by the mother's native language, as heard by the child in the womb (Mampe *et al.*, 2009). This has been interpreted as evidence that the newborn has a reflex to imitate her or his mother. There is considerable observational evidence to support this (Simpson *et al.*, 2014).

There is also evidence that carers imitate the infant for whom they are caring and strong evidence too that the ebb and flow of imitation between mother and infant is an important determinant of the speed of the infant's social development (Wiik *et al.*, 2011) and, later, her or his language development (Masur and Olson, 2008). Mimicry of this kind has been thought to be the major evolutionary jump that has enabled the cognitive development of more recent species of Homo (Zlatev, 2014). A recent reviewer of mimicry studies commented, 'People both mimic and are mimicked in nearly every social interaction, though neither the mimicker nor the mimicked are generally aware of its occurrence. People mimic what they observe in others, including facial expressions, emotions, behavioural movements, and verbal patterns' (Duffy and Chartrand, 2015, p.112).

be unaware that this was not a kind of spontaneous mirroring, thinking it was a deliberate act by the sales person. Training for other kinds of work, for example interrogation, might go in the other direction, with the interrogator being trained to consciously suppress involuntary smiling.

Perhaps mothers might also be taught how better to mirror their babies. But there is a kind of revulsion against this. Mirroring, we think, should be 'spontaneous' and we make a distinction between, for example, the mutual smiling of two friends who have met up after a separation, and the false or social smile of the salesman who smiles only when we smile. The former, we think, means something; the latter not. It may sometimes be difficult to tell a social, feigned smile from an unforced one, even though there is a simple rule: involuntary smiles are smiles with the eyes or at least smiles in which the muscles around the eyes, the orbicularis oculi, contract. But we can feel the difference between true and intentional mirroring from our own emotional reaction to it. We may think that one person comes across as truly friendly and another person as trying to be friendly but not really meaning it. Another way of describing this is when someone says about the former kind of mirroring, 'I felt a real connection with her or him.'

Real and not-so-real connections

Roberta's mother rang and Roberta said, 'I was just thinking of you.' 'Yes,' said her mother, 'we do have a connection, don't we?'

Many daughters have a strong intuition that they have a link with their mothers (rather fewer sons feel this about their fathers, in my observation). But it's not easy to know what to make of this particular intuition. It is the same problem as the one presented by the person who argues that horoscopes are effective predictions of the future because he read a horoscope recently that uncannily predicted what happened to him the following day. And the same problem as when people believe that coincidences are meaningful or that if two bad things happen, a third can be expected. The problem is that there are many possible events that could be predicted or coincidental. We overlook many events that occur in our lives but do not fit in with our expectancy of an exceptional or supernatural fulfilment of our prediction, but focus on any that do seem to fulfil it. Even so, we are usually quite lax about what amounts to that fulfilment. The chances are therefore quite high that out of a large number of events, one will seem related enough to meet our criteria. Once we have chosen it, it becomes invested with an aura of specialness, as if just this one event was the one that we predicted – which of course it wasn't.

It is easy in this way to find confirmation of a belief by ignoring all of the disconfirmations and then fallaciously argue that the confirmation justifies the belief. We should therefore be sceptical when people claim that 'there is more to the world than these scientists know' (for example, that we are all being used for the purposes of a higher being) or perhaps, 'My daughter and I are not just ordinarily close; we are especially close, in a way that few mothers and daughters are' (for example, by telepathy).

This kind of 'wishful' intuition is not involuntary but is motivated by our reflective desires. It makes some people suspicious of all intuition and by extension of anything spontaneous. I will be arguing that there is another kind of

intuition that is not wishful but originates from our involuntary
– interbrain – connections with others, that cannot be feigned
because they arise before we can reflect on them: intuitions
like 'he likes me' or 'I can't trust him'.

Philosophical intuitions about connectedness

David Hume[9] found himself faced with the insight that he
genuinely cared about strangers, even if their destiny had no
impact on his. He attributed this to sympathy, which arose
from the automatic connection with someone who you
resemble and can therefore imagine yourself to be. His friend,
Adam Smith, in his discussion of markets, developed this idea
as the basis for the otherwise inexplicable commitment to fair
dealings[10] that made free markets possible.

Theologians like Schleiermacher were also faced with an
inexplicable giving over of self-interest in themselves and
their congregations, not in the workings of free markets but
in relation to the religious experience. There were times when
a religious person felt a oneness with God and with other
worshippers.* The experience though was not knowing God
as one might know another person because it was predicated
on the assumption that God knows each of us through and
through. So God knows us in all our subjective richness and,
in touching the mind of God, we believe that we know as
much of Her as is possible, or at least as much of Her love as

---

* Schleiermacher argued that there was a specific pre-reflective Gefühl or
  mood, which he also calls 'higher self-consciousness', which was associated
  with being with others. I would interpret this to be a specific mood that arises
  when the interbrain connection is open and active. Schleiermacher considered
  that a religious experience occurs when this mood is present and combined
  with persisting self-awareness (Roy, 1997). This is an unusual situation, as the
  emergence of a theory of mind typically requires the suppression of interbrain
  influences on actions (Launay *et al.*, 2015).

is possible for us. So our relationship with God is not like a subject with an object but like that of two subjects, hence the need for a new term: 'intersubjectivity'.* Intersubjectivity goes beyond empathy because it is a kind of fusion.†

---

* Schleiermacher wrote, 'I entreat you to become familiar with this concept: intuition of the universe. It is the hinge of my whole speech; it is the highest and most universal formula of religion on the basis of which you should be able to find every place in religion, from which you may determine its essence and its limits. All intuition proceeds from an influence of the intuited on the one who intuits, from an original and independent action of the former, which is then grasped, apprehended, and conceived by the latter according to one's own nature' (Schleiermacher and Crouter, 1988, p.24) and later, 'every intuition is, by its very nature, connected with a feeling. Your senses mediate the connection between the object and yourselves; the same influence of the object, which reveals its existence to you, must stimulate them in various ways and produce a change in your inner consciousness' (*ibid.*, p.29).

The hinge to which Schleiermacher refers is what Merleau-Ponty calls 'intersubjectivity', although, for Schleiermacher, intersubjectivity can only exist when subjectivity has emerged and set itself against the oceanic absorption in the community of other beings, through the action of 'fantasie' or imagination.

Husserl was the philosopher who made intersubjectivity best known. Husserl's ideas were complex but became clearer and sparser later in his career, and are spelt out particularly clearly in lectures given at the Sorbonne. In these 'Cartesian Meditations', Husserl grounds intersubjectivity, and the existence of a shared, known world, in 'empathy'.

Husserl does not make the distinction that Schleiermacher does between the two ways of knowing other people: 'intuition' and 'imagination'. His students, Edith Stein and Martin Heidegger, did distinguish them, or at least each championed one or other interpretation. Edith Stein (Stein, 1989) thought that empathy provided us with our knowledge of other people; Williams (2016) provides an updated version of this; Heidegger (1962/1927) thought that we simply find ourselves in a world with other people and that we have to escape from that to find our 'ownmost' (eigenste) potential. Zahavi (2016) has provided an argument against this. The tension over Husserl's intended meaning originates from the editorial disagreements between Stein and Heidegger as they were arranging Husserl's papers for publication in the book that was eventually called *Ideen II*. It mirrors the tension that Schleiermacher imagined between intuition and imagination or, one might say, between affective and cognitive empathy. I shall come back to this tension in the next chapter.

† It is interesting, and challenging, to note that both sexes enjoy this kind of mutuality but that men can only experience it after a drink or two (Fairbairn *et al.*, 2015). I shall argue later that men are often stuck in a different mode of

Daniel Zahavi, a prolific writer on this topic, describes it as follows:

> when I empathically grasp the trepidation in the other's voice or the intentions in her actions, I am experiencing foreign subjectivity, and not merely imagining it, simulating it or theorizing about it. That we can actually experience (rather than merely infer or imagine) the minds of others is, however, not to say that everything is open to view.[11]

The term 'subjectivity' that Zahavi uses refers to the special quality of experience that we have when we are in the thick of an experience, rather than aloof from it. Other epithets for this added experience are 'self-conscious experiencing', connoting a difference between reacting to something and experiencing/ knowing it; and, to refer to the extra element brought in by experiencing, 'qualia', a term emphasizing the quality of depth with which we experience, for example, a beautiful landscape and our affective or aesthetic responses to it. The philosopher Frank Jackson invented a well-known illustration of a quale. He imagined[12] that there was a neurophysiologist called Mary who had become the world expert on the physics and biology of colour vision, having read every book and paper on the subject, but who had always lived in a black and white environment. He then considered how Mary would react if she was shown a colour television or simply went outside. He thought it inconceivable that she would not discover something new. Other commentators have imagined Mary saying things like, 'So that's what "red" is like.' If we believe, with Jackson, that

---

being in which they are prepared for challenge, and therefore less open to an interbrain connection.

mere knowledge can never add up to what seeing 'red' is like, then we are asserting that there is a quality of colour, a quale, that cannot be described in books or measured in experiments on wavelengths of light. This indescribable component is the subjective experience of 'red', and having this experience is bound up with being conscious of seeing 'red'. Mary, it is supposed, would only have experienced the 'quale' of redness once she saw something red.

Consciousness is distinct from self-awareness, that is being conscious of inner experiences, including the inner experience of 'being conscious'. Being conscious of being conscious seems to be a whole new developmental stage, and may, as philosophers have traditionally assumed, be limited to human beings, angels, and gods. Being conscious, on the other hand, is now something that many animals are thought to be, at least by the participants at a 2012 conference at the University of Cambridge, described as a prominent international group of cognitive neuroscientists, neuropharmacologists, neurophysiologists, neuroanatomists, and computational neuroscientists, who signed the 'Cambridge Declaration on Consciousness' on 7 July 2012.

Other scientists have argued on the basis of a case study that human consciousness – but possibly not self-awareness – may be preserved despite a massive loss of brain tissue in what are often termed the 'higher centres'. Their research collaborator, Roger, had suffered a severe herpes encephalitis that had destroyed both of his temporal lobes along with adjacent structures like the insula, the anterior cingulate cortices, and parts of his medial prefrontal cortex. Yet, despite this, the authors of the case study show by a series of tests customarily used to detect consciousness that Roger still had it and, furthermore, that he still had self-awareness, which they describe as the 'core of consciousness'.[13]

Nonverbal communication and connectedness
Types of nonverbal communication

'Little Annie is so clever,' says her mother. 'She is only one and yet the other day we were in the kitchen and I was making some pancakes, and I could swear she was making the same movements as I was, like she was beating the batter.' Then, with a laugh, she said, 'I expect that she imagined she was making pancakes, too.'

Intuition orientates us to important observations (although, as I already noted, these are open to the bias of being wish-fulfilling) and many developmental psychologists would agree with Annie's mother's intuition that Annie was probably imitating her, as the evidence indicates that children from a young age do imitate key people in their social environment. But the inference that Annie's mother draws from this is less plausible: that Annie was imagining making pancakes. It would, for example, be hard to work out how Annie could know what making pancakes was, let alone how to do it.

Broadly speaking, there are two theories about what causes mirroring and other nonverbal communications. The first is that a stimulus – like someone else smiling – is appraised and then an appropriate response is chosen that, if it is a smile, results in a responsive smile. This is sometimes called the 'reflective' kind of nonverbal communication. The other theory is that communications from others evoke an immediate, rapid, 'reflexive' response,[14] sometimes called 'emotional contagion' or 'affect diffusion'.[15] This account was anticipated by the 20th-century philosopher Edith Stein,[16] who considered that emotional contagion could be the basis for a kind of empathy (that we would now call affective empathy), but she rejected this because empathy was not just about having the same emotions as another person, but having them and at the same time knowing that they were not one's own.[17]

Decety and Lamm[18] have given one convincing explanation of how emotional contagion might support affective empathy if a further process of self-other identification were added in. They argue for a common process of emotional generation produced by the firing of mirror neurons but with the additional activation of a flag for self-generated or for other-generated. They propose that the temporoparietal junction might be particularly involved in this flagging.

Emotional contagion does not amount to a connection between people, as Edith Stein noted, unless it is reciprocal. The affect diffuses from one person to the other, but their response diffuses back, reinforcing the expressions of both and indicating that a connection has formed. Take the smile of a person being handed a baby. The person smiles as he or she looks down at the baby in their arms, or perhaps the baby smiles, and then the person or the baby might smile more, and if the baby does, a communication or a connection takes place.*

Reflective or top-down nonverbal communication

Some nonverbal communications fit this model well. The signs that deaf people use to converse, or that builders use to

---

* Although reciprocal, the signal in one direction may be stronger than in the other. Evidence is given in articles by the following: for images of faces (Alshamsi *et al.*, 2015; Mosek-Eilon *et al.*, 2013; Tracy, Randles, and Steckler, 2015) and for gaze direction (Rombough and Iarocci, 2013).

communicate to crane drivers who are out of hearing high above them, are learnt as replacements to words. A builder might shout 'lower the load', realize that the crane driver can't hear, and so make the sign for 'lower the load' instead. The meaning is the same. Although these are described as *non*verbal, they are equivalent to words. One can tell a story with them, or a joke; one could dream in them or sign a thought to oneself with them. We can say with exactitude what these signs mean. They are generated by the same processes that generate words.[19]

At a certain age, when little Annie is no longer so little, she might deliberately imitate her mother, knowing that her mother always made pancakes in a certain way. Her use of the same movements as her mother, at this later age, might now be deliberate, a parody. It would be under her conscious control. Tackling pancakes herself, she might also ask herself how her mother mixed the batter and call to mind her mother's movements in order to emulate them.

Annie's mature use of imitation is under conscious control and is an extension of language. It has a meaning, although perhaps not quite so conventional as that of the sign for 'yes' in sign language.

Top-down theories of nonverbal communication

Annie's mother's explanation of Annie's actions is attractive because we automatically attribute intentions to behaviours that are not obviously caused. The wasp that executes a random search pattern whilst smelling for nectar seems to be deliberately aiming at those particular people who say, 'Wasps always go for me.' Something as basic as an animation involving triangles is elaborated by observers into a story of thwarted aims and conflict.[20]

Top-down[*] explanations of nonverbal communication assume that the communication has to be decoded by some kind of interpretative system. Sometimes the meaning might have to be encoded too, as in the language-like signals to the crane driver, and sometimes it is assumed that the communication is not really a communication at all, but an inadvertent leak, like the 'tell' that we have been told the clever poker player learns to associate with his opponent taking a risk or feeling triumphant because of having a strong hand. This interpretative system is at a higher level than the neurons that register that another person has made a gesture or movement.

Higher and lower, in this context, refers not to spatial location (although in a person who is standing, higher centres are at the top of the body and lower centres are nearer the feet) nor to some kind of evolutionary superiority (although the brain does, to some degree, seem to have been organized like a ramshackle building with each newer extension being piled on top of an older foundation). Perhaps the easiest definition is that a higher centre has more neurons between itself and any actions that result from its activity. The highest centres, by this definition and by customary usage, are in the prefrontal cortex,

---

[*] Recognizing and responding to another person's emotion involves a succession of processes, up to and including conscious awareness. Traditionally, this process was thought of as 'feedforward' (Gilbert and Li, 2013) in which visual stimuli were interpreted in more and more complex ways before a motor response took place. Thinking was at the top level of this processing, supported by activation of the temporal cortex, where the neuronal networks that support language are located. Current ideas are that local processing is much more complete than this traditional model recognized, and that, though they are influenced by top-down influence from higher centres (*ibid.*), even local processes can lead to directed motor responses.

Top-down processes are much more likely to apply to narrative connections than to interbrain ones (Senzaki, Masuda, and Ishii, 2014).

or the area of brain behind the forehead. This is not because they are linked to the eyes but because they are linked to the nose. The input from the eyes gets carried to the back of the brain for processing, but the receptors in the nose contact a thin extrusion of brain tissue directly.

The area of the brain that is closest to the nose is the orbitofrontal cortex. It *might* be there because so many of our most basic connections to other people are via smell. It *may* have remained there during primate evolution, because it required room for expansion and the forehead could be tented outwards without much change to the rest of the skull.

Communication central: the orbitofrontal cortex

The position of the orbitofrontal cortex *perhaps* enabled it to develop newer associations, with those areas of the brain that directed gaze, and therefore in primates attention, and those other areas in the temporal cortex that analysed and recreated complex sequences that enabled speech and language to develop from simple vocalizations and gestures. The orbitofrontal cortex's development was *possibly* further stimulated by taking over the function of tracking perspectives and then the people having those perspectives. It is large not only in primates but also in elephants, who *seem* to mentally track the movements of other members of their herd when they are far away, and whales, who communicate by shared 'songs' over great distances. In human beings the orbitofrontal cortex is also close to the speech and language areas of the brain and *can* draw on the representative possibilities provided by language to give names to people and places and to use more abstract 'perspectives' such as descriptions of attitudes, opinions, or emotions.

Of course, the association between prefrontal cortex and communication at a distance is merely that: an association. It may be spurious. I have italicized the '*seem*', the '*can*', the '*might*', the '*may*', the '*possibly*', and the '*perhaps*' above, because the stories from evolutionary psychology about why we are built as we are, are but stories. They imply a kind of purposiveness that seems to be lacking in unreflective nature. But the hypothesis put forward by Robin Dunbar that the orbitofrontal cortex is the size that it is because it plays some crucial role in us being able to converse with our acquaintances does seem to hold up.[21] Perhaps it is also true, as suggested by Dunbar and others – way back to Mesulam[22] – that it does this through its support of a 'theory of mind'.

What is theory of mind?

A commonly used expression for the ability to characterize other people is 'theory of mind'. This derives from the idea that the basis for grasping that another person has a character is that they 'see' things differently. Seeing differently might mean being able to extrapolate from the axis of another person's gaze to identify what objects are in their visual field: 'visual perspective taking'. This is a capacity that many animals have. Vultures circle at a considerable height and at some distance from each other over a terrain. When one sees a sick or dying animal, it will stoop onto it. Other vultures, seeing the stoop but not able to see the target, will also stoop down onto the same spot, having extrapolated where the vulture is aiming from its posture and direction of its glide. This is why vultures cluster around a dying animal; not because they hunt in packs – the opposite is true as they are solitary – but because they are aware of, and imitate, other vultures.

'Seeing things differently' also means having different thoughts about the same observations, and it is being able to infer these different 'inner' perspectives that is nowadays usually attributed to a putative 'theory of mind'.

The expression 'theory of mind' – ToM as it is sometimes called – was coined by primatologists[23] who were not convinced that only human beings could think. They showed that chimpanzees could correctly select photographs of people solving a complex motor problem and used this as evidence that these chimps could not only think but also recognize thinking in others. They took this to be evidence that chimpanzees understood what 'minds' were – they had a theory of mind.

Wimmer and Perner developed a test of what they called deception using puppets.[24] This test was later repurposed by Uta Frith as a test of theory of mind in children, and Uta and her then PhD student, Simon Baron-Cohen, applied it to children with an ASD. The test – termed the Sally-Anne test – required a child to watch two dolls play with a marble and then hide it. One doll, called Sally in the test, left, and the other one, Anne, hid the marble in a new place. Sally then came back and the observing child was asked where Sally thought that the marble was. Children with an ASD, and children younger than four, said that Sally thought the marble was where the child thought it was, in its new hiding place. Older, neurotypical children said that Sally would think that the marble was where she last saw it, in its old hiding place. They had, so the researchers thought, acquired a theory of mind.[25]

This important study has stimulated many others, and even led to new schools of psychological treatment based on the ability to apply theories of mind or 'mentalize'.

The original hypothesis of Baron-Cohen *et al.* was that a part of the brain, a 'module', turned on and provided the capacity for minds to be theorized, some time after the second year of life.* One might imagine it would be like adding memory to a computer, except on the memory chip there would also be some software that ran theories of mind. A much more straightforward explanation has been emerging in recent years: that children develop a theory of mind when they can say to themselves, 'Now what would Sally be saying to herself about where the ball is?'[26]

Being able to have this kind of conversation with oneself – or with another person – is, of course, very important to

---

* All of the hypotheses about the development of theory of mind have to take into account the timing of its first appearance, which is at an age when a child is beginning to show other evidence that she or he is using narrative speech. This seems unlikely to be mere coincidence but indicates that the development of one leads to the other. I think that it is most likely that the development of narrative ability, arrived at through practice in conversations, leads to a child having a mind; having a mind is an obvious prerequisite for having a theory of mind. There is some evidence for this, both in normally developing children (Fernández, 2013) and in adults with developmental disorders (Brown and Klein, 2011). Theory of mind, sometimes also called perspective taking, is acquired later in people with language delays, even when those are due to deafness and not intellectual disability. Its acquisition is also delayed in people who have conditions that reduce time spent talking to oneself about emotions (Neumann et al., 2014), and a growing body of research suggests that theory of mind is linked to the acquisition of language, particularly the acquisition of syntax (Andrés-Roqueta et al., 2013; Rakhlin et al., 2011).

Somewhere between the ages of two and five, depending on the child, children begin to use 'I' statements and manifest pretend play. Infants at this age are usually able to walk, climb, and run independently. They exercise volition about where they go (although they may have to be guided by a restraining adult in dangerous situations). They may not answer questions immediately or do what they are told immediately, but, unlike animals, are able to give reasons for not acting immediately, reasons like 'Don't want to'. This then is the age range during which 'mind' itself first shows itself, not as a theory but as a manifestation. It is the age range at which spectators recognize this and start to say things like 'She's become a little person in her own right', or 'He's certainly got a mind of his own'.

These newly formed mental capacities can be put to work to extend empathy through imagination. Mothers can tell a child who might have inadvertently stepped on one of their stuffed toys that 'Teddy is hurt. Kiss Teddy better', and the child might then spontaneously kiss Teddy better the next time he is walked on.

our social understanding.* Mothers commonly engage even young infants in one-sided conversations about what their infant was trying to do or why the little boy at play group pushed the infant. We keep track of our social world through an ever-evolving narrative that, like a good novel, contains both plot and characterization. Unlike a novel, though, it has to be tethered regularly to what we observe in reality. When we expect a person to grin when we make a joke, and they look offended, we have to change our characterization of them if we do not want to offend them again.

Cognitive empathy

Sam was not sure how she should put it to her father. He knew that she had been going steady. He liked her boyfriend. But he also wanted her to finish her college course and had no idea that she had been in two minds about it. And now she was pregnant. She decided to tell him when the rest of the family were busy. She was surprised that he took it as calmly as he did, but then she noticed the tic of his cheek that had always appeared when he was really upset. She wondered what she could do to head off the storm that she now knew would be coming. Then she had a brain wave: she'd play on his guilt and his hopes at the same time. 'I know you would have preferred me to be a boy, Pa,' she said, 'but now you can have a boy in the family after all.'

---

* I shall argue later that theory of mind is dependent on language and in particular on the speech and language functions that are required to tell a story. See the following for reviews: De Villiers and De Villiers (2014); Gamannossi and Pinto (2014); Siller *et al.* (2014).

Top-down nonverbal communication is linked to what is called 'cognitive empathy'.[*] The short fiction about Sam and her father is an example of how it is assumed to work. Sam needs to persuade her father to accept an unpalatable truth. She tells him it and then pays close attention to his face. She is concerned that her father is not upset with her – this may indicate compassion for him, or simply self-interest, but neither are themselves empathy. Her empathy is what enables her to anticipate his possible reaction, check his facial expression against it and find it puzzling, and then to use his familiar tic as a clue to his inner state. She uses this to imagine what her father is feeling, and then runs through what her father has previously said about parenting and what has previously worked to inhibit his anger. She reminds him of something that he regrets – in this case that he has secretly wished she were a boy (or at least, so she believes) – and also a hope that he has never expressed but she thinks he harbours – that he might have a grandson who will make up for him never having a son.

A mind of one's own

Sam's relationship to her father is not unlike a novelist's attitude to a character in a novel she is writing that is based on someone the author knows. The character can be more or less well realized, and its delineation lies under the constraint that the person who has inspired it might recognize themselves

---

[*] Baron-Cohen, an originator of the theory-of-mind theory of impairment in autism, writes, for example, that 'cognitive empathy…is also called theory of mind' (Rueda, Fernández-Berrocal, and Baron-Cohen, 2015, p.86), although his definition of affective empathy is very different to mine. In his view, and the views of others he quotes, affective empathy includes having an appropriate emotional response triggered by the other person's emotion: a definition with which I would not agree.

and might be flattered, or offended. However well the novelist succeeds, her picture of her acquaintance will remain that, a picture. In contrast, her narrative about herself will seem to be based on direct knowledge of an unshared inner life to which she has a kind of private access that no-one else could. Having this kind of mind of one's own is tied in to what most people think is entailed in being an individual human-being.

Sam thinks of her father with fondness and with compassion, but he is only a partly opened book as far as she is concerned. She has to reconstruct what he feels and thinks from his expressions, but it is an error-prone process. Rather like an analyst looking at images captured by a satellite, she has to work out what is going on in his mind, and there is always the danger that the images are completely misleading – perhaps there is no father at all or even no other person.

It has often been remarked that a major theme in the recent history of Western culture is the rise of individualism.[*] This is, equally often, compared to the history of Eastern culture.[27] Both cultures have emphasized the importance of mental development and literacy. Literacy, or reading and writing, allows for greater exposure to narratives and greater opportunity to create novelty than oral story-making, contrary to expectation. Oral story-telling often involves efforts to preserve a story invariantly. 'Working people out', as Sam tries to do with her father, is a discovery or perhaps a re-creation of their individuality.

---

[*] Individualism takes little account of relations with other persons, but there is a philosophical school, personalism, that starts from some of the fundamentals of modern individualism such as interiority, freedom, autonomy, and subjectivity but develops these along with the inevitability of relationship for fully human individuals. Conspicuous commentators on this approach have been Karol Wojtyla (Pope Paul II) and Roger Scruton.

Theory of mind and self-awareness

I suggested already that I agree with those who argue that having self-awareness is probably dependent on having a language-like system of communication in which narratives or stories can be constructed.* One key element of such a language-like communication system would be, as one of the founders of psychology pointed out,[28] the ability to refer to non-existents as predicates allowing for counterfactual deliberations like, 'If Mum were alive, what would she think of me now?'

As theory of mind, too, relies on narrative, it is not surprising that theory of mind and self-awareness are interrelated.† In my view, the explanatory value of theory of mind for an understanding of one kind of connectedness – cognitive empathy – will turn out, in spite of the current emphasis on cognitive empathy, to be less important than the particular theory of mind that is a theory of our own mind. Enriching our theories of mind benefits both cognitive empathy, or empathy for others, and the amplitude of our narratives about ourselves.‡

---

* For a detailed discussion of this, and one supportive of many of the philosophical points that I consider later about consciousness and belief, see Hacker (2013). Of course, language might not be the first step that humanity took away from its un-self-aware hominid cousins. Zlatev argues that conscious imitation comes first (Zlatev, 2014).

† But narratives are not just about intentions or reasons; they may also be about facts and causes (Carney, Wlodarski, and Dunbar, 2014).

‡ I am conscientiously avoiding using words like 'self' or 'self-concept' here because I think that these reifications are objectifying and restrictive. I prefer – as an influential psycho-analyst once exhorted (Schafer, 1976) – to use reflexive verbs. An apocryphal story about Carl Rogers provides an illustration of the difference. Rogers had a patient who was hard-going (one assumes). Rogers would ask him, 'How are you today?', and the client would ask him what Rogers meant. So Rogers would clarify this by saying, 'I meant how are you feeling today. How are you in yourself?' After a few repetitions the client would respond by talking about how his self was doing, and Rogers just let him.

So in psychotherapy, personal insight – the ability to provide a plausible narrative for our own actions – is often seen as a step towards greater empathy for, or insight into, other people. But an internal narrative – what we tell ourselves about our hopes, desires, and aims – creates an encapsulated inner world. We may share some of this narrative with other people, but there will usually be some part of it that is not disclosed. It is this internal narrative that creates a sense of agency and positions us in the various social constructions, themselves the products of a narrative consensus, that matter to us – our status, the esteem that others hold us in, our capacities as social actors, and so on.

Theory of mind therefore both provides and takes away connectedness. It takes it away because it creates an 'inner world' of unshared narrative, the contents of minds or souls that we believe are known fully only to each of us (and possibly a supernatural agency). Children have, it seems likely, only started on this process of self-narration. They may still find that adults do seem to anticipate what they are thinking and can, as it were, read their minds (perhaps this is the origin of the fiction of the supernatural agent who can see right through us). But as the narrative deepens and branches away from standard cultural and family stories, our inner world seems to expand and, as it does so, the barriers between us and other people may seem greater and greater and our connectedness to them seem to shrink.*

---

* I have already suggested that mind and brain are opposed, and I shall be providing much more evidence later in this book. One of the pre-conditions of mind, I shall argue, is that it is solitary and self-centred. I am taking mind to include our thoughts and narratives including those thoughts and narratives about our own thinking. If we are verbal thinkers, we typically begin these thoughts with the word 'I' or frame them within our own personal perspective. If I think about someone else, it is my description of the someone else. If I think in images, these are typically images that I am looking at. If I am touched, it feels very different

Bottom-up nonverbal communication

Cognitive empathy seems like an effort that is open to mistakes. We can easily be mistaken in our valuation of other people's feelings because language allows us to converse about what is not real or not true just as easily as what is true. We can conceal or deceive using cognitive empathy and can equally be deceived. On the other hand, we can grasp exactly what we think motivates someone else, because our narrative about it is already couched in the same medium – language, or something language-like – that we use for thought.

Other kinds of connection are different.[*] Smells connect people, as they connect animals, into groups,[29] and they move us in some way or another. But it's difficult to say what they mean. We can be mistaken about a smell, but it has a given-ness that speech lacks. Most of the time when we smell something we take it that we know we are smelling it and what kind of smell it is. Smell is non-specific, and smells are not emitted in order to communicate. Nor do we reply to a smell by emitting a smell ourselves (I exclude the gross farting exchanges that some drunken men seem to enjoy because here the smells are deliberately produced). Alarm cries, eyebrow flashes, and tail flicks in deer or rabbits also trigger actions non-selectively in conspecifics, and sometimes transspecifics,

---

to me touching someone else because it is me touching. If I see something, it is from my viewpoint, i.e. somewhere just behind my eyes. I hear something and I sense its distance and direction from me. To be asked to think about my brain being multi-local simply defies thought and imagination.

[*] Lübke and Pause (2015, p.141) conclude from a detailed review of chemosensory signals between people that 'The ability to sensitively detect relevant chemosensory social information, accurately process this information and then show appropriate responses meeting the given situational requirements might thus inevitably underlie successful formation and maintenance of social groups.'

too, who can observe them. They are arguably most influential in human beings at the ends of life when smell becomes an important determinant of behaviour.

An anecdote from Christopher Ricks' life of the poet John Keats[30] provides an example of the operation of a signal similar to the tail flash but in human society. Keats was exquisitely sensitive to shame or embarrassment. Keats would become increasingly uncomfortable in company, Ricks writes, if others around him began to touch or rub their noses – usually without any awareness that they were doing it – sometimes to the extent of blushing or having to leave. Contagious nose touching, like the tail flick of the deer, is a signal of danger, although in this case the social danger of someone behaving badly. This kind of social danger, like the threat of predation in deer, wants to make people run away and leave the source of the shame behind. Keats was so susceptible to this danger that he would run away long before other people thought that the danger had reached a level where flight was required.[*]

Why non-awareness leads to denial that bottom-up nonverbal communication occurs

Top-down nonverbal communication is, like speech, mediated by reflection and, as such, we deliberate about it and are consequently able to be aware of it. Tail flicks, nose rubbing, and other signals are not deliberated upon, they are 'reflexive'. As a result, we only become aware of them by naturalistic

---

[*] A psychiatrist would probably consider this an example of social phobia. Social phobia is often described as 'morbid self-consciousness'. Interestingly, Keats had his own related theory about this. He argued that a poet must cultivate their negative capacity (Meares, 1983): his or her ability to set their own dispositions aside to allow into their poetry aesthetic elements that the verse needs but the poet finds repugnant.

observation. Most of the time they are not kept in mind, as the expression goes.* Our awareness of our ability to feel for others bears no relation to the strength of our connection with them.[31] This might be one reason that bottom-up nonverbal communication has received so much less study than verbal communication.

In many cultures, individuals are imbued with a sense that they are unique, autonomous, selves. They are held responsible for our uncoerced actions from an early age and told that they cannot blame others for choices that they make. As a product of this culture, we might know that Hegel argued that in every relationship there is an element of the master and the slave, but we pride ourselves (if we can) on not being anyone's servant, let alone their slave. Our bodies in particular should be inviolate, we consider. Rape, child abuse, and forced prostitution seem

---

* This becomes clear from studies of people with 'split brains'. Split brains are not really split. People who are described as such have had an operation to sever a very large bundle of nerve fibres that is the principal connection between the two halves, or hemispheres, of one part of the brain, the neocortex. Experiments on people who have had hemispherotomies have demonstrated that both sides of the brain can deal to some degree with language, although it is overwhelmingly one side (normally the left side) that processes language and is therefore particularly important for much of what we conventionally term mind. The right side of the brain does have access to the senses independently of the left and can provide a person who has had the operation with answers to problems. However, if one problem is presented to the left eye, linking to the left brain, and another to the right eye, linking to the right brain, and neither eye can see into the other's visual field as a screen is placed perpendicular to the forehead of the person being tested, the results suggest that momentarily the person has two brains acting independently. The left brain does not get information about what the right brain is working on and is not able to make that available to be 'talked about' mentally. To put it another way, the person is unconscious or unaware of what the right brain is doing but not what the left brain is doing. The person deals with this by ignoring what is being presented to the right eye, even denying that anything has been presented at all. It is otherwise just too difficult to think of having information from two partly connected brains. One mind, one brain seems to be the implicit rule that our minds live by.

to us particularly abhorrent. 'Our bodies, our own' has been the slogan of the women's movement but extends further to this idea that it seems so obvious a statement that it forces us to think more deeply. Could our body really be shared? Or could we share another person's body? Of course, our bodies are separate from other bodies. We cannot, except in stories or video games, of which there are many, be transferred into a different body.*

---

* Bodies are not so entire or separate as we would like them to be.

Somewhere along the way our human cells were not inviolate and fused with another organism to form a composite. Most organisms with a nucleus ('eukaryotic organisms') are composed of cells carrying a colony of ancient symbiotic bacteria that live inside the cell and have been passed from one generation to another for at least 1.45 billion years (Martin, 2010). Cytologists consider them to be intracellular 'organelles' and call them 'mitochrondria'. Different organisms have paired with different bacteria. Our cells may contain quiescent viral particles too. Some are potentially dangerous parasites, although at least one, HERVH, is a vital symbiont: it turns primate cells into stem cells that can then become other kinds of cells (Lu, 2014). Viruses may be more helpful to bacteria, as they may latch on to bacterial genes and transport them from bacterium to bacterium. Some people think that some human DNA has got there from other organisms, carried by viruses.

Separateness is much less of an issue to some other organisms. Slime mould that exist as single amoeba-like cells can join together with other individual organisms and form a unified body. This can later break apart into cells again, each of them behaving as individuals (Bonner, 2009). Of course, these are, as we say, very primitive organisms. No animals with a skeleton could pull off a trick like that. Or could they? Viviparity, giving birth to live young, means that for many weeks – on average 40 in the case of people – foetuses grow inside a mother, one body inside another. There are special arrangements to ensure that each has a separate blood supply, but these blood supplies are connected by diffusion, in the same way that our lungs are connected to the air we breathe, and our bowels to the food we eat and the waste that we excrete. The foetus gets its food and oxygen that way, from the mother's blood, and also passes his or her waste products back to the mother. So a pregnant woman is pulling off the same amazing feat as a slime mould: turning one body into two.

It used to be thought that the foetus was a kind of parasite at worst or a commensal organism at best: growing at the expense of the mother but not contributing anything to the relationship. Some pregnant women do feel that way, but most feel happier as a result of having the baby (Tyrlik, Konecny, and Kukla, 2013). Mothers think of their baby a lot as the pregnancy progresses

The tail flick of one deer causes the gluteal muscles of other deer nearby to stiffen, ready for a leap and then a run. We could make a kind of case for saying that the deer who was

---

(Lara-Carrasco *et al.*, 2013) and, indeed, fathers may, too. Some mothers may talk to the baby, and many mothers feel a particular sense of contact when the baby starts moving. Parents become emotionally 'attached' (van Bakel *et al.*, 2013). So babies in the womb do give something back, even if it is not DNA like viruses, or energy like mitochondria.

In a way it is strange that we describe this as attachment, because the baby is literally attached to the mother, but not to the father, and yet the same word is used for both. What people mean by this kind of 'attachment' is not, though, a physical one. This kind of 'attachment' was first described by two founders of the science of animal behaviour, Konrad Lorenz and Nico Tinbergen. The concept was extended and applied to people by the psychoanalyst John Bowlby (1969). It starts with some kind of link – Bowlby called this a bond – between the carer and the baby. Lorenz studied birds, particularly birds like geese or ducks that are born in rudimentary nests on the ground. These birds have to be able to run almost as soon as they hatch and are already developed enough to do so (this is called 'precocial' development by biologists). Human beings are 'altricial': we require a lot of continuing parental care before we can run from a predator. Precocial birds have to bond very quickly, over a distance. Lorenz called this distance bonding 'imprinting' (not to be confused with the same term used for quite different purposes by geneticists). Other animals can bond more slowly, and smell plays an important part in this, although maternal recognition also develops quite quickly in people, too.

Foetuses are physically attached to their mothers by the placenta (which is embryologically derived from the embryo and not the mother) but they can only communicate chemically, via diffusion within a 'portal system', an intermingling network of blood vessels, some belonging to the mother and some to the foetus. No nerves run from mother to foetus or back. The mother cannot see the foetus, although she can feel its movements. The foetus can feel the mother and can hear her (as well as hearing some environmental sounds). The foetus produces hormones that affect the mother and is in turn affected by the mother's hormones (Guibourdenche *et al.*, 2009). The mother influences the foetus in surprising ways: the flavour of what she eats creates taste preferences in the foetus that are disclosed only after birth (Schaal, Marlier, and Soussignan, 2000); and foetuses discriminate between the voice of their mother and another woman (Kisilevsky *et al.*, 2003), apparently being calmed when their mother reads poetry out loud, as demonstrated by a slowing of their hearts, but not when someone else does it (although their heart rates do speed up then). Maternal stress and cortisol levels also have substantial effects on the development of the foetal brain (Glover, 2007).

the source of the signal was controlling the brains of the other deer, inasmuch as the source deer's signal caused the gluteal contractions of the other deer. We could even say – if we were not so sure that the physical separation of two bodies was the major criterion for each having a separate identity – that the source deer had for a short time usurped the action controller in the brain of each of the other stiffening deer and had for a short while taken over the other deer's brain. Of course, this is not like 'taking control' in the sense of a deliberate action. It is quite possible that the source deer does not link the movement of the haunches of other deer around it as a consequence of its own tail flick.

We tend to exaggerate intention and diminish the importance of 'wired in' or habitual responses. This may be because neurotypical individuals tend to apply mentality to any movements of unknown cause as noted previously, although the same bias does not seem to apply to decision-making.[32,*]

The bottom-up hypothesis of nonverbal communication is that there is a class of nonverbal communications that are mediated reflexively. Though involving many more neurons than the dog's scratch reflex, these reflexes are already present in the newborn, well before the development of language, and well before the higher centres that appear to be required for

---

* A dog scratching an itch with its hind paw looks very purposeful. But Charles Sherrington, a Nobel prize winning physiologist, demonstrated that when dogs scratched an itch with their hind leg, it needed only two neurons: one to carry the input from the itch receptor and one to carry the impulse to the muscle that worked the leg (Creed *et al.*, 1938). This spinal reflex is about the lowest level one could get in the hierarchy of the nervous system. The dog may become aware of the itch, and it may make other movements to rid itself of a presumed flea. Or it may stop itself scratching if food is presented that requires a different kind of movement. But the original action, the scratch, comes first, and the notice of this is then sent up the nervous system where it may engender some further top-down control.

deliberation are fully connected to the rest of the brain. This class of communications includes the signals mentioned above, but also includes communications that are based on similarity or complementarity.*

We are not conscious of this kind of nonverbal communication, just as we are not conscious of many of our interactions with the physical environment.[†]

Bottom-up nonverbal communication that is non-reciprocal

There are many nonverbal expressions that elicit involuntary or reflexive behaviour in receptive conspecifics. They span olfactory, auditory, tactile, and visual modalities.

Olfactory signals are probably less important in humans than in other vertebrates but, even so, we respond emotionally[‡]

---

* This kind of 'iconic' communication was first described by Peirce (Peirce *et al.*, 1883) although in the context of connections in logic and not connections between people. It occasionally reappears in discussions of signification, for example in early Freud (1913).

† An example of complex interactions with the environment is provided by people with 'blindsight' walking through a littered room. Blindsight results from damage to the visual cortex and can also be produced temporarily by magnetic stimulation of the back of the skull, under which the visual cortex lies. People cannot see, i.e. not see consciously what they are looking at, without the relevant area of the visual cortex processing the stimuli before sending them forward to the front of the brain. But they may still perceive and react to objects in their visual fields and move to avoid them, because another area of the brain – the lateral geniculate bodies – also gets visual information and processes it well enough to alter locomotion (there are other areas of the brain that also get visual information that alters brain output, and some researchers have implicated them in blindsight, too).

‡ One well-worked-out example of this is the characteristic smell that is linked to each of the cell-surface proteins in the group of proteins called human leucocyte antigen (HLA) proteins, each coded at a genetic locus called the 'major histocompatibility complex' (MHC). Having a particular MHC gene confers increased immuno-effectiveness against a range of pathogens, and having

to the smell of ourselves and other people. Smell is also important in the first few hours of life as a neonate human has enough locomotor function to be able to crawl up the

---

another gene confers increased immuno-effectiveness against a slightly different range. So it is advantageous to have two different alleles at this locus on each complementary chromosome, i.e. to be heterozygous. The chances of this are greater if one parent has one allele and the other parent has another. As it turns out, women find the smell of men with a different MHC gene (or allele) to themselves more sexy and, presumably, are more likely to reproduce with them. Tiny fragments of nine peptides long can be prepared by fractionating HLA antigens, and, in another study, researchers have found (controversially) that people can also detect tiny amounts of these in that they can say that water containing a nonapeptide that is derived from their own HLA protein is more 'self-like' (Milinski *et al.*, 2013). Smell may be a factor that influences parental care, in that fathers exhibit more affection for children who smell like them and therefore appear to be kin. Mothers punish children less if the child has a smell that indicates that the child is kin (Dubas, Heijkoop, and van Aken, 2009). For a review see Lübke and Pause (2015).

Detection of non-volatile smells such as the HLA proteins (in the experiment quoted above, participants had to sniff their armpits, so ensuring physical contact between the nose and the cloth impregnated by the nonapeptide solution) is carried out in other vertebrates by a special olfactory organ in their noses called the vomeronasal organ. This is linked to mid-brain areas, such as the hypothalamus, that control hormone production. There are five genes for the synthesis of vomeronasal receptors in humans, and one specific stimulant, hedione, has been discovered (Wallrabenstein *et al.*, 2015). Although the existence or otherwise of the vomeronasal connection in humans is contentious, it may operate in the womb, when the foetal nose is submerged in amniotic fluid.

Olfaction in humans largely involves aromatic substances that are carried by the air and which stimulate receptors in the nose that output to a specialized part of an area of the brain that has developed more recently in evolutionary history than the mid-brain, the olfactory cortex. The olfactory cortex, or to give it its Greek synonym, the rhinencephalon or 'nose brain', is itself much 'older' than the newer or neocortex. On the surface, this might suggest that smell was more important for our ancestors than for us, and indeed the canine sense of smell is a million times more sensitive than ours, and the grizzly bear's, seven million times more than that. Smell as a marker of disease, contamination, or decay remains a sense that has the important function of preventing us from eating rotten food and avoiding diseased and possibly infectious material.

The insula part of the olfactory cortex (Keller and Malaspina, 2013) has become linked to judgements about potential harms with a special link to 'digust' and 'nauseous' stimuli such as nauseating pain.

mother, and will do this towards the greatest concentration of the smell of the amniotic fluid, which is mimicked by the secretions of the Montgomery glands around their mother's nipple.[*] Neonates rarely have to do this of course: someone usually puts them on the nipple. Anosmic babies thrive just as well as babies with an intact sense of smell. Culture has taken over from most of our olfactory reflexes.

The hunting mammal needs to be able to evaluate smell to decide whether a particular smell is an indication of another bear, food, fire or other danger, and so on. This function is performed by secondary association areas, probably including the insula,[†] an area of the brain between the temporal, parietal, and frontal lobes that receives afferents from both the nose and

---

[*] Mother and baby, and probably father, too, connect through touch, smell, vocalizations, and mutual gaze. The smell of the breast may be particularly important in the very early neonatal period. There are glands in the breast around the nipple (Montgomery glands) that are attractive to infants and guide them to the nipple (Doucet *et al.*, 2009), augmented immediately after birth by the smell of the amniotic fluid that has spilled onto the mother's skin and to which the baby has become accustomed. The first intentional action of the newborn infant is performed if she or he is not moved to the breast. Called the 'breast crawl', the infant crawls up the prone mother's body following these smells to reach the nipple.

   Smell and lip sensation are both important in suckling, but only smell is essential (Yokouchi *et al.*, 2007). Mothers with more Montgomery glands have babies that thrive faster than the babies of mothers with fewer, whose nipples are less smelly (Doucet *et al.*, 2009). As soon as the baby begins to suckle, it triggers a surge of oxytocin release, the 'let down reflex' that squirts milk from the milk ducts, giving the baby its first taste of mother's milk. Contact between a carer and the baby that he or she is caring for is intrinsically rewarding to both, with this contact – presumably a special kind of grooming – associated with a surge of endogenous opioids (Broad, Curley, and Keverne, 2006). Oxytocin and vasopressin also increase the calmness that a mother has when cuddling her baby (Uvnas-Moberg, 1996). It has been assumed that the pleasure that both mother and infant receive is a component in the development of the mother–infant bond (Gregory *et al.*, 2015), although if the contact is associated with breast-feeding, the infant's pleasure is also augmented by having a full belly (Nowak *et al.*, 2007) and the mother's by local stimulation of the nipple.

[†] Although there is some conflicting evidence (Boucher *et al.*, 2015).

taste buds in the mouth. This secondary association area has, with the dwindling of the importance of smell in hominids, taken over dealing with danger both within the organism and without, something that is mediated by smell, too.[33] Dangers within include eating bad food, and the insula mediates nausea and vomiting. Dangers without include the potentials for contamination or infection, for pain, or for social rejection. There are a variety of emotions that are produced by these external dangers including disgust (the nearest equivalent to nausea) and hurt.

The insulae are the areas of the brain that have enlarged most compared with the chimpanzee,[34] suggesting, perhaps, that there is something uniquely human about them. They have particular connections to the amygdalar nuclei, to the anterior cingulate gyri (from which they are not clearly differentiated), and to the orbitofrontal cortex. Their unique, spindle-shaped von Economo neurons are presumed to play a role in their actions, which include receiving internal input and mobilizing a response to distension in the viscera, for example nausea and vomiting if the upper gut is over-distended, and also appraising external threats to the person. It is sometimes said that the insulae are at the centre of a mirror network, but what is mirrored is not one person's facial expressions in another person's face, but the insides of one person with the outside environment of that person. So the sight of a mutilation may make us nauseated as well as disgusted, and the experience of being about to be sick may feel disgusting.*

---

* The link between smell and a response to disgusting multimodal stimuli continues to be preserved to some degree in human beings in that people born without a sense of smell (the congenitally anosmic) appear to compensate for this by being more accurate in their judgement of other people's facial expressions of fear and disgust (Lemogne *et al.*, 2015). Despite this, there is a link between acuity of olfaction and empathy (Mahmut and Stevenson, 2016), perhaps mediated by attachment.

We imagine that bears and dogs live in an olfactory world and that their experience is constantly changing as one smell comes and another goes. I imagine this being like playing a game of blind man's buff and hearing the referee shouting 'warmer' or 'colder' as one moves and turns, a constant commentary on what is in the environment. The insular cortex, I speculate, provides human beings with something similar, but it focuses on a person's status either internally or in relation to external threats to personal integrity, which would include threats from other people. Emotions that are linked to status are termed self-conscious and they include pride, shame, embarrassment, disgust, and hurt. These may be elaborated into emotional attitudes, such as Schadenfreude or pleasure in seeing someone else lose out. The insula-related network appears to be central to all of these.[35]

The insular network is a highly specialized receiver of nonverbal signals touching on the future receiver's health and well-being. It is not reciprocal, unlike the mirroring system to be considered below. It is not mediated by one person mirroring another – facial expressions of disgust are not involuntarily mimicked by other people.[36] Even so, it is often considered an empathy system, and this is primarily because of the importance of the insular network to vicarious pain.

Pain

Pain may be associated with a variety of facial expressions but they are only recognizable at no more than chance[37] by other people. Despite this, the insulae are the centre of a pain recognition network. Unlike the interbrain network, the insulae respond to signals and not to faces or other bodily cues: signals of injury, malformation, or situations threatening them that provoke nausea or disgust.[38] This is sometimes termed 'empathy for others' pain', and Decety and his colleagues regularly call this 'affective empathy'. But empathy is probably a misnomer; compassion may be more like it.[39] Compassionate responses to others' pain – 'feeling another's pain' is another way of putting it – are strongly associated with grey matter volume in the insulae[40] and with insular activation.[41]

Humean sympathy, identification, attachment, and attribution

David Hume was particularly interested in what causes a sympathetic response to other people in trouble. He[42] attributed it to a 'propensity we have to sympathize with others, and to receive by communication their inclinations and sentiments, however different from, or even contrary to, our own', and that if this communication is a persuasive strong one, we can readily start to think that those inclinations and sentiments are our own. Three factors strengthen the communication. Hume mentions resemblance and contiguity in this passage but later in the book also considers affection.

It is not always clear in Hume's use of the word which meaning of 'affection' he is using: what the Oxford English Dictionary terms '1a. The action or result of affecting the mind in some way; a mental state brought about by any influence; an emotion, feeling' or '2a. Favourable or kindly disposition towards a person or thing; fondness, tenderness; goodwill, warmth of attachment. Esp. in early use also more strongly: love (for another person) (*obs.*).' Perhaps for Hume they were linked in the sense that we are more likely to resemble and to be contiguous with other people for whom we have an attachment, and therefore the impact of their passions on us will be stronger, i.e. more affecting.

Hume's ideas have had long-standing, if indirect, influence. Freud put resemblance and contiguity (although he called them Verschiebung, 'displacement', and Verdichtung, 'condensation') at the centre of his early psycho-analytic theories, and identification was central to the later theorizing. Why we identify with some people and not others was not clearly spelt out by Freud, and Hume did not specify why a person had an affection for another, but both used the parent and the child as a paradigm. Attachment theory* provided a rationale for why we care for some people and not others: we become attached to them.

---

* Attachment has become a well-recognized, and well-researched, phenomenon since its original description by the naturalist Lorenz and the psychologist Tinbergen. As its name indicates, it is an example of an invisible connection between animals that behaves like a physical one. Other names for attachment include bonding, bond, or link. Group psychotherapists, sports and occupational psychologists, and cultural theorists also use a glue metaphor for something that they speculate holds a small group of people together – cohesion. Cohesion in group therapy is when, to paraphrase Yalom (1975), being in the group attracts rather than repels its members. It corresponds to the development of the kind of crowd described by Canetti (1984), when proximity seeking replaces the normal instinct for people to distance themselves from each other.

    Attachment is selective. Here, for example, is the account of a study by Manini *et al.* (2013) in which mothers watched their infants playing with toys provided by an experiment. The mothers were watching through a glass window and were being filmed, as their children were, by an infrared camera. Mothers watched their own children, and also other mothers' children. At one point during the play sequence, the children were given a toy that had been made to break, and the children were upset by this. Upset, in this situation, leads to an increase in sympathetic arousal, and blood flow in the nose is a good measure of this. So the children's noses became warmer, and this could be detected by the infrared camera. A mean of seven seconds later, the mothers' noses also got warmer, but – and this is where the selectivity comes in – with the increase being significantly greater if the mother was observing her own child than if she was observing another child. The authors interpret this to mean – and I agree – that mothers have a special link with their own children that, in this case, carries shame or embarrassment from one to the other. It is not a direct transmission, though. Seven seconds is plenty of time for the mother to observe the situation,

Hume's father died when he was young, but his mother never remarried. Perhaps she is the inspiration for an example he gives in both the *Treatise*[43] and the *Enquiry*[44] of how children would feel if their widowed mother would marry again. He was sure that their affection for her would drop and

---

evaluate it, appraise it as one that might lead to a negative judgement of her child and therefore possibly of herself, and become upset.

Attachment theory was developed by John Bowlby (1969) as an application of animal attachment theories to human beings. The function of attachment in mother and infant animals is apparently to maintain a safe distance between them: enough that the infant can explore, but not so far that the infant cannot rush back to the mother if threatened. There is a constant communication between mother and infant, sometimes involving specific vocalization on the infant's part and also, in the case of animals that are mobile from an early age like sheep, on the mother's part, too. Bowlby thought of attachment in humans as means not just of maintaining physical proximity but also of keeping arousal, or separation anxiety, at an appropriate level. Too little anxiety regulation and the child would stick too closely to the mother.

Attachment theory went beyond the existing ethological models in taking account of the child's representational system, their thinking. Some children had mothers whose proximity did not reduce anxiety because they were too preoccupied in some way to be aware of or to respond to threats to the child. Children with mothers like that stopped representing their mothers as a source of 'security' and became 'avoidant' of them instead. At the time that Bowlby and his students, Ainsworth and Main, were developing attachment theory, Harlow (Cross and Harlow, 1965) was carrying out experiments on surrogate mothering and showed that a particular kind of touch was essential for the social development of macaques. Attachment theory assimilated these ideas, paying attention to the mother's ability to soothe their infant, not just by proximity but also by touch. Anxious mothers tended to be less effective at this, it was argued, and so had anxious children – although another possibility was that anxious mothers had a hereditary disposition to anxiety and it was this that they passed on to their children (Kagan and Snidman, 1999).

Mothers provide soothing preferentially to their own babies, and indeed relate to their own babies differently to the babies of other mothers, as the previously quoted study by Manini *et al.* demonstrated. Sometimes this selectivity is imagined as being subserved by a quasi-physical link, the 'affectional bond'. Affectional bonds between mother and infant are created early in life, so suddenly in some animals that Lorenz called the phenomenon 'imprinting' and supposed that the first image that the infant saw was pressed into them as if into wax and became their mother.

therefore their sympathy.* Once again, Hume has anticipated a further influence on whether or not we feel for the person in pain as well as feeling for the painful situation. Our reaction to others' pain is influenced by cognitive factors, for example how we judge another person's previous actions. Our determination of whether or not we sympathize with another person is influenced by whether or not we think that they deserved the pain – whether, to revert to the gustatory focus for insular activity, they acted in good or bad taste or, to put it another way, whether to act for them or against them will leave a bad taste in our mouth.[45]

Recent neuroimaging studies using insular activity as an indicator of pain signalling have confirmed many of the speculations of Hume and Bowlby. Ethnic differences reduce our reaction to another person in pain,[46] as does whether or not we value justice,[47] whether the person is attractive and female,[48] and whether the pain is expected or unexpected.[49] Attachment also influences how sympathetic we are to victims, with people who have had difficult relationships with a carer as a child being less sympathetic. Oxytocin[50] may be one of the influences that switches towards considering the victim to be 'in our group and so to be sympathized with' or to be

---

* Hume here, as so often, sees it from the point of view of the male children. But what about the mother? It seems likely that her attachment to the sons by a previous marriage might also drop. Infanticide occurs in non-human primates when one mate displaces another in some circumstances (Broom, Borries, and Koenig, 2004) and also occurs in birds (Riehl, 2016).

The publication of observations of this kind of infanticide in primates produced such a storm that the primatologists concerned were impugned in what was known as the 'infanticide wars' (Sommer, 2006). Infanticide has only relatively recently been criminalized in Europe (Stein, 2016) and has still been sanctioned within living memory (Obladen, 2016), indicating the ease with which two powerful connections between mother and child, attachment and the interbrain, can be suppressed by cognitive factors.

'outside it' and so to be blamed for being in that situation.[51] MDMA also increases the interbrain connection.[*]

The insula and emotional flavour

The function of the insula in humans might be thought of as a sublimation of disgust from the involuntary reaction to rotten food, through an equally involuntary disgust at injury or malformation, to a final, ethical function,[52] in which other people's actions are evaluated as good or wholesome on the one hand, or bad and nauseating on the other.[53] These reactions can be overridden, not least by culture or individual preference. Masochists, for example, manage to turn some nauseating aspects of personal injury into pleasure.

Insular activation is regularly associated with activation in the anterior cingulate, and one hypothesis for this is that the anterior cingulate is the conduit into consciousness for different emotions, and the insula evaluates these in relation to the same issues of integrity to body and person that determine whether the emotions are a threat to that integrity. 'Self-conscious emotions', as these are called, include emotions like pride that increase personal security and shame or humiliation that threaten it.

Some time ago, I proposed that emotions that we experience are merged in our memories with key features of the situation in which we experience them.[54] These situations – or 'emotors' – can subsequently re-elicit the same emotions. In other words, the situation or person has become a signal. Smells and tastes act as particularly important signals, as Proust noted in *À la Recherche du Temps Perdu* and as I indicated in my paper.

---

[*] Or at least increases affective empathy and prosocial behaviour (Hysek *et al.*, 2014; Kirkpatrick *et al.*, 2014).

Research evidence for this has also accumulated.[55] Our taste preferences may be established like this,[56] although they are also influenced by the smell molecules that are excreted in our mother's milk. Phonemes,[57] morphemes, graphemes, and words may act as emotors, resulting in text becoming imbued with emotional connotations.[58] The insulae, with their particular relationship to the smell-brain and to signals affecting the integrity of the receiver, may play a particular role in mediating self-conscious emotions linked to memory, such as nostalgia, home-sickness, guilt, embarrassment,[59] peacefulness, hurt feelings, and compassion.[60]

Bottom-up nonverbal connections that are apparently innate

Some sounds, such as the vocalizations of infant mammals, elicit searching behaviour on the part of the mother until gaze is exchanged between the mother and the foetus. Sometimes this is preceded by the mother also making a species-specific vocalization. In people, the baby has an individual cry that mothers can discriminate from the cry of other babies. Very young infant humans cry in response to other infants' crying,[61] but this reflexive response only occurs in response to the cry of another human child of approximately the same age.[62] Gaze direction can also be 'caught' by emotional faces or by eye contact.*

---

* Facial expression is more effective when it is appropriate to the context or the mood of the person whose attention is caught by it (Kret *et al.*, 2013). Another person's gaze 'catches your eye' even if you are unaware of it (Stein *et al.*, 2011; Yokoyama *et al.*, 2014).

Bottom-up nonverbal connections based on similarity or complementarity: the interbrain

Examples of similarity include postural mimicry, mimicry of facial expression* (more usually called 'sharing' facial expression), mimicking rhythms (consider marching or walking in step), gestural mimicry (e.g. shaking or holding hands), mimicking sounds (e.g. singing in harmony[63]), shared gaze, and shared focus of attention (i.e. looking in the same direction and with the same focus as another person or persons). Complementarity is evident in many elements of dance, in which, for example, one partner moves forward and the other partner moves back, singing in counterpoint, and turn-taking in speech.

This kind of communication does not require us to think about it. In fact, thinking about it often disrupts the communication – think of dancing, for example, and being told to 'just give in to the music' or 'just let yourself go'. Because it is not the product of thinking, iconic communication has no propositional content.[†]

Although these reflexes can be inhibited by higher centres later in life, the highest centres are not required for the reflexes to be active.[‡] In other words, our brains may directly

---

* There is now considerable experimental support for widespread human mimicry (Duffy and Chartrand, 2015), although most of the work has related to faces. Involuntary facial mimicry has been repeatedly demonstrated and been shown to contribute to the accuracy of interpretation of facial expression (Rychlowska et al., 2014).

† Like all generalizations, this one has the odd exception: in some iconic signs, for example the schematic flames that signify fire risk, the sign does have a propositional content but only because it has become 'conventionalized'. If one just came across the sign for the first time, it might have multiple interpretations – fire up ahead, hot temperature, or furnace around here.

‡ Evidence for this comes from several sources. One increasingly prolific source is neuroimaging. Redcay et al. (2010), for example, scanned participants who were following the gaze of an experimenter. Doing this increased activation in the right temporoparietal junction, anterior cingulate cortex, right superior

temporal sulcus, ventral striatum, and amygdala – areas that are not associated with language or consciousness. The results indicate that the impulse to follow gaze originates in 'lower' centres.

A second source for evidence of the interbrain are psychological experiments in which the reflexive effects of mimicry are dissociated from awareness by giving participants a separate, conscious task to perform as a mask (see Duffy and Chartrand (2015) for a review of these and other methods). Chatel-Goldman *et al.*, for example, looked at the effects of mutual touching, i.e. a study of the effects of touch mimicry. Fourteen romantically paired couples were asked to recall emotionally charged past experiences. They did so either holding hands or forearms, or not touching. In either situation, they could not see each other. Touch increased synchronization of their hearts and breathing and also their sweating (electrodermal response) when recalling an emotional event (Chatel-Goldman *et al.*, 2014). What touch did not do was communicate emotional content. Even if the partners were instructed to remember events with an opposite valence, so one remembered something nasty and one something good, synchronization still occurred (*ibid.*).

A third source of information comes from clinical conditions in which the influence of higher centres is altered deliberately or inadvertently by disease (Bien *et al.*, 2009). 'Involuntary' facial mimicry or echomimia (considered to be a specific manifestation of a more general echopraxia) can be evoked by stimulating the supplementary motor cortex, where mirror neurons are found in monkeys (Finis *et al.*, 2013), presumably because the strengthened echopractic tendency then escapes top-down regulation. Schizophrenia, frontotemporal dementia, frontal lobe epilepsy, and Tourette syndrome (Yamamuro *et al.*, 2015) are all conditions in which there is reduced frontal lobe control over movement and are all associated with echomimia. Reflexive facial mimicry is held to be the explanation of the spread of emotions from one person to another – emotional contagion. Sturm *et al.* estimated emotional contagion using a self-report questionnaire that has been shown to be correlated with it and found that the level of emotional contagion increased with increasing severity of Alzheimer-type dementia, which is known to affect frontotemporal areas. The extent of overt emotional contagion estimated by the self-report scale was attributed by the authors to a reflection of up-regulation of emotional contagion and was correlated with loss of volume in temporal lobe, particularly on the right (Sturm *et al.*, 2013). Reduced emotional contagion is, however, associated with behavioural variant frontotemporal dementia (Giannitelli *et al.*, 2015), a condition associated with the specific atrophy of von Economo neurons (Cauda, Geminiani, and Vercelli, 2014).

Darwin described what he thought was echomimia in native Tierra del Fuegans who adopted the facial expressions of Europeans that they encountered (Darwin, 1989/1874). It seems likely from his account that he thought of this as a 'primitive' reaction, but it may also have been a deliberate attempt to communicate.

A fourth source of evidence, particularly in the study of facial mimicry, is to separate reflexive from deliberate imitation by response time, on the assumption that deliberation requires significantly longer processing, and therefore slower response time, than reflexive responses. One of the first studies to use this method was that of Sonnby-Borgstrom (2002). She showed 42 young people photographs of standard emotional expressions on a computer screen. The young people had fine electrodes put into two muscle groups in their faces, one associated with smiling – the zygomaticus major, which pulls up the corner of the mouth – and one associated with frowning in anger, fear, or disgust – the corrugator supercilii that wrinkles the brow. Sonnby-Borgstrom found that there were small and normally indiscernible contractions of the corrugator when some of her participants looked at frowns, and small and again normally indiscernible contractions of zygomaticus when some participants saw smiles – facial mimicry. The difference in response was due to a disposition to respond to others' emotions. Those who did not have a particular disposition to do so were non-responders. This may have been because their top-down regulation inhibited mimicry reactions. The response of those who were disposed to respond to other people's emotional states occurred within or shortly after 17 milliseconds: probably too soon for higher-level processing and indicative of local processing not involving the higher centres in the brain that deal with language or thinking.

There have been many electromyographic studies since this one (Likowski *et al.*, 2012; Reicherts *et al.*, 2012), sometimes coupled with electroencephalogram recordings or with temporary inactivation of the temporal lobe by an external magnetic pulse (Balconi and Canavesio, 2013), but their focus has been on the role of mimicry in recognizing emotions and not on the mimicry itself (Künecke *et al.*, 2014). The consensus is that facial mimicry is just one factor in facial responses to stimuli connected to seeing facial expressions of emotion, but it does occur. A second agreed conclusion is that mimicry, when it occurs, does contribute to the accuracy of interpretation of other people's facial expressions (Künecke *et al.*, 2014). Postural imitation may contribute to the accuracy of interpretation, particularly of negative emotion (Kret *et al.*, 2013). Some studies provide evidence for a fast pathway that leads to a response before a person is aware of the stimulus (Faivre, Berthet, and Kouider, 2012), a pathway that may also account for rapid emotional reactions to art, too (Cela-Conde *et al.*, 2013). Sato and others (2013) demonstrated that video clips of a facial expression as it develops were more effective in eliciting congruent facial mimicry (as evident in the usual zygomaticus or corrugator supercilii contractions) than static emotions, but the responses were less specific. Zygomaticus contraction occurred in response to positive emotions, and corrugator in response to negative emotions. Mimicry reactions occur even if the mimicker remains unaware of the emotion (Kaiser *et al.*, 2016); for a review see Xavier *et al.* (2017).

The final, fifth, source of evidence is from observational studies, for example studies of the response to direct gaze or averted gaze. Direct gaze, at least direct

communicate with each other, via bottom-up nonverbal communication, without any communication between minds taking place. I call this 'interbrain communication' or an 'interbrain connection' by analogy with the internet.*

Establishing interbrain connections

To establish the selective communication that is required for an interbrain connection to develop, the infant needs to orientate to the person that she or he needs to imitate and to select what to imitate from a stream of stimuli. Smell signals

---

gaze from a person who is not socially dominant, evokes more looks to the eyes of the gazer from the person being looked at than indirect gaze. Responding to direct gaze with direct gaze is taken to be a token of humanity (Khalid, Deska, and Hugenberg, 2016).

There have been several other studies replicating the occurrence of facial mimicry and exploring the notion of what has come to be known as 'embodied cognition'. I would argue that cognition is a misnomer, as these are reflexive and not reflective processes.

* This term (Tantam, 2009) has since been adopted by others (Chatel-Goldman *et al.*, 2013; Cheng *et al.*, 2015; Dumas *et al.*, 2010; Müller *et al.*, 2013). Mine is not the only proposal of this kind. Di Paolo and De Jaegher (2012) have proposed a similar 'interactive brain' hypothesis; Fiske and others, the concept of relational cognition (Fiske, 1992); Zahavi and others, 'direct social perception' (Herschbach, 2015); Krueger, the we-space (Krueger, 2011); Gallese and co-workers, 'embodied simulation' (Gallese, 2007); Froese and Fuchs, the 'extended body' (Froese and Fuchs, 2012); Watsuji, 'betweenness' (Yeo, 2013), 'intercorporeality' (Trigg, 2013), 'shared reality' (Echterhoff, Higgins, and Levine, 2009), 'enkinaesthesia' (Stuart, 2013) and 'the perception-action model' (de Waal and Preston, 2017); and, arguably the father of this approach, Merleau-Ponty, the concept of 'relationship tissue' (Verissimo, 2012). The interbrain concept is making its way into what has previously been thought to be purely solopsistic cognitive operations (Badets, Koch, and Philipp, 2016). Hobson, Reddy, and Trevarthen (in chapters in Braten, 1998) have also emphasized the importance of early nonverbal interaction between carers and the infant in the development of empathy, although they do not propose the strict delineation that I am making between brain-based interaction, which is essentially reflexive, and actions that involve a primitive degree of reflectiveness of mind. Consequently, they do not develop a hypothesis, as I do, of the potential opposition of the interbrain and cognitive empathy.

established during 'bonding' play a role in this. Infants imitate an object more when their mother has handled it and imbued it with her smell, than if a female stranger has handled it.[64,*]

Gaze reflexes: orientating to the eyes and gaze following

The carer her or himself also helps the infant to tune in to what is important by imitating sounds or actions that will assist in interbrain connection, for example by responding with smiles to proto-smiles or echoing sounds that are the precursors of vocalization. But most infants come pre-adapted to latch on to an interbrain connection, by orientating first to a carer's face and then to her or his eyes. Other imitative tendencies reveal themselves later, with facial mimicry and gaze following

---

* Smell's direct role in influencing human social interaction has dwindled compared with its role in other mammals, possibly because human beings rely so heavily on visual stimuli in social interaction. It lingers on in odd places though, for example in sexuality and particularly sexual deviation. Urolagnia, for example, is common in oestrus mammals such as cows. A bull in a field with cows can often be seen smelling a cow's vagina and sometimes drinking her urine. Cows lack obvious visual signs when they are in oestrus (unlike many primates). So an easy way for the bull to tell if a cow is in oestrus is to smell the presence of pheromones and hormone derivatives in vaginal mucus and urine.

I have argued elsewhere that the apparatus for detecting smell, especially the insula, has become adapted to scent in the same way that the word has a meaning beyond smell, to include 'trace of' (viz. 'the detective has picked up the scent of the killer'), and that the traces are created by the conditioning effects of strong emotions. Stimuli ('emotors') that were incidentally associated with previous strong emotions become 'scented' or 'flavoured' with that emotion, so that re-exposure to the emotor reproduces the emotion (Tantam, 2003). A similar theory has been advanced by Low (Low and Espelage, 2013). Smell remains a particularly powerful emotor (for examples of the smell of familiar partners reducing separation anxiety, see McBurney, Shoup, and Streeter (2006) and Croy, Bojanowski, and Hummel (2013)).

having particular importance.* I proposed in a much earlier publication[65] that gaze is especially important in connecting the infant with the carer and that two reflexes subserve this: the first gaze reflex,† in which babies are predisposed to look at human eyes looking at them, and a second, innate, gaze reflex ('gaze following') that leads the infant to follow the eyes that they are looking at when the gaze of those eyes is diverted to

---

* I am going to generalize about 'people' throughout this book, with little attention to individual differences, although these, and their effect on the connections that people make with each other, are obviously very important. Facial mimicry provides a case in point. Children who have been maltreated (or abused or traumatized, since several roughly equivalent terms are used) show reduced activity of their corrugator supercilii, i.e. less expression of anger or fear when putting on different face expressions of emotion but raised parasympathetic tone when compared with non-abused children. The researchers attribute this to the maltreated children's greater preparedness to run away when experiencing negative emotion (Ardizzi *et al.*, 2016).

† Infants from birth onwards look preferentially at human faces and the eyes in human faces looking at them from birth (Batki *et al.*, 2000; Farroni *et al.*, 2007), at their mother's eyes, and at their mother's eyes when their mother is smiling. Mothers also attend preferentially to their infant's gaze. Mothers looking at their infants whilst their infants look at them have larger P3 waves (a measure of attention) than when looking at their infants whose eyes are averted or when looking at other infants (Doi and Shinohara, 2012). Mothers who spend more time gazing at their infant have higher levels of the so-called bonding hormone, oxytocin, than other mothers (Kim *et al.*, 2014). Mothers and infants who look at each other synchronize their heart rates and make more synchronous vocalizations (Feldman *et al.*, 2011). More positive emotional expressions and more vocalizations are produced by infants when they are looking at, and being looked at by, their mothers (Colonnesi *et al.*, 2012). Eye contact continues to be important throughout life. For example, pairs undertaking a joint attention task showed correlation of the activity of the inferior frontal gyrus in each of their brains that coincided with gaze exchange and, the authors concluded, provided the basis for establishing their joint attention on the task (Voorthuis *et al.*, 2014).

   Direct gaze retains this special significance throughout life, but not apparently in people with an ASD (Georgescu *et al.*, 2013). This may reflect the underdevelopment of what Georgescu *et al.* (*ibid.*) call the social neural network (SNN). The SNN is also involved in recognizing human-life movement (Georgescu *et al.*, 2014), something that people with an ASD may also have difficulties with.

another focus, with the result that the infant focuses on the same thing as the other person.*

In a recent review, Frith and Frith[66] came to the same conclusion as I had: that gazing at another's eyes and gaze following are reflexes.† A more recent study showing intact

---

* Frischen, Bayliss, and Tipper (2007) have reviewed the evidence for this. Gredebäck, Fikke, and Melinder (2010) used eye tracking to demonstrate that infants begin to follow gaze at between two and six months of age. In an EEG study, six-month-old infants showed greater emotional arousal to fearful faces when the faces were looking at a potential object of the fear but not when the apparent gaze of the faces was averted, indicating that the infants had seen the facial expression and then followed the direction of the gaze (Hoehl and Striano, 2010). A detailed study of the impact of gaze following on altering attention has been conducted on 222 children and young people, showing that gaze orientation increased from the age of seven (the youngest child tested) to a plateau from age 13 onwards. The disposition to follow gaze was not correlated with a theory-of-mind task (Neath *et al.*, 2013), and develops in both human infants and chimpanzee infants in the first year of life, and by 18 months, i.e. before theory of mind has begun to develop, chimps and human infants will move in order to be able to accommodate an obstacle that prevents them from seeing what someone else is looking at (Doherty, 2006). Infants at nine months are more likely to follow the gaze of someone who is smiling (Niedźwiecka and Tomalski, 2015). Gaze following may be suppressed as children get older in response to the injunction 'It's rude to stare' (one example of the suppressing effect of what I will call 'common knowledge' on our behaviour). People are still alerted to interesting activity in their environment, but because of this and similar injunctions do not overtly look but instead 'look out of the corner of their eye' or attend covertly (Laidlaw, Rothwell, and Kingstone, 2016). Following another's gaze to its expected target can also be covert (Perez-Osorio *et al.*, 2015). Gaze following appears to be integral to predicting movement direction, but is under top-down control (Ondobaka and Bekkering, 2013).

† Mutual gaze has been of interest from the first studies of nonverbal communication (Kendon, 1967), as its use by humans to express affiliation differs from other animals in whom it mainly communicates challenge or threat. The amygdala is activated in mutual gaze, perhaps to evaluate the level of threat, but the amygdala is also involved in initiating reflexive looking at another person's eyes. In one case example, functional amygdalectomy resulted in a woman failing to recognize facial expressions, but this was partly offset by instructing her to look consciously at the eye region of the photographs that she was evaluating (Adolphs *et al.*, 1994). The gaze direction of another person modulates the significance of their facial expression: for example, a fear expression coupled with direct gaze does

selective gaze at human eyes, and subsequent gaze following, in the children of blind parents[67] is further evidence that this behaviour is not copied or acquired but exists at birth. The only difference that Senju found between the infants of blind parents and those of sighted parents is that, although the infants that they studied showed the usual increased propensity to look at the eyes of sighted interactants as infants with sighted parents, they looked less at the eyes of their mothers, suggesting that later learning had altered the innate gaze reflex. More evidence about gaze and gaze following is available in a review by Schilbach.[68]

Facial and other imitation

The two gaze reflexes are a kind of imitation: when eyes look at me, I look at them, and when eyes look at something

---

not produce fear in an observer being looked at, whilst a facial expression with an averted gaze does (Soussignan *et al.*, 2013). Afferent information about gaze direction and facial expression is integrated sub-cortically (Wagner *et al.*, 2012). Direct gaze can be detected even when gaze is being consciously fixed on something else and the direct gaze is detected 'out of the corner of one's eye' (Stein *et al.*, 2011; Yokoyama *et al.*, 2014).

Changing from averted to direct gaze at another person alerts the other person to something novel being about to happen (Böckler, Hömke, and Sebanz, 2014).

Looking at another person's eyes increases the accuracy of affective empathy (Cowan, Vanman, and Nielsen, 2014). Mimicry of pupil size occurs, contributing to intuitive judgements of trustworthiness, with pupillary dilation signalling greater, and constriction lesser, trustworthiness (Kret, Fischer, and De Dreu, 2015). Later in life, withholding eye contact or bidding for eye contact by looking at another person's eyes mediates social inclusion and exclusion (Böckler *et al.*, 2014).

Gaze direction indicates direction of movement (Becchio *et al.*, 2007) because gaze is processed as if it is a reaching movement, like grasping (Pierno *et al.*, 2006). This may be why people who walk while looking at their mobile phones provide such an annoyance on crowded pavements.

else, I look at that, too.* Imitation does not just involve the eyes, although the eyes do have special importance for social interaction, but, as already noted, the voice, movements, postures, the face, and touch.

Imitating another person's facial expression is another social reflex that is present from birth.† Like the exchange of gaze, facial imitation may be intrinsically rewarding: just think of the pleasure that a warm, responsive smile gives. We like someone who imitates us more, and we feel more for them if, for example, they are in pain.[69]

Interactional synchrony is a kind of mimicry in which pauses or movement frequency are the same between two or more people.[70] Music performance is another example of interbrain synchronization.[71] Marching in step is one example that I have already used.‡

---

* There is no single term that captures the particular kind of imitation that is relevant here. Mimicry is one synonym, but most often this does not apply to communication but to the use of resemblance non-communicatively, for example in the mimicry of wasps by hoverflies that erroneously lead predators to consider that the hoverflies have a sting because they have the same yellow and black banding as wasps. Imitation is often used for copying deliberately, for example by the comedian who portrays a well-known character. Mime relies on copying recognizable actions but out of context. The British Navy used to acknowledge a message sent by flags by having the ship intended to be the recipient to display the same flags in the same order. Identification, internalization, copying, and impersonating are all related to imitation too but are used in specific contexts and involve additional elements of processing.

† The original observations (Meltzoff and Moore, 1977) that supported this have come under fire recently, with arguments that they were a misinterpretation of the infants practising oro-pharyngeal movement sequences. Neonatal imitation has also come under fire by philosophical psychologists (Lymer, 2014), but the balance of the evidence is that an imitative reflex develops early on in infancy, even if it is not present from the moment of birth.

‡ Imitation of repeated movements has been tracked in one study by frontal EEG recordings in both participants in a synchronized finger-tapping task. The participants were tapping in time to either a metronome or to each other. When tapping to each other – when their interbrain connection was active – there

The mirror neuron paradigm

The human body has features that suggest evolutionary pressure to support gaze reflexes and mimicry.*

The notion that the human, and probably the primate, brain is hardwired for mimicry[72] has received a considerable boost from the discovery in macaque monkeys of neurons in the supplementary motor that fire when a particular action is initiating by the monkey and also when the monkey sees another macaque initiating the same action. There has been considerable debate about whether such neurons occur in people, but general acceptance[73] that there is, at least, a network of neurons that behave in this way[74] and, indeed, another

---

were fewer fast waves in the EEG of one of the pair who was on eight or nine occasions the 'leader' of the rhythm (Konvalinka *et al.*, 2014). This interesting result suggests that the interbrain connection is not entirely two-way, but there is an embedded polarization reflecting who initiates the communication (the leader) and who responds (the follower). The relationship of leader and follower may of course switch rapidly from one person to another as the task changes. In another study of rhythmic synchronization in dance, touch between expert and naive dancers reduced the regularity of the expert's rhythm, suggesting that the novice was leading the expert or, rather, that the expert was trying to fit into the novice's less regular beat (Sofianidis *et al.*, 2014).

* Consider the following human characteristics. People walk erect, bringing the face into prominence. The eyes both face forward and are highlighted by eyebrows. The forehead is hairless, increasing its potential participation of facial expression. The face is flattened and so the features are all equally visible. It is mainly naked but with key features, like the eyes and the lips accentuated by hair or, in the case of the pupils, the surrounding white sclera (Perea García, Ehlers, and Tylén, 2017). These features are further heightened by the use of make up. The pinnae of the ears are not flat against the skull, but stick up so that the direction of the head can be more easily detected at a distance. Nearer by, the ridge of the nose assists in judgements about head posture. Gaze towards the eyes is either at the eyes, or at least ten degrees of arc away from them, so that gaze at the eyes can be more unequivocally detected. There are strong sanctions in many cultures against hiding the face, and mild sanctions against using dark glasses that obscure the pupils and sclerae.

network that is required to inhibit them from initiating actual movement when that is not appropriate.[*]

It has been hypothesized that a failure to inhibit mirroring causes a rare syndrome, of as yet uncertain nature, called mirror-touch synaesthesia.[75] Mirror-touch synaesthesia does not, however, at first seem to involve over-imitation as its name suggests, but vicarious sensation.[†] This is an example of what might occur: This may mean that one person feels another person's pain. It may be related to the discomfort that a 'squeamish' person feels on seeing a painful procedure, such as an injection. There may be movements associated with this, often the movements associated with bracing oneself for an expected noxious stimulus, but it may not be the shared movement that causes any associated discomfort but the shared discomfort that leads to the same movement

---

[*] See Hari *et al.* (2014). More information about mimicry is available in a recent review by Duffy and Chartrand (2015), and for more information about mirror neurons and imitation see Hamilton (2015).

[†] Writing about a neurology resident, Dr Joel Salinas, with mirror-touch synaesthesia, Hayasaki describes Salinas examining a patient. "'Any numbness?' asked Joel Salinas, a soft-spoken doctor in the Harvard Neurology Residency Program, a red-tipped reflex hammer in his doctor's coat pocket. "Like it feels funny?" Josh did not answer. Salinas pulled up a blanket, revealing Josh's atrophied legs. He thumped Josh's left leg with the reflex hammer. Again, Josh barely reacted. But Salinas felt something: The thump against Josh's left knee registered on Salinas's own left knee as a tingly tap. Not just a thought of what the thump might feel like, but a distinct physical sensation' (Hayasaki, 2015). Mirror-touch synaesthesia occurs in the phantom limb of some amputees if the counterpart limb is touched in another person (Goller *et al.*, 2013). One hypothesis is that it is due to an impairment in the normal system of inhibition of imitation (Santiesteban *et al.*, 2015). It is more common in people with high affective empathy (Seiryte and Rusconi, 2015) or, as I would interpret it, the bandwidth of their potential interbrain connection.

The 'enfacement illusion' is a related phenomenon. This occurs when an observer views another person's fearful face being touched at the same time as the observer's own face is being touched, resulting in an increased contagion of fear to the observer (Maister, Banissy, and Tsakiris, 2013).

in the person about to be injected and in the observer. The connection appears to be mediated by the signal network centred in the insula.[76]

Emotional contagion

The interbrain, like the internet, is content-less. It is a connection. What this connection enables is a sharing of mental states, particularly of emotion[*] and attention. The sharing is reciprocal. So, for example, if I make a slight smile towards someone, and they frown back, both of our mental states are altered and we arrive at some kind of compromise between pleasure and negativity (the exact balance will depend on the memories and the interpretations that are called into play to resolve the conflict). If, however, the smile is reciprocated, my own smile is likely to broaden, along with the smile of the other person.

The particular term that has been used for this kind of emotional sharing is 'emotional contagion'[†] after the expression 'contagion mentale' coined by Gustave Le Bon[77] to explain how crowds can seem to get whipped up into a single emotion shared by all the members of the crowd (although Le Bon focused on the spread of opinions and beliefs, rather than emotions).

Preston and colleagues[78] have provided a detailed account of how facial mimicry might lead to emotional contagion and

---

[*] Emotional expressions, as Darwin argued, probably started out as serving a purpose, but this became subsidiary to their communicative value at some point during human evolution – see a review by Tracy, Randles, and Steckler (2015) for more information.

[†] 'Emotional contagion' was applied by Hatfield, Cacioppo, and Rapson to the spread of emotions in any human interaction, not just in a crowd situation (Hatfield, Cacioppo, and Rapson, 1994). This was not the first use of the term in this context; the existential philosopher and saint Edith Stein, who studied empathy with Husserl, had already used it.

therefore to affective empathy.* The steps are as follows: seeing a facial expression in another person (other factors being equal) triggers an answering emotional expression as a result of mirror neuron activation. These neurons are the effectors for emotion pathways but are also afferents to emotion pathways. So activation of mirror neurons for smiling create, according to this hypothesized second step and other things being equal, the affect that goes with smiling.†

---

* Their account was anticipated by Edith Stein (Dullstein, 2013). She had concluded that affective empathy could not just be due to emotional contagion, because empathy did not mean simple, direct experience of another's emotions as if they were one's own but to experience another person's emotions directly and at the same time knowing that they were not one's own (Aaltola, 2014). Decety and Lamm (2007) have given one convincing explanation of how this might happen. They have argued for a common process of emotional generation. Motor neurons may be activated in order to produce a facial expression or in order to respond to another person's facial expression, but although the two streams are processed in the same way, there is a separate channel that flags whether or not the activation is intrinsic or extrinsic. They propose that the temporoparietal junction might be particularly involved in this flagging (*ibid.*).

† Evidence that imitation of a facial expression produces activation in the areas associated with mirror neurons is provided by Braadbaart *et al.* (2014) and that imitation of a facial expression can create the congruent affect by Lee *et al.* (2006). As had been found in earlier studies, Lee *et al.*'s participants showed additional activation of areas of the brain that were associated with the emotion being imitated. This may have been because the subjects conjured up the relevant emotion in order to imitate better, but it may also have been that imitating the emotional expression aroused the emotion. Indirect evidence that reflexively mimicked facial expressions change affect was provided by a study of Foroni and Semin (2011) who subliminally presented pictures of happy and angry faces to participants and then asked them to judge a cartoon. Participants' facial muscles were blocked in half of these trials. Perhaps not surprisingly, having one's facial muscles blocked led to more angry interpretations of the cartoons under all circumstances. But more relevant to this note, in the unblocked muscle condition, seeing happy faces increased positive ratings of the cartoon over seeing angry faces as a covert priming stimulus. Sato *et al.* (2013) performed a similar experiment, with similar findings, to those of Lee *et al.* and Braadbaart *et al.*, but were also able to show that reflexively mimicked expressions produced an appropriate change in affect. Seeing negative clips made participants feel more negative, and positive clips made them feel more positive.

Perhaps one of the most rigorous tests that show emotional contagion does not involve interpretation by higher centres that support deliberation is a study by Tamietto *et al.*[79] in which two patients with unilateral destruction of their visual cortex, and therefore blindness in one half of their visual field, were studied. Pictures of bodily expressions and facial expressions of emotion were presented alternately to their sighted field and the other non-sighted side. Because their blindness was cortical, some basic processing of the stimuli on their blind side was taking place but was not relayed to higher centres where it could be named or described consciously. The usual set up for electromyographic recordings of facial muscles in mimicry studies was in place and pupil dilatation was measured by a device incorporating a camera, a pupillometer. The stimuli presented to the blind side, as well as the sighted site, resulted in mimicked facial expressions and a change in pupil size, indicating an emotional response to the expression. In other words, facial mimicry and emotional contagion occurred even though the participant had no awareness of seeing anything. In fact, the response to the 'unseen' image was more rapid than to the 'seen', consistent with the expected suppression of an immediate reflexive mimicry response when top-down control is intact so that a response is only manifest when some further cortical processing has taken place.

Shared attention

Consider this scene. An infant is being held by her or his mother who is holding a rattle and shaking it. The mother wants the infant to look at the rattle or perhaps stretch out to it; in other words, to get the infant's attention. Now picture the scene a few months later. This time the mother is entertaining a friend. The infant is holding the rattle and shaking it and after a while appears to want to get the mother's attention. She or he looks at the mother, but she is caught up in her conversation with her friend. So the infant waves the rattle in front of her eyes, and then the mother does look at the rattle and smiles at the infant, who perhaps smiles back or gives the rattle an extra-big shake. Both of these interactions are based on the mother and infant tracking each other's gaze, but in the second instance the infant is also aiming for the moment when not only are mother and infant looking at the same thing, but also they each know that they are looking at the same thing.

The first scene is of a mother directing her infant's attention using movement and noise as a stimulus, and also using her own gaze as she looks repeatedly at the rattle. The gaze-following reflex is the foundation for shared attention.[80] In the second scene, gaze following has been established and the child has learnt ways of diverting his or her mother's gaze onto what the child is attending to. This builds on gaze following and on face mimicry, as looks at the object alternate with looks at the mother's face.[81] The infant is interested in the rattle, and has drawn his or her mother's attention to it and established that she is now interested in it, too. Each of them now has the same shared interest mediated by 'joint attention'.

Shared attention confers some protection on vulnerable conspecifics,[82] which is an important foundation for language learning and, later, for initiating cooperative play with peers.[83] It is also another kind of bridge between the people who are sharing the connection and so another aspect of the interbrain. Shared attention increases emotional contagion[84] and imitation,[85] but it also means that, whilst it is established, two people have the same outlook on the world without ever having made any kind of decision or choice. At its simplest, this means that what one person spots is likely not to be missed by someone else, but at its most developed it means that two or more brains can automatically come to share the same emotions and the same objects of attention, creating the basis for the 'intersubjectivity' that I have already discussed.

What makes the interbrain?

In this chapter, I have tried to bring together the evidence for two kinds of connection, exemplifying them by focusing on two kinds of knowledge of other people – the mental connection and the interbrain.* These two kinds of connection have their approximate corollary in two kinds of empathy. Mental connections via the theory of mind (which I will later generalize and refer to as 'proto-commonality') are essential for cognitive empathy, but affective empathy requires an interbrain connection.[86]

---

* The distinction between these two types of connectedness was captured elegantly in a study in which participants were placed in a scanner and shown film clips of someone putting a cup down and either apparently involving the participant or 'acting privately'. The actor involved the participant by looking directly out of the frame, apparently at the participant, and reinforcing this with a nod and an eyebrow flash. The 'private' clip had the actor just looking at the cup. The researchers (Tylén *et al.*, 2012) thought of the first condition as a 'collective, inter-personal process where individual cognitive components interact on a moment-to-moment basis to form coupled dynamics' (*ibid.*, p.1) and the second as 'a self-contained individual cognitive process aiming at an "understanding of the other"' (*ibid.*, p.1). Participants in the former condition showed greater eye dilatation, taken as a symptom of coupled dynamics, and also showed greater activation in the right posterior temporal sulcus, an area associated with affective empathy (Redcay *et al.*, 2010). Participants who were watching an actor who did not apparently acknowledge them showed activation in the inferior parts of frontal and temporal lobes, which the authors conclude are the areas particularly implicated in cognitive empathy.

    This study provides a clear – almost too clear – neurophysiological contrast between affective empathy and cognitive empathy. Their stress on the involuntary, other-determined aspect of affective empathy was foreshadowed by the French philosopher Merleau-Ponty (1962/1945). He in turn referred back to a longer tradition of 'intersubjectivity', an explanatory concept also used by other phenomenologists such as Scheler and Gadamer (Van Deurzen, 2009).

Mental connections involve imagination, often in the way of stories, and they start from the point of view of a solitary agent discovering connections with the social world. Interbrain connections start from sharing, with the experience of an individual agent coming later. This is possible because the interbrain connection is not like a letter or text in which one person sends a message that requests a response but like a mobile phone or networked computer that is always connected when the power is on and wherever there is a compatible signal. Both the personal computer and the internet provider's server influence each other constantly: they are reciprocally connected, even if no discursive messages are being sent to the other.

This always-on feature was anticipated by the sociologist and criminologist Gabriel Tarde in the 19th century,* but its significance as a brain connection has only tangentially been taken up, perhaps because much of the science then was from the perspective of the individual scientist sensing and evaluating the world, rather than the phenomenological position espoused by Husserl, according to which the world is disclosed to us by our activity within it,[87] of reaching out to grasp as the world affords.

I consider that some intractable philosophical problems become clearer when the contribution of the interbrain to

---

* The French sociologist and criminologist Gabriel Tarde also thought that people were connected through imitation (Tarde, 1903/1890), although he thought that it resulted purely from a contagious spread of imitation 'rays'. Tarde emphasized that the rays acted on people who were unaware of them. When later authors have had this same intuition of the spread of fashions, ideas, tastes, or psychological disorders (for a review of these see Sampson (2012)), they have often suggested some degree of conscious imitation. Tarde did not. Like me, he thought that people were influenced unconsciously, although, not having the internet as a metaphor to fall back on, he used what to him was the contemporary idea of invisible physical influences, 'rays' or radiation.

our universal experience is taken into account. These include 'altruism', or the puzzle of why people should, and do, act generously towards others; 'solipsism', or on what grounds we assume that other people exist; and 'animacy', or why and on what basis we make a distinction between what has a motivating soul or intent and what is inanimate matter. I will consider each of these later in the book.

The first consideration, in the next chapter, will be the consequences of the interbrain for human behaviour.

Notes

1. Fessler and Holbrook, 2014
2. Valdesolo and DeSteno, 2011
3. Valdesolo, Ouyang, and DeSteno, 2010
4. Wiltermuth, 2012
5. van Baaren *et al.*, 2009
6. Fawcett and Tunçgenç, 2017
7. Fridland and Moore, 2015
8. Kokkinaki and Vitalaki, 2013
9. Hume and Flew, 1988
10. Smith *et al.*, 2002
11. Zahavi, 2014, p.140
12. Jackson, 1982
13. Philippi *et al.*, 2012
14. Hecht, Patterson, and Barbey, 2012
15. Peters and Kashima, 2015
16. Dullstein, 2013
17. Aaltola, 2014
18. Decety and Lamm, 2007
19. MacSweeney *et al.*, 2008
20. Abell, Happé, and Frith, 2000; Klin, 2000
21. Powell *et al.*, 2012
22. Mesulam, 1998
23. Premack and Woodruff, 1978
24. Wimmer and Perner, 1983
25. Baron-Cohen, Leslie, and Frith, 1985
26. Fernández, 2013
27. Nisbett and Masuda, 2003
28. Brentano, 1973/1874
29. Low, 2013
30. Ricks and Wing, 1975
31. Ainley, Maister, and Tsakiris, 2015
32. Newell and Shanks, 2014
33. Lübke and Pause, 2015
34. Bauernfeind *et al.*, 2013
35. Jankowski and Takahashi, 2014; Roth *et al.*, 2014
36. Fischer, Becker, and Veenstra, 2012
37. Bartlett *et al.*, 2014
38. Shenhav and Mendes, 2014
39. Seara-Cardoso *et al.*, 2015
40. Eres *et al.*, 2015
41. Decety, 2015

42. Hume, 1978, p.158

43. Hume, 1978

44. Hume, 1999

45. Decety and Moriguchi, 2007

46. Cao et al., 2015

47. Decety, 2015

48. Jankowiak-Siuda et al., 2015

49. Raz et al., 2014

50. Bos et al., 2015

51. Smith et al., 2014

52. Eskine, Kacinik, and Prinz, 2011

53. Hutcherson et al., 2015

54. Tantam, 2003

55. Smeets and Dijksterhuis, 2014

56. Schaal, Marlier, and Soussignan, 2000

57. Whissell, 1991

58. Poria et al., 2014

59. Müller-Pinzler et al., 2016

60. Immordino-Yang, Yang, and Damasio, 2014

61. Sagi and Hoffman, 1976

62. Martin and Clark, 1982

63. Cummins, 2014; Pearce, Launay, and Dunbar, 2015

64. Parma et al., 2013

65. Tantam and Whittaker, 1992

66. Frith and Frith, 2011, pp.293–294

67. Senju, 2013

68. Schilbach, 2015

69. De Coster et al., 2013

70. Chartrand and Lakin, 2013

71. Henning, 2014

72. Simpson et al., 2014

73. Avenanti, Candidi, and Urgesi, 2013

74. Morelli, Rameson, and Lieberman, 2014

75. Banissy and Ward, 2007; Ward and Banissy, 2015

76. Lamm, Decety, and Singer, 2011

77. Le Bon, 1930/1896

78. L. Preston, Shumsky, and Goldberg, 2002; S. D. Preston, de Waal, and Post, 2002

79. Tamietto et al., 2009

80. Frischen et al., 2007

81. Burnett-Zeigler et al., 2012

82. Lemogne et al., 2015

83. Yuill et al., 2014

84. Shteynberg et al., 2014

85. Shteynberg and Apfelbaum, 2013

86. Shamay-Tsoory, 2014

87. Husserl, 1970

Chapter 2

THE INTERBRAIN
IN ACTION

Both smell and interbrain connections are most often transitory, and on the rare occasions that they linger, they involve an additional step of 'frozen' memory in which a memory is made but not processed sufficiently for it not to recur in consciousness. This might be the explanation for outbreaks of 'epidemic hysteria' where, for example, a physical symptom of psychological origin spreads and is 'caught' by one person after another who display the same symptom as described in the quote at the beginning of this chapter, or the famous descriptions of Proust of the effects of the recall of smells such as the smell of madeleines that he describes in *À la Recherche du Temps Perdu*.

Two further difficulties arise when we want to isolate the effects of the interbrain. One is that the theory-of-mind connection is inextricably linked through language and inner language with our awareness of ourselves.* So it may be the only connection that we are directly aware of. When we think of ourselves, we think of a deliberating, decision-making agent, a unity.† Masicampo and Baumeister provide a sophisticated explanation of how this might be: they presume that conscious thought scans various inputs, including one from society, and selects just one to 'present to the executive', which then,

---

* This is a long-standing and largely accepted philosophical assumption that has only recently become testable. It is not quite the same as asserting that we are always conscious of 'thinking', which we are not (Bastian *et al.*, 2017), but whether we can be conscious of our thoughts or choose consciously to think about something without having recourse to inner speech. This is not to say that inner speech precludes thinking in images. Both kinds of thinking probably normally co-exist (Amit *et al.*, 2017), but language probably does play a key role in attending to our thoughts and so being conscious of them and being able to focus them on some particular content (Ünal and Papafragou, 2016).

† My sense – and this appears to be true of others (Stillman, Baumeister, and Mele, 2011) – is that my awareness extends to the very fringe of my thinking and experiencing. This 'executive self' emerges with the use of language and the ability to pass theory-of-mind tests at around 18 months at the earliest in neurotypical children (Miller and Marcovitch, 2015). This is not when cognition in its broader sense begins. I know that when I walk upstairs some complex motor calculations are happening outside of my awareness, but I do not experience myself doing anything 'really important' without it passing under my scrutiny. Yet, this assumption flies against issues, cases, and thought experiments raised continually since the mid 19th century, when Robert Louis Stevenson's 1886 novella *The Strange Case of Dr Jekyll and Mr Hyde* became an instant success. It continues to be read and dramatized today. He imagined what might happen if two different people occupied the same body, a Dr Jekyll and a Mr Hyde (although Mr Hyde was able to access a much greater proportion of that body's strength and endurance). Developments in psychology in the 20th century have made the issue even more acute. Freud's formulation of an unconscious, later reformulated as the 'das Es' or the 'It' and the 'uber-Ich' or 'over-I' (Strachey translated these as 'the Id' and the 'Super-Ego', respectively), allowed that this unconscious might be an agent in opposition to the agency, the Ich or the ego, that was disclosed to the actor. Behaviourism elevated habits to a level at which complex decisions might be made out of habit, effectively creating another kind of unconscious agency.

presumably, gives the go-ahead for action,* via the chief executive officer (CEO) or self. We can only maintain this metaphor of the self as CEO by suppressing or ignoring the contribution of the interbrain to our motivation. This works well most of the time because the interbrain and our theory-of-mind connection usually work in harmony,† but sometimes the interbrain connection can be suppressed.[1]

Introjection

Not all events pass into the stream of experience and lose their integrity.‡ Some events are resistant to this processing

---

* See Masicampo and Baumeister (2013). Supposing for a moment that it is like this, and the executive is 'I', then it is not surprising we should feel this executive, the 'I', is in charge. But Baumeister had reached a rather different conclusion in a much earlier paper (Baumeister, 1987) where he had reviewed the historical development of the concept of an executive or, as he termed it in that paper, a 'self'. The self was, he concluded, the core of a developing individual consciousness that was increasingly at odds with the communal perspective that preceded it in the pre-modern era. I alluded to something similar in the first chapter, although describing it as the suppression of the interbrain connection by the narrative self. This suppression is another reason that we may be unaware of our experience of our interbrain connection: in order to bring our individual experience into focus, we need to tune out this interbrain, communal connection. This tension is, I shall argue later, a determinant of the very mixed nature of humanity, of how we can be the hybrid of animal and deity that our poets take us for.

† For example, Wlodarski asked people what their 'mating strategies' were and found that people who were more promiscuous, or more willing to contemplate promiscuity, had higher interbrain connectedness (as assessed by tests of 'affective empathy') and more cognitive empathy. But higher affective empathy was required for cognitive empathy to have an influence. High cognitive empathy in the absence of low affective empathy was not correlated with a propensity to have many sexual connections (Wlodarski, 2015).

‡ Emotional events may be recalled in detail for up to a few days in what is called working memory and may be scrutinized there by a process that is similar to scrutiny of an external scene. Normally they thereafter slide into the background of our thoughts, although they are recoverable by cues related to them, such as

and remain, like unshriven souls, in working memory from whence they can be re-experienced. This, it is speculated, is the problem in post-traumatic stress disorder. Rumination or repeated rehearsal of the event provides one explanation for this persistence.

Laughter is often described as infectious and, as I noted in Chapter 1, the interbrain is the vector of this infection. Most people will be familiar with 'fits of giggles' when infection and re-infection form a cycle that allows laughter to persist until participants feel physical discomfort. An epidemic of laughing was described in the *Central African Journal of Medicine* (which is still publishing) as follows:

An epidemic disease is defined as one that 'is prevalent among a people or a community at a special time and produced by some special causes not generally present in the affected community'. As the commoner epidemics are caused by the spread of viruses, bacteria, or parasites, there is a tendency to forget that abnormal emotional behaviour may spread from person to person and so take on an epidemic form. It is the purpose of this communication to report an epidemic in the Bukoba district of north-west Tanganyika. The epidemic was characterized by episodes of laughing and crying. It is not only of interest from the sociological aspect but as it has disrupted the normal life

revisiting the place in which the remembered event happened. The hippocampus seems to be the structure most involved at this stage. The hippocampus after a considerable time lag then somehow parks the details of the memory in the cerebral cortex although tagging it so that it can be recalled. The event becomes less and less like a personal experience in this process, and more and more like an experience that someone else observed. Taking this third-person perspective on events associated with negative emotions may hasten this process (Ayduk and Kross, 2010) and diminish re-experiencing the negative feelings (Muir, Madill, and Brown, 2016).

of the community for six months, it is of considerable public health importance.

The disease commenced on 30th January, 1962 at a mission-run girls' middle school at Kashasha village, 25 miles from Bukoba... From that date until the 18th March, 1962, when the school was forced to close down, 95 of the 159 pupils had been affected. Fifty-seven pupils were involved from the 21st May, when the school was re-opened, until it was again shut at the end of June.[2]

What happened to the girls has similarities to the fits of giggles (that may also turn into crying) in that those affected cannot explain what makes them giggle, but differs in that the giggling is not immediately transmitted but there may be hours or days between a person being exposed to helpless laughter and they themselves becoming infected.[3]

This then is the second difficulty: that, although an interbrain connection normally only exists in real time between people who are in active nonverbal communication and its effects are normally transient, this is not always so. Interbrain effects, like the epidemic of laughter as described in the quote at the beginning of the chapter, may persist after a real-time interaction is over and may be preceded by an incubation period during which no consequences are apparent. The only possible explanation for this is that an interbrain connection can sometimes induce a state of mind that is preserved as a snapshot memory.

Infancy

A great deal of evidence was provided in Chapter 1 about the interbrain connection of mothers and babies. But what these connections lead to in the infant's life is harder to judge. Memories of our past that we can recall reliably date from the age of about five.* So what it was like to communicate with other people purely by nonverbal means cannot be recalled. Nor is it possible for infants to describe their experience, as to do so would require the words that will already have created a separate means of communicating, although with a nascent theory of mind.

Observations of infants' reactions to their carers – usually mothers or grandmothers – indicate that infants look to their carer, particularly when alarmed or distressed, follow their carer about, and, later on, seek proximity to their carer again when alarmed (and mothers seek to find and hold their babies). These reactions are all so well known to us that we hardly need supportive research, but attachment theorists and others have, even so, been able to confirm them. Older but still preverbal infants demonstrate changes in nonverbal communication that indicate that expectancies of other people's behaviour have been created† and a preference for interbrain connection,

---

* Although many people claim that they can remember earlier years, and even infancy, the likelihood is that these are narratives about the past that become accepted and then rehearsed as verdical autobiographical memories (St Jacques and Schacter, 2013) as the hippocampus does not develop sufficiently until between four and six to play what seems to be a crucial role in storing episodic memory (Riggins *et al.*, 2016). Non-recallable memory does persist, and still influences behaviour, for example in influencing emotional reactions to smells (Sullivan *et al.*, 2015) and in remembering whether an object was handled in earlier years (Cunningham *et al.*, 2013), and the names of objects and other words are acquired at an earlier period in many children.

† Infants behave as if they recognize harm to other people (Chiarella and Poulin-Dubois, 2015), seek parental attention when another child is distressed (Campbell *et al.*, 2015), and look longer at a person's face when the expression is discrepant with the person's actions (Skerry and Spelke, 2014). Hamlin and others (Hamlin, 2014; Van de Vondervoort and Hamlin, 2016) make even greater claims for the moral perspicacity of four-month-olds, which somewhat strain credulity.

and imitation, with some people rather than others. These early preferences persist into adult life.[*]

Carers, as the term indicates, are given control of their infants' welfare. But mothers are also leaders, and one effect of the interbrain connection is that infants do not ignore their mothers but follow. Mother presents a nipple, and the infant (more often than not) seeks it out and suckles. Mothers initiate conversations and rhythmic movement interchanges with which the infant synchronizes. Mothers smile, and infants smile back. Of course, some smiles and interchanges begin with a smile or a sound that the infant makes, but it is not directed towards the mother until late in infancy. Mothers are emotional leaders, with the mother's overall mood affecting, maybe for a long time, their infants' characteristic mood.[†] In the still face experiment, mothers are asked to turn a blank face to their infant to which the infant first responds by greater efforts to communicate and then by distress or turning away.[‡]

---

[*] Hofman *et al.* (2012) demonstrated that in a bargaining game women stopped imitating the smiles of other women who made unfair offers, but did imitate their angry expressions. The reverse was true of fair bargain proposers whose angry expressions were less likely to be imitated.

[†] Mothers' facial responsiveness, and the 'still face' challenge in which mothers are instructed not to respond facially, have been used to demonstrate the importance of the mother in leading her infant emotionally (Bigelow and Power, 2014). An alternative and novel approach to illustrating this was provided by a robot with simulations of a mirror neuron system, somatosensory cortex, an insula, and the ability to interpret 'motherese'. Mothers who interacted with the robot used movement and motherese to communicate their reactions to it. Novel, happy human voices led to optimal battery use and temperature control ('flourishing' to use the authors' words) 90 per cent of the time, whereas when mothers had sad voices, the robot showed 'distress' 84 per cent of the time (Lim and Okuno, 2015).

[‡] The recognition of familiar faces, and a differential reaction to them, is recognized by carers as the period of stranger anxiety, which normally occurs at about ten months. Brazelton has demonstrated in vivid video demonstrations the distress and withdrawal of infants when their mother adopts a still, unresponsive face (Brazelton *et al.*, 1975). Heyes (2014) provides a detailed account of how novelty

Very young children, particularly at an age before speech has developed when the only connection with other children is via the interbrain, are not cut off from each other as older children are, who have already been influenced by the messages from their parents and other adults about who deserves sympathy and who does not.[*] Very young children mimic other children's signs of distress at a young age, perhaps shortly after birth.

Adults who relate to preverbal children fall back on the interbrain connection to communicate. This is most likely to be true of mothers and babies and it has seemed to many observers that it is as if there is no mother and no baby, but just a 'mother and baby'.[†] A protective attitude towards juveniles, primarily towards human infants but often extending to other juvenile mammals, is often taken to be an indicator of affective empathy and the interbrain connection that affective empathy requires. Affective empathy is particularly associated in Western culture with the role requirements of being a woman, who may be considered to be the emotional leader in families or social groups. Contrarily, when the reputation of out-groups is being blackened, their treatment of infants as foods, or objects, is often invoked as the most effective means of creating disgust or hatred.

---

might be the basis for later elaboration into more complex discrimination mediated by the interbrain.

[*] For a review, see Eisenberg, Fabes, and Spinrad (2006).

[†] A paraphrase of an expression used by the English psychoanalyst Donald Winnicott, but an observation also made by the phenomenologist Merleau-Ponty (Krueger, 2013).

Altruism*

The protectiveness of human beings towards infants, even infants of other species, is often taken as strong evidence that people are not solely concerned with their own good and indifferent towards that of others. This may be misleading. One good turn deserves another, and so long as fairness prevails, a good turn may be self-serving. It has been argued that the sacrifices that parents make for their children are an investment, designed to ensure that the children will look after them in their dotage.

Self-interest is not a plausible explanation for what Durkheim called 'altruistic suicide' in his book on suicide, although he noted that altruistic suicide, in which people sacrificed themselves, was usually not for another person but for a belief, ideal, or goal shared by an in-group.† Instances of mothers sacrificing themselves for their children are rare in practice but are widely thought to occur‡ and attributed to what Auguste Comte called 'living for others' or living

---

* Altruism is often presented as a problem, as if it is obvious that people are self-serving. So why should they give this up? This question seems to gain added force from the presumption that it is a law of nature that animals are in constant competition unless they are procreating. These assumptions are being called into question from many sides, including neuroscience. One study, for example, has shown that paralysing the so-called higher centres of the brain, the parts that are supposedly associated with civilizing influences, increases cooperative behaviour in games, rather than reducing it (Christov-Moore *et al.*, 2016).

† See Durkheim (1970). The term 'in-group' was introduced by a medically qualified anatomist, Arthur Keith (1948), who had a distinguished career in surgical anatomy (he co-discovered the sino-atrial node) and in physical anthropology. He contrasted 'in-groups' and 'out-groups' and also considered that there were two basic relations within them – amity in in-groups and enmity in out-groups.

‡ Including by airline companies, whose safety breaches always urge adults caring for children to put the oxygen mask on to themselves first and the child second in the event of a sudden decompression.

'pour autrui' (hence 'altruism').* Protecting a child is an understandable consequence of two of the types of empathy that I have already considered, the interbrain connection that increases emotional contagion and the insula-based sympathy reaction to pain or distress.†

A tendency to self-sacrifice that is active during the reproductive years, as altruistic suicide is, seems to run counter to the evolutionary principle that individual animals, and

---

* Altruism is an English coinage derived from the French for 'other', featured in Auguste Comte's recommendation that we should 'vivre pour autrui'. He wrote: 'The individual must subordinate himself to an Existence outside himself in order to find in it the source of his stability. And this condition cannot be effectually realized except under the impulse of propensities prompting him to live for others' (Comte, 1973/1851, p.565).

  Comte's principle would have been familiar to many devout Christians, whose religion encouraged self-abasement, but public and philosophical opinion turned against it, possibly because of its association with the new religion that Comte and his wife founded and possibly also because it made collectivities like 'Existence' and 'Society' pre-eminent over individual interests (Dixon, 2008). There is, too, Comte's relentlessly progressivist ideas about human history that have turned 'positivism' into a term of scorn for many social science researchers. Cynics also suspect that behind apparent altruism there is some kind of selfish motive, and some research claims to bear this out (Cialdini *et al.*, 1987).

  Comte makes clear that, for him, there are two elements to the development of altruism. For example, he writes about education (Comte, 1973/1851) that, 'Over and above the several means of repressing personality, the essential condition of purification is the exertion of sympathy, which regulates individual existence by the family relations, and these again by the civic' (p.253).

  It is the first principle – the suppression of the personality – that has provoked the greatest animus in intellectuals as diverse as Nietzsche (2001/1882), Sartre (1969), and Ayn Rand (Campbell, 2006).

  Comte's notion of personality is probably closer to what we would now call 'celebrity' or simply 'self' (as in self-worth or self-interest). I also see in it some foreshadowing of the conflict in the title of this book between the brain and the 'selfish mind'.

† An example is provided by a study of Japanese children whose help-giving behaviour towards disaster victims was correlated with the extent to which films of these victims evoked facial expressions of distress (Shuto, 1985). Another study, this time of adults, provides evidence that altruistic behaviour also requires that one has concern for the other person (Van Lange, 2008).

their genes, thrive only if they multiply. Inhibition of any tendency for an adult to attack a child can easily be seen as of evolutionary value as a means of reducing attacks by irritated parents on their or others' offspring. A genome that confers a tendency to fatal self-sacrifice, though, would seem to offer little survival advantage and be selected out. There are many possible explanations for why it has not,[*] but the commonly expressed idea that altruistic concern for another is ultimately self-serving does not work.[4] An alternative explanation is that it is having a high-bandwidth interbrain connection capacity that is selected for[†] and that this conveys benefits that outweigh the rare side effect of altruistic suicide.

Altruism is also sometimes applied to situations in which a person foregoes a reward to spare suffering to someone else or

---

[*] Including kin-selection: see Eisenberg, Fabes, and Spinrad (2006). More altruistic individuals have enhanced activity in interbrain-related centres when making judgements about other people's emotions, as one might expect. They tend to be more sociable (i.e. to score higher on extraversion and agreeableness) and to have more grey matter in areas that are often implicated in contagious emotion. Altruism may therefore be a consequence of the capacity for an interbrain connection (Edele, Dziobek, and Keller, 2013), and it is the latter that selection favours, because of its value in group formation and infant care, and not the former.

[†] Pfaff has also attributed altruism to a function of the brain (Pfaff, 2015) but he does not consider that this is mediated by communication as I do. Instead, he proposes the brain represents the image of the self and an image of the other, and that these representations (that are somehow encoded as patterns of neuronal excitation) get blurred. So when I rehearse doing something nasty to another person, which requires, Pfaff thinks, the requirement that the representation of that other person is active, it is a representation of me, too. This inhibits me from doing something bad, but instead biases me to be kindly. The interbrain theory arrives at this same conclusion too, but on the basis that making someone else fearful results in me instinctively picking up that fear via our interbrain connection, whilst making someone smile results in me contagiously picking up their happiness.

to punish them for bad behaviour.* Even infants at the age of 12 months show rudiments of this,[5] and it has been suggested, although not supported by some studies, that chimpanzees, too, and even rats,[6] show this kind of altruistic behaviour.

Giving over to the other

Altruism involves putting another's needs before one's own, but, at the same time, giving that other person – or those other

---

* Comte was right in thinking that a principle other than selfishness or social control was required to explain people's collective behaviour. Economics posed an early example of this problem, singled out by Adam Smith, who wondered why fairness should be sufficiently entrenched that bargains could be made and markets established (Smith, 2002/1785). Economists still wonder about this and still refer to 'altruism' as an explanation (Fehr and Camerer, 2007).

Economic altruism does not preclude self-interest and so deviates from Comte's formula. Take the commonplace example of giving a tip to a server in a restaurant. One might give a tip: as a reward for good service; because the waiters seem very hard-working and underpaid (possibly the closest motive to Comte's altruism); or because it creates a reputation for oneself that may bring benefits (quicker service, better table placing, and so on) when one next goes to that restaurant. People do leave bigger tips, at least in thought experiments, if they plan to go to a restaurant again, but they still anticipate leaving some tip even if they never want to return. The motive might be fairness or to create a virtuous cycle of generosity ('paying it forward') (Watanabe et al., 2014), both of these motives being enhanced by the possibility that the fairness or the generosity might come back to benefit the self. The common feature of all of these altruistic actions is that their most direct consequence is the benefit of someone else, irrespective of whether or not the actor benefits, too.

Neuroeconomics is a new branch of economics that searches for these altruistic motives in the brain and not in the mind. Fehr and Camerer (2007) review brain studies of people playing one of the classic 'games' that elicit either opportunism or fairness, such as the classic Prisoners' Dilemma Game. They conclude that there is a consistent activation of those parts of the brain that are activated by other kinds of reward when the players in a game play cooperatively rather than selfishly, even though selfish play is the way that the greatest reward can be achieved. Choosing to cooperate rather than choosing to maximize the chances of winning is a good example of winning. Fehr and Camerer locate the cause of this in the brain, although it is true that they also credit the dorsomedial prefrontal cortex, an area of brain that has been proposed as the medium in which internal narratives run, with an important role, too.

people – the power to determine one's conduct.* We admire it, associating it with virtues such as loyalty or self-sacrifice, but we recognize that uncritically following a leader can also lead to fanaticism. It may be particularly problematic when the tendency persists even when the actual leader is no longer in direct contact but has become an introject. When several people share the same introject, it is a switch that has been thrown that suppresses individualistic thinking and replaces the individual with the follower. This is most obvious in crowds, which I go on to discuss later in this chapter. The susceptibility of the follower to carry out every expectation of a determined leader has, in the past, been attributed to a predisposition called suggestibility, because it was first studied during the height of psychological and psychotherapeutic interest in hypnosis. Some people could be easily hypnotized and would carry out instructions – 'suggestions' – made under hypnosis, whilst other people were much less susceptible.[†]

The example of altruistic suicide given by Durkheim is of someone throwing themselves under a juggernaut, a heavy carriage containing an image of one of the Hindu gods being pulled in procession by an elephant; an example, perhaps, of this kind of followership becoming destructive.[‡]

---

* Hence Sartre's excoriation of 'être pour autrui' as a form of self-deception in *Being and Nothingness* (Sartre, 2003/1943).

† The sensitivity to oxytocin seems to be associated with suggestibility: carrying the GG genotype, which confers greater oxytocin responsiveness, increases suggestibility, and carrying the A genotype, which confers reduced oxytocin responsiveness, is associated with lower suggestibility (Bryant *et al.*, 2013).

‡ Other examples abound. One of the most often cited is the Jonestown massacre, in which a paranoid leader inspired a crowd of followers and their children to drink cyanide-laced Kool-Aid.

Crowds

Like many CEOs, we imagine that we are in charge of all that we do. So, just as many CEOs would boast that they make decisions for themselves without being swayed by the changing mood of individual directors, we might not be aware of being taken over by our interbrain connection, although we are often more able to observe its effects.* These are most obvious when the interbrain connection is strongest or when our narrative self is weakest. An obvious candidate for a strong interbrain connection is being tightly packed in a crowd and being open to connection with the others with us. So not in a crowded train where we are trying to find our little space, or on a crowded beach where we are trying to feel as if we are on our own with our nearest and dearest, but in a demonstration or at a football match where we are proud to identify ourselves with our fellow supporters or demonstrators.† Sartre, the philosopher of everyone who feels lonely in a crowd, imagined what it would have been like to have one of the sans-culottes storming the Bastille at one of the high moments of the French Revolution. He described this as a moment of fusion in which each person thought that it might be them or it might have been someone else who cried 'à la Bastille'. Individual awareness was dissolved

---

* The idea that our self-awareness plays catch up with our actions, providing justifications for them only after they have been initiated, was first proposed by Wegner (2002).

† This notion of giving in to being a part of a crowd by adopting a shared social identity has been developed by Reicher, Spears, and Postmes (1995). It does not quite do justice to the force of crowd intoxication that can catch up people who would think themselves resistant to it, but it does give weight to the inevitable corollary of the crowd, that at a certain stage of its development one might side with it, or set oneself apart from it. If the latter, one becomes, more often than not, the crowd's potential adversary.

in the hysteria of the crowd or, as Sartre himself put it, in the 'constellation of mediated reciprocities'.[7]

Crowds have been the subject of a considerable literature, but the concept of crowd psychology probably originated with Le Bon.[8] His treatment may have been influenced by his viewpoint, a condemnatory one, on the Parisian crowd during the second Paris commune of 1871. Le Bon anticipated that the 20th century would be the age of the crowd and that individuals who could dominate crowds would be the new kings and rulers.

Le Bon thought that crowds had three main characteristics:

- 'the disappearance of conscious personality'

- 'the turning of feelings and thoughts in a definite direction' (and of course the same direction for each person)

- 'being brought together'.[9]

Deindividuation

Le Bon's idea that crowds are characterized by the 'disappearance of conscious personality' is the reason that I have started with them as one of the manifestations of interbrain communication between people. People in crowds may lack conscious personality but they do not lack drive or feelings, even though they do share them with everyone else who is part of the crowd. This 'deindividuation', as it has come to be called, continues to be recognized as a common denominator of crowds of people.* Sartre referred to it as 'fusion'.

---

* This 'deindividuation' hypothesis (Festinger, Pepitone, and Newcomb, 1952) has been extensively tested (Diener *et al.*, 1980) and the correlation between immersion in a crowd and reduced self-consciousness has been upheld. Le Bon's

There was a movement against this deindividuation hypothesis in the 1960s because, it has been argued, it ran counter to a sociological and political conception of the public, or groups of the public, being composed of autonomous agents.* Some current researchers have criticized the word because, they argue, there is no loss of identity in a crowd but only a shift from a personal to a social identity.† But this shift is a crucial one because it is a shift from an individual with a personal story who is separate from others to an individual who is fused with others and in whom, as I argue, the interbrain connection with others is potentially very strong. Just being placed in a crowd does not mean that one automatically becomes part of a crowd (notice our customary shift to the metaphor of the crowd being the whole and a person being a part). Each person in the crowd has some power to focus more on themselves or more on other people, which influences the amount of deindividuation that they experience. Crowds are also more immersive, or perhaps we are more willing to throw ourselves on the protection of numbers, if there is an external

---

corollary hypothesis, that this would always lead to disinhibited and therefore aggressive behaviour, has not (Reicher *et al.*, 1995).

* Borch (2012) provides a wide-ranging account of the ups and downs of this argument and of why sociologists no longer seem so concerned about the crowds that fascinated the father figures of their discipline such as Tarde, Taine, Simmel, and Durkheim.

† Reicher *et al.* (1995) argued that deindividuation removed one kind of self but left another 'level' of self-hood ('the social' or 'collective identity') reinforced. Many might think that a collective identity falls short of what might be understood as self. To say that 'I was there, ourselves' is not a coherent statement.

Deindividuation is increased by group collaboration. Bowman compared two experimental groups, one that had completed two exercises requiring their cooperative completion of tasks and one that did not. The former scored lower on tests of self-awareness than the latter and were twice as likely to go to help the experimenter who had appeared to hurt himself in a fake accident as the latter group (Mayer *et al.*, 1985).

threat. The greater the nonverbal communication between parts of the crowd, the more immersive it is, too. As nonverbal communication is enhanced by similarity, more homogeneous crowds are more immersive. Nonverbal communication also gains weight when there is reduplication of the same expressions or movements in different bodies. So the larger the crowd that one is immersed in, the more deindividuating it is.[*]

Although for the purposes of contrast I am going to be focusing on crowds that make extreme demands of their participants to deindividuate, in many situations the narrative self may partner with the interbrain to create a willing immersion in a partly imagined crowd.[†] This is most clearly

---

[*] More recently, Reicher and colleagues have shifted from considerations of individuals' self-awareness to the social context of the crowd. Proponents of Reicher's Elaborated Social Identity Model (ESIM) have emphasized the role of opposition, particularly opposition from the police. In one of the more recent studies of ESIM (Van Hiel *et al.*, 2007), the 'measures' of social identity used were two statements that participants (football fans in Belgium before a match) were asked whether or not to endorse: 'I am proud of our side' and 'I resemble the other members of our side'. The idea is, I think, that individuals choose to align themselves with the other members of the crowd, as opposed to earlier ideas that the crowd controls the individual. My own view is that both may happen and that there are crowds based on shared ideas and those based on shared emotions. The latter can subvert individuality if the shared emotions are strong enough. On the other hand, self-focus opposes deindividuation. Even the presence of a mirror may be enough to increase self-focus in children (Ross, Anderson, and Campbell, 2011) and thereby increase individuation.

[†] It might seem to be special pleading to argue that the imagination can supplement the interbrain, as I am so firmly asserting that the interbrain requires person-to-person contact sufficient to enable mimicry and emotional contagion. Sight or sound of other people, even when recorded, may afford some one-way traffic of that kind, but not text – the usual social medium. Text is the medium of 'theory of mind' or narrative. I am also arguing that interbrain connections are anterior to reflective cognition, whereas imagination is clearly reflective. I have set out a possible way that imagination of interbrain communication might work in the chapter on 'cacheing' in my book *Can the World Afford Autistic Spectrum Disorder?* (Tantam, 2009). I argued there, and will argue later in this book, that we memorize a great many of our interactions with other people, at least in a schematized way. We are able to recognize other people's faces, their clothes, or even their homes.

seen in internet-based crowds where extremes of grief or enthusiasm are exchanged on social media.*

Organismic analogies

Le Bon, who was medically trained, approached the psychology of crowds as a psychopathologist. He anticipated many of the subsequent observations of crowd behaviour, and it was from the point of view of a doctor viewing a patient. For example, he described 'ideas, sentiments, emotions, and beliefs' infecting crowds like microbes. He wrote that the spread was a kind of contagion and that it was spread not by the transmission of an infectious agent but by imitation, but did not explain further why imitation would be so powerful and would result in individual thinking being dominated by imitation of others –

We also remember their facial expressions sufficiently well that we can notice if they are not their usual ones. It is a perfectly meaningful expression to say 'You're not looking yourself today' using some kind of internalized image as the comparator. We can also tell ourselves or others, 'I can just imagine what he would look like if I wore that', and be put off our stroke even by the image of that thunderous brow or lecherous eye. So we have a plentiful stock of memories of embodied interactions that can be activated by our motor rehearsals. In this way, some of the features of interbrain communication can be preserved with people who had made a strong person-to-person impression, even when those people are not physically present any longer. I called this store a 'cache'. The cache is of limited capacity, and so its memory of particular interbrain connections gradually fades and needs to be replenished.

Another way that memory amplifies the interbrain connection is through familiarity. As interactions with a particular person take place over time, and emotions become associated with them, the interbrain connection with that person becomes more readily established and persists for longer. Interactions become subsumed into relationships and they develop a valency of liking and seeking out interaction or disliking and avoiding it (Scheidel, 2017).

I do not really consider these more complex features in this book, else it would turn into a social psychology textbook.

* The internet also enables the opposite process, of hyperindividualism, exemplified by the troll who cares nothing for received opinion except to insult, mock, or otherwise gainsay it.

it has taken a century for the explanations that I have alluded to in Chapter 1 to be worked out.[*]

Our vocabularies include numerous singular names of collectivities with multiple members. This makes it easy for us to talk of many people or animals as if they have a single mind. We can say that the flock of sheep panicked and ran down the hill or that the shoal of fish veered away from the sinister mouth of the grouper. For a variety of reasons, some trivial, some much more serious, engineers, IT specialists, animators, and others have become increasingly focused on what holds such collectivities together. This is how a programme developer describes the development:

> Animals flock, swarm, herd,[†] school, pack,[‡] and, also, crowd. Some of them have specialized means to ensure that they act as one when they do so. More and more of these behaviours are being investigated, often by creating models or rules that can be instantiated by robots or virtually, by a computer program that creates virtual agents that follow simple rules or a robot or 'boid'.[§]

---

[*] Le Bon's contagion model is described in Le Bon (1930/1896). A regrettable implication of the model was that psychiatrists might catch madness from their patients, and Le Bon, in a rare moment of questionable judgement, commented as evidence of this that '[t]he frequency of madness among doctors who are specialists for the mad is notorious' (Le Bon, 1930/1896, p.73).

[†] Zhang et al. (2016) use 'herding' to refer to clumping in crowds, for example around one water supply when there are others that are underused nearby.

[‡] Canetti (1984) uses pack for 'a group of men in a state of excitement whose fiercest wish is to be more' (p.93) and says that it does not need a leader, as each of the members of the pack shares a direction.

[§] Boids are virtual birds, so named by their inventor Reynolds (1987).

It is assumed that if boids can be programmed to flock in a life-like way, the rules that each boid implements may give clues to the biological principles behind flock behaviour, including human-crowd behaviour. 'Keep together' and 'avoid collisions' both seem universal, but rather obvious, examples.[10] More complex algorithms have developed spontaneously in social insects, enabling swarms to perform complex behaviour without a leader. Termites build ventilation systems, and honey bees have developed a logistic system for exploiting nectar and pollen sources with the greatest effect, despite the numbers of active worker bees varying. This, the honey algorithm, has been applied to server traffic management,* reportedly increasing the efficiency by a quarter,[11] and all of it based on the behaviour of swarms of worker bees communicating with each other by means of 'waggle dances'.

In the 19th century, crowds were assumed to be a danger under all circumstances, and public gatherings over a certain size were often proscribed. One example, etched into 19th-century English history, is the proscription of crowds protesting the repeal of the Corn Laws. Despite this law, a large crowd gathered in Manchester and the local military commander gave the order for the militia to fire on it in order to disperse it. This 'Peterloo massacre' brought down the government, but did not stop other governments in the UK and abroad from enacting similar regulations about public assemblies.

The same distaste extended to people's behaviour in crowds – or as I would say, to the behaviour of people whose interbrain connection with each other is more active than their

---

* The banks of computers that handle requests from users linked to them via the internet who may be requesting search results, their bank account details, or a weather forecast have to shift these tasks about between themselves so as to be most efficient – this is called 'traffic management'.

narrative connection. Sidis, for example, wrote this in 1903: 'This subconscious or subwaking self is regarded as embodying the "lower" or obviously brutal qualities of man. It is irrational, imitative, credulous, cowardly, cruel, and lacks all individuality, will, and self-control.'[12,*]

Today, crowd behaviour is being studied from a less fearful perspective, partly because governments have again embraced the governing principles of Roman emperors: that cities are safer when you provide 'bread and circuses' (although smaller crowds, or 'gangs', continue to be a challenge to security). Sports, entertainment, and the vicarious participation in 'events' have become, once again, stabilizing rather than dangerous features of city life because the crowd experience is rewarding.[13] Studies of crowds focus, in consequence, on crowd management as much as on crowd dispersal.[14]

People enjoy crowd participation

Crowds enable emotional contagion that has an amplifying effect on the emotions of anyone in the crowd who is not opposed to the prevailing mood. Individuals who enjoy a particular performer or who follow a particular team and are caught up with joy or sorrow in the performance experience this as consummatory, an effect that Aristotle attributed to catharsis.[†]

---

* Sidis (1903) is clearly influenced by Sigmund Freud, as his formulation of the unconscious as the residuum of our animal nature and of the importance of hypnosis in uncovering it are consistent with early Freudian theory, although Freud had, by 1903, turned away from the idea that hypnosis could uncover the unconscious, having come to believe that it increased resistance to unconscious expression, not diminished it.

† Catharsis involved building emotion and then releasing it, a process that Aristotle thought could be induced by watching emotions enacted in a tragedy

Surprisingly, there is a lack of information about whether there are more immediate rewards to being in a crowd[*] and, by extension, immediate rewards to opening up the interbrain connection. This may be because social interaction is potentially dangerous as well as potentially rewarding. Proximity to another person can be a challenge or a comfort. Eye contact can be a threat or an invitation.

Primate groups deal with this ambivalence in two ways, by differentiation or fission[15] and by grooming. Differentiation means separating from candidate group members that might be challenging or threatening. Its effect is to create an out-group that becomes the repository of difference, conferring a property on the out-group and its members that might be called 'alien', 'foreign', 'strange', or simply 'other'.[†]

Interbrain connection with 'other' groups is minimized compared with the connection with in-groups, perhaps for the very simple reason that reading nonverbal expressions in familiar others is quicker and more accurate than with unfamiliar others.[‡] Defining someone as a member of an out-group increases the risk of conflict with them[§] and is often a

---

(Straton, 1990), and there is some empirical evidence for this (Rennung and Göritz, 2015).

[*] See Godman (2013) for evidence on this point.

[†] More examples of 'othering' are provided by Çelik, Bilali, and Iqbal (2016).

[‡] But also because of the lingering effects of blame for the past, even if the past is the past of previous generations (Yang *et al.*, 2014).

[§] Family cohesion reduces adolescent involvement in sectarian conflict (Taylor *et al.*, 2016) and enhances task performance requiring collaboration (Schouten, van den Hooff, and Feldberg, 2016). Cohesion and conflict are reciprocally opposed. In group therapy, a setting in which cohesion has been studied as an important therapeutic factor, excessive cohesion can result in the group becoming stagnated, with any disagreements being suppressed and the separate development of individual group members being stultified.

precursor to denigration,* but including someone who is in conflict with the in-group may increase the threat to the in-group and lead to its dissolution.

Grooming establishes and cements the in-group in many primates. It is associated with the release of oxytocin,† with activation of the amygdala and down-regulation of the threat receptors there, and also the release of endorphins associated with pleasurable sensation. Being disconnected from an in-group causes pain.‡ Grooming also served the function of removing ectoparasites, but this function has largely disappeared from human groups, although European travellers sent back messages that the Mongols they met ate lice and fleas,[16] which may have been a misunderstanding of ectoparasite control in domestic Mongol groups. Ectoparasites must have been a major irritation in peoples who lived in close proximity to horses and dogs and who dressed in furs. Mongols were also tolerant of people who were willing to become subservient to them and join their in-group and notoriously

---

* There is a considerable literature on this, including many publications by Haslam and colleagues, for example Haslam and Loughnan (2014). Gutsell and Inzlicht propose that the in-group and out-group distinction applies to a very early stage of processing. Desynchronization of the EEG over the supplementary motor cortex occurred during an action and when a person was watching another member of their in-group performing that action, suggesting the activity of mirror neurons. When a member of an out-group performed the action, there was no EEG desynchronization (Gutsell and Inzlicht, 2010).

† Oxytocin is closely related to the very similar nonapeptide vasopressin, but it is possible that they act as antagonists in some circumstances and that vasopressin increases distancing from an out-group, just as oxytocin fosters inclusion in an in-group. Mancke and Herpertz (2014) provide some indirect evidence for this. Gastrin-releasing peptide is also an oxytocin antagonist (Kent *et al.*, 2016), but it has not been much studied up to now.

‡ See Eisenberger (2012). The pain is similar to that associated with activation of the insula and so is possibly linked with the pain of being shamed ('punched in the gut' as people sometimes describe it) or being disgusted or wounded (Masten and Narayan, 2011).

savage to those who they perceived as belonging to an out-group. This is possibly another consequence of the importance and regularity of clan members grooming each other.

Grooming persists in the 21st century but more often with a focus on improving personal appearance, reducing arousal ('relaxation'), or as part of sexual foreplay. It usually involves skin stimulation, which at a certain level of intensity and rhythmicity results in the release of endorphins and a sense of pleasure.* Shared laughter and probably other vocal aspects of social interaction can also increase well-being, possibly by the same pathways that grooming activates.†

Swarms and mobs

Alongside the perception that crowds are necessarily dangerous is the judgement that they are always stupid or rather that people become stupid in crowds. Here, it is important to think a little more about what a crowd is. There is the crowd described by Le Bon, which for the sake of clarity I am going to call a swarm.‡ This is the crowd most spoken of in past discussions of crowd psychology and is considered to be irrational or 'stupid'. Swarm members follow leaders readily, a phenomenon that seems to echo the behaviour of

---

* See Nummenmaa *et al.* (2016). Skin contact also reduces distress caused by pain (Inagaki and Eisenberger, 2012).

† See Dunbar *et al.* (2012). Evidence for call exchanges between affiliated Japanese macaques as a kind of 'grooming at a distance' has been provided by Arlet *et al.* (2015).

‡ It's difficult to find a 'good' word for this kind of crowd, as every possible synonym has a pejorative quality, precisely because membership of this kind of crowd is thought to induce irrationality and inhumanity. I am choosing swarm because it is the social unit of many Hymenoptera whose social organization requires olfactory and non-communicative networks with some formal similarity to the interbrain that I am discussing.

a person who has been hypnotized, as Trotter observed at the beginning of the last century and as has been repeatedly noted since.[17] Members of swarms are often said therefore to be suggestible. Members of swarms do not deliberate or plan but follow and obey. To make swarms do anything without a leader is difficult, and their behaviour with a leader is usually a reflection of the leader's personal agenda rather than action produced by the interbrain itself.

What makes a large co-present group of people into a swarm is high emotion that spreads through the group. This requires that a sufficiency of people in the group are disposed to feel that emotion. Unless the emotion is one that is linked to movement, the fact that a group has turned into a swarm may not be obvious. The feeling of cohesion that a great musical performance produces in a crowd, for example, is a moment of swarming that may not be recognized even by those present.* But if the emotion is one that is linked to movement then the swarm is disclosed. Three particular movement-related emotions are: adoration, when each member of the crowd wants to touch the object of their adoration; terror, when the movement is away from a threat or towards safety; and rage, when the movement is towards removing the source of the rage. I discuss terror at some length later in the book.†

There is another type of crowd that is drawn together by shared knowledge. This is the kind of crowd that used to sit outside department stores the day before their January sale was due to open. There was a camaraderie there and a readiness to share knowledge about which department had

---

* Swarms also play a role in the redirection of attention. When a majority of people look in one direction, everyone else does too (Sun *et al.*, 2017), especially if the faces that are already looking are trusted (Strachan and Tipper, 2017).

† Terror-driven swarms are sometimes called 'stampedes'.

the best bargains or to pass along a flask of coffee. But as soon as the doors were opened there was a rush to get inside that led, every year, to some tale of a fight that had broken out between hopeful shoppers fighting over a heavily discounted item. This kind of crowd comes together because of a shared purpose, not a shared feeling. I shall call it a 'mob'. Like crows mobbing a hawk, the members of a mob may act together, even selflessly, if the end result is to their personal advantage. This contrasts with the members of a swarm who selflessly give up their lives for others. The connection between individuals that makes them into a mob is not their interbrain connection but a commonality of purpose that they discover through their 'theory of mind'.

There is a third kind of crowd, which is probably the most common one. It is where people feel the pull of the swarm or the mob, but observe themselves doing so and so remain, to some degree, aloof. They may get caught up momentarily in the crowd experience, but they can also separate themselves.

I am not clear on whether it is the interbrain connection that shuts off individual rationalization or whether it is the intense emotion, or perhaps it is both.

Swarm-like behaviour can also operate over time, with secular rather than immediate effects. Paths across fields get established by successive path users, who might be sheep, people, or both, who follow in each other's footsteps often enough to kill the grass and make a groove in the underlying earth. These paths may lead to a distant stile that is not obvious when first entering the field, and the walker commits to the path knowing that it feels more comfortable to do so but also trusting that the path exists because it is the right path.*

---

* Paths can be created in different ways. In one experiment, a slime mould, Physarum, was placed on a Petri dish and glucose was added regularly at points

Equality

The first person to break a path could be anyone, chosen by happenstance. There is no need for it to be an expert or an official. Path-breaking is an equal-opportunity activity.

Philosophers such as Henri Rousseau and legislators such as Thomas Jefferson, the author of the US Declaration of Independence, have taken it to be, in the words of the Declaration, a self-evident truth that all men (exceptions were made for women and slaves) are created equal. We take this sentiment so much for granted that we do not question why it should be self-evident.

Yet many people in private conversation will admit to beliefs that some people are inferior in some way and others superior. Not only is this taken to be a fact, but many reasons are given to justify this view and as many reasons are given for ensuring that society is organized around this fact.

I shall argue in this section that we take equality to be self-evident because that is how we experience ourselves in relation to other people in certain situations in groups – situations that favour our interbrain connection with other people.

But one might similarly argue that groups are the very situations in which the worst kinds of violent behaviour towards

---

on the dish that corresponded to the cities making up Greater Tokyo and its surrounding cities. The mould at first sent feeding tubes in all directions (barring some that were strongly illuminated in order to mimic impassable geographic features like lakes and the sea), but then the tubes connecting the points where glucose was added increased in size, and those going elsewhere atrophied. The resulting pattern of the mould closely resembled the grid of the Tokyo subway system (Tero *et al.*, 2010).

The Tokyo grid was made by planners who could project forwards from the Tokyo terminus to the map references of the cities that the line was serving. The Physarum could not know its destination before it started, but reinforcement of the tubes that found glucose, coupled with atrophy of the ones that did not, had the same result. More regular tread on the path that correctly leads to the stile is another way of finding the right path.

out-groups occur. In their book on 'social dominance', Sidanius and Pratto give several egregious instances of this, including the Klu Klux Klan's racist persecution of people of colour and the Serbian army's treatment of Croatians during the civil war that broke up Yugoslavia.[18] Social dominance theory rests on the assumption that the most powerful will not only exercise that power to their advantage, but also support others doing so, whilst the weak will not just submit, but also actively collaborate. Social dominance theory is an ethological one, in that its main argument is that this is just how people are. The earliest records of human groups are about kings or gods, not ordinary people, suggesting that this may be how people have always been. And this does not just apply to people; it is also how chimpanzees and other primates behave. There is a dominant male, and often a dominant female, too, in any stable chimpanzee group.

The people who framed the constitution were speaking for a nascent nation of people who were, in many cases, strangers to each other. Their model was that of the spontaneously arising crowd that might spring up around some grievance – an example from the US is that of increased taxation by George III, king of Great Britain. The protest meetings and their actions were not organized at first but carried out by anonymous crowds. Organization of these crowds led to the formation of stable groups in which dominant individuals and in- and out-groups were identified.

Equality in spontaneous groups

Elias Canetti,[19] in his magisterial *Crowds and Power*, considers that crowds* have four main attributes: '1. The crowd always wants to grow... 2. Within the crowd there is equality...

---

* I think that Canetti is writing about the kind of crowd that I am calling a 'swarm'.

3. The crowd loves density... 4. The crowd needs a direction.'
The wish for density, for contiguity, is something that strikes
Canetti particularly because it is the reverse of how most of
us normally feel, which is to hold ourselves away from other
bodies.* I would go further than Canetti and argue that it is
from our experience of being in a crowd or spontaneous group
that we learn equality.† There is some evidence for this.[20]

Other animal swarms and interbrain connections

There are, apparently, two super-colonies of Argentinian ants in
the Mediterranean, one extending over 6000 kilometres.[21] We
do not think of this as a swarm, indeed we may even be unaware
of its existence, because it does not move en masse. Similarly,
observers may be unaware of the build-up of the population of
Norwegian lemmings under the Arctic snow until they break
cover and move. Argentinian ant super-colonies are divided
into nests with their own queens, who communicate with the

---

* See also Novelli *et al.* (2013).

† I already noted that it is the equality of its members that confers a potential
survival advantage on the crowd because each member can provide a different
perspective on the environment. This is also true of other primate crowds, and a
study by Strandburg-Peshkin *et al.* (2015) demonstrates this.

    Strandburg-Peshkin *et al.* fitted approximately a quarter (25 individuals)
of the members of a troop of wild-living olive baboons (Papio anubis) with
detectors and monitored the movements of the troop. The basic social unit of
this species of baboon is a harem: a single adult male with females and young
baboons. Older male children are excluded and live with other males who have
no female partner. The direction of the troop did not reflect this male dominance
pattern. A new direction could be initiated by any baboon. If two baboons
initiated a movement in two directions with an acute angle between them, the
troop would move in the direction that bisected that angle. If there was a wide
angle between two vectors of movement, some baboons would follow one and
some another until it was obvious which direction the majority was following,
when the whole troop would join up again and move in that direction.

nest chemically. But the queens also move from one colony to another, stitching together the connections that make the super-colony. Norwegian lemming females share child-rearing and are therefore alert to the welfare of neighbours' children, thus creating overlapping networks of social connections. Argentinian ants in their super-colony or Norwegian lemmings are, like locusts in their gregarious phase,* an immobile swarm or, in human terms, a cohesive group.

Are swarm-like crowds stupid?

Intellectuals have tended to look down on crowds, along with fashions and other fads. Even Freud, who promulgated the importance of the irrational (which he called the unconscious) in human behaviour, distrusted them.†

---

* Locusts provide a particularly interesting animal parallel to the opposition of interbrain and wilful communication, as they exist in two forms, or phenotypes, one solitary and one gregarious. The solitary form is green and the gregarious one, brown. The gregarious form has more resistance to infection (these facts taken from Simpson and Sword 2008) but is less fertile. From a purely biological point of view, the existence of the gregarious phenotype is evidence for a Lamarckian model of inheritance in that its offspring are also gregarious, although their offspring often revert to the solitary phenotype. The mechanism involved in this remains unclear but is probably a kind of imprinting, attributable to epigenesis. Solitary forms take some time to change colour but can switch behaviourally to the gregarious behaviour within hours. The trigger is touch stimulation of a part of the body as a result of crowding. The switch is probably mediated (in both directions) by serotonin (Ernst *et al.*, 2015).

† His major work on this subject was *Group Psychology and the Analysis of the Ego* (Freud, 1922) in which he develops the notion of the 'primal horde' that he had introduced in 1912 (Freud, 1955/1912), a propos of a comment of Charles Darwin. This has some similarities to my concept of a swarm, but rather than making the swarm the responsible agent for choosing or abandoning its leader, Freud makes the leader, and the fear that he (always a male for Freud) induces in the horde, the binding force. The horde does have some properties that explain this. It, for example, has 'a thirst for a leader'. Freud also opposes the ideas of individuals that lead to individual action through an individual's will and the emotional tie that connects members of the primal horde, which saps their

Swarms have the advantage over individuals or mobs when it comes to negotiating new territory.[22] The swarm has multiple viewpoints, and so long as at least one person sees a suitable way forward and others follow them, it does not matter if the ones at the back cannot see anything. Similarly, if one bird or one fish sees a threat, it does not matter if other individuals do not see it, so long as the flock or the shoal follows that one individual.* An interbrain connection overriding each individual decision-maker means that the whole collective can move very quickly to evade. The reciprocity of the interbrain connection also helps. The movement of the adjacent animal does not have to be interpreted and then a decision made to copy their movement. Copying the movement and understanding it are one and the same. If one could peer into the brain of a fish, it may even be that as far as that brain is concerned, there is no difference between initiating a veer from danger or following another fish veering from danger: they may be the same movement.[†]

---

individual will so that the horde can only act as an expression of the collective will. He wrote: 'What we have just described in our general characterisation of mankind must apply especially to the primal horde. The will of the individual was too weak; he did not venture upon action. No impulses whatever came into play except collective ones; there was only a common will, there were no single ones. An idea did not dare to turn itself into a volition unless it felt itself reinforced by a perception of its general diffusion. This weakness of the idea is to be explained by the strength of the emotional tie which is shared by all the members of the horde' (Freud, 1922, p.91).

* What does matter, though, is how connected one's neighbours are (Rosenthal et al., 2015).

† The action of the interbrain to ensure coordination between organisms may be one reason that, in emergency evacuations, crowds exit in a more orderly way than groups of disconnected individuals each seeking their own safety without reck for anyone else (Cocking, Drury, and Reicher, 2009). Models of emergency evacuations suggest that fear enhances coordinated movement so long as no-one panics and becomes immobilized (Lin and Lucas, 2015).

Cohesion, crowding, and swarming

Obviously, there is no physical connection that holds people together once the umbilical cord is cut. There are people who choose to live alone, as hermits, and they survive, although they are also prone to what our forefathers, who were more familiar with this tendency, called 'accidie'. Despite this, William Trotter, an early sociologist, thought it self-evident that people liked to be together, attributing this tendency of people to live and work in groups to a 'gregarious instinct'. Instincts have gone out of fashion as an explanation for behaviour, to be replaced by cognitive explanations. There are many thoughtful reasons for people to join together, for example to complete a task that requires more than one person or to find a mate. But, as I have already noted, Trotter got it right in one sense: there is something involuntary that pulls an in-group together.

There have been some studies of factors that influence nonverbal connectivity – or interbrain bandwidth – using one index of the interbrain connection: contagious yawning.[*] There have been a few, but not many more, studies of cohesion, and these results may give some idea of the factors that increase or decrease interbrain bandwidth. Proximity increases cohesion if the proximal others are experienced as sufficiently similar, but it is aversive and increases the sense of being different to the proximal others if there is insufficient basis for commonality.[†]

---

[*] A simple but effective measure of the bandwidth of the internet connection is 'contagious yawning' when one person yawning sets off yawning in other people. Women find yawning more contagious, apparently because of their higher empathy, and people find the yawning of family members or friends more contagious than strangers (Norscia, Demuru, and Palagi, 2016). This may be one explanation for the link between familiarization in a group and the development of cohesion.

[†] Described by Paulus (2015). In a book on the experience of concentration camp life, Sofsky (1997/1993) describes both of these outcomes as the result of being

We may be packed like sardines on a train and manage still to keep a psychological distance from our neighbours, or we may be in a packed concert and feel ourselves slipping into a sense of oceanic oneness as the music takes us over.*

There are many terms for a cohesive group of non-human animals, including the one that I shall use, a 'swarm'.

Louis Rosenberg, the creator of a 'human swarming' online platform, introduces his work in this way:

> It all goes back to the birds and the bees. The fish too. Even slime-molds. Really, it goes to all social creatures that amplify their collective intelligence by forming real-time synchronous systems. We have many names for these natural assemblages, including flocks, schools, shoals, blooms, colonies...† Certainly humans didn't evolve the ability to swarm, for we lack the innate connections that other species use to establish feedback-loops among individual members.[23]

---

crammed into a small space in a hut with other people whom the guards have selected: 'Social relations in space are no less salient. Homogeneous groups, bound together by familiarity, social similarity, shared convictions, are more likely to be able to transmute density into a sense of community – either by internal group pressure or by a shared attitude to external threat. In anonymous and serial mass formations, however, tendencies are intensified with the slightest degree of crowding... The more densely people are boxed together, the more powerful is the struggle for a modicum of distance, and the more virulent mutual aggression becomes' (p.70).

* Cohesion is increased by an external threat that is perceived by all the crowd or group members (Rothgerber, 1997). Cohesion is reduced by diversity and by the newness of relationships between group members (Zhang, 2016).

† And also troops, mobs, herds, hordes, charms, teams, swarms, packs, pods, and gangs... Wikipedia has a list of nearly 250 terms taken from the science of hunting or 'venery' to which might be added other anthropological terms such as classes, ethnic groups, races, and so on.

He goes on to describe his software that will enable people to swarm and so achieve the 'elevated hyper-mind' that would emerge if we could (a similar claim about the superiority of collective intelligence is made in a book that I will consider later – *The Wisdom of Crowds*). The swarming method that Dr Rosenberg has come up with is much like the one that was developed by Victorian spiritists who created the 'Ouija board'.*

Two things in Dr Rosenberg's blog make it particularly relevant: the allusion to the growing interest and research on the mass movements of animals or 'swarms'; and his belief that humans don't have 'innate connections that other species use

---

* Dr Rosenberg's UNUM software allows simultaneous users to influence the two-dimensional movement of the image of a puck. The majority of users will control the movement, although none of the users are privy to the attempted movements of any other user, as they are each at their own computer. The puck's movements can be used to poll opinions. For example, it has been used to predict voting patterns by having the users choose which of the names of the politicians who were standing, distributed in a circle around the puck, would win. The name that the puck ended up against represented the majority opinion.

In the Ouija board game, an easily moved object, a planchette – often a wooden or plastic object that could be placed on a table or board that is shiny enough for it to move easily – would be placed in the centre of the board or table on which there would also be the letters of the alphabet and, sometimes, numbers. Each participant would put their dominant index finger on the glass and a question would be asked of the 'spirit' in attendance. The glass would then move to indicate a letter, and then another letter, until an answer was spelt out. None of the attenders at what was often called a seance would own up to having moved the glass and indeed it does seem to move itself, i.e. it is not operated by any particular individual but by the collectivity. The Ouija (derived from the combination of the French and German words for 'yes') board is a commercial product, but planchette boards were described at much earlier times. The most common explanation of the Ouija phenomenon is ideomotor: that we make micro-movements when we recall memories but the micro-movement and indeed the memory may not be something that we are aware of (Gauchou, Rensink, and Fels, 2012). This does not fully explain why the planchette still moves even though several fingers are on it. This is best accounted for as a small-scale example of a leadership rule that I will discuss later in this chapter when I consider the work of Couzin.

to establish feed-back loops among individual members'. As I have demonstrated in Chapter 1, we do have these feedback loops, they work through imitation and contagion, and I am collectively terming them interbrain connections.

Thinking of us humans 'swarming' offends some people who believe that it is a pejorative term. David Shariatmadari, writing in *The Guardian* newspaper,[24] takes Mr Cameron, the then UK prime minister, to task for applying that word to immigrants fleeing the conflicts in the Middle East and West Africa. He considers it 'callous, misleading language'. But the language comes to mind because human migratory movements do resemble the movements of other animals that make mass migrations, such as ants, desert locusts, and Norwegian lemmings. We use these analogies regularly: we consider ourselves to be commuting to work 'like ants'; our children fall on food at family gatherings 'like locusts'; and we worry that we should not follow politicians too slavishly in case we follow them over some cliff and they lead us to disaster, like the Pied Piper did to the rats of Hamelin (like lemmings).*

---

* This is to slander lemmings. The apparently suicidal behaviour of lemming flocks was featured in a Disney film, *White Wilderness*. Lemmings were seen pouring over a cliff and apparently into the sea. It turns out the lemmings were being forced out of a truck over a bank into a river, and this was not done in the Arctic where they live but in Alberta (Woodford, 2003). It was a put-up job, but it seemed completely believable. Norwegian lemmings (but not the Canadian ones featured in *White Wilderness*) do emerge in large flocks from underneath the snow, but, unlike other voles, they can swim, and when they have been seen entering fjords it is most likely with the intention of swimming across and not drowning.

In- and out-groups

'When push comes to shove, you find out who your friends are.' This or a similar sentiment is likely to have been expressed by many readers who have gone through a difficult experience. It is a comment on the effect of threat or danger. As noted in the discussion on attachment, threat leads animals to search for and go to places of greater safety. In many infant vertebrates, the place of safety is in the proximity of an older, bigger conspecific. Not all older, bigger conspecifics will defend an infant: some might kill them. So the infant is primed at birth to bond with an attachment figure – typically the biological mother. Oxytocin plays a role in this bonding process. Later in life, the attachment function generalizes to other, connected conspecifics. In fact, as the adage quoted above has it, a threat to oneself might disclose the others with whom one has a positive connection when they identify themselves as defenders. These defenders may be merely connected by a common interest – they may be in one's 'mob' to use the term for this kind of group that I introduced previously – or they may be in one's swarm, i.e. my interbrain connection with them may be what mainly joins me to them. Threat increases interbrain connectedness, with oxytocin* playing a part in this

---

* The oxytocin story has become increasingly complex. The first use of oxytocin in medicine was to produce a contraction of the uterus after birth to reduce haemorrhage – hence the name. It was noted to promote milk let down and then to be involved in bonding between mother and child. The nonapeptide hormones – oxytocin and vasopressin – are still thought to be involved in the formation of affectional bonds, not just between mothers and infants but also between fathers and infants, and between friends and between sexual partners. Oxytocin is sometimes called the 'love hormone' (as if love could be reduced to a hormone's influence). Anecdotal accounts of people dating after insufflating oxytocin do not confirm that it induces love, although it may have something to do with sex, at least in female mice (Nakajima, Görlich, and Heintz, 2015). Transmitters do not have single functions: oxytocin itself is one of a family of peptide hormones that interact; the synapses in which it is active belong to many

as it does in increasing the primary interbrain connection with the attachment figure. Giving an extrinsic oxytocin boost enhances connectedness mainly in those who did not have a strong connectedness with their original attachment figure.[25] It is not unselective, but it increases already existing interbrain connections rather than creating them with strangers.[*] In fact, oxytocin administration may increase hostility to outsiders.[26]

---

neurons – in different systems and subserving different functions – including aggression in the service of the protection of dependants (Bosch, 2013).

Oxytocin switches the behaviour of some animals, including some people, into a more caring or more nurturant mode, and this may be associated with a switch towards greater affective empathy (Veening and Olivier, 2013) and therefore openness to affection. However, this may be modulated by whether or not the other person is already an affiliate. Men became more fearful, and therefore more behaviourally inhibited, if predosed with oxytocin before playing an economic game with strangers (Zheng, Kendrick, and Yu, 2016). This may be mediated by increased interbrain bandwidth. Oxytocin does increase activity in both the superior right temporal sulcus and the fusiform gyrus, areas associated with the interbrain (Haas *et al.*, 2016; Riem *et al.*, 2014). Skuse *et al.* (2014) found in a survey of probands of children with ASD that particular alleles of the oxytocin gene were associated with reduced performance on face recognition memory, discrimination of facial emotions, and direction of gaze detection.

Oxytocin administration increases focus on affective stimuli (Bate *et al.*, 2015), i.e., in the terms that I am using, increases interbrain bandwidth. Having the allele of the oxytocin receptor that binds oxytocin most strongly is associated with being more sociable generally but not with close relationships (Li *et al.*, 2015), indicating that oxytocin is not the 'love hormone' that it was once thought to be. Oxytocin insufflation increases performance on empathy measures (Carter, 2013) and increases post-hypnotic suggestion (Bryant *et al.*, 2012), another situation in which individuality is suppressed. In men, oxytocin makes empathic men more willing to put the interests of the group before their own in decision-making (Kret *et al.*, 2013). MDMA ('Ecstasy') releases oxytocin, and this is a likely explanation of its action as a party drug (Bershad *et al.*, 2016).

Oxytocin-induced empathy has been suggested as the explanation for altruistic behaviour that has no immediate individual reward (Zak and Barraza, 2013). Vasopressin enhances the ability to recognize whether or not others are familiar. It increases blood flow to the left temporoparietal junction, an area particularly involved in language, in contrast to the right temporoparietal junction, which is involved in the interbrain (Zink *et al.*, 2011).

* Mothers who are given oxytocin and then shown pictures of other mothers' infants show the neurological activation associated with the interbrain but are

Swarms induced by threats correspond to the in-groups originally described by sociologists on the basis of the higher-order category of 'relations' rather than the biosocial category of 'connections' that I am considering. What Tajfel and other sociologists established was that a separation into in- and out-groups immediately creates the potential for conflict and discrimination.[27]

In-group members may give more regular, 'warm' looks to each other's faces and this may be why judgements about the facial expressions of in-group members is more accurate than judgements about members of an out-group. This phenomenon is sometimes called 'ethnocentrism', because it was first noted in relation to the accuracy of judgements of facial expression of members of another ethnic group, but ethnicity may be a weak basis for group solidarity.* In college students, the accuracy discrepancy does not arise between students at the same university, who may have various ethnicities, but does when judgements of students of that university – the in-group – are compared with judgements of students at another university who are, for this purpose, an out-group.[28]

There has been a surge of interest in the hormone oxytocin (and to a lesser extent its closely related nonapeptide vasopressin) over recent years. Oxytocin is not the 'love hormone' that it was once imagined to be. But oxytocin does induce 'in-group favoritism and, to a lesser extent, out-group derogation'[29] (i.e. ethnocentrism in a number of mammalian species including people). Its effects, though, may be limited

---

not better at interpreting the expressions shown in the pictures (Voorthuis *et al.*, 2014).

* Although seven-month-old infants are more likely to have gaze cued by someone of their own ethnicity than by someone of another ethnicity (Xiao *et al.*, 2017).

in people who have had a consistently emotionally warm upbringing.*

The same epithets used to describe ethnocentrism – in-group favouritism and out-group derogation – could be used of the consequences of the coming together of a cohesive group, a crowd, or a swarm, since all of these groupings imply a boundary outside in which lie potential adversaries or rivals.†
These are all facets of the same phenomenon: the capacity of human beings to switch from being solitary individuals to gregarious followers, a switch that may partly be mediated by oxytocin.

In- and out-group mobs

Commonality, leading to in- and out-group formation, can, as I already noted, be based on connections of shared narrative. The groups that Tajfel and his colleagues were studying were based on such a shared narrative or, as they termed it, a shared 'social identity'.

In a famous experiment, Muzafer Sherif and his colleagues took 11-year-olds to a summer camp and divided them into two groups. The members of each group were encouraged to act as a team in competition with the other group. The

---

* See Riem *et al.* (2014). This is what attachment theorists would call securely attaching.

† Once an in-group has been created, its members' relationships change. In-group members have more empathy for each other – there is a stronger interbrain connection between members of the in-group – and less empathy for the out-group (Campbell and de Waal, 2011). In-group members also have more pain empathy for each other and less empathy for the pain of out-group members (Cikara *et al.*, 2014; Ruckmann *et al.*, 2015), or even pleasure at the pain of members of the out-group, a form of Schadenfreude (Cikara, 2015). Hate towards the out-group may be triggered by the perception or prejudice that the members behave immorally (Weisel and Böhm, 2015).

experiment got out of hand. There were attacks by members of one group on the members of the other, and Sherif and his team had to devise ways to fuse the two groups, which they did by giving them a common task.* It is likely that in-groups often have both swarm-like and mob-like features, i.e. that members are connected by both interbrain and narrative connections, each of which becomes more or less salient under different circumstances. Out-groups too may be alienated because they have opposing tasks or purposes and because this results in shutting down the potential interbrain connection between members of each in-group.[30] The disconnection of the members of each in-group may be modulated by the nature of the task, too. Experimental participants may feel more connected to someone of another ethnic group if they are focused on their expressions of pain than if focusing on their ethnicity.[31]

Religion and crowds

Groups – both 'swarms' and 'mobs' – are fundamental to much religious practice. Conversion to Islam is to join the 'umma', the fellowship of Muslims, and to accept its shared beliefs. Attending a Christian church is often described as participating in a fellowship. Many Buddhists aim to become monks or nuns, living in a close-knit community. Religion itself, St Augustine supposed, means binding together.†

---

* See Sherif, Hogg, and Abrams (2001).

† See Giner-Sorolla, Leidner, and Castano (2011). It is often supposed that religion is derived from 'religare', Latin for binding together. Modern commentators believe that it was Augustine of Hippo who originated the notion that religion was about creating community and who may have inspired this etymological reading. Most etymologists now consider, however, that religion originates from 'religere', referring to the duty to regularly repeat specified observances (Seitschek, 2012).

Fusing with a large and welcomed group is a constant component in the religious experience. Durkheim accepted Le Bon's concept of the contagion of emotions within a crowd and noted that participating in a crowd could lead to the emotional contagion of euphoria. Giving several examples drawn from anthropological observers of native Australian ceremonials, Durkheim also thought that euphoria would sometimes mount to higher, intoxicating levels, which he called 'effervescence'.* This particularly happened in mythic re-enactments, such as the enactment of the killing of the snake Wollunqua by two phratries of the Warramunga that Durkheim describes in detail in his book *The Elementary Forms of the Religious Life*.[32] He thought that ceremonies like this, with their associated effervescences, created the conviction that there was another powerful spirit world that people could sometimes experience, which was where divine beings lived. This, Durkheim thought, was the basis for religious belief. One element in this, although Durkheim did not mention it, was transcendence: the feeling that one could glimpse realities beyond the usual horizons.

In an up-to-date study, effervescent moods have been detected in a variety of situations in which people came together to do something that they considered to be for the greater good, including re-enactments of patriotic events and protests and demonstrations against capitalism and for the redistribution of wealth.[33] Participants in one of the world's largest religious events, or at least participants in a sub-group of it, leave with an enhanced sense of spirituality and well-being attributable to being with their co-religionists.[34]

---

* There have been several recent studies that support Durkheim's speculations: one study of participants in a Hindu festival (Hopkins *et al.*, 2016) and several studies of student demos (Páez *et al.*, 2015).

The abnegation of the self is an important component of transcendence, and that is what the crowd, or the spontaneous group, demands. As soon as we become aware of ourselves in a crowd, we want to take up a position in relation to it: to get away, to give it direction, to get one's friends around one, to be its mouthpiece, and so on. As always in this book, the focus on a theory-of-mind way of looking at a social situation is achieved partly by the suppression of the oceanic, reciprocal interbrain connection. One might be aware of this, and feel a sense of 'waking up' to one's situation, when the individualistic, personal narrative focus kicks in.

The sense of something greater, of something other but valuable, does not necessarily follow from absorption in the mergence that is a consequence of the interbrain connection. It requires something in addition to this.

Religious rituals increase the sense of group cohesion[35] and diminish individuality within the religious community. Religious practices are often aimed at increasing the interbrain connection of their participants, but to what purpose? One possible explanation is that the emotions that correspond to group immersion – giving up, going along with, being the servant of the group's will – create an expectancy of something greater that will provide leadership. If no actual leader steps forward, then this greater being, who can be both a product of the religious community and its inspiration, can be a reigning idea, a saviour, or a god. To create an image of this fantasy leader for themselves, each member has to conjure up something greater than themselves, cobbled together from miraculous events, from memories of being a child with apparently all-knowing parents, from depictions or images… from any suitable materials, in fact. But whatever that figure is, it transcends what a person thought possible before they 'got' religion. It will provoke awe, fear, humility, hope, joy, love, and occasionally rage and other emotions in varying proportions. It also seems to provide some satisfaction to those who think that life must be more than what is experienced in order to make it worthwhile.

Two types of leader

The experiment by Sherif and his colleagues has provided sustenance to the persisting claim that crowds are dangerous and to another claim that children and 'savages' both lack a controlling mental capacity that age or civilization confers.[*] Children's savagery was depicted in an influential novel by William Golding[36] that often comes to mind when issues about children's innocence and loving-kindness are raised.

Leaders who emerge spontaneously, who groups follow briefly, and who then fade away as the group chooses a new direction are, as I have already argued, one of the properties of mobile swarms that make them effective explorers of new territory, where no map is available.[†] Spontaneous leaders

---

[*] The fact that the prefrontal cortex, often considered the 'executive centre' of the brain, is the last part of the brain to fully develop, usually at around 27 years of age, seems to provide some spurious support for this.

[†] The interbrain as a direct albeit modulated connection between networks can be modelled by computer networks and can itself be applied to other involuntary group processes that involve swarm-like crowds, including emotional leadership in organizations and political change. These changes take place over a longer period since they involve change in established leadership, not just in spontaneous leaders. Changes in leadership in groups that are too large for all members to be in face-to-face communication can be modelled by computer and these models suggest that connections between a smaller leadership group remain important, acting as an alternative group of leaders in waiting to whom the swarm might switch (Mosquera-Doñate and Boguñá, 2015; Tucci, González-Avella, and Cosenza, 2016). Switches of leadership in organizations that are 'flat' in their hierarchical structure may be particularly appropriate in

only become leaders if enough group members follow them.*
Leaders in groups are often informal and readily replaced.
They are linked to groups by interbrain ties that pull the group
with them.

Leaders, even in animal groups, have a tendency to become
established although sometimes only in particular tasks or
ranges.† In human groups, leadership may become structurally
embedded with leaders having an authority or power to
enforce followship through obedience. So leaders like those in
the experiment by Sherif and his colleagues lead by standing
outside the group and at the same time creating fear within
it – albeit only the level of fear that is appropriate to their
authority. Another example of this is a short experiment
conducted by a teacher, Rob Jones, who ordered his students
to follow new rules, deliberately based on Nazism. It was a
very short experiment because the students adopted his
'dictatorship' so zealously that other members of staff and
parents were alarmed, and the students themselves became
frightened of being informed on by other students. Jones had
to devise a ceremony to end it.‡

---

community organizations (Liang and Sandmann, 2015). The same phenomenon
of spontaneous leadership of connected units can be observed at the micro
as well as the macro level, for example in the movement of cell monolayers
(Reffay *et al.*, 2011) and artificially grown neural networks (Eckmann *et al.*,
2008; Ham *et al.*, 2008), which become synchronized as they become connected
(Cohen *et al.*, 2008).

* If the behaviour of brown lemurs (Jacobs *et al.*, 2011), sheep (Pillot *et al.*, 2010),
and musk oxen (Ihl and Bowyer, 2011) are anything to go by.

† For example, in heifers (Dumont *et al.*, 2005) and musk oxen (*ibid.*). Leaders are
not always the strongest physically. In fact, in foragers it may be the weakest in
joint foraging groups who sets the pace (Rands *et al.*, 2003).

‡ See Renata Aron (2017). The experiment has also been the subject of a
documentary and, in fictionalized form, of two other films.

Families and familiarity

Few mammals abandon their young completely after birth. The young continue to feed selectively on their mothers' milk whilst the mothers are lactating, and the mothers and sometimes also the fathers provide protection against predators,[*] guidance about danger, and so on. These behaviours are most observable in the nuclear family group, but the more extended family participate as well. It is increasingly recognized that there are advantages[†] in extending this network more widely

---

[*] And also protection against infanticide. Infanticide is a highly emotive topic, even among primatologists (Sommer *et al.*, 2006), but it appears to be a regular feature in primates, with infants at risk of being killed by their mother's new mate (but only if the mother is likely to be able to procreate again) (Broom, Borries, and Koenig, 2004). In primates where the females and not males migrate from their natal groups, the rule in mountain gorillas for example, stepfathers can 'bond' with older chimpanzees and immature gorillas, and, if they do, they contribute significantly to the juvenile's upbringing (Rosenbaum *et al.*, 2016).

Infanticide is even more controversial in humans than it is in primates. The risk is low and the data are hard to get. Coroners may misclassify infanticide on the day of birth (when the risk is highest) as still birth, the birth certificate may not carry the name of the biological father but the man with whom the mother is currently living, and the relationship with that man is rarely specified (Hrdy, 2016; Overpeck *et al.*, 1998). It is clear though that there are circumstances in which the interbrain connection between a living human child (I am not considering abortion where the same biases apply) and adult humans, which would normally invoke protective behaviour, is suppressed. Children who are born as the result of a rape are more likely to be killed (Theidon, 2015), for example mothers who cannot cope with a child may abandon them. There is also a common belief that stepfathers are more likely to be violent to a baby that they have not fathered, but direct evidence of this is lacking.

[†] Allomothering, co-breeding, or fostering has been studied more (Palombit, 2015). It is one example of what has been called mutual aid or even altruism in animals. Hamilton's law of the selfish genes is one explanation of the evolution of allomothering by the extended family ('kin selection') but not of allomothering by familiars who are not related. 'Group selection' would explain this, but only after so many generations that the initial reduction in breeding potential for alloparents cannot be offset. Various suggestions have been made including the chance survival for a long enough period of even initially adverse mutations (Constable *et al.*, 2016) or the protective effect of altruism such

to foster-mothers or 'allomothers'.* Allomothering is one indication that a species is social, although great apes, unlike ourselves, do not allow other females to handle their young. Parent and child recognize each other's kinship through smell in many mammals, but this is much less well developed in humans, and other connections are needed.

Alloparenting is common in us, human beings, and English reflects this. 'Families' and 'familiarity' clearly come from the same root, but family means kin, and familiarity extends more widely to include our inner circle of friends.

Summary so far

Immersion in a crowd opens up the interbrain connection to its fullest, most untrammelled connectivity. There is a price to pay: a loss of individuality and all that goes with it.† But there are also gains.

The experience of transcendence is one, and this might be the root of spirituality and, indeed, what many people would consider the meaning of life.

The interbrain connection between crowd members of many species, including people, enables them, like flocking sheep or schooling fish, to adapt to threats from unexpected directions and to remain coordinated even in emergencies.

---

that the beneficiaries are less likely to attack the altruist (Becker, 1976). One alternative is that the disposition that makes allomothering possible has other and immediate advantages for selection. Increased interbrain bandwidth may, for example, increase both the chances of offering successful allomothering and the chances of survival of one's own children.

* Allomothers may include other males attached to polyandrous groups.

† The Warramunga, who belonged to the phratry that had Wollunqua as their totem, had to give their wives to the other Warramunga to lay with before the ceremony, as described by Durkheim (1915/1912).

Being in crowd mode may also make us experience what it would be like to transcend our perspective, our time, our place, and our capacity, and to feel, for a moment, like a divine being.

Why this chapter is about the brain, and not about, say, extended cognition

Gallagher and Varga[37] make useful distinctions between theories about how we know what other people are thinking and feeling. They consider that there are three main approaches. Two are customarily considered to be theories of mind. 'Theory theory', they consider, involves making theoretical inferences from behaviour. Simulation theory 'depends on simulating the other's mental states within one's own mental or motor system'.* Their last category corresponds to what I call 'the interbrain'. They call it 'interaction theory' and define it as looking:

> to embodied processes (involving movement, gesture, facial expression, vocal intonation, etc.) and the dynamics of intersubjective interactions (joint attention, joint action, and processes not confined to an individual system) in highly contextualized situations to explain social cognition, and disruptions of these processes in some psychopathological conditions.

Although interaction theory is described as a theory, the components that Gallagher and Varga describe are 'embodied'. 'Interaction theory' is brain-based. In fact, it is another name for what I am calling 'the interbrain'.

---

* I have called this 'the cache' (Tantam, 2009).

There are many alternative formulations of how people link together and I have referenced some of these already. Gallagher and Varga make the same clear distinction between mind-based and brain-based conceptions that I am trying to make when I distinguish theory of mind and interbrain theories.* They do not focus on the implications of the distinction, though, as I am trying to do. Even more important, in my view, is the possibility that there are not two hypotheses about how links are made as they suggest, but there are at least two ways that links may be established (actually, I proposed in the previous chapter that there is a second brain-based link between people based on our reactions to pain or disgust in ourselves and in others).

Not all theories of mental connection fit well into Gallagher and Varga's trichotomy. There are theories of extended cognition that call for the use of cognitive prostheses ranging from simple memory aids, like notebooks, right up to futuristic notions of computer chips or the internet being implanted in people's brains. Connection here would be via a visually accessed code ('writing') or a direct neural interface (which has yet to be invented). Extended cognition theorists have mainly reflected on its contribution to the use of material objects, but they have also extended cognition to what I have described as the elements that constitute the interbrain, arriving at this idea by a rather different route.[38]

There is another group of theories that focus on intersubjectivity, but they base this on theories of connection between minds. Modern formulations of these theories have typically alluded to the same communicative abilities of infants that I have connected in my theory of the interbrain but have

---

* Turner and Maryanski (2012) provide evidence for a brain-based theory or, as they put it, a neurological basis for group formation.

considered these to be precursors of the development of mind and not alternatives to it.[*]

There is a close kinship between these theories and my interbrain theory, but there is one substantial difference. I consider that the interbrain connection has a much stronger influence over individual behaviour than do the advocates of intersubjectivity, so much so that two states of human functioning can be discerned: Homo individualis and Homo socialis. These two modes of function can alternate, can blend,

---

[*] Trevarthen's treatment of intersubjectivity (Trevarthen, 2005; Trevarthen and Aitken, 2001) refers to all of the interbrain factors that I have mentioned but describes them as merely supportive of the development of 'companionship'; others (Hobson, 2002; Reddy, 2008; Rochat, 2001) also refer to the same phenomena, with some variation, but attribute them to mental activity. Hobson, for example, subscribes to the Kleinian view that the infant is born with 'unconscious phantasies' about other people that are attributable to an innate mental ability (Ogden, 1984). These authors have changed their views somewhat recently to allow for neuroimaging research that seems to gainsay the need to presuppose representations of perceptions mediating intersubjectivity but fall short of postulating mindless, brain-to-brain communication. Many of them have contributed to an edited volume, *The Shared Mind* (Zlatev, 2008), in which intersubjectivity is attributed to mental activity. Of course, there is no hard-and-fast definition of mind and, according to one definition, mind gradually emerges phylogenetically. This assumes that the interbrain and the development of mind are a seamless continuity. That may be so if mind is taken to be a system of representations. Baboons and other primates that see a stick and see it as a representation of a long, thin finger that can be inserted into a narrow hole to remove a grub clearly have a mind in this sense. I am confining mind to its implied usage in the expression 'theory of mind', i.e. mental activity that, in Trevarthen's own terms, allows a person to grasp the point of view not just of another person, but also of a third person watching that interaction (a crucial moment in many developmental theories, called 'third person relations' by John Rickman (1957); 'être pour autrui' by Comte and later Sartre; and 'the name of the father' by Lacan).

This particular definition of mind is, I argue, particularly linked to narrative and to narrative language.

Zlatev *et al.* (2008) contrast the intersubjective model of empathic interaction with the theory of mind as follows: 'Human beings are primordially connected in their subjectivity rather than functioning as monads [I think that they are using this term in its current everyday usage rather than its original and

or can be in conflict. I wish that I could claim that this is an entirely original thought, but I discovered after beginning this book that something very similar had been advocated a century ago.[39]

Notes

1. Likowski *et al.*, 2011
2. Rankin and Philip, 1963, p.169
3. Rankin and Philip, 1963
4. Slote, 2013
5. Sommerville *et al.*, 2013
6. de Waal, 2012
7. Sartre, 2004/1960, p.379
8. Le Bon, 1930/1896
9. Selective quotes from Le Bon, 1930/1896, pp.13–14
10. Yu *et al.*, 2015
11. Ab Wahab, Nefti-Meziani, and Atyabi, 2015; Nakrani and Tovey, 2007
12. Sidis, 1903, p.3
13. Zumeta *et al.*, 2015
14. Cocking, 2013
15. MacCarron and Dunbar, 2016
16. Frankopan, 2015
17. Trotter, 1909
18. Sidanius and Pratto, 2012
19. Canetti, 1984, p.29
20. Castelli and Tomelleri, 2008
21. Blight *et al.*, 2010
22. Strandburg-Peshkin *et al.*, 2015
23. Rosenberg, 2015
24. Shariatmadari, 2015
25. Riem *et al.*, 2014
26. De Dreu *et al.*, 2011
27. Tajfel, 1982
28. Stevenson, Soto, and Adams, 2012
29. Blight *et al.*, 2010
30. Hein *et al.*, 2015
31. Sheng *et al.*, 2014
32. Durkheim, 1915/1912
33. Páez *et al.*, 2015
34. Tewari *et al.*, 2012
35. Watson-Jones and Legare, 2016

---

opposite Leibnizian sense] who need to "infer" that others are also endowed with experiences and mentalities that are similar to their own; The sharing of experiences is not only, not even primarily, on a cognitive level, but also (and more basically) on the level of affect, perceptual processes, and conative (action-oriented) engagements; Such sharing and understanding is based on embodied interaction (e.g. empathic perception, imitation, gesture, and practical collaboration); Crucial cognitive capacities are initially social and interactional and are only later understand [sic] in private or representational terms.'

What they do not say is that mind, in the sense that I am using it, arises out of conflict and eventually suppression of the interbrain connection.

36. Golding, 1954

37. Gallagher and Varga, 2015. The
    Quotes that follow are from p.5

38. Krueger, 2011b

39. Trotter, 1909

Chapter 3

BEING DOMINATED BY THE THEORY-OF-MIND CONNECTION

Summary so far

In Chapter 1, I showed that our primary connection with others is the result of innate, reflexive connections with them. These connections include 'bonding', which is the basic expression of other connections mediated by smell and the visceral brain, imitation, and gaze. It is the combination of the latter two that I am terming the interbrain. A later set of connections is discovered by children in the social use of the language that they acquire as they gain awareness of themselves as persons in the social world.

Theory-of-mind connections are the ones that inform our conscious judgements. They may build on the interbrain or be independent of it, in which case the action tendencies emanating from the interbrain are inhibited. In Chapter 2, I considered the rare cases in which actions are dominated by the interbrain connection. I noted that a certain kind of leader may inhibit theory of mind in the led, allowing the led to act more on their interbrain connection. I come back to this later, where I also consider the corollary that suppressing the interbrain is a prerequisite of being able to develop autonomy and individuality. This creates the potential for conflict between the effects of the interbrain and the theory-of-mind relations with the world, and it is this inevitable, as one would say 'intrapsychic', conflict that I consider in this chapter.

I suppose that there will come a day when this conflict could be described in some kind of neurological diagram in which mirror neuron areas and prefrontal cortex areas mediating narrative are in balanced opposition,[1] but for the moment the conflict has to be inferred from behaviour.

Inner conflict

None of us can doubt that society is riven by conflict. Our media bring us shocking images of that from countries all over the world: at the time of writing this there are deaths in internecine conflicts in Ukraine, Afghanistan, India, Pakistan, the Central African Republic, Iraq, Syria, Egypt, Somalia, Venezuela, and no doubt many other states where the scale is not enough to hit the headlines. Consensus social theorists consider that there are manifestations of imperfect social constitutions or social systems in transition. Society can be mended, and cultures can be peaceable.[2] Conflict theorists, who outnumber them, believe that conflict is natural. Some of them are social Darwinists who argue that evolution in society, as in the natural kingdom, is driven by the opposing interests of predator and prey, host and parasite. Marx thought that the inequitable distribution of wealth, capital, or surplus value could only be resolved if everyone could own the capital, although, in practice, this meant that it was owned by the state but controlled by a small number of individuals. Neo-Marxists see this struggle more generally as one between people – each competing for the same desired but scarce resource.

Individuals too are so frequently in conflict that it seems unlikely that this is merely a stage in human evolution that will eventually lead to universal cooperation. Primates are, as a family, not a peaceable clade, although the splitting off of pygmy chimpanzees, Pan paniscus, who live in a small area of central Africa from the main group, Pan troglodytes, gives some people a paradigm of possible human destiny. Pan paniscus, or bonobos, are matriarchal, frugivorous, rarely violent, and have lots of homosexual and heterosexual sex. Chimp groups are dominated by a few males, go to war with other chimps, are omnivorous, and maintain order within a group by aggression. Conflicts are frequent. Chimps are the more numerous and widely distributed species. But perhaps Homo will go in the direction of Pan paniscus and not Pan troglodytes.

Some evidence for this was adduced in a persuasive book by Belk.[3] In his book, Pinker[4] argued that violence is gradually diminishing and may even be destined to die out (to use a violent metaphor). Pinker adduced several historical and social factors for this but also proposed that we are more knowledgeable nowadays about the factors that motivate violence or aggression and the factors that prevent it.[*] We could

---

[*] Motives for violence cited by Pinker are instrumental for gaining an end, becoming dominant (although it is not clear why this should be motivating), revenge, sexual sadism, and ideological reasons (essentially this is the first motive, but it is pursued by a group and not an individual). Restraints move towards cooperation and altruism. They are: empathy, which 'prompts us to feel the pain of others and to align their interests with our own'; the moral sense, which 'sanctifies a set of norms and taboos that govern the interactions among people in a culture' – these sometimes decrease violence but can also increase it 'when the norms are tribal, authoritarian, or puritanical'; reason, which 'allows us

make more explicit use of them to guard against violence. Three out of the four preventative factors cited by Pinker involve individuals' connections with each other: empathy (defined as the experience of vicarious pain); awareness of, and obedience to, shared social norms and rules; and having a wider knowledge of different cultures on the assumption that doing so leads to sharing their beliefs and values.

Many people consider that conflict is almost as reprehensible as violence, but even if violence was no longer required as a solution to conflict, it would be hard to see how conflict itself could be ended. Just to give one example, Pinker's fourth preventative factor against violence is self-control. But self-control is a biological impossibility for juvenile humans, humans with dementia or delirium, or humans in altered states of consciousness like sleep, coma, or intoxication. Inevitably, there will be occasions when other people will have to restrain people who lack self-control, and there will be a conflict between what the un-self-controlled person will want and the restrainer will want for them. Many other examples of an unavoidable conflict of interest will come to mind, including the differing reproductive instincts of men and women, or the conflicts that we euphemize as competition in sport or trade.

As in most books that set out a plan for humanity, Pinker treats individual human agents as single minded. But none of us are. We are often ambivalent, wavering, or muddled. We may be ataractic, lacking the strength of will to carry out our intentions. We might harbour desires that can unexpectedly arise and overwhelm us, throwing over plans in favour of impulsive actions. We change our minds, and we do not act

---

to extract ourselves from our parochial vantage points'; and self-control, which 'allows us to anticipate the consequences of acting on our impulses and to inhibit them accordingly' (Pinker, 2011, p.xxiv).

consistently. One explanation of this is that we are internally conflicted. Freud famously argued that this conflict was between our sexual desire and our civilizing impulses but was only repeating an old assumption that had been made many times before. I have argued in the past that civilization is just as likely to arouse our sexual desire as to quench it, but many people believe that it is the beast in us that civilization is at war with – Pinker himself seems to be suggesting this.

Freud, in his later structural theory, suggested that individuals are also inevitably in conflict with the society around them. This too has been a long-standing theory. Rousseau argued it, as did Schopenhauer and Nietzsche.* 'Society' is no more a unitary entity than is an individual. It is made up of many different and overlapping groups and institutions. So our obligations to one society of which we are a member may conflict with those of another of which we are also a member, and this conflict is played out inside us.†

The correct balance between individual freedom and autonomy and the obligations and duties of members of

---

* Nowadays their stance would be considered individualistic, as opposed to the collectivist stance of, say, ancient Greek philosophers.

† See Hirsh and Kang (2016). Political rhetoric often focuses on both sides of this conflict. Individuals are portrayed as seeking to be free and uncoerced. Societies are portrayed as being justified in protecting vulnerable members from antisocial acts by limited coercion and to enforce rules to prevent free-loading, an especial concern at the time of writing this book when developed countries are seeking to cut spending on residents of working age who do not earn but rely on benefits provided by the public. Identifying people who do not 'deserve' benefits or who are fraudulently claiming them, i.e. free-loading, has been the least controversial method of reducing the cost of benefits so far.

One metaphor that is applied to this tension is that of 'boundary'. Anzieu (1990) imagined that our minds are surrounded by a kind of skin, just as our bodies are. It holds us in and keeps us safe from psychological 'pathogens' (Oaten, Stevenson, and Case, 2009), but it also acts as a barrier against other people. Too thick a skin, and we are likely to find ourselves isolated. Too thin a skin, and we are likely to isolate ourselves as a form of protection.

a society to other members is undoubtedly a potent source of conflict both within society and within each of us, too. However, I want to explore a related but separate cause of conflict in this chapter: that between the consequences of our different connections to other people, the conflict between our theory of mind and our interbrain connections.*

When does the opposition between the interbrain and the theory of mind begin?

The interbrain connects the child with other people at birth or at most hours after birth. In people, a theory of mind develops over a period usually considered to be between two and four years of age. So the behavioural manifestation of the interbrain needs to take account of its additional development and refinement during the first two years of life.† The basic properties of actions linked to interbrain connections – speed of response, reciprocity, and intersubjectivity – persist, but their expression is modified by additional interbrain functions. Infants start to use the gaze of others to predict others' actions, and the exchanges of gaze with carers become smoother and more coordinated.[5] Infants four to five months old can correct for head orientation in discriminating direct and averted gaze.[6] Infants also become more similar in how they visualize a scene (a convergence that is fully established in neurotypical individuals by the time that adulthood is reached).[7]

Infants are curious at around three months and may look at strangers' faces more than their mothers'. However, this is

---

* Which connection dominates may be partly determined by our culture (Markus and Lin, 1999).

† In a cross-cultural study, imitation by children became much less frequent after they were older than two (Lieven and Stoll, 2013).

only the case if the infant's mother is not anxious and if the strangers pass some basic tests of authenticity, including a match between their facial movements and their voice.[8] But soon after this, their response to strangers is an anxious one and this period of stranger anxiety gradually increases and then reduces. Curiously, developmental research has largely ignored this phenomenon and so it is not possible to be sure what drives it and why it has persisted. I will therefore offer a speculation: that it is the origin of 'familiarity'.

Once speech and inner language develop, the interbrain connection, and the nonverbal communication that mediates it, come partly under deliberate control. Conscious imitation, as opposed to reflexive communication, only begins at this age, as do deliberate gaze shifts in response to signals.[9] The affiliative use of imitation ('over-imitation')* also develops. It is only at this stage that an explicit recognition of in- and out-groups appears, alongside the first awareness of social identity and of social status.[10]

Three examples of the impact of both the interbrain and the theory of mind on social interaction

Play

Play is an activity that we associate with young children and, if we count carers playing with babies, it begins at a very early age. Gaze games, like peek-a-boo, are enjoyed by children from the age of three months, and children respond to the emotional expression of the other player in the game from

---

* In one study, for example, children copied another child undertaking a task to the extent of copying that child's superfluous actions even though they had demonstrated that they left out the superfluous actions when they did the task alone (McGuigan and Robertson, 2015).

when they are four months old.[11] The peek-a-boo game relies on the interbrain connection having been established. Its development in children who have a restricted interbrain connection may be delayed until mid-childhood.[12] Play becomes more organized and rule-bound as childhood progresses, but we still use the same word to apply to adult, organized play, even when it has become an organized sport (cricketers speak, for example, of the 'close of play' when they mean the end of a day's cricket). Caillois[13] contrasted these two forms of play, which he called 'paidia' for the elements of play that are spontaneous and unplanned and 'ludic' for the rule-bound, game element of play. Paidia, spontaneous play, involves the exercise of the interbrain in an unplanned interaction with another person or, by extension, an object. Its culmination is flow or 'fun'. Ludus is regulated play as in sport or games. Its culmination is winning.*

Adult play involves being able to combine the flow of paidia with adherence to the regulations of a particular ludus. It reproduces social interactions in which interbrain communication and narratively informed communication have to be combined to achieve both the ends of the interaction and the feeling of flow or harmony that indicate an uninterrupted interbrain connection.

---

* In a philosophically orientated discussion, Henricks (2016) discusses Caillois' distinction in relation to related distinctions going back to the playwright Schiller and the sociologist Weber. He contrasts the emotional satisfaction of paidia, which he calls 'fun', with the gratification with successful achievement provided by ludus. He assumes that ludus has increasingly become the public face of paidia, which has suffered as a result. He concludes: 'But our adoration of technical competence should not occlude an awareness of personal and public existence. This means experiencing – and feeling – the multi-fold possibilities of living. Understanding this joins together Weber, Huizinga, Caillois, Sutton-Smith, and most of the other great commentators on human expression' (p.321).

Conflicts arise when one or other channel of communication predominates. Winning 'at all costs' may mean hogging the ball, harming other players, or putting one's own achievements before those of the team. Going with the flow can mean impatience with the rules or a fear of winning over other people. There is, too, the link between losing and being hurt or humiliated that in childhood can seem to run counter to the interbrain connection. Children who toss board games on the floor because they are losing do so not just because that brings the game to an end before they can definitively lose, but also because they expect other people to minimize their chances of losing just as they expect other people not to physically harm them. When the game itself is a more important consideration than the child, it feels like a betrayal of the child's sense that they come first and society and its conventions should come second.

Or, to put it another way, games only work because their rules are shared by the players as part of the shared narrative about the game. They are an example of a narrative connection between the players. One of the rules – the fairness rule – is that no-one gets an exemption. Interbrain connections do not support fairness rules. When applied to children, the only rules are that the adult responds positively to the emotions shared on the interbrain, or the child is rejected. The fairness rule, and its suppression of the partiality of the interbrain connection, can only be interpreted as rejection by a child who has not got a sufficient theory-of-mind connection with others to be able to use the fairness rule themselves.

The correct balance between individual freedom and autonomy, and the obligations and duties of members of a society to other members, is undoubtedly a potent source of conflict within both society and each of us.

Titus Livius

Livy (Titus Livius) gives an account of the overthrow of the hereditary ruler of Rome and the creation of the republic in his history of the founding of Rome.[14] The last kings were Tarquins, the very last being Tarquin the Proud.

An inauspicious event occurred during one of Tarquin's public building projects* and it was considered to be too disturbing to be dealt with by the local Etruscan augurs. Tarquin therefore applied to the oracle at Delphi for an answer to the question 'Who would be the next king?', sending his sons on the mission along with a nephew, Lucius Junius. Lucius was aware of the risks of condign punishment if the Tarquins took against him, and he was worried about being in such close proximity to them. So he played the harmless fool and became known as 'Brutus' (an epithet that has taken on a different connotation nowadays as 'a brute' but then meaning the dimwit). Brutus came back from Delphi, having fulfilled the terms of the prophecy himself on the sly, and joined the Roman army that was investing a neighbouring city. At a dinner that Brutus and another son of Tarquin, Sextus Tarquinius, attended, bets were laid about which of the attenders had the best wife. The young men agreed to ride round each other's homes and check the wives out. Cotellinus won because his wife was busy with household tasks when the youths arrived.

Sextus agreed that Cotellinus's wife, Lucretia, was the best. He had taken a fancy to her. Sextus came back to Cotellinus's home a few nights later on his own and raped Lucretia.

---

* Like many dictators (Mr Ceausescu comes to mind), Tarquin invested in huge, memorable public building projects. This policy made him very unpopular with his subjects, who wanted public monies to be spent on individuals, in the here and now, and not vanity projects.

Presumably believing that she would not get satisfaction from Tarquinian justice, Lucretia summoned her father, her husband, Brutus, and other witnesses and, after denouncing Sextus, stabbed herself to death.*The others were overwhelmed by grief but Livy has Brutus say:

> By this blood, most chaste until a prince wronged it, I swear, and I take you, gods, to witness, that I will pursue Lucius Tarquinius Superbus and his wicked wife and all his children, with sword, with fire, aye with whatsoever violence I may; and that I will suffer neither them nor any other to be king in Rome![15]

Brutus managed to persuade a crowd to follow him to Rome, where more rebels joined and, eventually, so did the army that was besieging a neighbouring city. The rebels returned to Rome where they drove the Tarquin family out. Brutus and Cotellinus were elected as the two praetors of Rome, but they no longer had a king over them, so they effectively became the rulers of the city. Not everyone was happy about this. Young bloods who had been favourites of the king's sons missed the licence that this gave them and being above the law. Livy puts these words into their mouths:

> A king was a man, from whom one could obtain a boon, whether it were just or unjust; there was room for countenance and favour; a king could be angry, could forgive, could distinguish between friend and enemy. The law was a thing without ears, inexorable, more salutary

---

* This whole incident becoming the topic of famous paintings by Tintoretto, Rubens, and others, a long narrative poem by Shakespeare, and an opera by Benjamin Britten, among other artworks.

and serviceable to the pauper than to the great man; it knew no relaxation or indulgence, if one exceeded bounds.[16]

Some of these young men, including two sons of Brutus, were overheard plotting to reinstate the Tarquins. They were arrested and, the following day, stripped, tied to a stake, beaten, and then beheaded. Livy writes, '...while through it all men gazed at the expression on the father's face, where they might clearly read a father's anguish, as he administered the nation's retribution.'[17]

Livy started writing *Ab Urbe Condita Libri* (Books about the Founding of the City) in about 27 BCE. Marcus Junius Brutus, the younger of the men who assassinated Julius Caesar in 44 BCE, claimed to be a descendant of Lucius Brutus and to be acting, like him, to prevent another tyrant from rising in Rome. Augustus, or Octavian as he was then known, pursued Brutus as the murderer of his father, Julius, and drove him to suicide. So Livy's treatment of the overthrow of rulers was highly politically sensitive and that, no doubt, coloured his treatment. It would be unwise to take it as an accurate history, but Livy's account does graphically describe a shift in the importance of a kinship connection.

Brutus made connections with his fellow citizens through their joint adoption of laws. These connections were based on explicit rules and therefore what I have been calling theory-of-mind-type connections. He broke his loyalty to the Tarquins who were his kin (he was a cousin in fact) with whom he had an interbrain connection of familiarity. I presume therefore that he may have felt some pain at their discomfiture on being exiled, but the tragedy of the story is that his sons remained loyal to the Tarquins.

Livy gives another example of a conflict that threatened to overturn the nascent Roman state, but this one was resolved by an appeal to the interbrain connection and to kinship, and a rejection of the usual legal penalties that would have followed abduction and rape. He describes (in Volume 1 of *Ab Urbe Condita Libri*) a ruse by which the all-male founders of Rome got wives. They organized a festival and the population of the local villages attended, with particular interest being shown by the Sabines. Once the festival had started, the Roman youths abducted the Sabine women and drove away their parents. The Sabines got together an army and attacked a Roman army, defending the new city. According to Livy, the Sabine women ran between the two sides shouting:

> 'If,' they cried, 'you are weary of these ties of kindred, these marriage-bonds, then turn your anger upon us; it is we who are the cause of the war, it is we who have wounded and slain our husbands and fathers. Better for us to perish rather than live without one or the other of you, as widows or as orphans.'[18]

Their intervention resulted in a cessation of hostilities and the fusion of the Roman and the Sabine populations into one group, of Romans.

Sympathy or law?

The connections to the Tarquins of favoured youths were an extension of the connections between Tarquin and his sons (his daughters are not mentioned in the account), i.e. the same connection that the Sabine women had argued connected them to both their husbands and their fathers (again, no mention of female relations) and therefore connected their husbands and their fathers: an interbrain connection. People who were not so connected to the Tarquins (or to the Sabines) were potential enemies ('a king could...distinguish between friend and enemy', Livy wrote[19]). Each member of the connected group would act on behalf of the others, and each member therefore stood for the whole in-group. Brutus recognizes this when he promises (emptily, as it turns out, as he was speared to death by one of the Tarquins a short while after these events): 'I will pursue Lucius Tarquinius Superbus and his wicked wife and all his children, with sword, with fire, aye with whatsoever violence I may...'[20,*] Each family member was, in his eyes, equally responsible.

Tarquinians dealt with each other according to the emotional reactions of their leader, the king. As Livy says, 'A king was a man, from whom one could obtain a boon, whether it were just or unjust; there was room for countenance and favour; a king could be angry, could forgive...'[21] The worst that happened to the rapist, for example, was that he was excluded from the family and did not go into exile with the other Tarquins but attempted to find another city that would take him in.

Livy contrasts the connections within the Tarquins with those between Roman citizens – another, but differently constituted, in-group – who were bound by the laws that they created. 'The law was a thing without ears, inexorable, more salutary and serviceable to the pauper than to the great man; it knew no relaxation or indulgence, if one exceeded bounds,' writes Livy.[22] Brutus was elected praetor according

---

* A similar sentiment motivated the murderers of the family of the Russian Tsar in Ekaterinburg in 1917 when great pains were taken to round up and kill every member of the household.

to the procedures that had already been established and, under the law, he had to watch his two sons being gruesomely put to death. His emotional, interbrain connection to them, Livy assumed, would have led to him experiencing intense emotional contagion of their fear. Livy writes that 'men gazed at the expression on the father's face, where they might clearly read a father's anguish,'[23] but Brutus was ushering a new stage in the social development of Rome, where conduct was ruled by rules and norms that were applied, or should be applied, to any citizen. So Livy has him administering 'the nation's retribution', inexorably.

Brutus's connection with his fellow Romans, and his disconnection with his sons to whom he was still clearly attached, was through their shared belief in Roman virtues, including the rule of law. But he could only act on these principles by overriding his interbrain connection with his sons.*

In this instance, most of us would argue that Brutus was right and that fairness should prevail. We would probably think that this was particularly important at this foundational moment, when new laws that applied equally to the poor as well as the rich, as Livy noted, were being established.

These principles of 'blind justice' are deeply entrenched in Western culture and it is hard not to agree with them. Livy clearly did, portraying Brutus and the nascent republic in glowing terms. But what of the rules that govern others, say the Sunni militants, who at the time of writing have banded together in the 'Islamic State'? Isis, or Daesh, have reinstated

---

* I will take up these issues again when I discuss kinship and the interbrain ties that connect kin, forming a special kind of in-group. Brutus's stance that politics should be 'fair', 'equitable', and 'democratic' would be heartily endorsed by today's politicians, who would consider the Tarquins a prime example of corrupt rulers.

Sharia laws against apostasy, and in 2016 a woman, Lena al-Qasem, was found guilty and sentenced to death for this 'crime'. She was publicly executed, by gunfire, by her son.[24] That strikes many people as brutal (and not in its original sense of stupid but in the newer sense of animalistic* or inhumane). But it is a comparable act to Brutus ordering the death of his children and supervising their execution, but, on this more recent occasion, many of us side with Ms al-Qasem and not the Sharia court.

Both the Isis and the Roman killings are situations in which our interbrain connection, and our wish to avoid the shared pain and grief of the victims, wars against our commitment to the rule of law, whether Roman or Sharia. Our narratives about how to treat other people incline us to fairness or to scripture or law. Our kinship connection spurs us to greater efforts on behalf of family elders and not just our children. It is children, however, who benefit the most, especially very young children, who are at risk of being abandoned to die.[25]

The trolley problem

The philosopher Phillipa Foot has become posthumously famous for her advocacy of virtue ethics, for her relationship with her fellow Oxford philosopher Iris Murdoch, and for what later came to be known as the 'trolley problem'.† The

---

* I am aware of the arguments of those, like Mary Midgley, who have pointed out that actions by other people that disgust us are often explained by the idea that there is a mysterious substance within each human being that all animals have and that we assume, quite wrongly, results in cruelty or selfishness. In so doing we falsely attribute purely human motives to animals that could not possibly entertain them.

† The trolley problem was just one of a whole series of moral dilemmas exemplifying the doctrine of double effect that Foot was using to disentangle the ethics of

original formulation was as follows: You are the driver of a runaway tram which you can only steer from one narrow track on to another; five men are working on one track and one man on the other; anyone on the track the tram enters is bound to be killed.

Foot writes that 'we should say, without hesitation, that the driver should steer for the less occupied track'.[26] Judith Thomson modified this scenario and termed it 'the trolley problem':[27] George is on a footbridge over the trolley tracks.

> George knows that the only way to stop the out-of-control trolley is to drop a very heavy weight into its path. But the only available, sufficiently heavy weight is a fat man, also watching the trolley from the footbridge. George can shove the large man onto the track in the path of the trolley...[28]

---

abortion (Foot, 1967). The doctrine of double effect distinguishes between our intentions and where we foresee that our actions will lead. So the tram driver in the original formulation wants to preserve life and yet is willing to shed it. Later in the paper, Foot gives a clearer example of the doctrine of double effect: that of such severe disproportion between the mother's pelvis and the foetal head that (it being presumed that a Caesarean section is not possible for some reason) the child's head must be crushed ('cephalotripsy') and the child killed to allow a safe delivery for the mother. Foot argues that the Roman Catholic doctrine would be that to do this would be unethical, even though it is likely that the mother would die as a result. The child's death would be directly intended by someone performing cephalotripsy; the mother's death would be just as inevitable if cephalotripsy is not performed, but it would not be intended and so would be ethically more acceptable.

Foot's distinction of harm by inaction from the more heinous harm by action has continued to preoccupy ethicists and lawyers (Woollard, 2008) and also to confound the ability of the trolley problem to distinguish utilitarians from deontologists (Crone and Laham, 2017).

What would you do? Most people say, 'Well I just couldn't push someone off a bridge. It would be too horrible.'* The difference between the two scenarios, most commentators agree, is the hands-on nature of the second condition. Touching someone makes a connection with them that makes it much harder to kill them,[†] evoking perhaps some of the disgust that deliberately cutting off one's own arm would induce.[‡] This is borne out by alternative trolley problem formulations in which the tram is coming up to points and can be diverted onto a branch line on which there is a man tied to the track. Suppose in one of these alternatives, the lever for the points is next to George on a gantry adjacent to the footbridge. A higher

---

* See Miller and Cushman (2013).

† So far as I know, this aspect of the thought experiment has not been varied to test out the connection hypothesis. Rather than a large man, one could have a baby harnessed in a perambulator with no time to remove the baby, a pallet of baby monkeys, or just a pile of bricks. Or perhaps the large man had actually been a robber who had attacked me with a knife, and I had just disarmed him.

‡ The trolley problem has led to a number of neuroimaging studies (Greene *et al.*, 2004) and some have a (limited) bearing on the topic of this chapter. These are studies in which the function of the brain at the temporoparietal junction (TPJ) is either stimulated by a positively charged current to an anode placed on the scalp above the right TPJ (Mai *et al.*, 2016; Sellaro *et al.*, 2015) or inhibited by a negatively charged current or by a magnetic pulse (Jeurissen *et al.*, 2014). The right TPJ is implicated in three aspects of the interbrain: imitation of another person (Sowden and Catmur, 2015), redirecting attention, and empathizing (Krall *et al.*, 2015). Inhibition of the right TPJ disrupts the interbrain network, just as inhibition of the left TPJ disrupts language production (Pobric, Lambon Ralph, and Zahn, 2015).

People with an ASD have reduced interbrain bandwidth, as I have argued elsewhere. People with a frontal lobe deficit in the ventromedial prefrontal cortex (VMPFC) area lack narrative ability. There is an interesting double dissociation between these two conditions when it comes to moral judgements. People with an ASD tend to give less weight to intention and more to outcome. They are rule utilitarians. People with a VMPFC lesion take no account of intentions but only focus on harm. They are act utilitarians (Koenigs *et al.*, 2007).

proportion of people are willing to switch the tram onto the branch line than were willing to push the large man off.[*]

The trolley problem has become a sort of touchstone for empathy theorists. The more compassionate the person faced with the problem (in the laboratory), the more distress they experience making the decision about what to do.[†] The decision to throw the large man off is often taken to be a utilitarian and rational choice, and not to throw him off to be the deontological, or emotional, choice.[29] The utilitarian choice is not lacking in empathy. A lack of empathy would be as likely to lead to non-intervention as not. But it is a choice that few people in the laboratory make – although perhaps that is because they do not take the problem seriously.[‡] Leaving aside the practical problems of manhandling a large, resisting man over a parapet, there is, for many of us who do take the problem seriously, a disgust about killing someone in the flesh. Miller *et al.* found that disgust has two components in this situation,

---

[*] See Bleske-Rechek *et al.* (2010). Interestingly, this proportion increases the more drunk that people are (Duke and Bègue, 2015).

[†] Several studies have come to this same conclusion. In one, distress was measured by self-report, using the personal distress sub-scale of the Interpersonal Reactivity Index and by a positive wave on their EEG, the P260, whose amplitude is correlated with emotional arousal (Sarlo *et al.*, 2014). Sometimes it is taken that it is emotionality and not empathy that limits people taking the utilitarian route, but it is difficult to see why the scenario should arouse emotion, except through empathy. Even if the fear is of making the wrong decision, there has to be an awareness that the decision is not merely an executive one. Wilson and Scheutz (2015) created a computer-based model for predicting the likelihood of making the trolley switch to the track with just one person on it. They added a connectedness factor and compared likelihoods that participants would choose to switch with the degree of their connectedness to the potential victim. When both the computer model and the participants took the degree of connectedness into account, the computer's predictions of what people would choose were nearly completely correlated with what the participants did choose.

[‡] People who are drunk are more likely to prefer the utilitarian option (Bauman *et al.*, 2014).

which they call 'outcome aversion' and 'action aversion'.[30] If we take the thought experiment a little further, the difference between the two becomes clear. If we realize as we stand next to him that the large man is not a man at all but an equally heavy, and surprisingly life-like, sculpture of a man, would we be happy about throwing him off? People with outcome aversion should be quite willing to do so: no blood or guts would appear on the track as a result. But people with action aversion in Miller *et al.*'s experiment felt disgusted at the idea of an actor stabbing another actor with a dummy knife in the course of a play. So some people may feel so disgusted by the idea of throwing a person in front of a tram that they could not do it, even to save lives.

Although interest in the trolley problem had been dying in both the philosophical and the neuroscience communities, it has suddenly become live again with the likely adoption of driverless cars on our streets. It is relatively trivial to programme a car to deliberately crash itself into an obstacle, most likely killing the driver, rather than hit and possibly kill more than one pedestrian. It would even be possible to programme the car to minimize the number of people killed in the event of a collision. But this might involve turning in a direction that would ram a pedestrian or killing passengers in the car who may include children. Perhaps too the people with which the car will collide unless it deviates are standing there with weapons, or perhaps they have run into the road with suicidal intent. All of these are scenarios that involve, as we would say, 'human judgement' and, as I would say, an interbrain connection between the actor and potential victims.*

---

* One can experiment with making new trolley-type problems created by driverless cars at http://moralmachine.mit.edu. Some speculative research has already

Kinship

One could solve the self-driven car problem by interrogating the internet to obtain an up-to-date figure for the economic value of each of the potential victims, taking account of their age, their likely earning potential, and so on. Perhaps in a few years' time, it would be possible to have access to the details of what they were carrying, or what was in their cars. A driverless car might then decide that the value of the irreplaceable artwork in the bag of one pedestrian outweighed the value of the other five pedestrians who were the alternative victims, and collided with them rather than with the single pedestrian and the artwork. I suspect that this would be enough to prevent the widespread adoption of driverless controls. Some have suggested that people do solve the trolley problem taking these features into account, or rather by computer the 'evolutionary fitness' of the person who could be deliberately killed to save the five workers.[31]

There are, as it turns out, many different sides to empathy involved in the trolley problem. There is the interbrain connection with the large man, which triggers disgust about pushing him onto the track. There are complex judgements about the evolutionary value of the person to be sacrificed and of the consequences for George of taking active steps to kill this person rather than passively watching five other people be hit by the tram. But the trolley problem only works if I can imagine being George. And if I were really George standing on the footbridge, I could only see the danger of the oncoming tram, because I could think about the consequences of men being on the track, and present it to myself as something I should try to do something about. And to reduce the problem

---

been conducted (Bonnefon, Shariff, and Rahwan, 2016). Google engineers seem unconcerned, however, arguing that the problem will not arise in practice.

to its nub, it only works if I know that the tram driver does not know what I know, which is that there are people on the track – and that I know that he cannot know it.

What I am calling the nub of the trolley problem is an analogue of the test that has made 'theory-of-mind' studies so important in studying child development over the last 30 years.

The original theory-of-mind studies

The 'theory-of-mind' paradigm was not originally about empathy but whether 'mind' was a purely human property. The tests proposed by the primatologists who posed this question were:* 'An individual has a theory of mind if he imputes mental states to others', and they defined mental states to include 'purpose or intention, as well as knowledge, belief, thinking, doubt, guessing, pretending, liking and so forth'.[32] These tests are clever because an individual who attributes these properties to another must understand how they manifest. In other words, to have a theory of mind requires having a mind, as well as being able to get into the minds of others.

Premack and Woodruff's demonstrations of whether or not Sarah, the chimp participant, had a theory of mind of the keepers, Kevin and Bill, whose recorded behaviour Sarah was watching, were not unambiguous. They required Premack and Woodruff to make theory-of-chimpanzee-mind judgements about Sarah, and it is difficult in this situation to avoid speciesism. When theory-of-mind tests were developed

---

* Premack and Woodruff's research participant was Sarah, a chimp who lived in a colony in which she had a lot of contact with people (Premack and Woodruff, 1978). Other studies indicate that chimps who have contact with people become more human-like than wild chimps. So there is some doubt about how typical Sarah would be of chimps as a species.

for humans,* it became easier to define tests that were more intuitively convincing. Wimmer and Perner developed the first example of the so-called false-belief tests,† and subsequently more subtle tests have been developed, for example the ability to detect faux pas.‡

As noted in Chapter 1, Frith proposed the Wimmer and Perner false-belief tests to colleagues in the MRC Cognitive Development Unit as a means of exploring why people with autism had difficulty in telling lies, but the results were

---

* One interpretation of the original Premack and Woodruff findings is that Sarah, the chimp, chose a photograph of what she would have wanted for the human she saw in the video. She wanted some help for Keith, and had the knowledge to know what that was, but she wanted something bad for Bill. A different kind of theory-of-mind test that makes use of self-report was devised for testing infants. This is based on a 'false-belief' paradigm of Wimmer and Perner (1983). False-belief tests simply establish whether the testee knows that although they have a true belief, another person, or character, can have a false belief about the same situation. These are not tests of what another person doubts, guesses, or pretends, to name some of the other mental states that Premack and Woodruff thought constituted having a theory of mind. Another type of theory-of-mind test, the Strange Stories Test developed by Happé, tests the imputation of some of these mental states. A newer test acknowledges that theory of mind is a function of narrative capacity and bases scores on testees' ability to follow the plot of a short story (Dodell-Feder *et al.*, 2013). Nonverbal tests of theory of mind include replications of false-belief tasks in which the testee indicates her or his expectations by means of gaze direction (Senju and Johnson, 2009) and tests requiring participants to arrange cartoon pictures in an appropriate sequence (Porter, Coltheart, and Langdon, 2008; Vollm *et al.*, 2006). Tests of self-recognition (see Chapter 2) and of inference from gaze direction or biological movement have also been used as tests of theory of mind. Some tests, like the reading the mind in the eyes test, are tests of naming facial expressions of emotion and should be considered to be tests both of naming emotions and of picking up on emotional cues.

† Which normally developing human children pass after an age threshold, but great apes never do (Call and Tomasello, 1999).

‡ Many of these tests were developed in an attempt to track down the social impairments in autism – although this is not, in my opinion, the right track to take. One of the leaders in this has been Baron-Cohen who has reviewed the first ten years of this research (Baron-Cohen *et al.*, 2009).

interpreted as an indication that children with autism did not have a 'theory of mind'. The test appeared to be extremely successful in reliably showing a difference between children with autism and typically developing children, was replicable in many different ways, and has opened the door into many new studies of empathy.[*]

The theory-of-mind paradigm is still going strong and has been taken up by research workers who have coined the terms 'empathizing' and 'systemizing' to examine gender differences,[†] and by practitioners who have used theory-of-mind measures to assess 'mentalizing' in a wide variety of conditions.[‡] The original, anticipated breakthrough into autism has proved a disappointment, however.[§]

Theory of mind was always a strange appellation for the stage at which human children would start to understand

---

[*] See, for example, the recent review by Happé and Conway (2016).

[†] See the empathizing summary by Christov-Moore *et al.* (2014).

[‡] For example, schizophrenia (Chung, Barch, and Strube, 2014).

[§] Autism in people with specific intellectual disability, which was for a long time the most common presentation, is actually two disorders: autism and specific language impairment. Theory-of-mind impairment is easily demonstrable in this group but not in people with autism whose language has developed normally, although some degree of social use of language is often still impaired (Colle *et al.*, 2008). Autism is much more common in people who are blind from birth (Jure, Pogonza, and Rapin, 2016), and theory-of-mind difficulties are more common in people who are congenitally deaf (and have not learnt to sign) (De Villiers and De Villiers, 2014). Failure on theory-of-mind tests is particularly associated with syntactical and pragmatic errors, which cause particular impairment in narrative, i.e. in telling and following stories (Ketelaars *et al.*, 2016), irrespective of whether these are or are not associated with autism (Spanoudis, 2016).

My own view of autism was developed contemporaneously with that of Uta Frith and Simon Baron-Cohen, at a time when I, like Simon, was a student of Uta's at the MRC Cognitive Development Unit. My instinct at the time was that theory of mind would turn out to be a narrative product and I wrote to the unit's then head, John Morton, to explain my ideas to him, at his request. There was no rancour or competition between students in the unit, and I did not press my views at the time, which was circa 1981 or 1982.

the differences in their beliefs and desires and those of other people. Attempts have been made to find a better form of words, such as 'simulated theory of mind' rather than theory of mind, but these do not solve the problem: that we do not apply a theory to other people. We develop the theories after we know other people.

Narrative

Bruner* noted the quantum leap that normally developing children seem to make around their third year of life and itemized many characteristics of this period, including deception. This included refusing to do things, being able to move around freely without help, being deceitful, pretending, wanting things, and expressing agency and desire in other ways.[33] All of these actions are indications of personal agency and when put into words require the use of verbs in the first person.†

Chimpanzees up to the age of 18 months are ahead of human children in many of these abilities, but the consensus is that although great apes can be taught nouns and even

---

* It does seem, as Bruner had suggested originally, that there is a quantum leap in young children's connections with other people at some time between 18 months and four years (for a neurotypical child).

† Although whether or not a shareable narrative is required, I am not sure. One of my grandchildren, at the age of 18 months, had a small, holophrastic vocabulary but could extend this to differentiate requests from descriptions or greetings by intonation and context. He muttered to himself a lot but not using recognizable words. In games, he would regularly make a wrong choice, for example trying to put a triangular shape through a square orifice, but would be able to choose the right orifice on other occasions. It seemed as if he was deliberately doing the task unsuccessfully, and it seemed, by his looks at the person he was doing it with, as if it was a kind of deliberate deception about his ability, a 'tease'.

adjectives, this is as far as they get in syntax.* Spoken language appears to be the crucial acquisition that enables children to

---

* Consider tools which are used by chimps and other animals. Chimps use sticks to dig grubs out of trees. Sea otters select a pebble, hold it in an armpit when they dive, and then use it after they surface to smash the shells of shellfish that they have torn off the seabed. Chimps copy other chimps in their tool use, and they try to use a tool that works in one way in other related ways, too. So there is learning, creativity, and culture around chimp tool use. But no chimp has ever called for another chimp to pass him or her a tool or even drawn a tool with charcoal on a stone and passed it to another chimp to find an actual tool (at least, none has been reported to have done so; and if this had happened what would the chimp have come back with? The tool depicted or another stone?).

　　Chimps, along with the related sub-species of bonobo, are very like human beings in other ways than tool use. Their diet is not dissimilar (they are omnivores, too) and their aggressiveness, including their use of war, sexuality, care for offspring, preoccupation with social status, viruses, opposable thumb, ability to walk upright, and longevity are all highly reminiscent of Homo sapiens.

　　Despite all these similarities, people consider that chimpanzees are animals and we are an order of being so above them that we have routinely assumed that we have something god-like about us. These self-bestowed accolades are not out of keeping if evolutionary success and population size are considered. There are between 150,000 and 250,000 chimps left in the wild (WWF, 2017) compared with 7,000,000,000 human beings estimated to be alive in July 2015 (Population Reference Bureau, 2015).

　　What is the crucial difference? There are many possible candidates, and many seem convincing at first yet melt away with further research (Frederick, 2015). Menstruation rather than oestrus, menopause, persistently upright gait, mastery of fire, memory for objects that are no longer perceptible (a key developmental moment in the history of psycho-analysis and Freud's observation of his infant nephew playing the Fort-Da game or the emphasis placed by others on the peek-a-boo game) (Bohn, Call, and Tomasello, 2015), and greater hand-eye dexterity – perhaps linked to lateralization of the brain (Fitch and Braccini, 2013) – all have their advocates, but speech has the strongest support. Speech requires a more flexible vocal tract than chimps have, and it also requires grammar, including the use of personal pronouns. Chimps can be taught to sign the names of people and objects, but even Nim Chimpsky, a champion in this area, failed to learn grammar (Yang and Marchetti, 2015).

　　Although I am referring to speech, there are other symbol systems that function, for a minority of people, as if they were speech. Equations may do it for a mathematician; musical notation or the sound of musical themes in the mind for a musician; and visuospatial images for engineers and artists. What all of these symbols have in common is that they are able to be summoned up by 'inner speech' (Vygotsky, 1966, 1971).

realize that other people have different beliefs and opinions, as the delay in developing a theory of mind in children with special language impairment indicates.

But I am not sure that it is even useful to call this the development of a theory of mind. This is the age at which mothers say, politely, 'He's becoming quite the little person, isn't he?' or 'She's becoming quite the little madam, isn't she?' because the infant is able to speak up for themselves. The crucial acquisition is the ability to connect with other people by speech and, more specifically, the narrative use of speech and the corollaries of acquiring the symbolic representational qualities of speech, meta-representations, inner speech leading to self-awareness,[34] and the ability to conjure up realities that go beyond what is to be found in the physical world.* Mastering pronouns in speech also means understanding that there are different persons but making it possible to connect them in myriad ways.

Inner speech allows one to have conversations with oneself and creates the possibility of introspection as well as grasping the inner nature of other people by telling stories about them.† Introspection enables the development of a self-conscious

---

* This property of 'intentionality' that Hans Brentano taught his influential students, who included Freud and Husserl, was the crucial test of mind. There are some who argue that ostensive gestures in great apes show 'intentionality' (Moore, 2015) but they are, I think, using the term rather differently to Brentano (Bara *et al.*, 2011; Slaby and Stephan, 2008).

† Blocking inner speech impairs performance on theory-of-mind tasks (Morin, El-Sayed, and Racy, 2015).

individualism,* and it is often stated that this perspective has become increasingly important over the last half millennium.†

Bruner contrasted the usage of 'self' in 'self-conscious' with the experience of oneself in a crowd, strongly connected with other crowd members via the interbrain. The experience of 'self' in the crowd, the 'social individuality' that I discussed in Chapter 2, is described by Bruner as placing 'us intersubjectively into a social matrix, and that, at the same

---

* Auerbach (1974/1946) in his magisterial review of European literature attributes the invention of the introspective method in literature to Montaigne, as is most evident in Montaigne's *Essays*. Montaigne argued that no-one could know more about himself than he, Montaigne, did and that what he wrote, since it was about himself, must be accepted as having the authority of truth. He thought that everyone should follow his example of searching introspection. This so-called sanctity of introspection has been effectively called into question by Nisbett *et al.* (1973). In his survey of the progression of different styles in European literature since the ancient Greeks, Auerbach (1974/1946) precedes his chapter on Montaigne with a chapter on Rabelais. He quotes from Gargantua and Pantagruel in which Rabelais describes the revenge of Pantagruel on a boastful merchant farmer, Dindenault. Pantagruel wants to buy a sheep from the herd that surrounds Dindenault and his shepherds on the deck of the ship on which they are all travelling. Eventually, and at an inflated price, Dindenault agrees and Pantagruel buys the bell-wether, which he picks up and throws into the sea. The other sheep immediately follow the ram, throwing themselves into the sea. So connected are they to their charges, the shepherds all follow, too, dragging Dindenault with them.

The anecdote relies on the unthinking and, as we would say, sheep-like behaviour that people also associate with crowds and, as Rabelais' literate audience would have thought, of impressionable and docile peasants, too. It is an anecdote about the potentially morbid effects of an interbrain connection and is in sharp contrast to Montaigne's connection with his readers from his lonely library room in his tower overlooking the Gironde valley and close to the city (Bordeaux) that had drummed him out of the office of mayor: an entirely imaginative connection mediated by the written word.

† There is a growing literature about the historical origins, and the changes in definition, of the self. A detailed account, albeit one ignoring the changing role of the self in common-sense psychology, is provided by Seigel (2005). This supports the Baumeister hypothesis, noted in Chapter 2, that modernism is marked by the rise of the individual, with a self that can be both the subject and the object of introspection.

time, it individuates us from the Other'. And he contrasts this with 'Self as a product of narrative, a product, indeed, of a form of metacognitive "omnibus" narrative'.* The mind, in theory of mind, is what Bruner calls the 'metacognitive omnibus narrative'. His speculation that the ability to narrate a story is the basis for our ability to know how others think and feel is increasingly borne out by research, including neuroimaging studies that show that theory-of-mind tasks, narrative, and language all activate the same areas of the brain.[†]

------

* The quotes are from Bruner and Kalmar (1998, p.308). He uses the word 'self' in these two quotes in two different ways. In the first quote, he uses it as we might do when we are dividing something up: 'Here's one for you, and here's one for me.' We might just as well say: 'These are your own, and these are my own', or: 'Here's one for yourself and here's one for myself.' Self and other are in this usage just differentiations based on some property or properties. There are no entailments outside this. Taking this a step further, I can say, 'I am looking for John. Which is he?', and be answered by, 'John's got red hair, no-one else in the crowd does.' Red hair is one distinguishing feature of John, and in this instance it individuates him. If John dyed his hair, he would still be the same John. The red hair is 'accidental', to use the term that has a particular meaning as used by 'self-psychologists' and another by person-centred psychotherapists. But, although it is sometimes said that Freud never had a theory of self, he would, I think, have recognized that his 'I' or ego would be what a person expressed if someone said to them, 'Tell me about yourself.' This same 'self' is also the perspective from which a person formulates the answer to this same question, for example 'Well, I am on good terms with my family, I work in the oil industry…' This perspective has been called a narrative centre of gravity, the 'être en soi' (by Sartre, who contrasted it with an ungraspable 'être pour soi' that frames the word 'I'). All of these different usages have different connotations but share the common sense that there is some entity, substance, or quale that is self-aware and that makes executive decisions. Since it is not the purpose of this book to example consciousness in any way, I shall often conflate these terms without too much care about what they each entail for models of consciousness.

† See AbdulSabur *et al.* (2014). The same networks may also be required for autobiographical or experiential memory (Yang, 2013).

Deceit

An interbrain connection provides limited personal information, but what it does provide cannot be deliberately dissimulated under ordinary circumstances. One can disguise one's features but it requires forethought and care and, as one says, the mask often slips. It is also possible to inhibit involuntary nonverbal expressions and replace an interbrain cue with a deliberate, planned one, for example looking at something designed to throw another person's attention from the real object of one's own interest or deploying a social, rather than a Duchenne, smile.* One can mask oneself in other ways, too, by using make up or special clothing, but it is not easy to pass the concealment off as genuine.

Theory-of-mind connections are, unlike interbrain connections, much more open to error, obfuscation, and deceit. Narratives are also subject to revisions when more information becomes available, for example when the given reasons and intentions of actions change. Although psychologists have often followed Montaigne in arguing that we are privy to our innermost selves in a way that others are not, a considerable literature demonstrates that we can be as deceptive of ourselves as we can be towards other people.†

Emotional differentiation and development contributes to this.[35] The truth about other people, or even about oneself, becomes an elusive quarry in these circumstances, rather than something apodeictic. No wonder that the goal of proving that other people even exist has proved beyond the arguments

---

* See Calvo *et al.* (2013). In interaction, we judge a smile to be genuine if it 'spreads' to us, making us want to smile, too (Rychlowska *et al.*, 2014).

† DeLay (2016) argues that it is the intersubjective, the one disclosed through the interbrain, and not the narrative self, that is our moral centre.

of any philosopher who does not rely on their interbrain connection to say, 'I just know that there are other people.'*

Further problems with 'mind'

There is no difficulty in assuming that an entity that can use language to participate in developing a convincing narrative has a mind.† But minds may not have the one-to-one correspondence to individuals that theory of mind implies. Huebner[36] has reviewed theories of 'extended minds' or 'macrocognition' and considers that mind can be shared out between several individuals, for example the CERN research team, although he does consider that 'maximal minds' cannot be shared between individuals.

The possibility of extended minds challenges the monist assumption that minds and brains are in some way coterminous, and that mind is a product of brain activity. This is usually taken to mean that minds can be extended over a brain and additional cognitive appendages, like a calendar or a diary. But it also means that one mind can also extend over several brains if, as I am arguing, that brains may act in tandem with other brains. Arguably the computational organ of the human body is not the brain but the body itself, which has autonomic and sensorimotor reflexes that pre-process information before it

---

* I do not agree with the critics of this approach (Gangopadhyay and Miyahara, 2015).

† This is the basis of the Turing test. A striking example is given in the *Dark Cloud*, a science fiction story written by the then Astronomer Royal, Sir Fred Hoyle (1959). Hoyle imagined a giant black cloud approaching the earth and potentially obliterating it. The cloud's movements suggested that it was self-aware. The hero of the book searched frantically for a way of communicating with it. He was asked how this could possibly help and said something along the lines of, 'Well, if an ant suddenly spoke to you and said "Please don't step on me" wouldn't you avoid doing so?'

reaches the brain. Mind clearly requires a functioning brain but it also requires the repositories of narrative, cultural, and discursive that are made available by the acquisition of language and speech.[37] Brains may be extended by physical connections and minds by tapping into additional information. Clearly, they cannot be interchangeable concepts in any sense and some kind of dualistic account seems inevitable.

Other people

Other people are normally 'there', connected to us via the interbrain. But we have to discover that these presences are what is called 'other people' and that we are 'another person' to them through the accumulation of stories about the actions and intentions of people, including of ourselves. Without an interbrain connection, we have to make this discovery without any kind of awareness that there are other people at all. Whether or not this would be possible has fascinated people from ancient times to the present.[*] There are instances of 'feral children' who have been isolated from a very early age, but some, including the most famous, the wild boy of Aveyron, lack language and so cannot tell us of their experience. Given that one of the foundations of language use is likely to be a connection with other people through the interbrain, it is possible only to guess at what it would be like to have been forever without this connection.[†] However, it is possible to consider the experience of someone for whom their interbrain connection is inhibited. I have already mentioned one example of how this might come about, which is through the

---

[*] Herodotus considers this, for example (Herodotus, 2003).

[†] The closest situation might be someone with an ASD, and I have written extensively about that in a previous book (Tantam, 2009).

suppression of the interbrain connection one way or another. I will consider this in more detail in the next chapter.

Theory-of-mind connections are associated with greater adherence to the impersonal or universal principles that language provides and that are available in narrative. This is in contrast to the interbrain connection that can only be made in full with people in the immediate vicinity.* An interbrain connection is, by its nature, reciprocal, but theory-of-mind connectedness is not, although some kind of reciprocity is provided when interactants share a common language. Reciprocity may be marked when the shared language is a minority one, if that shared language is used to convey beliefs and ethical principles that are particular to that language group.[38]

As children progress towards adolescence, they drop specific rules governing moral behaviour as their speech incorporates more universal concepts.† The development of stronger theory-of-mind connections with other people accelerates the acquisition of these through shared narrative but also makes this possible. Dunbar's limit of the number of different face-to-face connections that can be managed by the prefrontal cortex applies to different people that one can have conversations with over time while still retaining a narrative about each of them.[39] It is substantially larger than the number of people with whom it is possible to have a face-to-face connection. Durkheim made a similar point about the

---

* As an example of this, Miranda and Kim (2015) were able to reduce the (illegal) sharing of pirated music between Canadian college students by increasing their 'mindfulness'.

† For a review of this shift to more universal rules given an evolutionary perspective, see Krebs (2012). For the impact of the development of theory of mind, see Sommer *et al.* (2014). For a discussion of what happens when the two moralities conflict, see Royzman, Goodwin, and Leeman (2011).

shift in relations between working practices from the smaller, reciprocal 'mechanical' relationship to the larger, 'organic' one.

Inequality

Equality is a natural feature of a mature interbrain connection, i.e. when the nonverbal communicative apparatus of both interactants is fully matured[*] and is not suppressed. One paradigmatic example is the uncoerced, mutually satisfactory act of sexual intercourse.

But the mutuality and egalitarianism of interbrain connections via the interbrain may be inhibited in favour of universal, group identities that speech can create. The battle of the sexes if played out in the bedroom might be one example. Identities within crowds include very basic roles such as leader and follower; within families, roles such as mother, grandfather, task leader, emotion leader, and child; within organizations, more nuanced roles like foreman, store-keeper, secretary, chair, and so on; and within societies, a multiplicity of roles. None of these roles are personal characteristics, although personal characteristics may influence who occupies them, but a particular kind of status.[40] Take the example of a foreman having her father in her team at work. She may have an equal relationship with him at home, but at work she has to be the boss. Work identity has to be maintained, and this can only be done by suppressing the equality of informal sharing that

---

[*] So far as I know, no-one has studied the maturation of nonverbal communicative ability, but the onset of social play with peers is likely to coincide with mutuality of nonverbal exchange as I am describing it (Wang and Hamilton, 2012). Primate groups are structured, like human groups, according to social status. Chimpanzee groups have dominant and sub-dominant males and females, like other primate groups, but interestingly these emerge later, once the period of peer play is over. Until then, equality amongst peers is the rule (Sandel, Reddy, and Mitani, 2016).

would be the norm at home. This will often lead to tensions between the two kinds of connections – the formal, contractual one at work and the emotion-sharing, informal relationship at home (I discuss this in the next chapter).

Unlike an interbrain connection, which is immediate and real-time, narrative connections can be maintained in the absence of the person with whom the connection has been made. But this 'person' is more like a person described in a diary entry. Even if the person is not encountered again, or for a long time, they may remain 'in the mind's eye' or 'in memory', as we say, as they were when they were first described. They may not age, wither, or bloom as people do in actuality.

Gramarye

Sir Walter Scott popularized this Scots term, meaning enchantment. It originated from the word 'grammared', meaning to be able to read ('grammar', 'grammar school'), but has morphed since into the term 'glamorous'. This interesting link – between the use of language, enchantment, and attraction to others – casts another light on the theory-of-mind connection. It demonstrates how words or narratives may change our connection with other people to make that other person into something we want them to be and away from what they are. Scott would be familiar with this, as the most well-known European author of his generation who took semi-mythical stories and turned them into the acme of romantic tales.

Interbrain connections can be influenced by art. Eyes can be widened and cheeks brightened. We all learn social smiles, sympathetic expressions, or fake frowns, but as I already noted in Chapter 1, they are much less likely to trigger contagious emotion than to lead to conscious misjudgements. Make up, clothing, and other artifices can fool us in our conscious, theory-of-mind judgements and these can override – through their glamour – our instinctive reactions that stem from the shared emotions of the interbrain.

In everyday life, both interbrain and theory-of-mind connections are valuable, and each may complement the other. But sometimes, too, they can be out of sync, and this can turn out badly for us.

Notes

1. Cross and Iacoboni, 2014
2. Basabe and Valencia, 2007
3. Belk, 2016
4. Pinker, 2011
5. Daum *et al.*, 2016; Nomikou *et al.*, 2016
6. Otsuka *et al.*, 2016
7. Franchak *et al.*, 2016
8. Figueiredo *et al.*, 2010; Taylor, Slade, and Herbert, 2014
9. Chevalier, Dauvier, and Blaye, 2017
10. Azzam, Beaulieu, and Bugental, 2007; Oostenbroek and Over, 2015
11. Bruner, 1976; Montague and Walker-Andrews, 2001
12. Ueda, 1969
13. Caillois, 2001
14. Livius, 1919
15. Livius, 1919, book 1, section 59
16. Livius, 1919, book 2, section 3
17. Livius, 1919, book 2, section 5
18. Livius, 1919, book 1, section 13
19. Livius, 1919, book 2, section 3
20. Livius, 1919, book 1, section 9
21. Livius, 1919, book 2, section 3
22. Livius, 1919, book 2, section 3
23. Livius, 1919, book 2, section 5
24. BBC News, 2016
25. Abrahams *et al.*, 2016
26. Foot, 1967, p.3
27. Thomson, 1976
28. Panahi, 2016
29. Gleichgerrcht *et al.*, 2012
30. Miller, Hannikainen, and Cushman, 2014
31. Bleske-Rechek *et al.*, 2010
32. Premack and Woodruff, 1978, p.515
33. Bruner, 1986
34. Morin, 2011
35. Jablonka, Ginsburg, and Dor, 2012
36. Huebner, 2014

37. Fusaroli, Gangopadhyay, and
    Tylén, 2014

38. Deffa, 2016

39. Dunbar, 2004; Powell *et al.*, 2012

40. Durkheim, 1984

Chapter 4

CONNECTING TO
FINNEGANS WAKE

'Theory of mind' is, as its name indicates, about theorems and not connections. A theorem is a conception about something that seeks to explain the behaviour or other properties of that something.[*] Theorems may be written in a natural language,

---

[*] Note that a theory is a species of argument. Fisher (1987) was the first person to pull these different objections together and explicitly formulate a 'narrative paradigm' for argument (a general feature of argument being persuasion) that he conceived as an alternative to the rational paradigm in which propositions and their entailments are weighed up according to carefully gathered evidence and a decision made on the balance of probabilities. The narrative theory of argument was resisted at the time of its introduction but has gained ground since. It has proved to have surprising reach, even being applied to the resistance to the introduction of toilets in rural India (Clair *et al.*, 2016 (this paper also contains an excellent overview of the narrative paradigm, its critiques, and its relation to empathy)). The narrative paradigm in relation to empathy and to conceptions of the self was also the topic of Goldie's posthumously published book *The Mess Inside* (Goldie, 2012). Argument has also been put forward as a model of reasoning, leading to a view that reasoning is a collective product, a view that is very similar to my use of 'common knowledge' as a connecting process, although this is not stated in one of the best recent expositions of this view (Mercier and Sperber, 2011, 2017), nor in a recent summary of experimental evidence for the priority of group connectedness over disconfirmation (Sloman, 2017).

or in an artificial one, such as mathematical notation. The connection between a theorem or a proposition and its propositus is that the one predicts causal properties of the other. Not an obvious basis for empathy, even though for a while cognitive empathy has been thought to be explicable by theory of mind.

Languages have properties that make theories couched in them efficient. Words and phrases can be bunched together and the bunch then given a name or a function.* Mathematical expressions are particularly useful for this, as are computing languages. In the human sciences, bundling of this kind leads to the creation of concepts like personality, impulsivity, or, indeed, empathy that can be used instead of the exhaustive list of behaviours and behaviour settings that they stand for. This bunching is presumably represented within neural networks that are linked to the left temporal lobe where the language centres are located (in 95% of the population). Neural networks perform similar tasks but the performance of the neural network is quite often impossible to back translate into a theorem or procedure. So the labels for the bundles created by natural languages, unlike the functions in mathematical language, refer to something ineffable and the class of this kind of ineffable label also has a label or rather several labels. One of these is 'essence'.

Thought has, as Brentano argued,[1] the capacity for being cast on to labels of this kind, that is labels that do not refer to existents. Brentano termed this capacity 'intentionality'. It is a property of the language that thought is conducted in, too.[†]

---

* Categorization of this kind apparently develops early in the acquisition of language (Cimpian, 2016).

† These few sketchy paragraphs are obviously an oversimplification of a very complex field, and I have featured the connectionist accounts of the 'language

Language can create a purely conceptual world that does not have to map on to the perceptual world. But this presents both a problem and an opportunity. The opportunity is that the world created can go well beyond the perceptual world. The challenge is how to make this world created by one person's thought available to others. Availability is straightforward if that person's thought wholly refers to the perceptual world and properties of causal interactions within that world, i.e. if the thought can be straightforwardly communicated.* But how does *Finnegans Wake* communicate what James Joyce was thinking when he wrote it? Many readers have concluded that it is 'gibberish'. Others have struggled with skeleton keys and thesauri and found meaning embedded in some of the words on the page. But the conclusion of those who learn to enjoy the book is that it is best listened to and the sound world that it then creates is evocative and moving, which makes it possible to make deeper exploration of possible meanings for Joyce's many neologisms and onomatopoeic expressions.†

Music is pure sound or, as E. M. Forster puts it in *Howards End*, 'It will be generally admitted that Beethoven's Fifth Symphony is the most sublime noise that has ever penetrated into the ear of man.' Forster also considered it a narrative or at least Forster has his most sensitive character, Helen Spengler, hear a narrative in this symphony – '…a wonderful movement

---

of thought' without considering objections to them (Tillas, 2015) such as the existence of 'home signers', although, even in the case of home signers, key features of language that are likely to be related to the connectionist account, notably the development of syntax, play a key role (Coppola and Brentari, 2014).

* The picture theory was Wittgenstein's original account of communicability (Wittgenstein, 1922) but he revised it to a socially embedded theory in his second account (Wittgenstein, Anscombe, and Wittgenstein, 1953).

† Michael Chabon gives an interesting and insightful account of his struggle with *Finnegans Wake* (Chabon, 2012).

[the Scherzo]: first of all the goblins, and then a trio of elephants dancing'. Forster makes clear in this passage that, as an artist, he is making statements about how 'the sublime noise' changes its hearers by 'making the passion of your life' 'more vivid'. But that is not by communicating meaning but by some other means. He writes:

> All sorts and conditions are satisfied by it. Whether you are like Mrs Munt, and tap surreptitiously when the tunes come – of course, not so as to disturb the others – or like Helen, who can see heroes and shipwrecks in the music's flood; or like Margaret, who can only see the music; or like Tibby, who is profoundly versed in counterpoint, and holds the full score open on his knee; or like their cousin, Fraulein Mosebach, who remembers all the time that Beethoven is echt Deutsch; or like Fraulein Mosebach's young man, who can remember nothing but Fraulein Mosebach: in any case, the passion of your life becomes more vivid.*

I have titled this chapter 'Connecting to *Finnegans Wake*' because reading the book tells us almost nothing about the author; no more than connecting to Beethoven's pastoral symphony tells us anything about Beethoven's age, his celebrity status, his inability to make a lasting romantic relationship, or his abusive father. But even without this knowledge, one can connect to the music. On the other hand, one can learn about Beethoven or Joyce through the many books about either of them, and this kind of knowledge may help to connect to their work.

---

* This passage opens Chapter 8 of *Howards End* (Forster, 1910). All quotes are from p.90.

In previous chapters, I have referred to theory of mind as being based on narrative. Narrative is not theorem based, and not propositional, but a means of inciting or instructing actions (I am using 'action' widely to encompass remembering, experiencing emotion, practising, planning, and so on), just as Forster has Beethoven inciting actions without specifying the content of those actions.* Although data from the Sally-Anne test are often interpreted as an indication that Anne knows what is in Sally's mind, the results can equally be described as Anne being able to successfully anticipate where Sally will look (I have described this test in detail in Chapter 1).

If other minds are opaque to our narrative, as I have noted above but also suggested in earlier chapters, and if, therefore, direct connection is not possible, how can communication occur? How, for example, can we understand music or art? My suggestion would be that these art forms create a world of imagination that we can inhabit. Whether or not we experience this space as the artist created it to be is in one way beside the point.† But we can ask whether we are receptive to the aesthetic or emotional intentions of the artist, just as we can ask if we are receptive to the intentions of our friends or family.

Shared narratives are of particular interest to psychotherapists, who work on the assumption that the co-created narrative is a clue to the reality of their client. This is a particular challenge for the psycho-analytic psychotherapist, who in addition assumes that the narrative is partly located

---

* This is not to say that speech cannot have a propositional basis (Soames, 2016) but that, contrary to philosophers such as Corballis (2015), 'Language can then be viewed as a device for sharing thoughts' (Corballis, 2017, p.229).

† This was one of the points made by Derrida in his deconstruction of the theories about speech or writing being methods of conveying meaning (Derrida, 1988/1972).

within a mythic place inside the mind of the client, the 'unconscious'. It is perhaps not surprising therefore that a psychoanalyst, Donald Spence, addressed this issue by creating a new kind of 'truth': narrative truth, to be contrasted with 'historical truth'. Historical truth is, Spence argued, buoyed up by discoverable facts that are open to any investigator.* Narrative truth is true by virtue of its aesthetic.

---

* Spence (1984) called these 'referents', and contrasted historical truth with the narrative truth that prevailed in psycho-analytic interpretations. Propositions have a content and a referent, thought Spence. Historical truths have a verifiable referent: for example, the proposition that Huguenot Henry of Navarre was the same man as the Roman Catholic Henry IV of France can be verified by contemporary accounts that Henry of Navarre converted to Roman Catholicism and succeeded to the throne of France after Henry III died. But historians are nowadays much more interested in interpretations. They will be less interested in the exact date of his accession and more in whether or not he deserves the accolade of being the greatest king of France. The greatest king of France is not a referent. Spence thought that narratives could be propositions, and have a content, but could also have a predicate that was non-existent and certainly not verifiable. We are familiar with narratives like myths and folktales that are about or refer to a god or a fairy that neither we nor the narrator believes. But Spence thought that the narrative might still have 'truth' or sense that we could believe in.

If this truth is not verifiable, how can we say it has a truth value? Spence is using truth as a synonym of sense, as in: 'What sense can we make of it?' Speaking about psycho-analytic interpretation, which was the particular narrative about which he was writing, he argued that the sense that we might make of a piece of music as an interpretation was a 'kind of artistic production, and as such, it becomes possible to consider its effect on the patient as a kind of aesthetic expression. What might be called its "beauty" need have no necessary relation to the truth' (*ibid.*, p.37). Spence later picked a specific artwork as the model for interpretation: 'Roshomon [sic]' (Spence, 1993). In *Rashomon*, a famous Kurosawa film of that name, a sequence of events is recounted from the point of view of each participant, leading the viewer to draw different conclusions about what was 'actually happening' each time. No one truth emerges, but there is a message, drawn out by a priest, that men and women are capable of altruism.

When narrative truth comes into play

Imagine that you are walking into a railway station and an apparently distressed person approaches you and says that she has lost her ticket and has no money for another. She further explains that she has to go about 150 miles and so needs £15 for a ticket. Would you help? She'll pay you back, she says: if you give her your name and address, she'll send a cheque. What do you do?

You could just dismiss the request as one of many, more or less ingenious, attempts to beg money for drugs. But you remember that you were once in a similar situation, and someone did help you out. So, you first try to test her narrative. Fisher has provided two tests of narratives that are regularly used to either dismiss or accept the narrative. These are coherence* and fidelity.† The narrative seemed coherent: she was right about the likely cost of the train to where she was going. A further test of coherence would be to go to the ticket office and actually buy a ticket to that destination to give to her, but you are already late for your own train and there is no time. You cannot think of any corroborating evidence that you could reasonably ask for. She would not be required to carry evidence of personal information around (no ID is required in your country). So you fall back on whether the story is plausible, that is consistent with other stories that turned out

---

* One possible test of coherence is that each event in the narrative has a plausible, causal link to the next (Sah, 2013). So had the postulant said that her journey was only ten miles and that it would cost her about £5, but she was still asking for £15, the narrative would have lacked coherence and therefore been less persuasive.

† Fidelity is a broader criterion than veracity or truthfulness (Fisher, 1984). It can be judged by 'knowledge of objects' but also by 'knowledge of agents', Fisher says, referring to Toulmin's studies of reasoning. 'Knowledge of agents' means that it has to be true to life as the auditor or reader hears it.

to be true or other stories that turned out to be false. You try to use information about her from her clothing and you look at her face, which looks convincing, but you know how you are (and everyone else is) at judging whether or not a person is lying. The very act of scrutinizing suppresses the interbrain connection and therefore blocks that source of input. In the end, you give her the money – and she doesn't, of course, send you a cheque.

This story may have gone differently if you had never had this experience yourself. It would almost certainly have gone differently if the woman had been a friend and not a stranger.* So what difference would these have made? Being a friend means having the likelihood of continuing contact, but also, in the longer term, the loss of the friendship if the loan is not repaid. There is also the damage to her reputation in the social network that she will have shared with her friend, the donor, to consider. As Adam Smith points out, this would be more damaging to her in the long run than dealing with the debt.† If you had never been in the situation that she was in, and she was not a friend, the likelihood is that you would

---

* I am leaving out the nature of the argument. Influential rules for argumentation or persuasion were formulated by Aristotle but they are so informed by the particular circumstances of Greece at his time of writing that it is less easy to apply them to the modern day than other aspects of his philosophy. Toulmin, inspired by Aristotle, formulated six steps to be followed in a good argument (Toulmin, 1958): 1. Claim; 2. Ground; 3. Warrant; 4. Backing; 5. Rebuttal; 6. Qualifier. Applying this to the plea made for money works like this: Can you lend me £15? (claim); I have to get home but I've lost my ticket (ground); I don't normally do this kind of thing, but I am desperate (warrant). If this is not enough, Toulmin suggests, then further stages in argument are invoked: I will pay you back (backing); I know you will be sceptical (rebuttal), but I'm not the kind of person to do this normally (qualifier).

† Smith (1982/1723) wrote: 'When a person makes perhaps 20 contracts in a day, he cannot gain so much by endeavouring to impose on his neighbours, as the very appearance of a cheat would make him lose' (pp.538–539).

have been less likely to consider helping because, as both Adam Smith and his friend David Hume argued, compassion follows from fellow-feeling and fellow-feeling follows from shared experience. This is because it is easier to imagine what someone like oneself is feeling than someone unlike oneself.

In the days following the incident, someone who had given her the money might wonder whether it would arrive and, at the stage when it obviously is not coming, think about whether they had been foolish or just generous. Their final judgement on this would hinge on the intentions of the beggar. Was she purely cold-bloodedly fleecing you, having worked out a clever patter? Might she have really been trying to get home but she did not have the money to pay her debts when she got there? Was she too ashamed to be in contact, or was she feeling condescending about the fact that she had successfully taken in another sucker?

Working out someone's intentions matters, because moral and ethical judgements hinge on these intentions. Such judgements are not unemotional. We are warmed by ethical actions, disgusted by evil ones, angered by people who fail to get punished...and so on. These emotions are engaged by our stories about another person's intentions, but despite the intensity of our responses, we make mistakes. Reviled offenders can be found after many years to be innocent. People who are lauded for their ethical actions may turn out to be morally despicable, despite their public image.

Emotional reactions like this influence our own actions, and, we imagine, the actions of others. Anticipated shame inhibits us from certain actions and may influence others, too.[2] But we can only reconstruct these motives. We have no direct knowledge of them, unlike our direct knowledge of emotions through the interbrain.

Our narratives can improve if we observe other people carefully and if we do not have too many presumptions of our own that get in the way. Generally, therefore, we develop accurate awareness of our nearest and dearest and can feel that we know how they think or what they are capable of. Even so, people still surprise us. It helps that our nearest and dearest develop a meta-narrative, a narrative about our narratives about them, and that they try to act according to that narrative,* unless it becomes 'stultifying' and then the opposite may happen: our nearest and dearest taking pleasure in showing us that they are more interesting than we thought.

Minds and 'theories of mind'

If a theory of mind is a narrative, and if it has no referent as Spence argued, what is the mind to which the 'theory of mind' is referring? The radical answer, with which I have sympathy, is that 'mind' is a useful fiction, developed in order to allow for an intermediate level of analysis of human actions that lies 'between' purely personal and purely biological accounts. That there is no entity called mind does not prevent us from using it as a category, and it would be strange to deny that there are certain experiences – thinking things through, planning, feeling hot, feeling impatient, feeling anger – that most of us would call 'mental' experiences. These experiences are also associated with the immediacy and quality that most of us would recognize as being described by the term 'self-conscious' or just 'conscious'.

This book is about connecting to people and communicating with people. So it would not be appropriate here to divaricate

---

* Laing and others have tried to develop a systematic account of this back-and-forth narrative process (Laing, Phillipson, and Lee, 1966).

into the seductive field of consciousness studies. But it is worth observing that none of the mental experiences that I have listed are necessarily private. I can think things through in conversation and, indeed, I am thinking things through now as I write to an imagined reader. We regularly plan with others. Thinking things through or planning are not dependent on the activity of our brains or even our brains along with any additional component of soul or spirit that the reader wishes to add in. So it is clear that the referent of 'theories of mind' is at the least slippery.

Communicating information

Arguably, being told a factual state of affairs by someone is not like participating in a narrative. If I ask someone 'How far is it to Leicester?', it might seem that I am seeking a datum that one person can call to mind, that can be communicated to me without ambiguity, and that can be checked against, say, my electronic route-finder. Spence would consider that it is a proposition that has historical truth. I can even say 'Google Maps makes it 23 miles, but you said 30', and the other person can give a specific referent or demonstration of veracity by saying, 'That would be if there were no deviation. But the road is closed at Nuneaton today. So by the time you go round, it will be 30.' Informative answers[*] can also be given by smartphones, as the example indicates.

But before we consider that this example of communicating knowledge about the roads around Nuneaton is an example of how minds can connect by means of the giving and receiving of information, it should be noted that even such simple

---

[*] I think that this use of 'informative' corresponds quite closely to Austen's term 'constative', which he contrasts with the much more socially embedded 'performative' (Austin and Urmson, 1962).

messages are rarely free of the requirement for interpretation in which the different perspectives of giver and receiver need to be considered. If, for example, I had been on a bicycle, I might have worked out that I could get through the road block as a pedestrian and that it would still be worth me taking the shorter route.

Information can, in principle, be checked, but it often has to be taken, as we would say, at its own value. This means that the provenance of the information is also an issue. I consider this in more detail in the next chapter. It is worth remembering, too, that we have to make a similar judgement about information that we present to ourselves and that we recall. This is not the case for motor memory. We make few errors when we get on a bicycle for the first time in years and never behave as if we are riding a horse and not a bicycle. We just set off. Errors can multiply, though, when we start to think about what we are doing, suggesting that the process of mentalizing is fraught with error, even when we are dealing with so-called facts. I think that this is yet another of the facets of the conflict of 'mind' and interbrain.

Perspective taking

'Theory of mind' is sometimes referred to as 'perspective taking'. Perspective taking at its most concrete means to be able to conjure an image of what another person can see, taking account of any obstacle to their line of sight. It is an ability that many animals, including humans, share. It develops progressively in children throughout childhood, first appearing at around the same time as children are able to pass simple theory-of-mind tests.[3] Perspective taking as a synonym of cognitive empathy is a simile, like 'seeing things from another person's point of view', or 'putting yourself in another person's shoes'. It does not mean that the same skills are involved. In fact, it seems very unlikely that they are.[*]

Working out what another conspecific can see is an important skill in many group situations where conspecifics have to coordinate a pack action, with each member of the pack having a different line of sight.[†] Perspective taking is also important in concealing a food source from conspecifics who might otherwise raid it, and primates have extended this ability to include being able to predict the behaviour of conspecifics.[4] Some have argued that this is evidence of theory of mind. It is obviously important in human societies, too, to predict how other people will react, but it does not require a theory of mind to do so. One could train a neural net, or a computer, to predict how another interactant might behave over a sufficient series of trials. All one would need to do is to have the neural net or the computer to predict the other person's responses and then compare those predictions with actual responses and make appropriate adjustments to the predictions. This is a process that begins in childhood. In one study, the unpredictability of care up to the age of five, but not thereafter, had long-term deleterious effects on social behaviour, suggestive of reduced competence in predicting other people's actions.[‡]

---

* The theory-of-mind test, the director's task, tests this directly (Rubio-Fernández, 2016).

† Canines have developed pack predation to high levels and have better visual perspective skills, at least on some tests, than primates (MacLean, Krupenye, and Hare, 2014).

‡ Doom, Vanzomeren-Dohm, and Simpson (2016) found that the unpredictability of mothers for children up to the age of five increased 'externalizing behaviours' in adolescence and young adulthood in a pseudo-prospective design. These results are only suggestive in the sense that the predictability of the mother's care-giving was not directly assessed, and nor was the proband's ability to make accurate judgements about other people's behaviour later in life.

Predictions like this are more accurate than narratives in many human situations, such as the prediction of whether or not someone who has been violent will be violent again or whether or not someone is likely to reoffend. So-called actuarial methods are less widely used than predictions made by experts for two reasons: they are less good at the prediction of the behaviour of an individual than of a group, and they do not take account of the intentions of the violent or offending person.

The evidence points towards intentions not being causes of actions, certainly not of impulsive actions, but being rationalizations after the fact. Rationalizations may alter the expectancies of future actions* but comply with the criteria for being narratives rather than causal explanations. Even more than other narratives, their efficacy rests on their ability to act as justifications to other people. To do this, they have to be revealed 'out there' in discourse with others and not hidden in a private domain of 'mind' unless that domain is the only way that an exculpatory or other self-deceptive narrative can be sustained.

Connecting feelings

So far, I have argued that we connect with other people directly through shared emotion and shared attention – through the interbrain – but not through any kind of mind-to-mind communication. This is one of the reasons that solipsism is so hard to defeat merely by argument. Were there to be other minds with contents, there would still be no means to reveal them to another person. This is not in

---

* There is a considerable literature on this, sometimes framed as the difference between reasons and causes.

itself a solipsistic position, because I have also argued that the co-creation of narratives constitutes a 'world' or 'domain' of social experience in which one can meet with other people and in which connections are possible. I am not arguing for an interpersonal theory such as that of Goffman in which we have public personas that interact on a public stage, leaving our private selves behind the scenes,* but one in which the private self is itself embedded in the public narrative, just as a skilful actor may hint at his or her character having private thoughts even whilst uttering his or her lines. Memory preserves and maintains the narrative and, to the extent that memories are privately rehearsed and amended, there is a private world too – but the private rehearsal of memory may be a recent feature of culture, developing alongside a stronger conception of individuality and independent-mindedness that has partly replaced community story-telling and public rehearsal and emendation of the past.

One root of narratives about actions and intentions is in face-to-face interactions that have actually taken place. If we are connected to the other people whose actions and feelings the narrative describes, we must assume that they would narrate the circumstances of our interaction with them in a fashion that was congruent with our own. We can test this by overtly comparing narratives, and also by the effectiveness of their ability to predict our actions, as well as our ability to predict theirs, and by the extent to which emotional contagion occurs. In other words, the strength of the interbrain connection validates the connectedness of our joint narrative.

---

* Had multi-user domains been invented during Goffman's lifetime, he might have used a different analogy: that we only exist to other people as avatars.

If there is no embodied interaction, is there any other means of connecting through a narrative?[*] Some narratives are truthful, that is they have a reference to some fact or datum that is recognized by the narrator and the auditor. But this is not required of many narratives about intentions. Earlier in this chapter, I quoted the authorial voice of E. M. Forster who suggested that a connection was made when mood was shared. This works well for embodied narrative because of the ability of the interbrain to channel emotions, but can it work for disembodied interaction?

In Chapter 1, I briefly referred to the stickiness of emotions and feelings that can transfer themselves to other elements of experience that occur with but are otherwise unconnected to a strong emotion. The scent of lilies may forever carry the feelings that we have at a funeral when lilies are laid all around a body, for example. I have called[5] these objects or perceptions 'emotors' when they become imbued with emotion in this way. There are some 'emotors' that are inherited, too: a cliff edge, the shadow of a hawk, or snakes. Colour has a subtle but consistent emotional effect and so does sonority in music. Words themselves may become emotors. The medium of

---

[*] In his excellent, posthumously published, book on narrative, Goldie (2012) discusses many aspects of narrative theory that touch on issues that I also mention from time to time. He discusses the question of 'objectivity' in narrative at p.155. He argues that narratives that reveal a person's intentions will usually be 'perspectival', a word he uses in the same way that I have referred to 'seeing another person's perspective', but he assumes that this will create a disconnection between the narrator and the auditor in the sense that the auditor may account for a person's behaviour in a very different way to the one that the narrator appears to be suggesting. But that, of course, suggests a connection of a kind in that the auditor may believe that they know what the narrator is trying to convince them of but at the same time be setting that aside. Goldie's explanation of the connection is the same as mine: that it is the appropriateness of emotion that enables the connection, i.e. a narrative that appears emotionally appropriate to the narrator's experience and that induces the same emotions in the auditor (or viewer).

disembodied narratives has the ability to conjure emotion, albeit one-way emotion, unlike the interbrain. Catching these emotions from narrative, being 'moved' by narrative, is a measure of connection with the narrator, so long, that is, that the auditor considers that the emotions match the situation experience by the narrator.

Consider this example:

A young person presents themselves at an emergency clinic and says that they want to die and, in fact, that if someone cannot help them, they will throw themselves from a bridge onto the railway. A few questions elicit the following story. The young person has run away from home. They are known to have taken several recent overdoses of the antidepressants that they have received. Before the last overdose, their father had said that he did not think that they were really depressed, but that their low mood was a reaction to getting drunk in the clubs that the young person went to most nights. He said that the overdoses were stressing out his wife (the young person's mother) and the other children in the family, and if the young person took another overdose, the father would insist that they left home and sorted themselves out. The young person had left home, had slept on a bench the previous night, but did not want to do that again and could not go home.

The nurse who obtained this information was touched by the young person's story, related it to a similar experience in his own life, and thought that his patient was deeply depressed and should be admitted to the hospital. His colleague thought that the young person's distress was skin-deep, that his story was exaggerated, and that the hospital would be full to bursting if it admitted everyone whose life was a mess and who could tell a good sob story.

Neither nurse could check the story and both knew that there was an outside chance that it was invented. But the first nurse thought that the hopelessness in the story was appropriate (to use Goldie's term) to the situation and consequently felt a connection with the young person. The other nurse felt that the mood of the story was not consistent with either the clubbing or the drinking and, far from feeling a connection with the young person, felt an antipathy. She had a sympathy (which she was careful not to express) with the father and imagined banning the young person from the A&E department, just as the father had banned the young person from their home.*

Emotional connection through narrative

Some of the richest elements of our world are constituted by disembodied elements. I have already mentioned music and art, but there is also recorded speech and writing. The most obviously realistic elements of our experienced world are

---

* It is possible that the second nurse was influenced by her own perspective on demanding young people. Inhibiting a personal perspective seems to be a prerequisite for seeing another person's point of view when it differs from one's own (Aïte *et al.*, 2016), but power comes into this, too. Perhaps the second nurse was much more senior and thus inclined not to see other people's point of view (Galinsky, Rucker, and Magee, 2016), or maybe they were just more anxious, which has a similar effect (Todd and Simpson, 2016).

empirical, but we rarely experience even those without some filter of interpretation or affect.

It is important that this world of experience is not just arbitrary or simulated, and this means that it matters and that it matters in the same way to us as it does to other people whom we hold dear or value.* Connection with others is an important contributor to mattering. When things do not matter, we describe ourselves as indifferent, uncaring, unconcerned, neutral, or, sometimes, on autopilot. We feel that our existence is an irrelevance to human life and, sometimes, that we have ceased to be human.

How narratives induce emotions

Sigmund Freud, in his profound essay on the interpretation of dreams,[6] used dreams to investigate what he thought were the vicissitudes of what he then called unconscious catharses. He imagined these to be packets of energy generated by extrinsic emotional stimuli and then moved from one neuron to another to be processed. By the time he was writing *The Interpretation of Dreams*, he had given up on his original aim of formulating the processing as a neurological process that linked the sensory system and evoked the desires that made up this energy and an effector process that acted to satisfy the desire. Instead, he substituted a semiotic mechanism.

Desire would arise from the sensory system, or possibly autochthonously, and would normally lead to a drive towards satiation. But to preserve sleep, an image of a situation leading to satiation would be enough of a substitute for this,

---

* I have previously referred to these affines as constituting our 'in-group', and although this is perhaps a rather approximate term, it is probably the most useful one to apply, without developing unnecessary neologism.

Freud thought, to preserve sleep. A hungry person might, for example, imagine eating steak and chips, or a thirsty person, drinking ice-cold beer. But the alcoholic who was aiming for abstinence might experience sufficient anxiety about drinking that his or her sleep would again be disturbed and so clamp down on the image of the ice-cold beer and imagine ice-cold tea instead. The desire for beer would have been displaced, according to Freud's usage of the term, from beer to something that resembled it, i.e. cold tea.

Freud thought that displacement moved along preferred pathways and that these could be retraced to the origin of the anxiety by using the method of free association. Normally, there were visual resemblances, homophones, parts of the things themselves, or other physical objects that belonged to the person. These associations would be disclosed in the process of free association.

The gaps in Freud's formulation (for example, an explanation of why being stirred by a feeling should be associated with increased energy in individual neurons)[*] will be obvious even from the previous summary, although I believe it to be faithful to at least some of Freud's thinking. But Freud was always on safer ground when he concentrated on semiology and mental 'operations'. His application of Peircean logic, which included a description of metaphor and metonym, did capture the way the emotion slides from one emotor to another on the basis of similarity. Think, for example, of a clever chef creating a dish out of chocolate ice cream and caramel sauce that looks exactly like diseased human faeces. Would everyone be happy to eat it? It would probably taste delicious but it would be so similar in appearance to actual faeces that most people would

---

[*] Although 'neuropsychoanalysts' still do argue this (Pfaff, Martin, and Kow, 2007).

say, 'That's disgusting. I couldn't eat that.' They would have a disgust-mediated action avoidance, to use the terms used by Miller *et al.*[7] and discussed in relation to the trolley problem.[*]

Once a displacement has occurred, it can be repeated and repeated again. So a person who has had the misfortune to spend a day judging which chef has produced the most life-like faeces from chocolate ice cream may become so disgusted that any ice cream, even in blocks, would start to seem disgusting, as the disgust has transferred from the representation to just one feature of the representation (a phenomenon that Freud called 'condensation'). Disgust is particularly likely to be transferred by smell, so it would likely be the smell of the ice cream that becomes disgusting. Disgust can be displaced onto words, too, and thereby influences the words we can use in our narratives about other people.

Upbringing also has an effect. Men who came home from fighting in the Second World War were both preoccupied and fascinated by firearms. Even my father, an engineer, brought home his service revolver. So when as a child I pointed my obviously fake child's revolver at him and made a shooting noise, he became very distressed and told me, 'Never, ever, point a weapon at anyone.' Both of us knew that this was a toy and not a weapon, but it looked sufficiently like a weapon that he acted towards it with the same fear as if it had been one, and he wanted me to do the same. I am sure that if I ever have to point a gun at anyone, I would have to overcome the action avoidance associated with that memory.

---

[*] Schiermer (2013) attributes a similar model of connection between people mediated by inanimate objects to Benjamin (1968), modified by the ideas of Durkheim.

Words or phrases can also acquire emotional resonance through conditioning, through their etymology, or by even more basic means such as onomatopoeia. And, of course, emotion words are not neutral. Their use raises the scent of their meaning.[*]

Even if our only connection with other people would be via the narrative that we exchange with them, or rehearse about them, it would not be emotionless. As I have indicated, words readily acquire emotional overtones, or connotations, through displacement, conditioning, and culture, and by direct instruction.[8] So even when an attempt is made in 'rational discourse' to purge words of their connotations,[†] it is likely to fail.

The example of embarrassment or 'cringe'

Embarrassment is related to disgust and shame and is in the self-conscious group of emotions.[‡] Finding someone's behaviour embarrassing can lead to a feeling of painful withdrawal – the cringe – if they are someone with whom one has a connection. It is a very similar reaction to seeing someone

---

[*] This can be a problem in psychotherapy. Suggesting that a client might be angry about something can inadvertently make a client angry and, even if no criticism is intended, can be taken to be an annoying criticism. Mentioning shame in any connection can also be perceived as shaming.

[†] Socrates stood at the cusp of the supplanting of the sophists by philosophers. Sophists taught rhetoric: how to move people and win arguments that way. Philosophers thought that this was illegitimate (and also disapproved of sophists selling their teaching). Philosophy has ever since been a fountain of technical terms, designed to purge itself of connotations, but its success has been in proportion to the dry-as-dust nature of philosophical technical writing that only engages other philosophers.

[‡] See Giner-Sorolla, Leidner, and Castano (2011) and Müller-Pinzler *et al.* (2015). The self-conscious group of emotions are said to depend on having self-awareness, i.e. a theory of mind (Heerey, Keltner, and Capps, 2003).

else get hurt, although it is not so bad that one feels nauseated. If the connection is a negative one, one might paradoxically feel pleasure of a kind, as happens when someone is humiliated by a practical joke that one plays on them. Embarrassment is, like shame, disgust, and panic, a highly contagious emotion. Embarrassment can easily be shared. Paulus *et al.*[9] have shown that this is associated with the temporoparietal junction, a part of the interbrain-connecting apparatus, being active. So the theory-of-mind experience of embarrassment is to be aware of the discomfort of someone else and to keep their emotions at a distance from oneself by a 'cringe' or, at an even further distance, by malicious pleasure or Schadenfreude.

Shame and pride are considered self-conscious emotions because their experience presupposes some judgement of social status: inferior and marginalized in the case of shame; superior in the case of pride. So, to get the less-contaminated view of the experience of the theory-of-mind connection with other people, it will be important to neutralize any interbrain connection and also to minimize the impact of any difference in status.[*]

---

[*] The social phase I refer to is not the same as the biologically mediated phase, evident in a 'swarm' or crowd of people. Here I am referring to a sociality mediated by shared narrative. Its origins can be traced to Herder and then the folklorists who assembled narratives that exemplified the spirit of their nation, according to the romantic nationalism movement. In the late 19th century in Germany and Austria, this 'völkisch' movement led to a study of how culture mediated shared meaning and the separation of the sciences of reasons (Geisteswissenschaften) from the science of causation (Gesellschaften), partly in response to the rise of scientific psychology. Schutz (1967), for example, described four life worlds: the Vorwelt (the past); the Folgewelt (the future); the Umwelt; and the Mitwelt. The Mitwelt is the world of people we know things about, and the Umwelt, the world of 'consociates' or 'people who share a community of space and a community of time' (*ibid.*, p.186). Umwelt approximates to what I am terming a connection between minds that is mediated through a shared narrative, or Lebenswelt. Mitwelt is constituted by relations between people that do not involve knowing, as we would say, how the other person feels, but we can predict their behaviour on the basis of rules or social expectations of how they will react. Buber's 'I-it'

Why do people chat to each other? Oftentimes nowadays people will say that they do it because it's always good to keep connected or because they are networking, i.e. adding new connections to their network. Not many people, I suspect, would think that it's good to chat to everybody and anybody. There's a proscribed list for all of us, and chatting to people on that list might lead to joining it oneself. The list is not generally put together by a clerk; it's created by a variety of negative emotions, such as fear, anger, disgust, distrust, or dislike, or by social judgements that impinge on us via guilt, shame, vengefulness, opprobrium, or hatred. At bottom, it is the membership of our particular out-group that is on the proscribed list.

This out-group/in-group distinction arises from but is also constitutive of our empathy. It is apparent in the stranger anxiety that affects infants when they are about nine months old. It is present in the choice we make about: whether to smile with our eyes or just smile; whether we are gratified by someone's gaze or negative about it; whether our relationship with another person is 'I-thou' or 'I-it', to use Buber's distinction;[10] and whether we feel disappointment at another person's joy or pleasure. It is so pervasive that it is useful to think of four, rather than three, modes of connection with other people: positive, negative, blocked, and untried. The out-group can be composed of people to whom any of the latter three modes of connection can apply. It can just mean people other than me, or people other than 'us',

---

relations belong in the Mitwelt and 'I-thou' to relations in the Umwelt. I have previously mentioned Rickman's idea that the infant develops from second-person relationships to third-person ones: from, as one might say, an Umwelt to a Mitwelt. Chisholm *et al.* (2014) provide a simple rule of thumb to distinguish these different connections. Second-person relationships (which they call first-person relationships) are marked by eye contact, i.e. by an interbrain connection; third-person relationships are not.

or it can refer to other people whose existence is so alien to us that it would require us to change our assumptions about the world. Levinas, in particular, is associated with the latter, for which he has coined a special term: their 'alterity', represented by the face of the Other.*

These dual perceptions of the world are deeply entrenched in many cultures, at many levels.[11] In many religions, the kindliness of a beneficent God who means well to humanity is opposed by the power of a great enemy of mankind, who in monotheistic religions is often portrayed as an enemy of God herself.[†]

Secular theories of sociology have also been divided between consensus and conflict theories, with conflict theories becoming dominant towards the end of the last century.

In philosophy, Hollingshead has traced a metaphysical problem from Thales to contemporary philosophy that he summarizes as '[t]his bifurcation of the world into the mundane world perceived and the transcendent, "more real" world revealed by thinking'.[12]

Psychology has been strongly influenced by Freud's theory of unconscious conflict. Freud adopted and extended Nietzsche's theory of the unconscious as it applied to society, and the unconscious struggle of will against resentment, applying it to a different conflict, that between lust and shame.

---

* Gallagher argues that it is the (interbrain) connection with the other's face that adds this transcendent element (Gallagher, 2014).

† Christians call this great enemy Satan, and Muslims, Iblis. In Zoroastrianism Satan or Iblis, or whatever name this fallen angel or demon has, stirs up all of the negative emotions, especially strife, wherever he goes. In Hinduism, many of the gods have aspects of eternity and wholeness, on the one hand, and activity, and therefore conflict, on the other. So although Nagas are often thought to be devils, they are in some ways essential to the successful evolution of the universe.

Freud's take on Nietzsche was that it was the disruptiveness of sexual desire that constantly tried to break through the conventional ties of civilization – that was the cause of the conflict. But there were many other candidates. Darwinians thought it was the struggle to survive, one product of the chaotic processes of genetic variation leading to rival phenotypes. Marx thought that it was economic struggle for control over the means of production. Sartre thought that it might be over any scarce resource, and since there was always something that people desired to have but was in short supply, there would always be conflict.

The ancient Greeks imagined that each person's life was determined by the fates: one of whom was gathering together the threads of life, another was ready to cut the threads, and the third measured.

The Greek view of the fates puts life and death at the centre of existence, and one might argue that this is the fundamental conflict. In his later life, Freud, for example, became interested in an idea put forward by one of his analysands, Dr Sabina Spielrein,* that there was a death instinct that opposed libido – the sexual and therefore the life instinct.

---

* One way to look at Dr Spielrein's life is that she was possessed of an unusually strong death instinct herself. She had been first the patient, then the research associate, and finally the mistress of one of the 20th century's best-known psychiatrists, Carl Jung. She subsequently became a correspondent and then a colleague of another, Sigmund Freud. But rather than these contacts leading to a long and successful career in Switzerland or Austria, she chose to return to her native Russia after being left by her husband. But the nursery that she founded in Moscow was shut down, amid allegations of wrongdoing that were almost certainly trumped up, and she went back to her hometown, Rostov on Don, to reunite with her husband who had been living with, and had had a child by, another woman. Her two brothers were arrested by the NKVD and died in a gulag. Her husband died, and she and their two children were shot in 1942 during a mass killing of Rostov Jews by the occupying Nazis.

Terrible as her life was, it is hard to see that Dr Spielrein was actively seeking death, and if she was, she chose a horribly painful route. We might say that it was a dreadful mistake to leave safe Switzerland to travel to a country where the intelligentsia were at risk of being killed by the secret service and, a few years later, the holocaust was going to burst over Eastern European Jews particularly. But that is to argue with the benefit of hindsight. In fact, we can never look ahead or aim at death, it seems to me, as it is a kind of nothingness. When people kill themselves, it is because life has become intolerable and not because they are wanting to possess death.

The professor of signs

A famous overseas professor came to Cambridge to engage in a sign-language debate.* Only a one-eyed miller would take him on. The debate went like this: the professor held up an apple, and the miller held up a piece of bread; then the professor held up one finger, and the miller held up two; the professor held up three, and the miller held up his fist. The professor accounted himself highly satisfied, as the miller had, he said, followed every turn of his thought. The professor explained that the apple signified the forbidden fruit that Adam picked, the bread stood for the Bread of Life that redeemed mankind, the single finger referred to the one God, two fingers meant that Jesus should not be forgotten, three stood for the trinity, and the fist to show that the Trinity was one. The miller said: 'The professor was quarrelsome and shook an apple he found in his pocket at me. He looked as if he was going to throw it at me. So I felt in my pocket, but I could only find a bit of

---

* This is a synopsis of a folk tale collected (in two versions) by Katharine Briggs (Anon, 2011).

stale bread, which I shoved under his nose. Then he poked his finger at me, as if to stab it in my eye. So I poked my two fingers towards him to show that, if he tried that, I would put out both his. Then he threatened to scratch my face. That was too much and I made a fist to show that, if it came to it, I would knock him down.'

This is a debate of fools on the surface. Both parties thought that they knew what the other was thinking, but each was using completely different signifiers or, as Spence called them, references: the professor, as befitted his dignity, used religious symbology; the miller followed the moves of a street brawler. But looking more deeply, there is a commonality.

Both participants knew that they were in an argument, with each step in the dialogue being a claim and counter-claim. Both participants recognized that their exchange of signs reached a climax at the end, with the miller ready to get physical and the professor believing that the dialogue had culminated in affirming one of the fundamental mysteries of orthodox Christianity, the Trinity. Both participants stuck to their turn. Both parties also needed just three turns to complete their debate, and, of course, three is a special number in folk tales. It is one of the most common tropes: three sons set out, three trials have to be performed, three years pass, and so on.* There is also a meta-narrative: put two men together and, whatever their status and whatever their circumstances, they will spar – but that is another story.

---

* One could argue that three encapsulates the theme of this book: conventional philosophy has us starting as one being or, as I am arguing, one being is what we achieve by breaking away from our connection with others. I am arguing that we are connected from the first, principally to our main carer as a couple, or, as Winnicott (1957) said, 'there is no such thing as a baby, there is a baby and someone'. Three is our condition throughout most of our lives when we relate to another but almost always in the context of having yet others who are observers.

The recognizable grammar of a story, its morphology as Vladimir Propp[*] called it, may be one of the methods by which narratives in music or dance as well as words can sweep us up into a shared world with the narrator.[†] One of the reasons for this is that similarities are significant to us at an early age. Similarity is one step up from imitation, after all. The relations of similarity that we act out in infancy are transferred to the inanimate world as correspondences before they further mutate into similar words and similar concepts.[‡] The gestural sequence of the professor-of-signs tale expresses another primitive relationship between signs, the metonym, the *pars pro toto* that Freud concluded was an important linkage in his own dream imagery: the sign that stands for something of which it is a part.[§]

---

[*] See Propp (1968) and the brief summary from Aguirre (2011) focusing on the role of iteration and giving an example of triplication.

[†] Sundararajan and Raina (2016) argue for the creation of a shared world, too, basing their account on the metaphor of entanglement from quantum physics and the rasa tradition of Indian aesthetics. They argue that the narrator or performer of a narrative is not doing something *to* her or his audience but *with* them. This might come about because the narrative only makes sense in that both performer and audience are mining a shared stock of imagery and emotion that Jung termed the 'collective unconscious'.

[‡] Max, at 17 months, could understand and act on simple phrases ('Bring the book to Daddy'), babbled and occasionally repeated a word clearly, said 'What's that?' unclearly but frequently, could say 'Mama' and 'Dada', had started to play pretend games like deliberately putting a puzzle piece into the wrong place, and would regularly and spontaneously point to an object in another place if he saw a picture of that thing in a book. For example, if he saw a picture of a tree in a book, he would turn and point towards a tree outside the window.

[§] I am touching here on a sophisticated tradition of the structural basis of language developed by de Saussure and developed subsequently by Piaget and others, but foreshadowed in Peirce's work on iconic and indexical signs.

Notes

1. Brentano, 1973/1874
2. Lickel *et al.*, 2014
3. Vander Heyden *et al.*, 2017
4. Whiten, 2013
5. Tantam, 2003
6. Freud, 1992/1900
7. Miller *et al.*, 2014
8. Clancy, 1999
9. Paulus *et al.*, 2015
10. Buber, 2003
11. Van Deurzen, 2015
12. Hollingshead, 1970/1851, p.12

Chapter 5

CONNECTING THROUGH COMMON KNOWLEDGE

James Surowiecki, a business journalist, has written a book in which he attempts to put an alternative view of crowds to the one that I put forward in Chapter 2. In order to differentiate his view of crowds from the 'swarms' that I was writing about, I will refer to the groupings that Surowiecki describes as 'collectivities'. Surowiecki argues that people, even people with little or no relevant knowledge, can out-estimate experts so long as they act independently but collectively. His book *The Wisdom of Crowds*[1] starts with a description of the 19th-century scientist and intellectual Francis Galton collecting the estimates made by the public attending a country fair. It was a competition to guess the weight of an ox; the catch was that the ox was alive but the weight that had to be guessed was what it would weigh after it had been 'dressed'. The ox was there, and anyone who wanted could pay a small fee and make an estimate. But the weight of the skin, horns, and other inedible parts had to be estimated and subtracted. Galton thought that someone in the abattoir business would make the best estimate. But he obtained all the estimates of weight made that afternoon, and, on averaging them, discovered that the average was within a pound or two of the correct weight.*

This is, at first sight, a surprising finding. There was no collusion between the estimators overall (there may have been some groups of which some of the members had a go), and there was variation in the estimates, but this variation fitted a normal distribution whose mean was pretty close to the correct weight. One can imagine how that worked to some degree: there will have been some pessimists who will have estimated too low, and optimists who will have estimated too high, and they would have cancelled each other out.

Attenders at country fairs in the 19th century were likely to be familiar with cattle raising, and one assumes that only a person who thought that they had a chance to guess correctly would hazard the cost of buying a ticket. So perhaps Galton's results are not so surprising. But there are many examples of groups of people holding systematically false beliefs about other topics, such as human anatomy and geography.

Surowiecki is, however, impressed by the ability of groups to make good decisions, and even suggests that groups regularly out-perform experts. He provides many other examples of groups of people making accurate judgements, but he also explains that these are only groups by happenstance. There is no discussion of each person's estimate by anyone else. In fact, the groups do not really meet at all. When individuals do meet in a group and try to arrive at a joint decision, persuasion by one or more influential group members sways the results and makes calculations less accurate. Having someone whose

---

* Galton wrote a short paper about this (Galton, 1907).

judgements are opposed to those of other people in the group reduced inaccuracy to some degree. But it is only if individuals make their choice independently that the best estimates are achieved, i.e. when individuals have not become lost in a swarm.[2]

Surowiecki emphasizes that, in this scenario, decision-making is most effective when no greater weight is given to any one person's opinion over another. It should be contrasted with an ineffectual example of group decision-making in which a group discusses a decision, coming to a more and more extreme and panicky formulation, a situation called 'group-think' by Janis.[3] This is a group situation in which the extended mind is embodied in a group connected by the interbrain and the contagion of emotion. Common knowledge is most effective if those who hold it do have some relevant expertise or if there is a degree of empirical knowledge included. Surowiecki may be wrong that one can do better without experts, but one can do better to rely on one or two experts when it comes to decision-making.

Cooperation and coordination

Surowiecki[4] discusses three types of outcomes of these collectivities, which he calls extended minds: calculation, described above, requires a special form of collective decision-making but not one involving crowds as I am defining them; cooperation; and coordination. Surowiecki's example of coordination is of how individuals move through flocks of people, for example on pavements or in restaurants.*

---

* There is a kind of generic rule here that applies to the behaviour of all of the individuals in a crowd, but it applies to keeping distance from others rather than proximity (Yu *et al.*, 2015). Proximity is essential for maintaining the interbrain

Surowiecki gives several examples of coordination in action in supply chains, for example how food production adjusts to food packaging, transport, and sales, each of which affect the speed of transmission down the chain and therefore the amounts of food demanded. He considers these to be an example of the ability of crowds to cooperate. This kind of cooperative activity is remarkable, but it depends on a multitude of individual transactions and individual predictions rather than a mass action of a coordinated group of people.

Each of these transactions does, however, require the people in that transaction to be connected to each other by a theory of mind that enables the motives of each of the parties to be considered. When the packager says that he cannot take as much chicken because it is too hard to get labour on the production line, is he saying this because he is taking chicken from some other farm at a lower unit price? Or is there a reduced demand for chicken, and the packager is switching to turkey? Such human insights ensure that longer term changes in supply and demand can be anticipated.

There need be no real connection between the people in the supply chain. The coordination is implicit in its efficient functioning at times of change. Coordination is more obviously required if people need to work together. Revolutions are often cited in discussions of the risks and benefits of coordination. Repressive regimes almost always have some opponents who may be shot, imprisoned, or silenced in some other way by the regime without regime change taking place. These individuals know the risks and are rarely motivated by the expectation that they will be successful. Regime change requires mass protests or mass violence, but mass protests and mass violence

---

connection in humans and other flocking species and is one of the rules that maintains cohesiveness of the crowd.

require the involvement of people who are willing to endure the regime rather than put themselves at risk. Repression by the regime is designed to maintain the common knowledge that revolution will not succeed. So revolution can only happen when that common knowledge gets replaced by the common knowledge that revolution is possible without substantial risk to the participants. There may even be a tipping point at which the common knowledge becomes known: 'The revolution will certainly succeed, and those who are seen to be supporting it will benefit.'

'Common knowledge' is also fundamental to any kind of social interaction in which one stranger may benefit or lose and the other or others may lose or gain reciprocally. To stand the best chance of gain, one party needs to know how the other party will react but, since the other party is a stranger, they must base this on whether or not the other party shares the same moral instincts and precepts – the same common knowledge – that will respect a bargain.* Many games that

---

* These ideas are not new. Adam Smith strongly emphasized the notion of bargains that worked to ensure that moral actions, i.e. altruistic actions, preponderated in society, and, in *The Wealth of Nations* (1805), that individual self-interest actually led to greater performance of the market and therefore wealth creation for everyone. Smith also used the same explanation, which was originally proposed by Hobbes, for the emergence of dominance hierarchies in human affairs. Giving a person power, via the social contract, ensured that they would then have the power to protect. Both explanations depended on reciprocity. This, like empathy, has two foundations: that harming others causes emotional discomfort to oneself because of sympathy, and that being in a market means having to maintain trade with others. Cheating another person is likely to lead to exclusion from the market in the future. If a person is trading for just a short time, it may matter less that they are not trusted in that particular market if they can move to another one. Patrons who expect to return to a restaurant will, for example, tip more than someone not expecting to return. Giambattista Vico's writings have been rediscovered as scepticism about empiricist approaches to epistemology has grown. He argued that science was only one kind of knowledge. The other was sensus communis – common sense – which was 'judgment without reflection,

people play with each other have this kind of element in them, and a science has developed to study them and apply these 'game theories' to decision-making in general.*

---

shared by an entire class, an entire people, and entire nation, or the entire human race' (Vico, 1968/1744, Element XII, section 145, pp.63–64).

* Lewis (2002) initiated the study of common knowledge from a game theoretic point of view. Binmore (2004) outlines some of the features of common knowledge in an unpublished but excellent paper on conventions. He traces the conception of common knowledge back to Hume, whose work, as I have already noted, also originated modern concepts of empathy. Binmore is concerned, in this paper, about convention, a common explanation for the rules that govern human interaction and, as Hume pointed out, ensure coordination and cooperation between people.

Binmore approaches common knowledge from the perspective of game theory. His views deserve respect not only because of his academic prowess, but also because he conducted the auction for frequency bands for 4G communications, which netted £22 billion. Game theory has developed procedures for studying human behaviour as if it is governed by the kind of rules that apply to games, although these are the rules of life or the rules of human nature. These rules are implicit in the choices that people make in simple interactions and can therefore be inferred from repeated playing of the game when each interactant's behaviour has become unchanging or, as game theorists put it, when equilibrium is reached. Binmore proposes two 'branches' of game theory: evolutive and eductive. Evolutive rules can arise out of trial-and-error adjustments until an equilibrium is reached. Hume's example of convention is one example: two men rowing a boat need to learn how to pull their own oar in coordination with the other rower or the boat goes round and round (the equilibrium condition here is that the boat moves steadily forwards in a straight line). Common knowledge does not have to be articulated and may not even have to be formulated, as it is implicit in the establishment of an equilibrium that both of the rowers know how to row.

Eductive theory is the branch that has produced the most often cited research, according to Binmore, but here the common-knowledge problem is more acute. He cites an example from Halpern (1987) in which two generals each occupy adjacent hilltops with an army. They are in league against an army in the valley that is too strong for either general to defeat on their own. Messengers have to cross the valley to get from one general to the other and are regularly intercepted. One general may send the other the message 'I am ready to attack' but cannot move until he knows the other general is ready too. But if he sends the message, he has no idea if the other general gets it until the other general sends an acknowledgement. But even if the acknowledgement arrives, the other general cannot know that it has arrived... The attack is therefore delayed until

It is unusual for people to be tested on their 'common knowledge', but it is done in *Pointless*, a quiz programme on UK television. Contestants have to answer questions by choosing the correct answer that is also the least likely to be answered correctly by a panel of 100 members of the public. So, the contestants are being tested on not just their general knowledge, but also the accuracy of their knowledge of what 'the public' knows, i.e. common knowledge.*

What knowledge is, and how people arrive at it, has been the key problem for epistemology since it emerged as a named branch of philosophy. But 'common knowledge' may not meet epistemological criteria. It may even be false,[5] as 'the madness of crowds' indicates.

The madness of crowds

Extraordinary Popular Delusions and the Madness of Crowds is a book written by Charles Mackay[†] and published in 1841. Mackay describes his subject matter on the first page of his Preface to the 1852 edition: 'We find that whole communities suddenly fix their minds upon one object, and go mad in its

---

the knowledge that each army is ready becomes common, which might not happen, given the recursive nature of the messaging.

* Studies suggest that people gain common knowledge from what have been called 'select crowds' (Mannes, Soll, and Larrick, 2014) in which more reliance is placed on the belief that people do not necessarily hold themselves but believe that others will hold.

† Mackay's book is still popular, partly because he is such a good writer. His popular songs are still known today, and in his journalistic career he rose to become editor of the *Illustrated London News* at the height of its fame. There have been many books similar to Mackay's examining 'mass phenomena', for example the recent *A Colourful History of Population Delusions* (Bartholomew, 2015). Bartholomew has also co-authored an account of mass hysteria in schools and *Outbreak! The Encyclopedia of Extraordinary Social Behaviour*.

pursuit.' He deals with the South Sea Bubble, crusades, the Mississippi bubble, and a variety of other inexplicable social movements. Some contemporary researchers have attributed these mad pursuits to 'the willingness of people to comply with social norms',[6] but the protagonists Mackay describes were typically trying to get an advantage over other people rather than to conform. They thought that they could do this by reacting more quickly than other people to what they took to be 'common knowledge', and by reacting to their beliefs, and by other people seeing them react, they widened the spread of that common knowledge.

But that did not make this common knowledge true; it was only a widely held conviction that could actually be traced back to influential individuals who had arrived at that belief without having good evidence for it and initiated the process of changing 'common knowledge'. In his book *The Tipping Point*, Gladwell calls them 'mavens'.[7]

How does knowledge become 'common'?

Gladwell takes the view that ideas spread by means of being remarkable (to use a term used by Gordin,* another subscriber to this model of top-down marketing). He argues that ideas can spread epidemically from person to person, basing this

---

* See Gordin (2003). Gordin also publicized the notion of viral marketing to name the spread of ideas through a population. Gladwell focuses on the originator of the idea; Gordin on the idea or the product itself. The latter is closer to the suggestion of Dawkins that cultural artefacts ('memes') spread through populations by a process that was originally conceived as being more like an evolutionary spread (Dawkins, 1976).

on research into 'degrees of distance' and sociometric 'stars',*
which Gladwell calls 'connectors'. Mavens come up with the
ideas, the connectors spread them widely, and if more than
150 people adopt them, a tipping point is reached that results
in widespread acceptance.

Gladwell's ideas work well for 'suggestions' that often
appear on help pages and, nowadays, on websites. How to deal
with small pieces of soap, what to do with matchsticks, and so
on. They do not apply to the life-and-death situations that I
have considered in earlier paragraphs on common knowledge.
If I were living in a dictatorship and got a message that
someone I did not know was asking me to join the revolution,
and this message had been passed on by acquaintances, I would
be very reluctant to declare my hand, fearing at the least that
the message might have been distorted (which easily happens,
as demonstrated by the game of Chinese Whispers), or that I
was being tested by an agent provocateur.†

---

* These terms are taken from an influential paper on the 'small world problem',
or why, despite how many millions of people there may be in my country, I can
connect with most of them. It is a means of quantifying the overlap between
social networks. Say I want to contact X; one of my acquaintances will know
one of X_1's acquaintances, who will tell X_1 that I want to contact X. X_1 will
know X_2, who will know X and will tell X that I am trying to be in contact. In
this scenario, there are three degrees of distance and a sociometric star, X_1, whose
large acquaintanceship I make use of.

† Common knowledge changes social behaviour more than personal belief. For
example, teachers discussing students are more likely to express consensus
opinions about them if they know that other teachers also have the same
information that they do, but their own judgements are not affected by
whether or not their knowledge about the student is common (Gigone, 1993).
In a study in Rwanda, a popular radio soap listened to by a large number of
people, about harmonious relations between Hutu and Tutsi, influenced social
norms about discrimination between the two groups but did not change private
beliefs (Paluck, 2009). Common knowledge was malevolently influenced in
Rwanda by community radio, too. It played a part in widening the involvement
of Hutus in the massacre of Tutsis at an earlier period (Yanagizawa-Drott, 2014).

Widening the group of those who share common knowledge is not just a matter of disseminating knowledge, but also of establishing that each person in that wider group knows that each other person has that knowledge. Contrary to the predictions of the Gladwell model of tips dissemination, common knowledge dissemination is more reliable if the connections between disseminators are strong and not weak. That is, there are fewer people but more interconnections between them in the networks being used for dissemination.[8]

Gaining common knowledge

One method for the transmission of common knowledge is by participation in a shared experience.[*] If I travel on the train and note that everyone buys and reads the same newspaper, I will assume that the statements printed in the newspaper, or at least those on the front page, become common knowledge amongst commuters on that particular train. Furthermore, the more that commuters linger on a particular story, the more 'important' that story becomes.[9] If commuters are the only people whose knowledge matters, and if newspapers print even convincingly knowledgeable information, this assumption may be well founded. But neither newspapers nor television broadcasts have the same degree of penetration that they did, and people who commute no longer catch the same trains at the same times, wearing the same suits, and considering themselves to be the establishment. Shared experience and psychological closeness are associated with each other.[10] But

---

[*] See Shteynberg (2015) for a review of experiments from his team about this. He calls the reinforcement 'shared attention', which is confusing, as he is referring to shared awareness of others' attention to a third party and not the interbrain connection that is referred to in the infant development literature and that I considered in Chapter 1 as a form of gaze following.

new media have taken the place of newspapers in creating common knowledge, and I shall be considering the role of these, particularly of social media, in the final chapter.

The special dress of city workers, the carriage of the furled umbrella, and the rolled copy of *The Times* newspaper were a source of fascination and amusement throughout the world. To dress up in this way was to participate in a ritual. Intrinsic to this ritual was the commute, from one well-heeled suburb or another to London Bridge and an office in Whitehall or the City of London. One function of ritual, Chwe has argued,[11] is to create common knowledge, as I am arguing that the ritual of the city commute did. He cites the eminent anthropologist Clifford Geertz's treatment of royal progresses in many parts of the world in which a large group of people turn out to watch a member of a royal family. Electioneering, in which political leaders engage in whirlwind tours of places, arguably has the same function. Among the audience, there will often be a few put there to note the names of those who are not celebrating as enthusiastically and even, in smaller communities, of anyone who is absent. The royal progress establishes the status and power of the royal but also the dissemination of that common knowledge, indeed the creation of the common knowledge that fealty and devotion are owed to the royal personage. Politicians on the stump may not be absolute monarchs, but they too impersonate a party and encourage fealty to it.

Common knowledge and the interbrain

Committing to a joint action with another person carries with it the risk that they might seek their own advantage at the expense of yours and that their commitment to the joint action is a ruse. Some people assume that no act can be selfless, as every person always puts their own interests first. I have argued already that an interbrain connection with another person or group of people makes it possible that each member of the connected group may act on behalf of the group, even if that action is harmful to the actor. The interbrain is one explanation for altruism or, to use another metaphor, self-sacrifice. Preserving the life of a child at one's own expense is an example of altruism that people might acknowledge as credible even if they otherwise thought that life was about 'looking after number one'.

I have also suggested in previous chapters that, as seeing others in pain is vicariously painful, there is a brake on how much pain we are willing to give to others.*

---

* Adam Smith (2002/1785) covered all of these different positions in his *Theory of Moral Sentiments* but did not make a distinction between them. His starting point is empathy – 'How selfish soever man may be supposed, there are evidently some principles in his nature, which interest him in the fortune of others, and render their happiness necessary to him, though he derives nothing from it except the pleasure of seeing it. Of this kind is pity or compassion, the emotion which we feel for the misery of others, when we either see it, or are made to conceive it in a very lively manner' (p.1) – and he refers to the three elements that I have but without differentiating them. So he writes, 'The mob, when they are gazing at a dancer on the slack rope, naturally writhe and twist and balance their own bodies, as they see him do, and as they feel that they themselves must do if in his situation. Persons of delicate fibres and a weak constitution of body complain, that in looking on the sores and ulcers which are exposed by beggars in the streets, they are apt to feel an itching or uneasy sensation in the correspondent part of their own bodies' (*ibid.*, p.2) and 'Grief and joy, for example, strongly expressed in the look and gestures of any one, at once affect the spectator with some degree of a like painful or agreeable emotion' (*ibid.*, p.2), which is an apparent reference to a direct connection like the interbrain. He refers to vicarious pain and the fear of injury – 'When we see a stroke aimed and just ready to fall upon the leg or arm of another person, we naturally shrink and draw back our own leg or our own arm...' (*ibid.*, p.1) – but he also stresses the connection of imagination that he says explains the rest: 'It is the impressions of our own senses only, not those of his, which our imaginations copy. By the imagination we place ourselves in his situation, we conceive ourselves enduring all the same torments, we enter as it were into his body, and become in some measure the same person with him, and

Being tuned in to common knowledge is not like being tuned in to another person via the interbrain. It is not about ensuring the welfare of both parties, although that might be its secondary upshot. It is about managing in a world where others will usually be seeking to put their own interests first, a world of risk.

The question arises: in such a world how can people afford to act cooperatively?

In the footnote on page 205, on game theory, I quoted a scenario sometimes known as the Byzantine army game. Two armies and two generals are on proximal hilltops. The army that they are attacking is in the valley, where its sentries can intercept any messages; the likelihood is that the army in the valley can be defeated if the two generals on the hilltops collaborate. But one general might think that if the other army went in first, and was decimated, all his army would have to do would be to mop up. So how can they trust each other to act together?

The coordination of action and inaction has been considered in a series of studies at MIT.* They concluded that risky

---

thence form some idea of his sensations, and even feel something which, though weaker in degree, is not altogether unlike them' (*ibid.*, p.1).

Smith extends the power of the mother's imagination to supply a narrative to the preverbal infant who is ill – 'In her idea of what it suffers, she joins, to its real helplessness, her own consciousness of that helplessness, and her own terrors for the unknown consequences of its disorder; and out of all these, forms, for her own sorrow, the most complete image of misery and distress' (*ibid.*, p.4) – and points out that we can even imagine what it would be like to be dead.

* See Thomas (2014, 2016). Both experiments contrasted the impact of having personal knowledge and sharing common knowledge. In the 2016 experiment, common knowledge that a person needed help but that this help would be a cost to anyone intervening reduced the chances of someone intervening below those when each person thought that only they knew that the person who required help. In the 2014 scenario, participants who shared common knowledge of a

collaboration was more likely to occur if the collaborators had common knowledge of the outcome (but altruistic behaviour was less likely to occur if there was common knowledge of the need for altruism and the price to be paid – the so-called bystander effect). Common knowledge does not increase altruism, but it does increase a willingness to engage in risky collaboration, i.e. trust or 'mutualism'.

In the MIT experiment, common knowledge was established by broadcasting the rules of the experimental game by speaker so that everyone could hear and by making it an experimental rule that this knowledge must be applied. But in real life, common knowledge is rarely articulated and there is no guarantee that the participants will treat it as knowledge, i.e. true. The problem for the generals is that they cannot rely on messages going backwards and forwards. They cannot know that the allied general knows the content of their message – it may be that the messenger was intercepted crossing the enemy valley.

The MIT researchers suggest an ingenious solution: that there is a class of nonverbal expressions – called displays by ethologists – that are developmentally linked to 'self-conscious emotions'.[*] Their foundation is probably the submission/ dominance family of expressions in other primates.[†] These

---

risky investment strategy were more likely to collaborate and accept the deal than participants who each had private knowledge of the deal but did not know that others also knew of it.

[*] Spite, grief, shame, guilt, embarrassment, envy, Schadenfreude, and Gluckschmerz are some of the self-conscious emotions.

[†] Negative self-conscious emotions always involve slumped posture and gaze aversion from the dominant figure (Weisfeld and Weisfeld, 2014) and this is also the case in chimpanzees. Rapid assessments of status are associated in the human brain with an N170 wave in the EEG whose magnitude is influenced by the facial processing apparatus in the right superior temporal gyrus, the right insula, and, surprisingly, the caudate nucleus (Santamaría-García, Burgaleta, and

expressions do not automatically induce corresponding emotions in others via contagion but, so the authors argue, are both involuntary and yet consciously perceived and accompanied by the belief that they have been transmitted to others. An involuntary smile in response to another person's smile may come and go on my face without me perceiving it, but if I smirk, i.e. if I smile in a sneering way to another person, which may also be involuntary, I am immediately aware of it and also sure that the other person will have registered it too.

The researchers use blushing as their example of a self-conscious emotion that might serve this function of communicating common knowledge. As any self-conscious person knows, blushing is involuntary but something that one can become only too conscious of, perhaps as a hotness of the cheeks, and is associated with the conviction that everyone else in the vicinity will have seen it, too. Let's say that I blush because I realize that I said something that I should not have done. Perhaps I let drop some private information about myself. A blush on my face tells any listener that this is something I believe to be true. It also calls forth a reaction, typically a verbal or nonverbal reassurance, that establishes that it has been heard and has become 'common knowledge'. I might even feel indignation if, at a later date, the other person has not retained my secret.

The public persona

Common knowledge is policed. To continue with the example in the last paragraph, a blush may not just indicate that I have

---

Sebastián-Gallés, 2015). The insula is, as I have previously noted, the core of the system that activates in response to vicarious pain. Self-conscious emotions are triggered by medial areas of the prefrontal cortex (Gilead *et al.*, 2016).

shared a truthful secret but also that I have shared a secret that I should not, or did not want to, share. Self-conscious emotions involuntarily reveal whenever I depart from common knowledge, and therefore expose myself to possible criticism or sanction, unless I ensure that I continue to conform, that is, to act on common knowledge rather than my own beliefs. So policing common knowledge presupposes that there is private knowledge too.

Many social psychological theories hang on this differentiation. Acceding to, or acting on, common knowledge covers the same territory as the already-mentioned conformity to conventions, or norms, but it may not mean giving up private dissent. Rejecting common knowledge is an expression of dominance that may be perceived as a threat to the established order, leading to retaliation.[12] Most of us choose the path of submission and therefore act as if common knowledge is all we know. Why so many people fall into submission needs some explanation, and I will return to this when I consider leaders in the next chapter.

Notes

1. Surowiecki, 2004
2. Kao and Couzin, 2014
3. Cannon-Bowers and Salas, 1998
4. Surowiecki, 2004
5. Fussell and Krauss, 1991
6. Coleman, 2007
7. Gladwell, 2000
8. Reagans, 2016
9. Shteynberg *et al.*, 2016
10. Boothby *et al.*, 2016
11. Chwe, 2001
12. Coleman, 2007

Chapter 6

LEADERS

Le Bon and other 19th- and early 20th-century 'crowd psychologists' were frightened of anarchy that they associated with crowds. Le Bon was also fascinated by the ability of leaders to control and use these anarchic forces for their own purposes. Le Bon's example was Robespierre, who not only inflamed the French Revolution so that it became 'The Terror', but also died by it.

The Terror began when the invasion of neighbouring countries, launched by French revolutionary forces in the early years of the revolution, was repulsed. Consequently, there was a danger that France herself would be invaded, a fearful prospect. The crowds of supporters that swelled the Khmer Rouge in its early days were terrorized by the US carpet bombing of Cambodian villages thought to be harbouring Viet Cong, by civil war, and perhaps even by the tergiversations of the king, long a crucial figure in Cambodian life.

The Cambodian peasants who swelled the ranks of the Khmer Rouge initially were not just in fear because of the

US bombings,* but also their fear was whipped up by a small group of French, educated party leaders, of whom the most prominent was Saloth Sar (who later renamed himself Pol Pot). Sar was of the bourgeoisie. His aunt, who fostered him during his childhood and adolescence, was a ballet dancer and royal concubine, as was Sar's own sister in later years. Sar did not do well educationally. Although he eventually won a scholarship to study engineering in France, he failed three successive examinations there and returned home without any qualifications but with an indoctrination into Marxism. His contempt for anyone who was not Cambodian, or anyone who lived in a town or lived by trade, dominated the policies of the Khmer Rouge party that he founded from Communist and anti-colonial groups with other friends that he had made in France. He became brother number one in Cambodia – renamed Kampuchea – until a Vietnamese army took power in 1979. Pol Pot continued to lead a guerrilla movement and died without being tried. In fact, one of the striking features of this period of Cambodian history is that, although around 1.4 million Cambodians died under the Khmer Rouge government, only one trial had been completed by the end of 2016.

How could a small group headed by Pol Pot have forced cities to be nearly emptied and ordinary Kampucheans to

---

* See Kiernan (2008). Kiernan is quoted as saying this in an interview with an Australian journalist, Bruce Palling, about the effects of the US bombings and how they were exploited by the Khmer Rouge: 'Every time after there had been bombing. They [the Khmer Rouge] would take the people to see the craters, to see how big and deep the craters were, to see how the earth had been gouged out and scorched... The ordinary people...sometimes literally shit in their pants when the big bombs and shells came... Their minds just froze up and they would wander around mute for three or four days. Terrified and half-crazy. The people were ready to believe what they were told' (p.225).

kill each other with spades, tipping the corpses into a mass grave? Why was there no uprising? Why did no-one tumble the guards into the mass grave, commandeer the lorries, and take back their homes? The Khmer Rouge cadres did not have superior technology. Although they were initially supported by the Vietnamese who did have access to Chinese weaponry, this was soon withdrawn. There was no great ideology underlying the killings, although Pol Pot and the other leaders did believe in a Rousseau-esque policy of a return to a rural economy sans capitalism and were partly inspired by Mao's cultural revolution. The ideology was not based on the usual religious, ethnic, or cultural differences, either.

Questions like these have, of course, been raised before in other pogroms, and many answers have been proposed.[*] The educated middle classes are often targeted first, removing many of the people who would have the organizational abilities to stage a counter-revolution. People are moved in masses, leaving their personal belongings behind, and families are broken up: all of these leading to deindividuation.[†]

Pol Pot's own motivation has eluded the historians, possibly because he never emerged as a public leader. The group that he led presented itself only as the anonymous 'Angkar' 'organization'. Pol Pot clearly did excel in the mobilization and direction of crowds. Whole villages and towns, including the capital Phnom Penh, were emptied out under the Khmer Rouge with masses of their citizens being forced to leave

---

[*] See, for example, Kissi (2003).

[†] Locard (2004) has collected some of the Angkar slogans and these tell a chilling story – on p.209, he cites this one: 'Better to arrest ten innocent people by mistake than free a single guilty party'; on p.210: 'No gain in keeping, no loss in weeding out'; on p.188: 'The sick are victims of their own imagination'; and on p.284: 'Hunger is the most effective disease' (a reference to the lack of resistance in people who are hungry).

property behind and march into unknown destinations in the countryside. But they were not provided with any national leadership, only propaganda.

One of the few perpetrators of crimes against humanity who has faced trial is Kaing Guek Eav (renamed Comrade Duch), a former schoolmaster who became the superintendent of prison S-21 where important prisoners were taken for torture to create mainly spurious but voluminous records of treachery. Prisoners, and often their dependants, were taken to a 'killing field' after their torture where up to 14,000 prisoners were executed or 'smashed' (a term previously used by the monarchy for executions). Only seven prisoners survived. One, spared by Duch, was a talented artist whose job it was to continually paint Duch's portrait. Duch sustained himself culturally by reading poetry. At his trial he vehemently protested that he knew all about the executions at S-21 and was not a dupe.

Duch is an interesting counterpoint to other actors in the Angkar. Before going to S-21 he had, for example, countermanded an order from the regional secretary of the Khmer Rouge and spared a Frenchman living in Angkor, François Bizot, who had been arrested but was allowed to escape. Most other people just seem to have gone along with party orders, whatever they were. Oddly, this obedience continues. The Extraordinary Chambers in the Courts of Cambodia appointed to try war criminals from the Kampuchean era has only completed the trial and conviction of one person, Comrade Duch. It has ordered the arrest of other suspects, but these orders have not been carried out, as if in the minds of the police they went against an earlier injunction to obey the Angkar.

Submission

The argument that has sometimes been made about the Shoah is that ordinary people did not know what was going on, although the facts are against this.* It is not clear how much ordinary people knew in Cambodia, as news media were abolished, S-21 and similar facilities were concealed, and most murders were carried out in 'killing fields'. Yet the universal starvation and the absurdity of the agricultural methods cannot have been hidden. Members of the Angkar must have known the slogans of the regime, and at least one of them – 'Better to arrest ten innocent people by mistake than free a single guilty party'[1] – must have reminded them that many people sent to S-21 were former cadres who fell out of favour and were accused of being Vietnamese spies. As the harvests failed and the economy nosedived, more and more apparatchiks were accused of treachery. Knowledge about the slogans, the risks, and the preferential targeting of educated people must have become common knowledge, and this is supported by survivors' accounts.† So it appears there was nothing wrong with this kind of connectedness (for those not too torpid with starvation or sickness to think) or with Kampucheans' common knowledge and therefore the mental connections, the theory of mind, that allowed its dissemination.

It seems unlikely that an impairment of 'cognitive empathy' was the explanation for the explosion of callousness that turned a great number of people into brutal killers. Indeed, anticipating how your superiors would react was probably an important survival skill. So what could be the explanation?

---

* See Gellately (2001).

† For example, www.cybercambodia.com/dachs/stories.html

Obedience

Many of the Cambodian survivors of the Khmer Rouge describe thinking that it was better to give in than fight back. The only high-ranking member who has been convicted so far, Comrade Duch, also gave 'following orders' as his reason for committing atrocities. Submission as a defence to charges of 'crimes against humanity' was brought to the world's attention by Nazis who originated the argument that following orders was an exculpation at the Nuremberg trials at the end of the Second World War.

In a dramatic experiment to probe obedience, Stanley Milgram demonstrated that a majority of ordinary people will, if ordered to, deliver what they think might be lethal shocks to another human being under laboratory conditions.* Milgram supervised these experiments wearing a white coat and assuring the naive participants (or 'subjects') that, 'Although the shocks may be painful, there is no permanent tissue damage.' He also said, 'Whether the learner likes it or not, you must go on until he has learned all the word pairs correctly. So please go on.' The 'learners' were ostensibly being taught paired word associations but were actually confederates of Milgram who simulated expressions and sounds of fear, pain, or death

---

* See Milgram (1963). The quotes that follow are from p.376 of Milgram's article. There has been considerable controversy about these experiments since, and some have tried to discount them because they were deemed unethical. There have also been limited replications, some using avatars as the apparent victims of the shocks (which are sham shocks but result in behaviour that appears as if the victim has been shocked) rather than human confederates to get round some of the ethical objections. They have supported Milgram's findings. One study has suggested that feeling ordered to do something does reduce personal responsibility, although this seems like something we already knew (Caspar *et al.*, 2016). Another study showed complex changes in the brain when avatars were 'punished' (Cheetham *et al.*, 2009), but the evidence was more towards inhibition of the interbrain-associated areas and was more marked in participants who were more affective empathic.

according to the 'voltage' of pseudo-shock being induced. In total, 27 of the 40 subjects administered shocks at a level of voltage above that which was labelled as 'Danger: severe shock' and above the level at which the learner, who was tied into an apparatus like an electric chair, could be heard groaning and kicking against the partition of his room.

Subjects sometimes pleaded with Milgram not to give the shocks, and many of them became very anxious during the experiment. But it was this connection with Milgram, the authority figure, that mattered and not the connection with the 'learner'. Milgram carried out other experiments in which the connection with the learner was reinforced, resulting in reduced compliance with Milgram and fewer high-intensity shocks being delivered (but some subjects still delivered them).[2]

One conclusion of Milgram's experiment is that the interbrain connection can be focused on the leader to the exclusion of others in an authority situation if one submits to the dominant. There have been a number of replications of Milgram's experiment, with more recent ones often using an avatar in place of the human learner, which have all come to the same conclusion.[3] One, conducted in an fMRI scanner, showed reduced activation of the areas that I indicated in Chapter 1 as being associated with the interbrain.[4]

Obedience and submission are closely related concepts, as is appeasement. All of these words describe a reaction to a threat or demand in which a mammal[5] – including a human mammal[6] – responds with displays indicating yielding to the conspecific making the demand rather than counter-attacking. Adams[7] has suggested that submission displays and behaviour are coordinated by a very primitive part of the brain, the central grey, and that this receives inputs from higher centres that, presumably, determine whether the animal can defend itself or whether the potential attacker is a familiar, in which case a defence attack is inhibited. Whether or not Adams' neurology is correct, the notion is that evaluating the threat of an aggressor and the recognition of a demand from a familiar are independent, and perhaps competing, pathways that can both activate submission. This was the situation of Brutus that I discussed in Chapter 3. He watched his sons being executed because he was so ordered by the senate. He was, Livy makes clear, moved by their plight but not enough to spare them.

Focusing on an aggressor in order to appease them, and so increase the interbrain connection to the aggressor at the expense of the connection to non-threatening others, makes a kind of evolutionary sense.* After all, the next target after the animal or person doing the appeasing is likely to be even more vulnerable family members.

Pre-emptively killing one's own children 'out of love' is one rare motive for 'murder-suicides', usually carried out by mothers who fear that their children face suffering in the future.[8] There is some similarity between this and the situation mentioned above of protecting children or family members at the expense of tuning in to their feelings. In this kind of murder-suicide, the mother is overtaken by an overwhelming belief of future harm that attenuates her immediate connection with her children. A similar situation arose in Jonestown in Guyana.† Reverend Jones had told his followers that the US

---

* It has been claimed that leaders in a crowd can be identified by automatic processing of films and programmes that track who initiates movement and who follows (Solera, Calderara, and Cucchiara, 2014).

† The Jonestown massacre is just one mass suicide of the members of a religious sect (Dein and Littlewood, 2005). The number of deaths (about 900) was probably exceeded by the number of people killed in a series of mass immolations (dramatized by Mussorgsky in his opera *Khovanshchina*) of Skoptsy. There were

was planning a military attack on the community and a plane, actually containing an investigating group from Congress, was spearheading this. Families were ordered by Reverend Jones to drink cyanide-laced Kool-Aid. Some families ran away or hid; others gave their children the Kool-Aid before drinking it themselves.

The saving idea

Jones, like Pol Pot, had run out of options. His community was disintegrating of its own accord, and the methods of education and agriculture that he instituted were failing. Cambodia was also a failing state, and the number of people tortured on the suspicion of spying for the Vietnamese or for other powers was increasing. Leadership was replaced more and more by one insistent idea, a saving idea in the sense that it gave meaning to the contagion of fear that groups and families felt in both settings. The insistent idea in Cambodia was that once all of the traitors had been killed, a Rousseau-esque agrarian paradise would come true. In Guyana, the mood was a great deal more hopeless, as befitted the failing mental state of Reverend Jones, until the saving idea became: 'We must escape this life to gain an eternal paradise.'*

---

probably various motives for the Jonestown suicides (Black, 1990), but those who killed themselves and their children at Jones' behest had previously been dominated by him and his lieutenants. Interestingly, children were also often used as informants in Jonestown.

* Many of the ideas in this section go back to classic writings on groups: Le Bon stressed the craving that groups of people appear to have for authority; Freud, the harm that paranoid leaders can lead their members into; and McDougall, the 'suggestibility' of the 'group mind' (McDougall, 1920). These ideas were dismissed in the rationalist reaction to these classical ideas (Borch, 2012) when crowd actions were lauded as being valuable forms of social protest. But it is not so much the understanding of crowds that has changed but that crowds are a regular

The connection between the leader and the group

It seems likely that obedience, or submission, is wired into us as human beings, just as the interbrain is, and that, as I already suggested, one consequence of this is that the interbrain bandwidth of followers becomes disproportionately taken up with the leader* or dominant person.† There are obvious similarities‡ with the child's attachment to a parental figure, another wired in connection.§

---

feature of human living and serve many functions. I am focusing on dysfunctional crowds in order to illustrate some of the problematic issues about 'connections'. This very dysfunctionality has again become a preoccupation according to some sociologists in the 'post-modern period' (Borch and Knudsen, 2013). According to Borch in his introduction to a review of these new developments (Borch and Knudsen, 2013), post-modern crowds are characterized by 'ecstasy' and 'affective immersion (loss of self)', but this involves a concentration on the body that can result in crowds of people becoming crowds of bodies, as in human shields being used to screen armies. He also mentions the 'stagnant crowds' of people queueing or waiting and, of course, the non-interactionist crowd connected by the internet.

* A similar phenomenon occurs in fish, where it is called 'frontal bias' (Bumann and Krause, 1993). In humans it takes the form of a disproportionate amount of time spent gazing at the leader (but only when they are leading, not when they are threatening: gazing at them would constitute a challenge at that time) (Holland *et al.*, 2017).

† This focus is not entirely positive. The reaction to dominants in pain was suppressed – as estimated by activation of the anterior insular – compared with the greater identification with a lower-status individual in pain in one study (Feng *et al.*, 2016).

‡ Oxytocin or equivalent nonapeptide (isotonin in fish) enhances attachment, increases the bandwidth of interbrain connections (Tollenaar *et al.*, 2013), and reduces dominance and submission displays, at least in rats (Wesson, 2013), increases submissiveness in fish (Hellmann *et al.*, 2015; O'Connor *et al.*, 2016), and also makes it less likely that men characterize faces as angry (Lynn *et al.*, 2014).

§ One proponent of the persistence of the connection of mother and child into adult life to explain persisting empathy is Preston, who has provided evidence for this in a number of publications, for example Preston (2013). Stress reduction, as would follow from the resolution of a potential confrontation between two

Leadership in other primate groups may be temporary. Similarly, leadership of a human crowd may be taken by the person who happens to know the way or whose voice is the loudest. Leaders' connections with their followers also have to change temporarily, since it is unlikely that a leader can give enough interbrain bandwidth to all of the people who are gazing at them, alert to their every expression.* As a group gets larger, it becomes impossible for the leader to maintain a connection with as many people as are connecting with her or him. So the leader increasingly disconnects from the interbrain connection with the group that she or he leads and increases her or his connection with the group through a common knowledge that reflects her or his values, goals, or ideology. Not much is known about what brings about this change, but there is some suggestion that it may be an increase in testosterone levels.†

---

individuals vying for dominance, also increases connection (in this case measured by the extent of emotional contagion) (Martin *et al.*, 2014). Interestingly, 'stress' itself appears to be contagious (Buchanan *et al.*, 2012; Perez *et al.*, 2015; Waters, West, and Mendes, 2014).

* Temporary leaders may also change the emotional character of a crowd, particularly towards the unruliness or turbulence (from one Latin term for crowds, 'turba') of the kind of destructive crowds that Le Bon described. Such crowds and such attitudes to crowds have not gone away. Wall, for example, covers the 'kettling' or confinement of a crowd of about 100,000 protesters in the UK in 2001 and the justification of that confinement by Lord Hope, a judge sitting in the House of Lords, who in 2010 referred to 'human nature being what it is', i.e. destructive if released by the deindividuation of crowd participation (Wall, 2016).

† Testosterone has been implicated in many studies as a correlate of empathy, with claims that foetal exposure is associated with the trait of empathy and that blood levels of testosterone correlate with empathy scores. It is also the basis for the assumption that human beings are sexually dimorphic, with women, and low testosterone, being associated with success on empathy tasks but less success on constructional tasks, and men, and high testosterone, being associated with the reverse. More relevant to the point that I am making now is that testosterone administered to a sample of young women reduced the connectivity of areas of

Leaders are likely to have a task that may require their gaze, for example in scoping out a new route or looking out for danger. So their interbrain connection to their followers needs to be suppressed, although for dictators it seems to go further than this, and their emotional disregard for their followers seems to be in their job description. But leaders cannot afford for their followers to disconnect from them. One way the asymmetry can be maintained is by creating common knowledge that the leader is still connected.

Temporary leaders are more likely to become permanent if they are dominant over conspecifics. Dominance becomes important as groups become more than temporary aggregations, as they develop some kind of structure, including who is, and who is not, eligible to be a member, and as a status hierarchy develops. Species differ considerably in how these arrangements are managed. Human beings are unusual in that any one individual belongs to many groups, and these groups exist not just as physical collectivities, but also as constructs in which there are 'roles' and 'memberships'. The political groupings that I have already mentioned in this chapter trump all of these smaller groups because their leaders have the power of life and death over their members.

How does a leader gain a more permanent connection with others who become followers?

One basic requirement is that leaders remain connected to the groups that they lead, but they cannot do this via the interbrain and must rely on their connection with the common knowledge

---

the brain implicated in the interbrain connection (Bos *et al.*, 2016), with the likely consequence that their interbrain connectedness was also reduced.

of the group. Common knowledge has, I have already noted, roots in self-conscious emotions and also shared convictions.

Emotions of obedience

There is a specific set of self-conscious emotions that cement common knowledge links with a leader. Extreme positive emotion, like worship, veneration, devotion, and adoration, are most commonly associated with the intense worlds of fandom or religion but are in action, too, in this manner for other communities organized around a leader, such as nations.[9] Other linking emotions include pride in community, honour, and patriotic fervour.

Leaders may cultivate such emotions towards their own persons by various means, including ceremonies, public showings, and, increasingly, sharing 'secrets' about themselves sometimes presented as if they are special privileges for the viewer or the listener.

Leaders of very large groups cannot make enough such appearances to refresh binding emotions but can use proxies, such as lieutenants or deputies, images (such as the picture of the sovereign, the president, or the archbishop on the wall), films, icons (the American eagle, the Russian bear), flags, chants, logos, books, and so on.[*]

The emotions that obedience induces charge these symbols and, as noted in Chapter 1, these emotions are able to be re-evoked when the symbols are experienced in the future.[†]

---

[*] More examples can be found in 'ethnosymbolist' accounts of nation building, for example Smith (2015).

[†] See Reeck (2015) who describes the creation of a Hindu saint and how his body became an object of veneration.

Common knowledge

Common knowledge is based on shared emotions but comes to comprise beliefs, convictions, or even just cognitive habits. What appears to be knowledge might sometimes be something much simpler. Golden shiner fish shoals move into shadow and, as the shadow disappears, race to the next pool of shadow. Do the fish think about keeping out of sight of predators? It's obviously a good survival strategy. Do they follow an intelligent leader? It appears that what they do is stick together (maintain their interbrain connection) and swim more slowly in shadow. When one fish finds itself in shadow, it slows down and other fish swim close to it, also slowing down. When the shadow disappears, the first fish in the light starts to swim more quickly and the other fish swim to be close to it until one fish in the shoal finds itself in shadow again, and so on...[10]

Swarms, however big, do not require fixed leaders to remain connected so long as each member is physically adjacent to another, but, if animal swarms are anything to go by, extended groups are subject to splitting and that leads to breaking off the connection between the two sub-groups. Once members are separated, or even physically isolated, the group will cease to exist, as with many spontaneous crowds, unless connections can be established in some other way. Snapshots, minutes, follow-up phone calls, and the other means that we all use to make an occasion live on cannot do this. Even having a common, shared purpose is usually not enough. A leader is required. The leader may maintain a connection with the members of the group by scheduled appearances, either to the group as a whole or to some members who thereafter connect with other less-privileged members of the group to report on what the leader said or did. Leaders often write texts that connect groups together – often called manifestos – and the texts themselves may develop a holiness that creates a connecting network of shared emotion.

Moral convictions are beliefs that influence a wide range of behaviours. They may connect disparate individuals who share the same convictions but divide individuals who would otherwise have many potential connections.[11] Moral convictions are a major element of common knowledge, often being taken as indubitably true and universal by those who hold them and as false or parochial by those who do not. The ability to weigh up what others tell children, and therefore whether or not to take it as knowledge, begins at the same time as children pass theory-of-mind tasks. The criteria that both children and adults use are not those of epistemologists. Truth is not essential.*

There is the possibility that moral convictions arise through acculturation into a group, but I think it more likely that moral convictions arise through the influence of, and sometimes identification with, a leader. Surprisingly, there has been little research on this point. There is the suggestion, that is sometimes traced back to Max Weber, that charismatic leaders are charismatic because either their example or their preaching leads others to adopt or accept certain moral convictions (note that I am not using 'moral' in its normative sense of what is good but in its descriptive sense of considerations of what

---

* Epistemic 'vigilance' is the term that Sperber *et al.* (2010) coin for vetting common knowledge or what Sperber (1997) elsewhere calls 'reflective concepts and beliefs'. Sperber *et al.* (2010) consider that vigilance is achieved through an initial trust that a proposition is true, judging that the source of the proposition is both competent and well disposed, the internal logic of the proposition and its consistency with existing beliefs, and support from additional new propositions or observations.

is good or bad; many people may have 'moral convictions' that other people think are actually 'immoral').*

In an informal attempt to find out how some of my work colleagues gained their moral convictions, I asked each of them to tell me, if they were happy to do so, one of their moral convictions. I gave the example of dietary prohibitions. Few of my colleagues would admit to having any moral convictions (although I know them to be very moral people) and no-one was sure whence they would have obtained any that they did have, although two who did volunteer a moral conviction thought that it was inspired by a particular person.

My small survey is, of course, only an anecdote, but it does establish that charismatic leaders can connect to groups of followers or rather can inspire moral convictions that create common knowledge linking the followers with the leader. Once common knowledge has been established, followers as well as leaders may ensure unswerving adherence to it on pain of exclusion. Doubters who want to maintain that connection might be forced to avow the same moral convictions on pain of exclusion.

Oaths are one means of transmitting common knowledge and of binding people to it. The Nicene creed that is repeated and affirmed by worshippers in many Christian churches is an example. It originated as a means of binding followers of Alexander, the Bishop of Alexandria, to his formulation of the divinity of Jesus of Nazareth and dissociated them from the views of Arius whose Arian heresy that Jesus was merely a man was one of the most popular of the many deviations of the doctrine at the time (the 4th century).

---

* An example of a moral conviction that I would find morally objectionable would be an activist who believes that it is right to burn down a research centre because the researchers are experimenting on animals.

Maps, like creeds, purport to tell us how the world is, but always subsume a point of view that we can easily overlook as the map itself becomes part of our common knowledge. The paths that maps depict may themselves depict a kind of common knowledge.[*] Maps are intended to be informative and of limited scope, as we can only take in a geographically limited map view at any one moment. A better example of how partaking in a shared, but imagined, world can create a connection between people is when people come together and share a narrative that conjures up a shared world. This world does not have to be grounded in the 'real',[†] phenomenal, or 'objective' world but may be 'subjective'. This shared subjectivity is often referred to as 'intersubjectivity'. Earlier in this book I discussed in some detail what enables us to say that we do truly share the same narrative and I suggested that this required that the narrative induced the same emotions in all of the participants, that the participants could be sure that other participants had the same emotions as they, and that the narrative carried conviction. Some narratives are convincing because they convey a picture of the phenomenal world other people find plausible. Others convince because they are subsidiary to master narratives, for example that there are gods who can reveal reality to chosen individuals. Earlier I suggested some alternative tests of convincingness – 'true to lifeness', stylistics, being 'moving', and having wide explanatory or justificatory scope.

---

[*] It has been argued that, in non-urbanized areas, settlements are developed by one family and are therefore not just connected by paths between buildings, but also lineages between occupants (Hillier and Hanson, 1984).

[†] Although it can be (Eliastam, 2016).

Many psychologists and anthropologists consider man is a social animal,[*] but there is still controversy about this, perhaps because humanity's sociality does not neatly fit into biological categories.

E. O. Wilson originally made the controversial suggestion that humanity is eusocial, like ants, bees, and naked mole rats,[†] but many others have also made competing suggestions that we are parasocial. Arguably, though we manifest both types of sociality, eusociality does bind us to others who are not genetically related[‡] as a result of relationships built from groups linked via the interbrain in small groups (small groups may be composed of very distant individuals in the case of whales and birds,[§] but in people are usually only with others with whom we have face-to-face contact[¶]) and because we are linked to

---

[*] Fiske, for example, argues that this sociality is expressed in a different balance of four kinds of social relations: communal sharing (which corresponds to the relations of people who share a capacity to be linked by an interbrain connection); authority ranking (which I consider both in terms of leader and follower, and in terms of dominance and submission); equality matching; and market pricing. The latter influences the narratives that people keep of themselves or others (Fiske, 1992).

[†] See Nowak, Tarnita, and Wilson (2010) for a review. Crespi and Yanega give the following criteria of eusociality: 1. A reproductive and a non-reproductive caste (it has been argued that this could be women after the menopause) (Foster and Ratnieks, 2005), although there are potentially other explanations in those cetaceans who share this unusual biology uniquely with humanity (Croft *et al.*, 2017); '2. Altruistic helping by individuals in the non-reproductive caste; 3. Either behavioural totipotency of only the more reproductive caste (facultative eusociality) or totipotency of neither caste (obligate eusociality)' (Crespi and Yanega, 1995, p.110). Human eusociality is still contested (Liao, Rong, and Queller, 2015).

[‡] And therefore Hamilton's explanation of 'kin selection' or 'inclusive fitness' does not apply.

[§] It appears that birds may also be connected at a distance by a kind of interbrain connection (Perez *et al.*, 2015).

[¶] In one study, children aged between five and seven years used more moral, cognitive, and mental state terms when chatting on the phone than they did when they were face to face (Pinto *et al.*, 2016).

leaders via strong, but non-reciprocal, connections mediated by our narratives about those leaders and their significance for, and expectations of, us. This is a kind of sociality that is characterized by our relationship with celebrities and other leaders and is often referred to as parasocial.* This kind of connection may be uniquely human. One consequence of having two different socialities is that humanity has a conflicted nature, each of us being split between our acquired, mental, egocentric connection with others and our innate, altruistic connection through the interbrain. Wilson makes the same point.[12]

The exploration of these two types of connection has been dominated by one particular epiphenomenon of connection, 'empathy'. Affective empathy is particularly derived from the study of small groups, and cognitive empathy from large group studies.

Disconnection

It turned out to be easier to define orthodoxy in Christianity for what it was not rather than what it was. But disconnecting (excommunicating, or removing from those who can receive communion) individuals or whole groups from the established church reinforced the connectedness of the remainder. This is not just true of the Christian Church, or of churches in general, but also of all collectivities organized around a central idea or ideology.

---

* See, for example, Banks and Bowman (2016).

Disconnecting

Groups, crowds, and swarms may spontaneously disperse and disappear just as easily as they appear. Even enduring groups may dissolve when their leaders die or resign and there is no successor. Such spontaneous collectivities may, indeed normally do, lose peripheral members, as the connection with the leader of peripheral members is inevitably weaker.* Conversely, foreign groups that were previously separate from each other may also sometimes merge under a single leader or ideology,† especially if they do not have competing connections with other groups.[13] Easy-going connectivity like this is the exception and not the rule. One reason for this is the problem of 'free-loading'. Even in slime moulds, the progress of the collective entity, known as a 'slug' in Dictyostelium, is slower if it includes organisms from different clones. The alien clones are cheaters; they get a free and much quicker ride on the slug created by another clone and then drop off when they scent a good food source. They do not contribute to the sporangium, of which 30 per cent is formed by merged slime moulds that die in the process, which will disseminate the clone and perpetuate it.[14] So with people as with slime moulds: free-loaders who

---

* In many mammalian groups, including human ones, the individual who is directing the movement of the group tends to move more slowly than the leading followers so that the leader comes to occupy the centre of the group. This strengthens the potential connection from all of the followers but also increases the number of weakly connected group members.

† I have referred in Chapter 2 to studies of swarms of insects and vertebrates that show these effects, but striking examples of merging and splitting are also shown by slime fungi whose reactions to environmental changes mimic some of the behaviour of human beings in aggregate despite having no macroscopic internal structure (Reid and Latty, 2016). It has been suggested that slime moulds constitute the biological version of an analogue computer (Mayne *et al.*, 2017) and can successfully model some aspects of human decision-making, such as anticipating supply and demand (Zhang *et al.*, 2017).

gain the benefits of human association but contribute no work are a challenge. The people who connect with members of a group may be monitored by other members, and any free-loaders who do become group members may be extruded.

Control over the connectedness of members of the collectivity is one of the means by which the collectivity endures.[*,15] Weakly connected members are poor transmitters of contagious emotion, and one way to create stronger connectedness is to exclude these 'uncommitted' members. But a greater threat comes from those who are connected to a rival leader or his or her proxy, or a rival ideology. Collectivities that want to survive must monitor this threat to their integrity and exclude these others. The key to doing this is negativity.

Disconnecting through negativity

Just as there are negative emotions such as anger and disgust that are fulfilled when another person is driven away, and there is a family of self-conscious emotions linked to following, so there is a family of self-conscious emotions associated with social expulsion. They include hate, revulsion, rage, contempt, hostility, disgust, and scorn.[†] These emotions suppress the interbrain connection with the person to whom the emotion

---

[*] For a mathematical treatment of this see Chakraborty *et al.* (2016). This paper is orientated towards the analysis of massive datasets. These can be modelled as graphs in which 'communities' (sometimes called circles) can be identified. Communities are detected where the intersection of graphs, or nodes, are more highly interconnected with other nodes within the community than with all other nodes (sometimes also called vertices) (Zakrzewska and Bader, 2016). The behaviour of social animals like ants has influenced the development of methods of analysis (González-Pardo, Palero, and Camacho, 2014).

[†] Burklund, Eisenberger, and Lieberman (2007) argue that 'rejection', which I am terming 'scorn', has a characteristic facies and induces neural activation suggesting that it is distinct from other kinds of fear.

is directed.[16] Disgust is an interesting case in point. Disgust is evoked by seeing others in pain as well as by looking at one's own wounds. This normally inhibits a person from harming others,* but feeling sufficient negativity for those others can shut off this disgust and make it possible to harm them without concern.† Schadenfreude is a similar reaction, albeit a more socialized one. Its inverse, Gluckschmerz, or distress at the good fortune of others, is an example of how these negative self-conscious emotions change the polarity of appraisals. Negative emotions like this and their effects are not scientific abstractions. The most striking feature of life in Cambodia during the ascendancy of the Khmer Rouge, which I discussed in detail earlier in the chapter, was its brutality. This was demonstrated in the many atrocities reported from this period. Torture methods at the main prison S-21, for example, included force-feeding faeces and exsanguination – being drained of blood until the heart stopped. The smell of blood and faeces, as well as the sight of these tortures, would have made the guards' gorges rise, unless those guards were under the thrall of some power that could turn their disgust off, making it possible to be disgusted by the prisoners and not by what the guards were doing to them.

---

* I am not sure that compassion is always required in order not to want to harm others. This could as easily be a self-protective reaction, i.e. to prevent further disgust to oneself. Compassion is a consequence of imagining oneself to be the victim. People who have experienced adversity themselves are more likely to feel it for others (Lim and DeSteno, 2016). For people who imagine they can right wrongs by aggression, the immediate reaction is likely to be anger at the aggressors rather than compassion with the victim (Fanti, Kyranides, and Panayiotou, 2017).

† See Bucchioni *et al.* (2015). Contempt, anger, and disgust at someone are a particularly toxic combination (Matsumoto, Hwang, and Frank, 2017) but disgust at feeling vengeful may inhibit the desire for vengeance (Richman *et al.*, 2014).

Hegemony and hate

Most of us are capable of hate but we are often also curiously preoccupied by those we hate. This comes to a head when people seek vengeance for some slight, often setting aside personal goals to do so. The preoccupation, though, is an intellectual one, as hated people are often kept at a physical distance and, even when they are physically present, hate blocks the interbrain connection and the connection is cognitive rather than effective. We cannot feel, indeed it enrages or disgusts* us to feel, as the hated person does.†

Oftentimes, we may feel that we would go mad if we did have to connect with a hated person. This may in part be because forgiveness is often an intermediary step in contemplating a situation from the point of view of a hated person.‡ Hate is created by demonizing the other person, and that means considering that they have nothing good to justify their hateful actions. If one can bring oneself to consider that there may have been some justification, the hate begins to dissolve.[17] The common knowledge that one shares with valued others may militate against letting go of hatred, because to do so might be seen as 'letting off' the hated person. Altruism may induce a person to continue to suffer the bad effects of their own hate to preserve the greater good of the knowledge that justice is upheld.

---

* Which may be partly determined by gender.

† Conversely, if we can do that, our desire for revenge diminishes (Berry *et al.*, 2005).

‡ To cite just some of the evidence: Fatfouta *et al.*, 2015; Lichtenfeld *et al.*, 2015; Mansfield, Pasupathi, and McLean, 2015; Nateghian, Dastgiri, and Mullet, 2015; Okimoto, Wenzel, and Hornsey, 2015; Zheng *et al.*, 2014. These studies also stress how difficult forgiveness is, partly because restitution is not seen as being enough and partly because to forgive is to forget. Forgetting, whilst it may improve health, may be seen as failing to get justice.

Morality, demons, and beasts

Holding on to suffering in commemoration of past harm, of which holding on to hate is one example, is an example of a narrative that sustains hate. Demonization is another.[18] For a very long time, human beings have explained harm coming to one person or to groups by attributing this to demons. Demonic possession is possibly the oldest explanation of psychopathology and is still widely held in Africa and other parts of the world.[19] Witchcraft is the other explanation, and witchery too continues to be an explanation of deviant behaviour. Demonization is also a way that followers turn on and displace their leaders.[20]

Demonization of offenders increases the public's desire to punish them retributively.[21] This is most likely because of common knowledge, which seems to be widespread, that demons exist, that they are evil, and that evil is contagious. So humans cannot, and indeed should not without imperilling their own morals, consort or connect with demons. Demons must be cast out of individuals, as the *Bible* has Jesus casting out the demons, and of society. Psychiatrists and psychologists have updated this demonology by postulating that types of people exist who cannot empathize and consequently act in a deranged or demonic fashion. There is also the presumption, as there often is when a person is said to lack empathy, that it is equally impossible to empathize with them.

I have been considering demonization of individuals by other individuals or by groups. But groups may also be demonized, leading to the disconnection of that group and all its members from the main group.[*] This may have the

---

[*] There are many examples of this – the demonization of: political groups in Thailand (Sripokangkul, 2015); criminals of colour in the US (Smiley and Fakunle, 2016); and opponents by the US (Ivie and Giner, 2015).

paradoxical effect of increasing the connections within both groups by increasing the power of their leaders or their regnant ideology, that is the 'common knowledge' that each group takes to be uncontestably true even though each of the new groups may have a different 'common knowledge'.

The demonized group may retaliate against the hegemonic group that disconnected from them in the first place by counter-claiming that it is they, the hegemonic group, who are demonic.

Casting another person or group as demonic is a moral judgement. Rejecting a group or an individual as immoral justifies, according to some, hating the immorality and, by extension, hating the demonized person or the demonized group.[22] Group morality may be determinative of the group's identity. Groups that differ ideologically and that consider the other group's ideology hateful are not just disconnected, but are also committed to maintaining that disconnection in order to safeguard their own identity.*

Dehumanization

Demonization is, for obvious reasons, a strategy that is particularly attractive to religious groups. Exclusion of heterodox groups has, over the centuries, resulted in fragmentation of the great monotheistic religions,† sometimes leading to persecution or wars, but the gain has been a renewal of religious zeal within each fragment. What unites the members of each fragment is a reaffirmation of their shared narrative concerning their identity and also an increased

---

* Participants in laboratory experiments who are reminded of their moral failings are more likely to avoid looking at the eyes in photographs of angry faces (Van Dillen et al., 2017).

† Norenzayan (2016) provides a detailed review.

interbrain connection with their leader and with each other. Shared hate of the out-group unites,* but so does terror of the leaders if there is a fear that you or your family might be placed on the hate list, too.

Demonization is just one of the ways in which an individual or a group can be disconnected from humanity. Groups may be denied an interbrain connection with the hegemonic group because the latter believes that the excluded are slaves, robots[†] or 'mechanisms',[23] sub-humans, or animals, as well as devils. One of the easiest ways that disconnection can be maintained on an individual level is to have a rule about gaze avoidance. Slaves, or even the courtiers of despots, were not allowed to raise their eyes to their masters or mistresses, and the latter would avoid looking into their slaves' eyes, too. I already noted that not looking at followers is a standard expression of dominance by leaders, but forbidding slaves not to turn their back on their 'owners' is an indication that they are even less than followers, and in the eyes of their 'owners' that they are even less than humans.

When the rule is not to look at the dehumanized, direct gaze has a special interrogatory function. This is not to share a connection, as it is expected that the dehumanized person will not look back, but to re-establish dominance. In primates, staring down a challenge is generally a signal that dominance has been re-established. In human beings it is also a means

---

* There is a considerable literature on conformity, dissent, and social deviance, which overlaps with my treatment but from the point of view of more traditional psychology. There is considerable evidence that dissenters are expelled from groups in order to maintain group positivity (Jetten and Hornsey, 2014), which directing negative feelings towards excluded others – the scapegoat effect – will do.

† Although robots are traditionally included in the list of infrahuman species, they, like animals, are increasingly considered to be potentially capable of agency and of feelings (Coeckelbergh, 2016). So it may not always be ethical to kick them.

for the starer to obtain information about the emotional state of the excluded person, notably self-conscious emotions such as pride or resentment, which would indicate the possibility of future challenge. Remorse or contrition are, on the other hand, often expected when punishments are given, and their absence may extend the punishment.* Gaze may be withheld from people who are considered inhuman because they are assumed not to be capable of self-conscious emotion.†

Two recent reviews[24] consider the steps that enable each of us to be able to dehumanize others.‡ Disgust seems to pave the way for dehumanization,[25] but an important factor also seems to be the belief that as neither animals nor robots have emotions (I am here quoting the belief, not asserting that animals do not have emotions nor that robots might not develop them), human beings who are robotic[26] or animalistic do not have proper, self-conscious emotions§ and are therefore unable to feel what happens to them or be aware of it. I stress that these provide us with exculpatory narratives for the harm we do to people from whom we disconnect, and that it is not they who lack feelings or awareness but that our disconnection from them prevents us from having the interbrain knowledge of it. Even when a group accepts collective responsibility for harming excluded members, this has the effect of increased

---

* Dehumanized people are typically assumed to be less sensitive to pain by those who dehumanize them (Riva, Brambilla, and Vaes, 2016).

† See Martínez et al. (2017). Even if a person is not considered sub-human but only lower in status, various studies have shown that higher-status individuals may consider lower-status colleagues less able to experience human emotions (Iatridis, 2013).

‡ Note that dehumanization of individuals does not always result in exclusion from an in-group (Renger et al., 2016).

§ See Haslam et al. (2008) in which the authors seem to be referring to self-conscious emotions, although this is not specifically mentioned in the paper.

connectedness within the group, sometimes even leading to glorifying malefactors within the group* but dehumanizing the excluded members further,[27] suppressing the possibility of an interbrain connection with any individuals that we should meet from that group.

News media are one means of disseminating common knowledge, and they have an ambivalent role in the relations between in-groups, to which they belong, and out-groups. It has been argued that they moderate violence[28] but they also dehumanize.[29] Just occasionally, media may depict 'counter-stereotypes': out-group members who seem like in-group members in their behaviour, attitudes, or emotions. Contemplation of counter-stereotypes is uncomfortable, leading to surprise and 'expectancy violation' but also a reduction of dehumanization of the excluded group.†

In- and out-groups

My gorge rises to imagine a woman deliberately executed by her son in a public square.‡ I feel a visceral sense of disgust – and recognize this to be due to the third, insular-involving,[30] pain empathy network that, with the addition of negativity, results in abhorrence of the people committing the act. I am inclined to attribute the atrocity to the crazed nature of Daesh as an organization, but I reflect that in Daesh's interpretation

---

* See Leidner *et al.* (2010). One could say that the group members become more connected to the perpetrators in sustaining the common knowledge that the group was right to act as it did. These members therefore become temporarily hyperconnected like leaders. Their position is unstable, unlike true leaders (Flinders and Wood, 2015).

† See Prati, Crisp, and Rubini (2015). A similar effect can be produced by not reducing the categorization of an out-group to a single dimension (Prati *et al.*, 2016).

‡ An event that was described in Chapter 3.

she had committed blasphemy for which some Hadith specify death. I also need to remember that the news medium reporting this has selected this piece of news to showcase. Their argument was probably that it would create greater connection with their audience – translated as viewer numbers to their funders – but it is also a reflection of the viewers' desire to be given information to reinforce their prejudice about Daesh.*

Vilification of out-groups rarely happens out of a clear, blue sky. Connections between people are not all or nothing, although they do vary from high bandwidth† to no bandwidth. For individuals who deviate from group values, disconnection from the group may be gradual and the individual may hasten the process from their side. Sometimes, this happens because a person starts to see themselves as less than others,‡ but other times it may be because they feel increasingly vilified by the members of what was their in-group previously.

In-groups

Once in-groups become established and stable, there is less need of leaders. Interconnections can become stronger between members of the in-group, and the homogeneity of the membership increases interbrain bandwidth between members. This increases the possibility of mutual joy but, regrettably, shared joy does not spread so readily as shared

---

* Providing reasons to reinforce prejudice is a popular strategy. Harper (2014) discusses a notorious case of arson in a similar light.

† There is no common or garden word that conveys the amount of information traffic in a communication channel. Close connection implies spatial proximity. Regular connection is simply a count of the number of times the connection is used, not how much information passes.

‡ Renger *et al.* (2016) call this 'self-dehumanization', although they justify this by suggesting that there are universal characteristics of being human and that any deviation from these makes a person less than human.

distress. In-groups, though, want to maintain this stasis and the hyperconnectivity that leads to it. New ideas do arise spontaneously in in-groups, but radical ideas are often suppressed if they are perceived as an ideological threat when the group is already under threat from an out-group.[31] Groups that are open to new connections become transformed into conservative groups that reject radical ideas and are threatened by new extrinsic ideological challenge.[32] This may contribute to the finding that periods of liberalism and well-being in groups and societies are interspersed by periods of fear and xenophobic conservatism. Individuals when threatened by out-groups do not retaliate as individuals, but when it is their in-group that is threatened they will fight back.[33]

Justice, obedience, honour, and duty

An external threat to an in-group, such as a threat to its core values, threatens each individual member's connection with the leader, or leading ideology, of the group. I have argued previously that there are similarities between attachment to a child and attachment to a leader. It is a matter of common-sense psychology that a threat to a mother with an infant can trigger aggression – even the boldest of sheepdogs will think twice about tackling a ewe with lambs at foot. So, if I am correct, it might be supposed that the reaction to a challenge to a follower's attachment to a leader might be similarly extreme and, consequently, a person's reaction to the fundamental beliefs of their in-group being challenged might also be vehement. A recent study suggests that this is the case, although it attributes this vehemence to challenge to 'protecting the aspects of our mental lives with which we strongly identify, including our closely held beliefs'.[34]

We justify this aggression sometimes by invoking cultural concepts, part of our common knowledge, that give us a sense of moral purpose. We speak of honour or duty. Oftentimes, we omit to notice that in going out to fight with the leader of an out-group, having cast them as an oppressor, we are leaving behind family and friends who might suffer from our absence. Yet, common knowledge has it that this is justified – or so our own leaders urge us – not just to 'protect ourselves' but also to protect our 'way of life' that is our ideology. I am not going to argue for or against this as a justification. I do accept the premise that absorbing or merging two groups that are each constituted around a strong ideological identity will result in a perturbation in the connections between members of each group and lead to an increase in terror.

Wars may also be justified by war leaders on the grounds that they are the only way to liberate the out-group from its despotic leaders if we, the in-group waging the war, expect the group that is apparently ripe for liberation to have the same defining ideology as ourselves: that the leader is a despot, that they are being denied fundamental human rights, and that they should be able to choose their own leaders. We do not ask them first if they want to choose or what they want from us. We assume that our common knowledge – our ideology – is the truth even though, in many cases, the cousins of the people we are 'liberating' have experienced discrimination and stigma in our own countries, to which they moved in order to improve their living standards. Were we to doubt the enterprise once our leaders have put it to us, we would be failing in our own patriotic duty, perhaps even be traitors.

Again, I am not denying the possibility that malignant leaders can instil such obedience in their populations that the only means to remove them is by the invasion of a foreign army. The removal of the Angkar by a Vietnamese army may be a case in point. But removing a leader also removes the focus of the shared connections that hold that group together. Without them the group members need to find other bases for connection or else terror supervenes. Those new connections may define very different groups that may turn out to have unexpected properties, as the coalition armies that toppled Saddam Hussein have discovered.

An example from Lodz

Table 6.1 shows data from a comparison of three Jewish ghettoes created by the Nazis during the Second World War as a preliminary to the population being moved to concentration camps.* The first column shows the city and the second whether or not an uprising occurred. One occurred in Warsaw, one was planned in Vilnius, and none occurred in Lodz. I have argued in this chapter that three factors might be relevant to a possible uprising that is an attack on the out-group (German occupation forces in this case). An attack is most likely if the leader or a leading idea of the in-group is under threat by an out-group. But the position of the incarcerated Jews was one of extreme fear, and many of them, including the leadership, held out for appeasement – for obedience to the out-group. The Nazis effectively isolated Lodz but not Warsaw. The message that the Nazis passed to the ghetto leaders was that everyone would be moved to work camps. But in Warsaw the young people knew that Jews were to be exterminated and they challenged the policy of appeasement, arguing that their defining ideology was defining one's own fate and not hoping

---

* The data are taken from Einwohner (2014).

for salvation.* So many fewer Jews in the Warsaw ghetto supported pacifism, and none turned traitor on the rebels. In Lodz, it was quite different. There was uncertainty about the Nazis' intentions, and it was not realized that they had adopted an extermination policy. The official leaders preached obedience to the Nazis, and the residents went along with it. In Vilnius, the knowledge had eventually got through and been believed, but it was too late for the policy of appeasement to be reversed.

Table 6.1 *Factors affecting armed resistance to Nazis*

	Uprising	Leadership	Communications outside the ghetto	Uncertainty about Nazi intentions	Obedience to leadership
Warsaw	Yes	Official leaders divided	Yes	No	+
Vilnius	Planned		To a degree	Yes	++
Lodz	No	Official leaders united	No	Yes	+++

Source: data from Einwohner, 2014.

These terrible but fortunately exceptional happenings underline the impact of group life on individuals. They must also give us pause when we consider pacifism and building bridges – or making connections – as the answer to all social fragmentation. Sometimes fighting the Other, the out-group, reflects rigidity, stigma, and fear, and sometimes it represents survival instinct, a correct recognition of the destructiveness of the out-group, and fear.

---

* For example in the film *Uprising* released in 2001 and directed by Jon Avnet.

Notes

1. Quoted in Locard, 2004, p.209

2. Milgram, 1965

3. Haslam and Loughnan, 2014; Reicher, Haslam, and Miller, 2014

4. Cheetham *et al.*, 2009

5. Ginsburg, Pollman, and Wauson, 1977

6. Burgoon and Hale, 1984

7. Adams, 1979

8. Knoll and Hatters-Friedman, 2015

9. Scheff, 2007

10. Berdahl *et al.*, 2013

11. Federico *et al.*, 2016; Skitka and Morgan, 2014

12. Wilson, 2014

13. Shang and Ye, 2017

14. Reid and Latty, 2016

15. Pond *et al.*, 2012

16. Underwood, 2004

17. Tuller *et al.*, 2015

18. Giner-Sorolla, Leidner, and Castano, 2011

19. Stefanovics *et al.*, 2016

20. Flinders, 2012; Flinders and Wood, 2015

21. Webster and Saucier, 2015

22. Weisel and Böhm, 2015

23. Moller and Deci, 2010

24. Haslam and Loughnan, 2014; Li, Leidner, and Castano, 2014

25. Hodson and Costello, 2007

26. Swiderska, Krumhuber, and Kappas, 2013

27. Castano and Giner-Sorolla, 2006; Čehajić, Brown, and González, 2009

28. Armoudian, 2015

29. Bleiker *et al.*, 2013; Dalsklev and Kunst, 2015

30. Cikara, Bruneau, and Saxe, 2011; Liu *et al.*, 2015

31. Capellini *et al.*, 2016

32. Kruglanski *et al.*, 2006; Nail *et al.*, 2009

33. Weisel and Zultan, 2016

34. Kaplan, Gimbel, and Harris, 2016, p.1

Chapter 7

CONNECTIONS AND MORALITY

Article 3 of the Universal Declaration of Human Rights states: 'Everyone has the right to life, liberty and security of person.'[1] Yet we all constantly come across situations or representations where one person kills another. Fortunately, few people are personally involved in these situations, but we hear of our government killing a terrorist, of serial killers, of terrorists killing people who represent a government, of wars where thousands, even millions, of people are killed, and of judicial killings as legally enforced punishments. We think that if our home were invaded, our children threatened, or our partners threatened with wounding or rape, we might kill a person, too.

There is clearly an opposition between what we tell our children – that killing people is wrong – and what we might conceive of ourselves doing in some (extreme) circumstances. How do we rationalize this? A lot of the time we might not even try, but we just accept that life is not simple or that we cannot always stick to our principles. If we dig more deeply, we might say that people are imperfect and that there are still some people who need to be stopped...but if we could all feel for each other, if empathy became universal, there would be no need of killing.

Empathy has become something of a fetish, and a lack of empathy has become an easy explanation for horrific or repeated aggression. 'Psychopaths' are thought to exist, whose monstrosity lies not in some horrible physical malformation, as in the stories about monsters that we tell children, but in their lack of empathy or, some psychologists would go so far as to say, their lack of the right functioning in parts of the brain. Wars, we sometimes suppose, break out because psychopaths convince gullible people to follow them. Genocide, too, is placed at the door of a few cold, calculating individuals,* although genocide may also be justified by groups who perpetrate it on the basis that the group who were being exterminated were 'infrahuman'.[2]

As has sometimes come up in earlier chapters, empathy turns out to be a pretty woolly category, and different people use it in different ways. It is often forgotten that its origins lie in aesthetics, although not by Patricia Highsmith, whose fictional character, Tom Ripley, is portrayed as a connoisseur entirely without morals and has been described by critics as a 'sociopath' or a 'psychopath'. But he loves classical piano.

Tom Ripley is in a long line of amoral characters in crime. Professor Moriarty in Conan Doyle's Sherlock Holmes stories is another example. In reality, paradigms of these literary stereotypes are hard to find. But perhaps we cling to literature and films because of their massive explanatory value. Like the

---

* Although I agree with Bartov (2003) that genocide is the result of an ideological split in a community between opposing values with the result that 'eradication... [of one group by the other] is not only justified but also lauded as a noble act sanctioned by God' (p.75). I look at the processes that lead to this later in this chapter.

fox people of Heian literature, the demons walking amongst us disguised as ordinary people, or the savage animals who still survive in our unconscious minds, psychopaths seem to explain whilst letting us all off the hook. Violence, denigration, and driving people out – these we would like to say are forced on us by these bad people, or done to us by them, and they are not really full people because they are damaged, they are psychopaths. So our image of true humanity as being free of hate, if not full of love for the 'brotherhood' (and sisterhood) of man, can be preserved.

So pervasive is this modern concept of empathy being our salvation, and the lack of empathy being the bane of civilization, that it is difficult to find research that actually tests whether a lack of empathy is associated with offending against others. I have only been able to find two examples, with one being an extension of the other. The results of the more recent and larger study found no relationship between affective empathy (closely related to the interbrain connection) and offending. Although there was, in the second study but not the first, an association between offending and cognitive empathy (or theory of mind or, as I have been calling it in previous chapters, common knowledge, narrative, or ideology, depending on the context), this was not strong enough for the authors to recommend that increasing empathy would reduce offending.[3]

In this final chapter, I am not going to provide a moral take on violence or judge whether or not violence is ever justified. Instead, I am going to try to set out how violent expression can very often be traced back to the conflicts between the two types of connection that I have been describing in previous chapters: the interbrain and shared 'common knowledge'. I am not going to comment on whether these conflicts represent a design glitch in humanity that we need to overcome or whether they have some evolutionary purpose. Nor am I going to put forward a path for a violence-free future or advocate some ethical position, such as the social Darwinism that soured Darwin's legacy. My account is, intentionally, primarily descriptive.

The injunction not to harm other people, and especially not to kill them, is deeply embedded in almost all cultures (although it is not an 'absolute' right within the territories of states within the European Union). In this chapter, I will be considering whether the different nature of the connections between people, and the potential of conflict between them, can throw light on those situations that bedevil humanity by revealing a capacity for violence that offends our aspirations to be of a finer nature than, as we sometimes say, mere animals. Few people question the axiom 'Thou shalt not kill', and yet deliberate or reckless killing of other people occurs every day.

Many of the connections that I have discussed in this book have been investigated because of their supposed relationship to empathy, and therefore the interest in empathy has had the useful side effect of providing a great deal of evidence on human connections on which I have relied. But this research has also created confusion, mainly, I think, because empathy is a concept but it does not map readily onto actions or brain functions. When we use it as an explanation, we are applying an idea that does not correspond to any intentions that a person might have, any commonality in their experience, or any system in their brains. Connections are created by an imagination, with whose properties we are familiar, or by areas and connected systems in the brain that can be reliably demonstrated by imaging. We can sense these connections, but we cannot feel empathy. When people say that they are feeling it, they are usually referring to compassion or sympathy.

War

When George W. Bush visited the scene of the destruction of the twin trade towers in New York on 9 November 2001 by deliberately aimed commercial airliners, he described it as an act of war. Had he described it as a criminal act, the individuals that perpetrated it and their accomplices would have been pursued and punished. By describing it as an act of war, Bush defined it as the attack of one formally recognized group on another. This implicated all Americans as the victims, as it was a war on America. But it also elevated Al-Qaeda from the terrorist network that it was into a kind of terrorist nation, a newly created status that Isis or Daesh was later to adopt, with more serious consequences. Nations fight wars by killing as many as possible of each other's combatants and squeezing the territory that they occupy until their leaders are exposed and either killed or captured. Nations fight crime by identifying ringleaders and removing them. President Obama's strategy has been to avoid pitched battles and target individual leaders as if they were criminals and not generals. Drone technology has made this increasingly possible, but the same policy was pursued before drones by targeted strikes by bombing or special operations teams.[*]

Some say that war is disappearing[4] and point out that the proportion of active combatants in an army has fallen progressively. But the number of civilian casualties killed or wounded by 'collateral damage' has risen progressively, too. The distinction between combatant and criminal is, in any case, blurred if the war is on 'terror'.

---

[*] For example, by the British Army against the Irish Republican Army (IRA) in Ulster.

Many people consider war an aberration or as evidence of human beings to be supernaturally evil. But wars, or at least intergroup violence associated with deliberate killing and wounding, have been observed in other primate groups. Evolutionary psychologists suggest that wars may have persisted because they have provided a means to deal with a surplus of males. An alternative idea is that wars force the exchange of resources and so reduce inequality between cultures. The rather older idea, that war is an expression of natural selection of which the disappearance of Neanderthal man (Homo neanderthalensis/erectus) is an example, has been undermined by the discovery that H. sapiens has benefited from incorporating Neanderthal genes into the sapiens genome, that Neanderthal and modern mankind lived in proximate settlements for substantial periods of time, and that it was natural circumstances that killed Neanderthal man off and not genocide by H. sapiens.[5]

It has also been suggested that war is an appetite,[6] and that nations, like people, have one.

George W. Bush is, according to at least some people who have met him, a charming person who people feel is really listening to them and is on their side. But as a new president, he started off with many disadvantages. He had won the electoral college by a slim margin but not with the majority of votes. The result of the election was so much in doubt that the matter was finally dealt with in the US Supreme Court. Just before the destruction of the twin towers of the World Trade Center in New York, his popularity was 50 per cent. Shortly after the announcement of the 'war against terror', it went up to 92 per cent.

There is no doubt that Bush was a weak leader (his popularity dipped again later and fell fatally after what was counted as the mismanagement of the effects of Hurricane Katrina). Perhaps only a very popular leader could have contained the fear that many people in the US undoubtedly felt after 9/11. The images of people spilling out of the collapsing buildings like tiny dolls and the recordings of people phoning family and friends on their mobiles as they awaited immolation saw to that. Aeroplanes are ubiquitous in the US, as are skyscrapers. It seemed for a time that havoc could be caused in every city by an aircraft taken over by a terrorist simply ploughing into such a building. The US seemed powerless. What could the military do? A policy of shooting down every aircraft full of innocent travellers that deviated from its flight path was unacceptable. For the president to announce a rigorous police and FBI investigation and an assurance that everything would be done to prevent further attacks must have seemed weak and likely to lead to further unpopularity.

So what he did was to announce a war and later invade first Afghanistan and then Iraq to create more battlefronts. Was this a rational strategy? It is very likely to have boosted his popularity, as that of leaders is increased when they give expression to the beliefs of their followers,[7] but it was not a rational one. According to one analysis published in the journal of the US Strategic Studies Institute, it has been 'largely ineffective' at a cost of 7000 US combatants over 15 years[8] (not to speak of allied forces or the very much greater numbers of civilians killed and still being killed at the time of writing by groups opposed to the US interventions).

Bush did not just declare war but also created a new narrative about the dangers on terrorism* within 'the

---

* I am here using 'terrorism' as a brand that has been applied to the actions of certain groups of dissidents who are assumed to be pursuing terror rather than some more traditional goal, like killing and wounding as many combatants as possible (Artelli et al., 2010).

Homeland' as the US began to be called. He stressed the closeness of every American to death from a terrorist, an idea that President Trump, the next incumbent Republican president, reinforced. Unexpected death is a constant feature in life. The likelihood of being killed by a foreign-born terrorist on the mainland of the US in the 40 years from 1975 was 1 in 3,609,709.[9] This is less than half of the lifetime risk of dying by being struck by lightning. The possibility of dying by lightning strike may seem a real possibility to people who have a fear of thunder storms, but it is just too low for most of us to worry about. Yet the substantially lower risk of being murdered by a terrorist is associated with disproportionate fear, a fear that has been called, by psychologists who adhere to a branch of psychology called 'terror management theory', 'mortality salience'.[*] Increased mortality salience has many interlinked effects: it increases the empathy of the in-group whose mortality salience has been increased for each other; it also increases conformity generally and conformity with an established leader who controls common knowledge. Studies conducted in the years following the declaration of the 'war on terror' showed a general increase in mortality salience in

---

[*] There was a similar ramping up of mortality salience in the UK when the prime minister of the time, Tony Blair, announced that Saddam Hussein could trigger weapons of mass destruction within 45 minutes. This was widely thought to mean that people in the UK might be in danger from these weapons within 45 minutes. There was a kind of vague memory of a previous threat from a giant gun designed to fire a projectile 1000 km or coat satellites with glue to disable them. This absurd project, although begun, was nowhere near being ready to fire, and the weapons of mass destruction were never found. But it created the kind of support that Tony Blair needed to send troops to invade Iraq during the second Gulf War that overturned the Ba'ath regime in Iraq and possibly caused the instability of the other Ba'ath party, in Syria, with massive civilian casualties in both countries.

the US, an increase in support for Bush and his policies, and reduced support for his electoral opponent John Kerry.[*, †]

The word 'terror' has become twisted from its original meaning of an emotion that people felt to being the name of an opponent. Something like this happened once before, as I mentioned in Chapter 6: 'The Terror' is the name given to the period between September 1793 and July 1794 in France, when France was threatened with external attack and internal revolt and was convulsed by mass executions. The Terror did not end there. Its architects were themselves executed, quite often by street gangs supported by the new authorities. The fighting only fully died down when a leader, Napoleon Bonaparte, emerged, who united all of French opinion in exaltation of his inspiring victories in foreign wars. These wars eventually engulfed the whole of Europe and parts of the Mediterranean.

George W. Bush exaggerated the risks to the US of criminal attacks by politically motivated individuals, as many leaders had done before him. But he also offered a solution: take the war to the enemy in *their* homeland. Make *them* quake in their beds.[‡] US citizens did not have to confront and deal with the danger in their midst and their own fear of death that this created. They could attack the outsiders who were infecting them with fear. It was important, too, that the authorities were not humiliated. So an invocation of war

---

[*] See Landau *et al.* (2004). And in a more extended discussion from the perspective of terror management theory, which I will be considering later in this chapter, see also Pyszczynski, Solomon, and Greenberg (2002).

[†] The cohesive effect of war has been tackled from a different, but related, angle in a recent book by Scheidel (2017). He argues that societies have shown a secular trend for wealth to become increasingly maldistributed and that war (or other catastrophe) has served to reduce wealth inequality and has thereby increased the solidarity of nations.

[‡] This has become known as the Bush doctrine and has been adopted by many Republican voters in the US as their preferred strategy (Ankony, 2011).

was also directed to this end: to convince the public that the ability of the three terrorist groups to hijack planes to lethal effect was not an expression of failure by the administration to protect American citizens from clever and well-organized gangs, but an attack by an enemy on every person in the US who considered themselves to be American. It was a means of shifting responsibility from an administration to an enemy. But it also enjoined loyalty to the in-group 'America' or, as some saw it, 'the Western World', or even the non-Muslim world, whilst making anyone who thought that there could be any justification of the crime a pariah. It created a connecting ideology that connected a high proportion of US citizens. Expressions of sympathetic grief were the order of the day in people who were not directly affected by the deaths, and people as far afield as California felt 'traumatized'. The tightening of ideological connections in the US also made 'America' into an even closer in-group with greater demands on conformity to the leaders of the in-group. Conformity meant going along with the dominant narrative that the atrocity was committed by irrational, bigoted, hate-filled people who had no grounds for legitimate enmity towards the US. Terror about being unconformist and extruded from the connectedness within the in-group effectively blocked any kind of discussion about what might have led people to plan and carry out such an appalling attack, because that would have meant crediting the out-group with rationality and justification. Even now, there is little analysis of this, beyond the paranoid suggestion (which paradoxically gives the US and US leaders even more power than was appropriate by the rhetoric surrounding the 'war on terror') that it was funded by US money, provided by the CIA to the opponents of the Russian occupation of Afghanistan.

What leads to war?

War is arguably one of the most complex organized human actions. It would be pretentious in the extreme for me to provide a total explanation for it or even a typology. Armed conflicts have been pursued to retain territory or to gain territory. They have been motivated by plunder, by the wish to gain slaves, or, as in the case of ancient Rome mentioned in Chapter 3, to capture women. The same complexity applies to the question 'What leads to war?' Obviously, many things. War always involves destruction, death, and the possibility of reward as a result of economic stimulus, plunder, and rape. Sometimes, individuals are said to be motivated by the latter rewards to put their lives at risk.* This kind of conflict is typified in European culture by buccaneers and pirates, although modern scholarship has challenged even that piece of common knowledge. Pirates often, historians now argue, started out as privateers fighting wars on behalf of states who wished to appear uninvolved in their activities.† Soldiers of fortune, similarly, rarely now just fight for money but, like the many young men who went to Spain to fight against Franco and the Republicans, fight for ideals, a motive that has troubled European countries who have experienced some of their younger citizens travelling to join Al-Qaeda or Daesh and becoming 'radicalized'.[10]

---

* A notion explored and rejected in Bertolt Brecht's play *Mother Courage and Her Children*.

† Dr Thomas Dover, a Bristol-based physician, is one example. He partly financed and led two ships on a long privateering expedition during which he rescued Alexander Falkirk ('Daniel Defoe'). Dover invented a famous and long-lasting treatment for fever ('Dover's powder'), which was used up until to the 1990s in India, although it has now been abandoned because of its opium content (Banatvala, 2016).

Nations continue to use armed conflict as a means of securing strategic resources. Examples include Hitler's attack on the wheat belt of Ukraine and southern Russia;[*] the UK's attempt to control the Suez Canal; the US invasion of Grenada; Russian involvement in reclaiming the naval bases of the Crimea and the coal fields of eastern Ukraine;[†] and, arguably, the first Gulf War to prevent Kuwaiti oil fields falling into Iraqi hands, and possibly the second Gulf War, too.

These are not just examples of purely instrumental or predatory aggression on a national level; it is important not to ignore emotional determinants for them.[‡] Humiliating a great power seems particularly likely to lead to war.

Modern war has new features. Civil wars have always put the non-combatant general population at risk, but since the

---

[*] The German invasion of the USSR provides examples of how the Nazi war machine used propaganda to create obedience and savagery in invading troops, by appeals to the protection of the fatherland and warnings about the 'barbaric and Asiatic' behaviour of Russian commissars. Frankopan (2015) describes the decisions made when Germany began to run out of food in 1941 and experts on agriculture suggested that the answer would lie in the fertile 'black soil' of Ukraine and the Caucasus. To get it would mean invading Russia, with whom Germany had signed a non-aggression pact. It would also mean cutting northern Russia off from its wheat supplies, leading to the death – the German planners predicted – of millions of people. The way to motivate German troops to do this was to tell them to imagine that 'food eaten by Soviet citizens had been torn out of the mouth of German children' (p.377) and that threats were to be expected from 'agitators, partisans, saboteurs, and Jews...to whom no mercy should be shown' (p.38). It was 'a war of extermination' (p.376).

Increasing both the affective and cognitive empathy for one's in-group and the expression of pro-in-group feelings work together to inhibit any sympathetic response to the suffering of the out-group for supportive evidence from laboratory studies; see the reviews by Eres and Molenberghs (2013) and Gonzalez-Liencres, Shamay-Tsoory, and Brüne (2013).

[†] Although it has been argued that this conflict, too, is an ideological one (Kiryukhin, 2016).

[‡] A point made, for example, by Scheff, although he focuses on shame or humiliation as a motive (Scheff, 1999). A similar, more recent analysis has been made of the armed conflict between Israel and Palestine (Gold, 2015).

Second World War and the development of intercontinental ballistic missiles, non-combatants are always at risk, even if the fighting is being carried out far away. So war always increases mortality salience in the populations of the belligerent nations nowadays. Modern ways are televised, too, and recently have been recorded and uploaded to social media by passers-by, local residents, and even combatants, and these videos can be accessed by anyone and everyone.

The involvement of everyone in a war means that everyone has a stake. Wars cannot be prosecuted purely for reasons of state. Combatants and their Facebook friends no longer carry out orders from above without considering their own beliefs. The common knowledge of the combatant has become coterminous with the common knowledge of the nation or community from which he or she comes. This, it has been argued, led to the end of the Vietnam War. It was not a military failure but a change in the common knowledge that the war was a moral one. The common knowledge grew that it was an unethical war in which people of colour or people who came from the poorest areas of the US were being sacrificed to no purpose against an enemy who were defending their homeland.[11] The well off did their best to avoid fighting, including recent US presidents: George W. Bush (who joined the National Guard), Bill Clinton (whose draft was indefinitely deferred), and Donald Trump (who had a 'heel spur' in his foot and so was declared unfit). The willingness for those in power to carry on with a war that was being fought by combatants who had no faith in it being just was jarring. I can personally attest to this, as I spent a short while working on a ward for the rehabilitation of heroin-addicted Vietnam veterans in a Veterans Health Administration hospital in California (a sister hospital of the one that was described in the book *One Flew Over the Cuckoo's Nest*). The deracination of these veterans was implacable.

The moral importance of war

Moral and morale have forked in English (although not in the French used by Marshal Foch, commander of the Allied Forces in 1918). Modern discussions of morale have mainly been limited to military units, where it has been noted in one study to be strongly linked to the cohesion of the unit and to leadership.* Morale in larger army units, which are connected by a shared ideological identity, do not protect individual soldiers from psychological stresses,[12] but the connectedness of smaller units in which the members meet face to face (and so have interbrain connections) do.[13]

Since the Boer War, wars have been played out in both their actual locale and the public consciousness. Winston Churchill played a part in this as a war correspondent. The relief of Mafeking by the British was welcomed by cheers in theatres in the West End of London. A performance of *Lohengrin* was halted at the Royal Opera House, and the audience burst into patriotic song, with the Prince of Wales, who was attending, beating time in accompaniment. Marshall Foch may have been the first person to point out the link between public opinion – common knowledge – and the outcome of war. He is quoted as saying, 'War = the domain of moral force. Victory = moral superiority in the victors; moral depression in the vanquished.'[14]

---

* Cohesion was not measured directly in this study but created from four of the survey items. The sample was, however, large, and the results are in the same direction as many other results (Du Preez *et al.*, 2011).

Terror management theory

Ernest Becker believed that existential philosophy had established that deep down all of us are frightened – 'terrified' – of death. This is not entirely consistent with empirical research, which demonstrates that, as people get older, they become less concerned about death itself and more about the process of dying.[15] Older people can defend themselves against the fear of death so long as they believe that they are valued by like-minded people who will keep those values alive, even after the individual has died. What is truly terrifying is that these like-minded people and these values will be annihilated.* Paradoxically, the fear of death reduces in most people as they get older, too, but the notion that the fear of dying is principally a fear of annihilation is upheld. The assumption that annihilation lies in the extinction of the individual body and mind neglects the potential destruction of social identity by the breakdown of social relationships.

One effect of periods of threat to social groups is that they draw together. This happens during periods of terror, for example after the twin towers attack. This occurs partly by increasing connectedness, as noted above, but also by excluding dissenters, increasing norm adherence, and favouring authoritarian leaders.[16]

What leads to terror?

The path from terror to war seems well established, but what leads to terror? What, for example, led George W. Bush to tilt the reaction to the terrible act of destruction and murder that

---

* There are many studies of 'self-esteem' as a balm to the fear of death. Solomon, Greenberg, and Pyszczynski (2000) summarize early studies and make the explicit link with annihilation.

was 9/11 towards it being an act of war? I have argued already that there were advantages to him and his administration in doing so, but it would be cynical to assume that this was a deliberate act (and I do not have any evidence to support this).

So what did lead to this switch to war being thrown? Why did the revolutionaries in France start a series of foreign wars? Actually, this turns out to be a very frequent occurrence. Despite the inevitable administrative and economic upheaval of a revolution, a foreign war commonly follows.[17]

Revolutions create a diversity of opinion and belief. Fortunately, the age of revolutions appears to have passed, at least for Europe. The issue is now 'globalization':[18] the irruption of new ideas, new ideologies, into Westernized nations through immigration and also through tourism. Increasing percentages of national populations travel to other nations motivated by curiosity, but when they are there find themselves offended or disturbed by the mores that they discover.* This fear has been played on in recent elections in many European countries, including Britain,[19] and has centred more and more on Muslim residents in Europe, their otherness, and moral panic† mainly driven by the fear of the collapse of 'national cohesion'.[20]

---

* Boa (2006) argues that these were the pressures that Thomas Mann imposed on his fictional character, Aschenbach, in *Death in Venice*, pressures that resulted in his breakdown and death.

† The first uses of the term 'moral panic' to refer to terror in a group of people can be dated to the 1830s. One early use was attributed to a French speaker. A report in the *Journal of Health* conducted by the Association of Physicians (1831) quotes him: 'Magendie, a French physician of note on his visit to Sunderland, where the Cholera was by the last accounts still raging, praises the English government for not surrounding the town with a cordon of troops, which as "a physical preventive would have been ineffectual and would have produced a moral panic far more fatal than the disease now is"' (Anon, 1832, p.180). Francois Magendie was a physician whose simultaneous discovery with Charles Bell, that sensory input returned into the spinal cord via the anterior root, and motor output exited via the posterior root, is now known as the Bell-Magendie law. He seems to

Nations do not have intentions. So it would be an error to claim that the revolutionary nation or the nation that is experiencing 'immigrant panic' intends to start a war just to deal with this panic. But in panic more credence will be given to anyone who offers to take the panic away, who reassures. So the person or group who campaigns to attack or blame another state for creating the diversity in the home nation, and confronting its members from disturbing alterity, is more likely to be joined by other voices rising in support, creating a community whose 'common knowledge' is that war is the only way to deal with the threat to cultural identity and ideology, a phenomenon long recognized under the name of 'war fever'.[21] The creation of a dominant in-group triggers the 'common knowledge' reconnection process of pushing dissenting voices to the margin, and even turning them into an out-group, whilst lining up the remainder behind a leader (typically the leader of the revolution), increasing the in-group's conformity and reducing diversity or 'otherness' in both the in- and the out-group at the expense of increasing the potential for conflict between them.[22,] * At the time of writing, this process seems

---

have had troubles with his hospital colleagues, though, and went into public health where he concluded that the cholera epidemics that were starting to ravage European cities were not caused by a contagious agent (now known to be false, as Vibrio cholerae is readily transmitted through faecal contamination of water and is often therefore transmitted by touch from hands that have been in contaminated water). He made a visit to Sunderland in 1830 and praised the government for not preventing egress and entrance to the town, as 'a physical preventive would have been ineffectual and would have produced a moral panic far more fatal than the disease now is'.

The history of moral panic as a concept has been confused since then (Sutton, 2015). Panics have been triggered by fears of economic collapse, 'white slavery', drugs, and street crime (one of the best-known books about moral panic was by Stanley Cohen and described the fighting in the streets of Brighton between scooter-riding Mods and motor-bike-riding Rockers).

* See also Koomen and Van Der Pligt (2016) for a discussion of the cycle applied to 'radicalization' and 'terrorism'. This is a similar phenomenon to the salience of

to be in train in the US again, but with two equally balanced communities,[23] each with its own 'common knowledge' still fighting it out electorally.[24,*]

How does war end?

War follows on from creating and demonizing an out-group and entrenches, sometimes by censorship, the connections between those people who share an increasingly concrete and homogeneous common knowledge, sometimes amounting to a creed, as I have discussed previously.[†] Wars have been fought as a kind of game or even sport – at least that is what novels depict – but most wars aim to stifle the ideas, beliefs, and values of the out-group. Sometimes both sides run out of resources, and the war halts but is likely to resume later. Perhaps, too, nations get 'tired' of war, as people often say, but there is no evidence for this. Sometimes one group succeeds in eradicating the other altogether. More often, the war takes on the lineaments of a championship: a moment comes when one power wins over another, and the loser submits not just to the demands of the winner, but also to the assimilation of the values and dominant beliefs of the winner.

There may have been a time when the championship contest could replace the war altogether, as in the proverbial Biblical story of David fighting the Philistine's champion,

---

hate crimes and the condign punishments that are entertained to prevent them (Lieberman *et al.*, 2001).

* One frightening alternative is that people might be 'treated' to remove ideological conformity by powerful magnetic fields applied to the frontal part of their brain (Holbrook *et al.*, 2016).

† For a discussion of the development of conflicting common knowledge in the Israeli-Palestinian conflict see McAlister and Wilczak (2015), and for the role of the media in this see Gvirsman *et al.* (2016).

Goliath. The trial by champion that Malory described in *Le Morte d'Arthur*[25] resulted from Guinevere being falsely accused of killing a knight, Sir Patrise, with a poisoned apple (it turned out to be Sir Pinel who poisoned the apple, who was anyway aiming to kill Sir Gawain, but killed Sir Patrise in error). Her accusers, knowing perhaps that her usual champion, the much admired and feared Sir Launcelot, had gone missing, demanded trial by combat. Sir Mador de la Porte, who was a kinsman of the murder victim, was down to fight Sir Bors, but in the end Sir Launcelot turned up, replaced Sir Bors, and overcame Sir Mador. Guinevere's innocence was proven and Sir Mador sued for her forgiveness.

This trial by championship succeeded in averting a war, but it was a trial of fact and not a trial of ideology. Some while later, Guinevere faced another threat of execution, but this time over an ideological issue. She was accused and found guilty of infidelity and therefore treachery to King Arthur, her husband. She was to be burned at the stake when Sir Launcelot intervened. This time he was not just her champion, he was also the lover with whom she had been unfaithful. He rescued her from the pyre but did not stay with the company of the round table, and he and Guinevere fled. This led to war. Trial by combat or 'wagers by battle' persisted officially in the UK until the 17th century, and its single combat version, the duel (named after the Latin for two), till much later, albeit without judicial sanction. Duels settle individual matters but do not settle conflicts between ideologically opposed groups.

The interbrain in war

Launcelot, Gawain, Mador, Pinel, and Patrise were knights at the fabled court of King Arthur. Guinevere was Arthur's wife. The determination of the trial for murder was conducted according to the ground rules of mediaeval chivalry, which assumed a brotherhood between knights based on fellow feeling and a connection with their leader, the king.[*] The combat does not create enmity but resolves tensions. When Launcelot rescues Guinevere from the stake, he goes 'berserk', killing 24 unarmed knights in the melee,[†] including one of his greatest admirers, Sir Gareth. Mediaeval values required that the senior member of Gareth's Scottish family, Sir Gawain, sought blood from Sir Launcelot's Breton kin.

As in Ovid's story about the fall of the Tarquins, rules of vengeance trump the empathic connection between the knights of the round table, who are pledged to support each other and still did so in the single combat between Launcelot and Mador. Combat of their kind of lances and swords is, after all, a kind of dance that relies heavily on the interbrain connection. Launcelot's behaviour is very different when rescuing Guinevere. He is dissociated and 'berserk', and his interbrain connection is cut off. He mows down his fellow knights, focusing only on his desire to rescue his lover. Arthur recognizes this shift in Launcelot's connection to him and the

---

[*] There has been a great deal written about the rules that bound cavalry men (chevalier, hence chivalrie) together and general agreement that much of it was a literary fiction fostered by the church to pass on Christian values. Its origins seem to date back to Moorish Spain and perhaps to the concept of the brotherhood of Muslims, the umma. Bourdieu used it as the basis for his conception of the unspoken habits or 'habitus' that determine an individual's behaviour and are derived from the group to which the individual belongs (Bourdieu, 1994). There is an implication that this habitus is derived from a kind of interbrain connection.

[†] Malory (1920) puts it this way: 'they were slain in the hurtling as Sir Launcelot thrang in the thick of the press; and as they were unarmed he smote them and wist not whom that he smote, and so unhappily they were slain. The death of them, said Arthur, will cause the greatest mortal war that ever was; I am sure, wist Sir Gawaine that Sir Gareth were slain, I should never have rest of him till I had destroyed Sir Launcelot's kin and himself both, outher else he to destroy me' (p.450).

round table, or at least Malory does, and puts these words into
Arthur's mouth:

> And therefore, said the king, wit you well my heart was
> never so heavy as it is now, and much more I am sorrier
> for my good knights' loss than for the loss of my queen
> for queens I might have enow, but such a fellowship of
> good knights shall never be together in no company.[26]

War, with its ideological demands that those involved (and
that is everyone in the nations involved in these days of
total war) are patriotic, unswerving supporters of one side
or another, and not being these things is to be open to a
charge of treason, suppresses the interbrain connections that
might previously have linked people who were close despite
differences in politics, ethics, or religion. Wars break families
apart and enable acts that in peacetime would be considered
viciously callous.

War does not release the brute in mankind, and is not an
aberration, but, as I have already noted, it serves many purposes.
One that may be becoming more important is the consequence
of a conflict of ideology and identity that leads to a sufficient
number of people feeling that their deeply held beliefs are at
risk, and their identities are being crushed. If a national leader
takes up their cause, a war provides the opportunity not just
to reflate that identity but also to reduce the threat to it in the
future by excluding or silencing those who disagree with them
on the grounds of patriotism or fraternizing with the enemy.

Even the interbrain connection between nationals may
be controlled. Combatants are encouraged to bond with the
strangers that the nation places in their platoon, ship, crew,
squad, or unit. Even though it is artificially put together, strong

interbrain connections may develop between team members, just as husband and wife may develop a strong interbrain connection even though their marriage was arranged. Unlike a marriage, the nation, through its officers, can just as quickly redeploy members of these groups, breaking the connections between them.

The patriotic message also enjoins the suppression of compassion for the transgressive enemy or the civilians who are seen as the enemy, too. No interbrain connection exists between the combatant and the enemy he or she is water-boarding or the civilian he (rarely she in warfare) is raping. The interbrain connection ceases to be a spontaneous human connection, but becomes something controlled by the common knowledge that is purveyed about the enemy.

'Mortality salience' also reduces affective empathy.[27] The effects of splitting in- and out-groups that I have described occurring in institutionalized or socialized conflict such as systematic oppression, prejudice, and war involves dehumanization, and the driving force is to create cohesion through the 'binding force' of purified ideology.[28] Dehumanization is associated with detachment from the suffering of another person and indifference to their emotions and interests.* It is not just the consequence of an abnormal state of mind induced by the fear or rage of conflict.

It may be an explicit policy. For example, in the Bosnian War it was the policy that Serbs raped Bosnian women so as to replace the Bosnian population with children with Serbian fathers. Thousands of men, many of them law-abiding, were involved, all of them participating in crimes that in civilian life would, no doubt, have revolted them.[29] Here an overt 'common

---

* Dastur (2008) makes the point that this indifference is the ultimate step in dehumanization, whilst hatred still keeps a kind of relationship alive.

knowledge' that Serbs were superior to Bosnians, and should replace them, reinforced the disconnection of the interbrain connections between Serbs and Bosnians having intimate contact. Some of the rapes were conducted with foreign objects, causing great and lasting harm, an additional effect of the terror induced by an increased awareness of mortality, which reduces the vicarious awareness of the suffering of others.[30]

What effect does war have?

To summarize, war creates an enemy, who is demonized, and allies, who are connected by a shared ideology or common knowledge that the war conditions exaggerate. This common knowledge becomes the most important connection between people, reducing interbrain connections and, in dealings with the enemy, sometimes entirely suppressing them.[31] Justice and tit-for-tat reciprocity increases as a motivation,[32] and compassion decreases, when people become more preoccupied by death, as they do in war, and the remote possibilities of harm can become exaggerated, as they do in panic about terrorism.[33] In-groups become more forgiving of the violence of other in-group members when their mortality is threatened.[34] Out-groups, on the other hand, can become even more alienated if the justice focus is not seen as applying to them[*] and if the sense of unfairness turns to bitterness.[35] Nations at war become more conservative and more determined to preserve tradition, which they see as being under threat.[36] Because war replaces

---

[*] Lerner and Clayton (2011) introduced an overarching theory, not dissimilar to terror management theory, about social alienation when the usual belief in a just world collapses to be replaced by the belief that the world is fundamentally unjust. One corollary of the just world assumption is that victims somehow deserve the harm that comes to them (Sullivan *et al.*, 2016) and that lucky people deserve their luck (Olson *et al.*, 2008).

the terror of annihilation with the salience of mortality, which has the same effect, it readily becomes self-sustaining.[37]

Does the contrast between types of connections provide any guidance about conducting peace?

The evidence that I have presented does have some implications for dealing with the unrestrained and unreflective reliance on connecting people entirely through 'knowledge' (actually conviction), whether or not it leads to war.

War cannot be prevented by attacking the common knowledge that fuels it. People cannot be persuaded by argument that their understanding of the risks of war and the grounds of war are wrong. Frightened people do not consider disconfirmations of what they believe but seek confirmation instead, especially if they have succumbed to the authoritarian values that often prevail in war. They want, and are urged, to keep their values simple and not entertain inconsistent facts. Timid people become more punitive when death threatens. People want to conform, to be conservative, and to go along with stereotypes.[*]

Increasingly, we assume that knowledge is obtainable through evidence and that if we pile more evidence on other people they will yield to our knowledge. Evidence, particularly the visual evidence on which we increasingly rely, is open to

---

[*] People look for more confirmatory evidence (Jonas, Greenberg, and Frey, 2003), especially if it is authoritarian (Lavine, Lodge, and Freitas, 2005) or reduces dissonance (Friedman and Arndt, 2005). These issues – of instances of collective intelligence and also of collective bias – were covered in a group of publications synchronous with the election of Donald Trump as US president: see, for example, Sloman (2017).

Less hardy people become more punitive when they are mortality salient (Florian, Mikulincer, and Hirschberger, 2001).

not only fraudulent manipulation but also multiple interpretations. What you make of a picture depends on the frame in
which you mentally place it.

An alternative approach is the Hegelian one: to find
a common knowledge that subsumes both the thesis of
my common knowledge and its antithesis in your common
knowledge. But history indicates that conflicts are never
resolved this way.

The championship approach to the prevention of war
sidelines knowledge but preserves the lineaments of conflict,
unlike diplomacy or mediation, and yet involves interbrain
connections. Champions do not nowadays demonstrate their
ability in the tilting yard but on the sports field. Football (or
soccer) might have become one of the greatest prophylactics
against war.

The bodily interaction between opposing football teams,
and the connection that binds crowds together, may work both
ways, leading to rage as well as affiliation. It is chancy, but it cuts
across national and ideological boundaries. Smaller groupings
based on interbrain connections – far-flung families, churches,
special interest groups – cut across communities built on
shared convictions. The more that individuals are connected
to others in the former, the more likely that the dominance
of moral panics based on stereotyping or rigid adherence to
imaginative connections is less likely to develop to the all-
encompassing level which is the harbinger of war.

Certain kinds of out-group contact increase out-group
intolerance. Package tourism, in which strongly connected
in-groups travel from place to place acting as disconnected
observers of the exotic weirdnesses of the places they visit,
probably increases xenophobia unless the travellers find ways
to break out of their alienation.

This is not to say that interbrain connections are good or that common knowledge is bad. But, in my view, they need to be in balance for human connections to be healthy and not war-like.

The connections of terrorists

Ideological wars are fought against supposedly evil groups, which nowadays are most likely to be characterized as terrorists. Terrorists create terror. That is their purpose.[38, *] Terror induces obedience in those most immediately in the power and therefore the sway of the terrorizer,[†] but in others it leads to panic. People may accommodate to panic and learn to live with it.[‡] But it induces a tendency to flee that many people give in to, leading to massive movements of displaced people that I called 'swarms' in Chapter 2. Because fear or terror are

---

* Terror, extreme fear, can have two effects. Most commonly it produces the release of epinephrine, norepinephrine, and corticosteroid, along with increased activity of the sympathetic nervous system. This is associated with flight, either away from the stimulus causing the terror or, as Sartre pointed out, towards a place that is imagined to be safe, a relict of separation anxiety. This is often termed panic or panic flight. Occasionally, if flight is blocked, an irruption of parasympathetic arousal occurs that replaces the sympathetic arousal and substitutes fainting and immobility for flight. This has been called 'panic-stunning', and is probably related to the sham death exhibited by birds and rodents.

   Terror can be induced by circumstances or situations that are potentially fatal. But it can also be induced by some stimulus that portends death: in ancient times, this could have been a sudden sound in an empty wilderness, particularly if one was surrounded by an army that could amplify that panic as it resonated in the faces and behaviour of other soldiers (in ancient Greece, this sudden sound might be attributed to the pipes that the demiurge Pan owned that had the special property of arousing terror). In contemporary times, when panic has become a disorder, the terror may be triggered by shortness of breath or pain in the chest that is taken to be the symptom of a heart attack.

† A consequence of 'panic-stunning', i.e. the combination of terror and the inability to escape.

‡ What behaviourists term 'anxiety reduction through prolonged exposure'.

contagious, the person who is most anxious in a swarm will transmit that to others. Swarms of people therefore maintain high levels of anxiety, and if they have moved into unfamiliar territory and are perhaps being threatened by new enemies, the swarm itself also becomes a kind of security. So the swarm perpetuates itself as a result of being a swarm: that is, a group of people who are interconnected by means of the interbrain.

Other people perceive the swarm itself as a source of terror. They note that it remains together, like some kind of indefeasible super-organism. It has biological needs. Like invading armies, although without the organization or the plethora of weaponry, swarms have to forage, commandeer shelter, and drive off attackers. Armies may travel with a swarm of camp followers and civilians who need protection but also need feeding and clothing. Swarms are often thought of as invasive, 'foreign', or alien, just like invading armies. What is known about invaders or displaced groups is not known directly through a face-to-face, interbrain connection, but through rumour – in other words, through 'common knowledge'.

So there is a clash of two kinds of connectedness: the interbrain connections within the immigrants that sustains companionship and security as well as fear, and the common knowledge connection between them and the resident population.

Of course, this is an over-simplification. The residents may form their own groups to resist what they see as the threat of the immigrants, with these groups being held together by their shared fear of the 'invaders'. The threat may not be negligible.* Human swarms may also be held together by

---

* A characteristic of Homo spp is that waves of newer, larger-brained hominids emerged from East Africa and spread through Europe and Asia assimilating

common knowledge. Successive crusades were composed of human swarms (of children on at least one occasion) loosely held together by the common knowledge that 'liberating' Jerusalem from Arabic rule would guarantee salvation in the afterlife, plus yielding abundant spoils.

Moral panic: impersonal and disembodied

Common knowledge relies on language for its propagation, and it can readily use general concepts like 'immigrants', 'invaders', 'Muslims', 'Christians', and so on. The connections between in- and out-groups mediated by common knowledge are usually impersonal, in contrast to interbrain connections between people who are face to face.

Images of long lines of immigrants that can be distributed to everyone's screen sustain this swarm-like idea. Reporters and cameramen on the spot do not share it, often recording interviews with named individuals who are urged to tell their personal story or photographing people coming ashore having nearly drowned on a capsized raft. But even though these images show bodies in states of exhaustion or distress, they are not themselves embodied. Rather than overcoming the anonymization of the members of a swarm, they may exacerbate it by showing quite how many individuals there are who are equally exhausted. At least when we are presented with images of the face, the sound of the voice (denied when a translator is dubbing a person's voice), or other identifying characteristic, we can experience emotion by contagion.

---

earlier hominids as they went – probably not just by murder, but also by mating with them, gaining valuable genes in the process. Homo sapiens have shown a similar tendency to expansion in waves, many originating in the Mongolian steppes, with assimilation of previous waves of expansion along with the retention of cultural elements developed uniquely by those previous waves.

But we cannot exchange emotions. There is no connection. We may feel compassion (or hatred or other self-conscious emotion), and sometimes an uneasy sense of wanting to do something, but this is without the fellow feeling that the interbrain would bring.

Moral panic or moral terror

I have previously considered what Mackay called 'the madness of crowds': crowd-like behaviour in pursuit of an object that common knowledge has identified as generally desirable. Its obverse is the vilification or persecution of an object that common knowledge labels a universal danger, a phenomenon known as 'moral panic'.* Immigration† is one example of a moral panic. Other examples include paedophilia, acquired immune deficiency syndrome (AIDS), political extremism, and religious fanaticism. Unlike panic triggered by a meaningless symptom, moral 'panics' are a reaction to significant threats, but the reaction is overblown. Moral terrors might be a better term.

Autarchs often come to power as a result of moral terror when they become leaders of the in-group united against some threatening out-group but then maintain their power by inspiring terror themselves, which they can do because once in power they command enough people and enough power over those people to hunt down, torture, and gruesomely execute dissenters.

Vlad III, the voivode of Wallachia, is a case in point. Wallachia now forms part of Romania and is separate from

---

* For examples of moral panic see Cohen (1973), Goode and Nachman (2009), and Scheinin (2010).

† See, for example, Martin (2015), McKay, Thomas, and Warwick Blood (2011), Saux (2007), and Welch (2003).

the Transylvania with which Vlad has become associated. Wallachia was originally a Celtic enclave but was, after the Roman empire withdrew, occupied by Hungarian, Bulgarian (Cuman), Turkish (Pecheneg), and Ottoman troops. It was a difficult place in which to be a prince. Vlad III was the son of one of the more successful princes, Vlad II, who was known as Vlad Dracul because he belonged to a society, the Order of the Dragons, dedicated to resisting the Ottoman empire. His task, and that of other Wallachian voivodes, was complicated by constant uprisings by local nobles or boyars and by pressure from the Catholic Saxons, who were German speakers who had been resettled in Transylvania and needed to keep trade routes open through Wallachia to the Black Sea.

As the son of Vlad Dracul, Vlad III was known as little Dracul or Dracula. He and his middle brother became Ottoman hostages for his father's good conduct, but his father and eldest brother were assassinated in a Hungarian invasion that installed their own puppet voivode. Vlad, with Ottoman support, displaced him and began a campaign against the boyars, the Saxons, and criminals, in which he used impalement as his method of crucifixion. Impalement was an ancient execution method, used widely in the Middle East and the Ottoman empire. Vlad III's officers impaled their victims transversally, through the abdomen and out via the back (evisceration was also an element of the English method of executing particular heinous malefactors, being the 'drawing' of hanging, drawing, and quartering). Other regimes, including the Ottomans, used vertical impalement in which the stake was driven between the buttocks, up into the chest, and outwards, sometimes through the mouth. Vlad also used impalement in a reprisal raid on Saxony following an uprising.

Like other terrorists, Vlad must have known that terror increases in proportion to the number of people killed, the use of modes of death in which pain is prolonged or the human body is made grotesque, and the defenceless or innocent people. Impalement was a common form of execution in the Ottoman empire, but his use of it may also have been influenced by these considerations (and perhaps because minimal preparations were needed to carry it out).

His reputation as a violator of human decency was fostered by the Saxons and later in Germany and other areas of Roman Catholic Europe. Vlad III adhered to the Orthodox rite (until persuaded when he was imprisoned by the Hungarians to convert) and was accused by the Saxons of drinking blood, an accusation made of other execrated out-groups in Europe and a Satanic twist on the Holy Sacrament in which wine is drunk that is mystically connected to the blood of Christ. Blood-drinking was also an attribute of the supposed souls of the undead, who could be observed sometimes flying at night and making unearthly sounds (their Romanian name, 'strygoi', is clearly derived from the onomatopoeic Greek word for owl, which was believed by the Romans to be a bird of ill omen that drank the blood of infants; the most likely 'culprit' is Otus scops, the Western screech owl).

Bram Stoker, a journalist, made Dracula into a household name by fusing the Germanic perspective on Vlad III's bloodthirsty nature with the strygoi legend and throwing in elements from werewolf myths, too. Dracula is 'undead'. So no longer human but 'other'.

Terror increases obedience, and the Romanian apologists for Vlad still argue that his massive use of impalement was the only way to pacify Wallachia. When no-one feels safe, effective opposition is restricted to those who are unusually capable of deception or are unusually resilient in the face of terror. Insecurity is increased not just by the risk of summary execution, but also by covert surveillance, as so graphically described in George Orwell's novel *Nineteen Eighty-Four*: the terror associated with the secret police and their informant network. I imagine many of today's terrorists must feel this themselves, with so many covert means of spying on their activities plus a means of execution at a distance by drone strike.

Some modern-day political and religious activists seek to induce terror, too. This makes sense for the few such groups that have set up alternative governments,[*] as it allows them to control potential dissidents. But it is less clear how terror helps otherwise.

In Vlad III's case, his notoriety, fostered by the Saxons who were clients of the Hungarian king, cemented Roman Catholic opposition to him and he was eventually imprisoned for 16 years by the King of Hungary (although after his release he served in the Hungarian army until his death). We need narratives to make sense of terror, especially if that terror is deliberately induced. We ask ourselves, how could one person do this to another person, how can a person be so callous? The most obvious answer is that the terrorist is inhuman, a monster – just as the historical narrative of Vlad III has been changed into 'Dracula', the vampire.

Creating monsters is a kind of 'othering'. Sharing a narrative about the existence of monsters creates a stronger connection between everyone else, who the narrative defines by exclusion as fully human. Oddly enough in the case of

---

[*] At the time of writing, examples of these include the Russian puppet government in Chechnya, the Taliban in Afghanistan and parts of Pakistan, and the so-called Caliphate in Iraq.

vampires, the narrative about our humanity is unchallenged by the traditional use of impalement as a method of killing vampires, although the fabled method involves a stake through the heart and immediate death, rather than a stake through the abdomen and a prolonged one.

The deliberate use of terror would therefore seem to be of limited value if it unites other people against you. Yet terrorists, particularly radical Muslim groups, work hard to project terror worldwide. They do this through the use of social media, through atrocities that are highly newsworthy, by targeting major cities, by targeting or using 'innocents' such as children, and by making the attacks as unpredictable as possible. It may be that the intention is to create a sense of impotence in the target population and turn terror into resigned obedience, but this seems like too great an ambition, as the dilution of the experience of being vicariously terrified is probably too great for emotional contagion to build. But it may be effective if it infects smaller groups of decision-makers and opinion leaders. Their job is usually to reduce panic and minimize terror,[*,†] but public pronouncements do not always have this effect.

The evidence, as I have already indicated, is strong that panic and terror trigger an urge to become better connected,

---

[*] One example of this comes from the mental health of Northern Irish people during the Troubles. Once the British Army had moved in, the UK government did everything it could to reduce the impact of terrorism. Statements by politicians linked to terrorist organizations or by spokespersons of those organizations were spoken by actors. This had the effect of substantially reducing their rhetorical impact. Although the Troubles had an effect on the mental health of the people who were directly involved, there was less of an effect for those who identified with the nation – those who were connected, one might say, were less likely to have been affected (Muldoon and Downes, 2007).

[†] The basis for the current panic about immigration, it has been suggested (Osang and Weber, 2017), is a consequence of dissimilarity between immigrant and native groups, and 'cultural friction'.

and this is achieved by out-grouping. Zygmunt Bauman's concept of the 'social construction of immorality' has some similarities with terror management theory's view of the use of out-groups as a means of sequestering and managing moral panic.[39] There may be a downside though: some people may identify more with the out- than the in-group. This may be another factor in the current use of terror by radical Muslim groups. It creates publicity that can be coupled with a religious message that appeals to the brotherhood of Islam – the umma – who may themselves experience religious discrimination if they live in non-Muslim countries. These already-alienated individuals and small groups may be drawn to the out-group and not repelled by it.

The lone terrorist

There was a time when new recruits had to be sent to training camp where they received military, political, and often religious training. Radicalization of these aspirants into active terrorists required some degree of interbrain connection to forge them together. It would be renewed by regional commanders in organizations like the Irish Republican Army (IRA) or Al-Qaeda who would interact personally with headquarters and with local cadres.

It took a long time for the authorities to admit that members of terrorist organizations were not mentally ill or even drawn from an offender group.* Terrorists who belong to organizations have close connections with other, similarly

---

* One clear indication of this has been the subsequent political careers of influential members of terrorist organizations, including Ariel Sharon in Israel, Martin McGuinness in Northern Ireland, and Nelson Mandela in South Africa, all of them implicated in murder as young men but dying as glorified heroes of their country.

minded people, albeit within small 'cells', and rather than being people who are on the edges of society, many 'terrorists' are happily married, are well educated, and have held down or are still holding down good jobs. Like prophets and other social innovators,[40] the members of terrorist organizations gain strength from their interbrain connections through which could flow the sense of grievance, of outrage, and of pride in accomplishment of a difficult and anxious task that reinforces their self-belief and their determination. This became even more obvious when many supposed IRA members were arrested and 'interned' in the Maze prison. Far from dissuading them from their revolutionary beliefs by torture disguised as interrogation, these beliefs were hardened.

The two factors that are often credited as defeating the IRA are the successful infiltration of their cells by members of the intelligence agency and the change in the common knowledge that they were acting on behalf of their communities. Infiltration meant that the supposedly close interbrain connections with other people could not be relied upon when a proportion of those other people were simulating their emotions, and the deviation of the narrative of IRA 'soldiers' that they were fighting to defend the Republican cause could not be sustained given the common knowledge that they were just causing mayhem because they were clinging on to an outdated Fenian glory.

The democratization of terror

Once explosives became widely available, anyone could aspire to be a terrorist. An early example of this is the Gunpowder Plot of 1605 organized by a small group of Roman Catholics angered at religious discrimination by the Protestant king James I. They placed 36 barrels of gunpowder in the crypt of the Palace of Westminster, intending to set them off whilst James I was attending the state opening of Parliament. Former British kings had killed each other and, with great trepidation, a court had ordered the regicide of Charles I. It must have seemed inconceivable that ordinary people might have the power to assassinate the king (although Parliament a few years later was to sentence James I's son, Charles, to death). The plotters were ordered to be hung, drawn, and quartered, a penalty reserved for traitors. The audacity of the plot continues to astound and shock, so much so that the traditional bonfire marking the onset of winter has been reinvented in the UK as a re-evocation of the near-burning of Parliament. The festival is still called Guy Fawkes, after the ex-soldier amongst the plotters whose job was to light the fuses in the barrels.

Since then, it has become commonplace that military materials have fallen into the hands of terrorist groups, along with small arms that are available to members of the public in many countries. Even so, buying explosives or enough small arms to create terror must require considerable organization. Manufacturing one's own explosive also requires technical know-how. But even this becomes unnecessary when everyday materials can be used as explosives, when an ordinary object like a car, a lorry, or an aeroplane can be a weapon, and when the blueprints exist on the world wide web.

Another story about monsters

Terrorists may belong to organizations or be loners. Loner terrorists may inspire fear and sometimes grudging respect, but they may also inspire revulsion, as indeed may the acts of terrorist organizations. Are they monsters? Driving a car or a lorry into a crowd certainly seems monstrous.

There is no doubt that some actions disgust or revolt us, even as they terrify us. We might refer to them as evil or depraved. I have referred to several already in previous chapters – the rape of Lucretia, the actions of Comrade Duch in Kampuchea, Vlad III's butchery of political opponents, and terror attacks by religious extremists of all religious persuasions.

I have indicated that such actions can induce moral panic that spreads through the 'common knowledge'. I have also argued that this common knowledge serves to connect people together in condemnation of the action but that connectedness becomes even stronger if it shuts off any fellow feeling for the person who has committed the action. This can be achieved by denying that person's humanity and turning them into a monster.

The paintings of Hieronymus Bosch are full of such monsters, sometimes engaged in unnatural acts and sometimes just depicted as frightening hybrids of human and animal. Visions of heaven and hell are also frequent in these paintings, as are demons, and the message is clear: allow yourself to be taken over by evil, and you become a monster destined for hell. The contemporary world no longer experiences this kind of moral panic. Secure in that knowledge, the town council of s'Hertogen Bosch has placed plastic effigies of some of the more grotesque monsters that its most famous son imagined along main tourist routes.

During the enlightenment, medicine began to vie with religion as an explanation for monstrosities. Degeneration of the brain over successive generations was one of the most persistent medical explanations. It was dwindling at the end of the 19th century, even in its strongholds in France and Italy, but received a new burst of energy from the rediscovery of Mendel's genetics experiments and the impetus that this gave to the eugenics movement, and degeneration, or depravity, as an explanation for actions that revolt us has never quite gone away since.

Some medical explanations other than those of the degenerationists have proved useful. 'Berserker' violence and the murderous attacks that were attributed to 'amok' in Malaysia[41] are both explicable, at least in part, by dissociation,[42] a half-awake, half-asleep trance state that can also be caused by epileptic activity (when it is called 'epileptic furore'), by an uncoupling of paralysis and sleep allowing dreams to be acted out ('sleep automatism'), or by 'dissociative drugs', such as phencyclidine. Not everyone in a dissociated state is violent. So dissociation is only a part explanation, but it does address the most troubling issue about atrocities, which is our disbelief that we could ever do this. We could not imagine, say, driving a car along a pavement at up to 70 mph in order to kill as many strangers as possible, as has happened in several European cities. But we might be able to imagine doing something like this in a dream. We can even imagine being half-asleep and not knowing the people around us are actually people – although we wouldn't be driving in this state. As there is some similarity between being half-awake and being in a waking dream, many of us might therefore imagine what it would be like to be so disconnected to other people that we could do something so callous. What is hard to imagine is doing it when we are connected to other people, seeing their faces and their eyes, and hearing their screams.

Similarly, an imperious voice telling us to stab someone because they are the devil is something we could imagine giving in to if we were convinced that the voice had greater knowledge than we did and must be obeyed, and if we believed that the person that we were stabbing was not really a person.[*] Neither becoming dissociated nor yielding to an authoritarian leader who gives callous orders is outside the normal range of human behaviour. What is difficult for others to conceive is that someone could become so disconnected from others that this kind of dissociation or delusion is possible. As I have suggested, disconnection might occasionally be one-way, for example if someone takes a dissociative drug, but normally it needs both sides to produce it: the in-group on the one side and the excluded person on the other.

An explanation for the state of mind that a person might be in that could lead to monstrous behaviour does not, though, tell us what kind of person a monster is. In fact, the people who run amok in the developed world, people like school shooters, might imitate other shooters' actions without necessarily being similar to them as people.[43]

Degenerationism has received a new boost from neuroscience[†] and from the current fascination with empathy. It is assumed that empathy, and not good, is what holds us back from exploiting other people, a hypothesis that is not more advanced than that of earlier ages, when people might have said it is conscience that stops us doing harm to others and that conscience was what was put in us by God for just that purpose.

These issues have come to a head because psychology has sought to take over and extend the territory claimed by psychiatry over offenders whose motivations and actions are

---

[*] Command hallucinations associated with delusions about the intended victim indicate violence (Taylor *et al.*, 1998) and suicide (Zisook *et al.*, 1995) risk in people with schizophrenia.

[†] Although it should be noted that neuroscientists do not use the term 'empathy' consistently. More generally it is also worth noting that the contribution of neuroscience to neurology is limited. Its contributions to psychology have been negligible, except as thought experiments.

inexplicable to juries, judges, and advocates. The high-water mark of this psychology project has been the reinvention of 'psychopathy'.

The psychopath

Psychopaths are presented as the successors of Vlad the Impaler: monsters whose actions reflect, it is assumed, their monstrous nature, a nature that can nowadays be measured by psychologists, or so they claim. My own view is that they are monsters because people choose to so label them and therefore distance themselves from the taint of the violence and depravity that ordinary human beings have shown under extreme circumstances at different times and in different places. But more of this below, when I consider our connections with 'psychopaths' and their connections with the rest of us.

'Psychopathy' was first used by German psychiatrists as an explanation of the repeated actions of people that they thought could best be considered unhealthy, but for which there did not seem to be an explanatory mental illness. The condition is sometimes traced back to a 19th-century Bristol GP who described what he called 'moral insanity'. Reading his case histories now, most of them are instantly recognizable as people with early dementia that is affecting their frontal lobes before other parts of their brains.*

---

* See Prichard (1835) and also Whitlock (1982). The term 'psychopathie' was introduced by a German psychiatrist, Koch, who, as a follower of the Continental trend for 'degenerationism', attributed certain kinds of social misbehaviour to degeneracy or, as he put it in 1888, in his *Short Textbook of Psychiatry* (*Kurzgefaßter Leitfaden der Psychiatrie*), to 'psychopathic inferiority' (Psychopathische Minderwertigkeiten). As degenerationism became discredited, 'Psychopathie' was extended to what is now called 'personality disorder'. The Scottish psychiatrist Henderson published an influential textbook on 'psychopathy' (Henderson, 1939) in which he described three types, one of which was 'creative psychopathy'.

The modern conception of psychopathy was synthesized by a psychiatrist, Hervey Cleckley, who also wrote an influential book on a condition that used to be known as multiple personality disorder (*The Three Faces of Eve*) and a book pathologizing homosexuality (*The Caricature of Love: A Discussion of Social, Psychiatric, and Literary Manifestations of Pathologic Sexuality*).[44] All of these themes were influential initially, but the latter two have been debunked as social constructions masquerading as psychiatry. Homosexuality as pathology is now considered to have been an expression of homophobia. *The Three Faces of Eve* inspired a film and a rush of professional as well as public interest, but the concept of multiple personality disorder is now considered to be the product of coaching by the mental health professional as much as disorder in the client, and the disorder itself, renamed dissociative identity disorder, is considered a manifestation of the ability to shut off from threatening reality and not mental illness.

Psychopathy has, however, thrived in the public and scientific imagination, even though it is not a recognized medical diagnosis (its nearest medical equivalent is antisocial personality disorder). Cleckley was a degenerationist, like many psychiatrists of the century before him. He believed that 'psychopaths' had brain abnormalities. Not everyone bought into the brain abnormality hypothesis. There were psychiatrists who accepted the principle that there were some people who offended against society repeatedly, but they thought that this was because of upbringing and not brain abnormality. They proposed the term 'sociopathy' as being preferable to psychopathy. Other people have since tried to maintain the distinction between these two terms,* but it has not been successful.

The persistence of the Cleckley reinvention of 'the psychopath' and its re-reinvention by his greatest contemporary exponent, the psychologist Robert Hare, can be attributed to two characteristics: the hiddenness of the psychopath and the so-called lack of empathy.

Cleckley's book was called *The Mask of Sanity*, and Hare's exposition of 'psychopathy', *The Snake in a Suit*. Both titles imply the same frisson of fear of what lies beneath the surface. Like spies, traitors, and terrorists, all of whom can legally be executed in many jurisdictions, the 'psychopath' is presented as a deceiver who lies in wait, hidden, only to pounce, like the great white shark, on its victim. Naturally, such people create disproportionate fear and therefore public attention. Like the effects of terrorism, the fear also has a unifying element. The common knowledge that people who are less than human exist as secret threats to any of us who might cross their path brings communities together in execration and shared horror.

Who is a psychopath?

The fear of the psychopath is exaggerated by the so-called lack of empathy of the psychopath. As noted several times already,

---

* An instance of what has been called 'labelling theory' – provide people with a term, and they will seek to find people to whom the term can be applied. Labelling theory failed as an explanation for mental disorder, not because it was wrong about this tendency but because of its presumption of 'secondary deviance', which suggested that the person so labelled also played up to the characteristics of the label. In fact, labels seem to have much more influence on the professionals who use and argue about them than on the clients or patients to whom they apply them. Much, I suppose, as the wren Troglodytes is indifferent as to whether it is called Troglodytes troglodytes in the South of England, Troglodytes indigenus in the North of England, or Troglodytes zetlandicus in the Shetlands.

empathy has become a confused concept, spanning what I have previously referred to as compassion (sometimes called sympathy), a functioning interbrain connection ('affective empathy'), an imaginative connection with others informed by shared or common knowledge ('cognitive empathy'), and repugnance to wounds, blood, or physical harm, whether to the self or others, with an associated impulse to alleviate the situation. I have already pointed out that men whose social behaviour is normally unimpeachable will lie, steal, rape,[*] assault, and murder other people in conditions of war. Otherwise normal people will also lash out at others, causing wounding or death, to protect a child, their property, or even their sexual identity.[†] Military drone pilots or artillerymen may carry out killings of people that are too remote to have an interbrain connection with them. Hunters stalk other mammals and hold their gory carcasses with pride to be photographed. Citizens may clamour for someone's execution or even go on to lynch them. There are other examples of extra-judicial killings, for example those carried out by militias as 'punishment' or by off-duty groups of policemen who are 'solving the problem' of roofless children in South American cities.

None of these actions lead to the people involved being termed 'psychopaths'. What does, according to Cleckley and later Hare and his co-workers, is some kind of fundamental

---

[*] Explanations of rape in war have generally focused on the assumption that this is a modern phenomenon, but historical evidence suggests that war and rape are ancient companions (Gaca, 2011), as Ovid's account of the rape of the Sabine women, referred to in Chapter 3, suggests. This kind of sexual exploitation was considered justified by the majority until the 18th century in Europe. Men and boys were regularly raped, as well as women.

[†] The term 'homophobic panic' used to be used as an explanation for assaults by male adolescents against men whom the adolescents perceived as attempting to seduce them (Bartlett, 2012).

deficit.* Confusingly, they are inconsistent about what the deficit is. It is variously argued to be a dimension of personality, an abnormal genome, or the consequence of structural changes in the brain.[45] Others have even suggested that 'psychopathy' is 'an alternative evolutionary brain development',[46] a scientific reformulation of the everyday idea that some people are 'inhuman'.

There is no doubt that some people are perceived as being callous or cruel by the majority, sometimes the overwhelming majority, of members of the society in which they live, that some offenders repeat their offences over and over without obvious gain,[47] and that some people hurt or kill others 'just for the fun of it', either for sexual arousal or just because they can.† A few

---

* Hare and Neumann (2008) discuss this in detail, rejecting Cleckley's assertion that 'the fundamental factor in psychopathy [is] an inability to participate in, or understand, the emotional aspects of humanity' (p.226). Having written that, Hare also said, in an interview for *The Telegraph*: 'It stuns me, as much as it did when I started 40 years ago, that it is possible to have people who are so emotionally disconnected that they can function as if other people are objects to be manipulated and destroyed without any concern' (Chivers, 2014). Hare and Neumann (2008) thought that psychopathy was more mixed: a single superordinate factor accounted for interpersonal problems (60%), affective detachment (82%), impulsive lifestyle (81%), and antisocial behaviour (60%) factors (the percentages of total variance of the factors loading on the superordinate factor are in parentheses).

† There is evidence that these behavioural dispositions might be set very early on in life. Psychopathy is not a diagnosis used in childhood. However, there have been several large follow-ups of children into adulthood that have focused on persistent offending in adults (Assink *et al.*, 2015), which is what 'psychopathy' is most often used to predict. Most of them uphold a suggestion first made by Kim-Cohen *et al.* (2005), based on their own follow-up of children born in Dunedin, New Zealand, that a small proportion of children – of the order of 5 per cent – do misbehave without consideration of others from an early age and the same children do go on to become repeat offenders long after almost everyone else has stopped offending (Zara and Farrington, 2016). It could be that this propensity to break the rules is due to upbringing, genetics (for example, less calculation of consequences as in attention deficit disorder or less anxiety

of these people have acquired lesions in their frontal lobes (although Hare argues that these 'secondary psychopaths' are not the same in their behaviour as the 'primary psychopaths' that he describes[48]). Hare's ideas have been so influential that they have become 'common knowledge' amongst forensic practitioners and lawyers who share the conviction that: monsters of depravity or cruelty exist;* their motives cannot be understood; their actions are not constrained by consideration of other people – in fact they appear to take pleasure in other people's pain; the only explanation can be that they have a kind of mental disorder; and the principal impairment resulting from this disorder is a lack of empathy. Looking back in history, this focus on psychological abnormality in the person seems to be recent, replacing earlier Christian ideas that people become evil only after they have been seduced by Satan. Satan

---

about them), or childhood trauma making these children into survivors at any cost (or perhaps a combination) (Farrington, 1989).

But there is no evidence that the same factors are responsible for this in every child. Nor what the effects of being an unpopular, uncontrolled child might be in later life. There is some evidence that being a bully is one step in this pathway, which suggests that persistent offenders might have discovered early in life that they are unable to gain their ends except by coercion or deception. Another is that life cauterizes these children's emotional responsiveness to fear (van Zonneveld *et al.*, 2017). The pathway to persistent offending does not apply to other people who would be called psychopaths because of repugnant, selfish behaviour: people like the television and radio presenter Jimmy Savile, who charmed responsible institutions into giving him privileged access to vulnerable people whom he abused sexually, or Ted Bundy, who had a promising political career and was the assistant director of the Seattle Crime Prevention Advisory Commission.

* An egregious example of this is a paper by Kiehl and Hoffman (2011, p.355), a psychologist with a particular interest in neuroimaging and a judge. In this paper, they write that 'Greek and Roman mythology is strewn with psychopaths, Medea being the most obvious. Psychopaths populate the Bible, at least the Old Testament, perhaps beginning with Cain. Psychopaths have appeared in a steady stream of literature from all cultures since humans first put pen to paper.' They go on to locate the first description of psychopathy by a certain Greek, Theophrastus, who referred to people who were 'unscrupulous'.

himself was invented by the early Christian Church possibly as a pre-emptive strike against earlier religions that believed in demons that could inhabit a person, changing them. To give this god-like power to evil was anathema to the Church but had been mankind's explanation for many bad things for millennia before that. We still enjoy and understand Goethe's *Faust*. After all, the role of Mephistopheles in that is no more than a literary account of an age-old belief that demons could take a person over, forcing them (or in Mephistopheles' case, seducing them) to do evil.*, †

Demons can be execrated, exorcised, aspersed, and sent back whence they came. It's not so easy to get rid of troubling people. One can execute people, of course, but that preserves their humanity, and even that might not abolish the imaginative connection that can be made with them and that can continue after their death. To break any possible connection with them, they need to be stripped of their humanity first. Modes of execution have sometimes been designed to do this. People have been flayed like animals, drawn and quartered like carcasses at the butchers, hung up on hooks like cuts of meat at the butchers, or spitted like fowl being made ready for roasting. These last two methods are both examples of 'impaling', a method of execution that I have already discussed.

---

* This idea has not quite gone. There are still people who attribute psychopathy to a lack of morality whilst also recognizing its connecting effect (Malka *et al.*, 2016), much like I am arguing that 'psychopathy' and its impugnment have a connecting effect.

† Other contemporary explanations also refer to personality, for example narcissistic personality disorder (Marissen, Deen, and Franken, 2011) and the 'dark triad' (Book, Visser, and Volk, 2015; Jonason *et al.*, 2012) of narcissism, Machiavellianism, and psychopathy. So-called narcissists, like psychopaths, are claimed to lack the ability to take others' perspectives and to be lacking empathy (Böckler *et al.*, 2017; Jonason and Krause, 2013), but they are also supposed to experience less contagious emotion (Czarna *et al.*, 2015).

Simply labelling someone as a psychopath may be enough to dehumanize them and even make their existence a kind of trick of fate. Cleckley discusses a well-to-do family whose ne'er-do-well son was a constant shame to them, who were reassured to be told that they need not take any responsibility for his conduct, as he was a psychopath. Jaspers, the famous existential philosopher, had a ne'er-do-well brother too, but Jaspers always tried to understand him and was grief-stricken when his brother killed himself after another failed venture. Doris Lessing's book *The Fifth Child*[49] describes a middle-class couple with four delightful children, all of them devoted to good works, whose fifth child is so antisocial in his conduct that they concluded (in a later book[50]) that he was an evolutionary throwback.

'Othering' the 'psychopath' as a monster, someone who is 'morally insane' to use Prichard's term, has many advantages for the in-group. For one thing, it suppresses our connection to them. That means that we are protected from contamination by those emotions that might otherwise shake up our 'common knowledge' that we are moral persons who would not stoop to such behaviour. The one disadvantage of this is that by cutting off our connection with them, and assuming that the other person has an inhuman motivation, we define that motivation as incomprehensible. That in the long run can make perpetrators more terrifying, less predictable, and harder to deal with.

Dangerous, severely abnormal personality disorder

Michael Stone was well known to the forensic psychiatry team in Kent, in the South East of England. He had a troubled upbringing, being placed in care where he was sexually and physically abused. He seems not to have been prepared to cope with life after care either, and he turned to heroin. He had already been shoplifting and stealing from childhood. He presented to the medium secure unit in which he had been previously detained and was assessed by the consultant. Mr Stone was not admitted, and, subsequently, three bodies were found nearby: a mother, Dr Russell, her daughter, Megan, aged six, and their dog, Lucy. Nearby was Dr Russell's other daughter, Josie, aged nine, still alive but with severe head injuries and not expected to live, although she did. She had no memory of the attack. The victims had been tied up with strips of a towel (they were all coming home from a swimming gala) and their heads were repeatedly struck with a hammer. Mr Stone was accused and convicted, but this conviction was quashed at appeal. He was subsequently tried again, after a fellow inmate claimed that he had heard Mr Stone confess and give details of the crimes. He was imprisoned rather than being given a hospital order.

Mr Stone had previous convictions and had also been diagnosed as a 'psychopath'.

The home secretary at the time, Jack Straw, was apparently outraged by the refusal to admit Mr Stone and announced that something would have to be done. A policy document (a 'green paper') duly appeared that referred to a new legal category of dangerous, severely abnormal personality disorder (DSPD). Judges were given new sentencing rules to apply to people with 'DSPD', and the government provided funding for new units to treat 'personality disorder'. Famous psychologists were recruited to spread the message that this was a great step forward – finally people with 'personality disorder' were not being neglected but were being given the treatment that they needed.

Little was made of the lack of evidence for a reliable diagnosis of personality disorder, for the value of treatment, or for the social harm of medicalizing deviant behaviour. What mattered was that these very dangerous people were being put away.

Myths about psychopathy and insights about connection

One of the many difficulties in analysing the term 'psychopathy' is that everyone who writes about it claims to know what it is, and yet those who do think that they know disagree with each other.[*] Another problem is that one nation's psychopaths are another nation's heroes.[†] But an even greater problem is the eroticization of famous people even if, or perhaps because, they have done evil things. Vlad III, or at least his reincarnation as the vampire Count Dracula, was portrayed as an almost irresistible seducer in Bram Stoker's novel, and his many cinematic and fictional characterizations since have been glazed with this same glamour (a term I used in Chapter 3).

Psychopathy has become a potent signifier in the common knowledge of the 21st century. Claiming to be a psychopath has become a route to successful authorship, but failing a 'psychopath test', if you are a convicted offender, increases the likely length of sentences by 150 per cent.[51]

---

[*] Fields (1996), for example, alludes to the Scottish psychiatrist Henderson's classification of 'psychopathy', which included: T. E. Lawrence as an example; Cleckley and Hare's degenerationist viewpoint; Duff's view that psychopaths are those without moral feeling; Smith's view that they are just people who take 'look out for number one' to its limit; and his own, that 'psychopaths' are weak-willed and therefore cannot inhibit their own 'self-regarding desires'.

[†] As an example of this, Adrian Axinte blogs on behalf of the Stanford University Romanian society about the veneration in Romania of Vlad III as a national hero: see https://web.stanford.edu/group/rsa/_content/_public/_htm/dracula shtml.

The othering manoeuvre

So what is common to all of the different usages of 'psychopath'? One is that the concept provides an explanation of behaviour that is contaminating. Like bloody wounds, food that has gone off, excreta, and, by metonymy, the smell or images of these things, there are some behaviours that we cannot allow ourselves to imagine us doing. They are so disgusting or so atrocious that even seriously imagining that we could do them makes us feel sick. We cannot get rid of the fact that these happenings occurred, but we can remove ourselves from their authors. We can disconnect from them and remove them from the species – human. In the past, we could say that the perpetrators were devilish, demonic, animals, beasts, degenerates, or monsters, but all of these categories have been vitiated by scientific scepticism. So it serves our purposes that we can say that they are 'psychopaths' and back this up with all of the pseudo-science and misapplication of neuroimaging[*] that gives this term scientific conviction.

If psychopaths existed, what would they be like?

In the 19th century, saying that someone was a psychopath, according to Koch, meant that they were a degenerate. In the 21st century, saying that someone is a psychopath still implies that they are defective – something is missing in their brain, a something that makes the rest of us more than animals. As I have already noted, different commentators allege that it is their soul, their capacity for empathy or their amygdala, depending on how each expert accounts for morality (I have already cited which experts make these claims). Being able to

---

[*] For a review, see Jalava and Maraun (2015).

connect with other people is common to all of these accounts. Of course, if we disconnect from someone, then they are not connected to us as much as we are not connected to them. So if, as I am alleging, our first instinct is to disconnect from anyone who outrages our morals, it is difficult for us to be sure whether it is they who are disconnected or us who has disconnected them.

Why do we connect to psychopathy?

As I have tried to show, there is little evidence that 'psychopath' is a useful psychological or psychiatric category. The main common feature of 'psychopaths' is that they have performed some action so tainted that 'common knowledge' is that they are abominable persons. The actions cover a wide range, may not be criminal, and may appear to have many motivations. And this continues to attract much scholarly activity. Of course, it does appear to explain a lot, but that is only because the 'common knowledge' is that atrocities can only be committed by atrocious people.

Despite this abomination of real-life monsters, fictional ones, or safely dead or captured ones, fascinate us. Hannibal Lecter, vampires, serial killers, cold-blooded Nazis, demons, and orcs populate some of our highest-grossing films. It is as if we need to measure ourselves against the inhuman.

What could we be testing? Compassion? Possibly, although we usually enjoy the annihilation of the monster at the end and our compassion for them is minimal. My own suggestion would be that we are testing our ability to connect to other people against the monster's disconnection from them. That we are not monsters ourselves but human beings. Experiencing horror vicariously makes us want to reach out and make human contact – more interbrain connections – to reassure ourselves that we can. There is nothing like watching a horror film with a partner to set up a romantic evening. So long as we can turn to a companion and share this interbrain connection, our humanity is reinforced by our brief sojourn with monsters.*

It may be that even the most vile actions do not make their perpetrator unable to make an interbrain connection, but we can imagine someone who cannot do so or someone who feels pleasure at another person's terror or rage at another person's fear.† I can suppose that many people could imagine feeling towards another person as we might towards a snake: having the category of psychopath in our imaginations reassures us that it could only be a temporary feeling and that we are, most of the time, in emotional and reciprocal contact with other human persons.

Internet connections

The internet provides greater connectivity between multiple, unrelated people (with internet access, which is a constantly growing percentage of the world's population) than we have ever known before, although none of its features are new. It has been possible to exchange communications at a distance – to connect to people far away – since the development of writing and, even before then, by messenger. But these methods were

---

* This may not be true for people who are socially isolated, who may be left angry or frustrated. Nor is it true for people who have some condition that impairs their ability to make an interbrain connection, who may feel compassion for the monster who is fundamentally alone.

† Paradoxical reactions that are associated with the works of the Marquis de Sade, who was writing, at least early on in his career, not about individuals but about the state, which might take satisfaction in the terror of its enemies or drive even harder during a rout when it sees the fear on the faces of an opposing force.

slow and throttled by the bandwidth of the medium. It has been possible to exchange emotions, too, by the use of images and emotive words, and that process was facilitated by the development of photography and film. But making images and exchanging them with targeted individuals is now routine. The internet has also incorporated telephony so that we can discuss with other people, broadcast to large groups, take questions, add images, and so on. Libraries have existed for a long time, too, but searching them required a classification system that was also a filter and the time and inconvenience of visiting them. Search engines potentially make much of the world wide web available and, for some hackers, much of what is on the internet too.

The internet is informative, but it is also a medium of exchange full of emotion,[52] but this is not corporeal emotion. It is not embodied. The svelte twenty-something person you think you might be befriending on your Facebook page, based on their posted image and their self-description, may, in fact, be a gaunt 80-year-old or an overweight eight-year-old. The face looking at you in the video chat is the face of someone seconds before. Even if you and they have an excellent bandwidth connection, it is their face milliseconds before. Emotional contagion occurs at the speed of light, not the speed of electronic transmission. Face-to-face, visual input is accompanied by sound, by gesture, by the smell of sweat, by the possibility of touch,* and by a context. So what is lacking in this vast network is an interbrain connection between its

---

* My wife and I have weekly chats with our son and his son, who is 20 months old (at the time that I write this). He has worked out where the camera is on his father's computer, and sometimes when we comment on one of his toys, he touches it to the camera, trying to pass it to us. He is still trying to make an interbrain connection with us, in which joint attention can be supplemented by shared handling of the object of the attention.

human participants. The emotions that are exchanged are not embodied ones but 'self-conscious ones' – emotions that arise from a person's narrative about themselves, their world, and their relationship to it.

On the other hand, the internet is the perfect medium for creating, sharing, and storing common knowledge. It supports localized 'common knowledges' or 'ideologies' readily, with social media splitting into camps or groups of friends who selectively share 'facts' that are congenial.

The absence of an interbrain connection means that being on the internet is being in the same state as someone – like the proverbial psychopath – who has inhibited their interbrain, like the soldier who is taken over by the fury of war confronted by enemies.* That people interact purely as a result of their 'common knowledge' connection on the internet, that they act 'psychopathically', does not mean that morality is suspended. Studies of so-called psychopaths have focused on repeat offenders whose morality cannot be expected to be the same as non-offenders, but even they have intact moral principles.[53] Moral philosophers do not, nowadays, consider that moral principles are wholly grounded in passions, *pace* Hume. Nor are people taken to be psychopaths found to be free of morally related emotions like resentment or indignation at being let down.[54]

Internet users do not entirely lose their memories of interbrain exchanges with the people they know and connect

---

* Recent research suggests that it is a testosterone surge that inhibits the interbrain connection (and reduces the bandwidth of the interbrain connection) (Bos *et al.*, 2016) reduces. It will be interesting to see whether the increasing number of female combatants experience the same loss of empathy as their male comrades – hearsay from the ancients – as well as the changing composition and behaviour of gangs – suggests that they do. Whether or not this too is brought about by a surge of testosterone will be an interesting study.

to online,* but as memories are non-reciprocal, and are not updated by interaction with an actual other, it is easy for them to become biased in favour of the internal narrative into which they are being incorporated.

Interactions can easily become more extreme online, perhaps because in actuality another person's expressions provide immediate feedback (if the interbrain connection is not cut off) that buffers emotional expression. Hatred may become more wild, but so may generosity.[†]

One of the most consistent findings in internet research is that unsatisfactory personal relationships – and therefore, as one might suppose, reduced interbrain connections – may increase dependence on the internet as a form of interpersonal connection but that, paradoxically, greater use of this form of connection as a substitute for real-world personal interactions increases the risk of pessimism and dissatisfaction with life.

The tension between our spontaneous interbrain connections with others with whom we have face-to-face interaction modulates our conscious appraisal of their motives, intentions, or beliefs, and vice versa. It is all too easy for connections that are only mediated through narrative, including those narratives that are shared on social media, to become unbalanced, as they refer to a world of imagination that might never have to stand the test of being enacted in the physical world.

Untrammelled interbrain connections, and the mobs and swarms that they enable, present their own challenges of being

---

* I referred to this remembered interaction as 'the cache' in a previous book (Tantam, 2009).

† Impulsivity is on some lists of 'psychopathic' characteristics, perhaps indicating that the fallacious concept of psychopathy does draw some of its characteristics from the more well-grounded neurodevelopmental attention deficit hyperactivity disorder.

ungoverned by rationality. Their subordination to a leader can also lead, if that leader has violent aims, to mob violence or swarm depredation. But the most permanent leaders are those who lead mobs vicariously, through an ideology or through terror that is sustained just as effectively through our theory-of-mind connectedness – that is, through our imagination – as it is through the immediacy of a physical crush of people around us.

The contagion of ideas and of self-conscious emotions presents society with as many problems as the contagion of bodily expressed emotions. The evolution of individuality is not something many readers of this book are likely to cast aside. But we need to recognize that we are now evolving again into a post-individual society in which people are connected through ideas and, sometimes, falsehoods. Interbrain connections are one corrective, but as people become more isolated, their interbrain connections weaken – a situation presaged in 1909 by E. M. Forster.[55]

Forster also anticipated what would happen to humanity's thirst for obedience if our interbrain connections withered: we would start to idealize the medium that enables our narrative connections with each other. As it is, the interbrain connections between us give us a sense of transcendence – or so I believe – that is grounded in the perception that each of us individually is but a shadow of something greater. If we believe that we are created in the image of a god, we might have a sense of godhead. If we belong to humanity, we might sense something frightening but inspiring that we call the human spirit. Or we may have a sense of family, or nature, or place. It seems to me that even if we ignore it, or even do not notice it, our interbrain connection to other people is fundamental to what it means to be human.

Final conclusions

Neither of the terms 'empathy' or 'psychopathy' are helpful in understanding human goodness or human evil, and I recommend that empathy is returned to the aesthetic theory from whence it came and that psychopathy joins 'masturbation insanity' in the nosological wastebasket.

People do act in terribly evil and inspiringly good ways. What makes this such a concern for all of us is that we want to increase good and reduce evil – although we cannot agree on how to do it, or sometimes even what good and evil are – but I have argued that human beings are truly social animals, connected not only in spirit through a culturally acquired shared or common knowledge about people (sometimes this is called 'theory of mind') but also via an innate connection provided by our brains, via specialized structures and networks that mediate nonverbal communication. This is prelingual, preverbal, and shared with other animals, including other primates. But rather than being an evolutionary relic, it has developed to a high degree in Homo sapiens. In fact, I suggest that it is this network that gives us the intuition of something beyond us, of transcendence, that is the foundation of religion and of our sense of meaningfulness and, ultimately, our humanity.

These two connections complement each other most of the time, but they occasionally work against each other, giving us the sense that we are creatures dogged by internal conflict – a paradigm that made Freud famous and has inspired psychotherapists ever since.

Denial of the interbrain connection's importance may be a consequence of the rise of individuality, which is only possible if we stress the agentive, autonomous aspect of human behaviour and not that aspect of ourselves that is best understood by being a unit in a super-organism or swarm.[*]

Notes

1. Resolution 217 of the hundred and eighty-third plenary meeting 10 December 1948 of the General Meeting of the United Nations, A Universal Declaration of Human Rights

2. Castano and Giner-Sorolla, 2006

3. Jolliffe and Farrington, 2011; Van Langen *et al.*, 2014

4. Gleditsch *et al.*, 2013

5. Vernot *et al.*, 2016

6. Hashikawa *et al.*, 2016

7. Cohen and Solomon, 2011

8. Goepner, 2016

9. Nowrasteh, 2016

10. Joffé, 2016

11. Vazansky, 2013

12. Breslau, Setodji, and Vaughan, 2016

13. Cacioppo *et al.*, 2016

14. Quoted in Strachan, 2014, p.191

15. Cicirelli, 2002

16. Asbrock and Fritsche, 2013; Pyszczynski, Solomon, and Greenberg, 2002

17. Colgan and Weeks, 2015; Walt, 1992

18. Sanderson, 2004

19. Vautier, 2009

20. Amiraux, 2013, p.794

21. McAlister and Wilczak, 2015

22. Saeri, Iyer, and Louis, 2015

23. Reed, 2015

24. Gibson and Hare, 2016

25. Malory, 1920

26. Malory, 1920, p.173

27. Crawley and Suarez, 2016

28. Malka *et al.*, 2016

---

[*] I have tried to show that there are dangers when either kind of connection dominates the other, reflected in the risks of submerging our individuality in a swarm or standing apart without sympathy for the fate of our fellow human beings. I have briefly touched on a third system, one based around the insula and anterior cingulate cortex, that is intimately related to the two networks that have been the main topic of this book. This system is principally an evaluative one that is linked to internal harm as well as to moral harm – it provides the link by which the words 'sickening' or 'nauseating' can be used of rotten food or morally reprehensible actions. This insula-based system evaluates communication itself, not what is being communicated. The latter has its own evaluative systems, which I have almost completely ignored. Most of the hypotheses about this kind of content evaluation seem to involve the amygdala, a relatively small and insignificant group of nuclei currently being given disproportionately great attention.

29. Skjelsbæk, 2012

30. Luo *et al.*, 2014

31. Jonas and Fritsche, 2013

32. Schindler, Reinhard, and Stahlberg, 2013

33. Kastenmüller *et al.*, 2013

34. Schimel, Wohl, and Williams, 2006

35. Rotter, 2011

36. Burke, Kosloff, and Landau, 2013

37. Chatard *et al.*, 2011

38. Cohen-Almagor, 2017

39. Eriksson, 2015

40. Tantam, 1984

41. Knecht, 1999

42. Vandevoorde and Le Borgne, 2015

43. Flannery, Modzeleski, and Kretschmar, 2013

44. Thingpen and Cleckley, 1992/1954

45. de Oliveira-Souza *et al.*, 2008

46. Boccardi *et al.*, 2011; Glenn, Kurzban, and Raine, 2011

47. Neumann, Hare, and Pardini, 2015

48. Hare and Neumann, 2008

49. Lessing, 1989

50. Lessing, 2000

51. Dutton and McNab, 2014; Dutton *et al.*, 2016; Hyatt and Black, 2004; Kiehl, 2014; Meloy, 2001; Ronson, 2012

52. Belk, 2016

53. Sinnott-Armstrong, 2014

54. Deigh, 2014

55. Forster, 1909

References

Aaltola, E. (2014). Affective empathy as core moral agency: Psychopathy, autism and reason revisited. *Philosophical Explorations, 17*(1), 76–92.

Ab Wahab, M. N., Nefti-Meziani, S., and Atyabi, A. (2015). A comprehensive review of swarm optimization algorithms. *PLoS ONE, 10*(5).

AbdulSabur, N. Y., Xu, Y., Liu, S., Chow, H. M., *et al.* (2014). Neural correlates and network connectivity underlying narrative production and comprehension: A combined fMRI and PET study. *Cortex, 57,* 107–127.

Abell, F., Happé, F., and Frith, U. (2000). Do triangles play tricks? Attribution of mental states to animated shapes in normal and abnormal development. *Cognitive Development, 15*(1), 1–16.

Abrahams, N., Mathews, S., Martin, L. J., Lombard, C., Nannan, N., and Jewkes, R. (2016). Gender differences in homicide of neonates, infants, and children under 5 y in South Africa: Results from the Cross-Sectional 2009 National Child Homicide Study. *PLoS Medicine, 13*(4).

Adams, D. B. (1979). Brain mechanisms for offense, defense, and submission. *Behavioral and Brain Sciences, 2*(2), 230–241.

Adolphs, R., Tranel, D., Damasio, H., and Damasio, A. (1994). Impaired recognition of emotion in facial expressions following bilateral damage to the human amygdala. *Nature, 372,* 669–672.

Aguirre, M. (2011). *An Outline of Propp's Model for the Study of Fairytales.* Madrid: The Northhanger Library Project.

Ainley, V., Maister, L., and Tsakiris, M. (2015). Heartfelt empathy? No association between interoceptive awareness, questionnaire measures of empathy, reading the mind in the eyes task or the director task. *Frontiers in Psychology, 6*, 554.

Aïte, A., Berthoz, A., Vidal, J., Roëll, M., *et al.* (2016). Taking a third-person perspective requires inhibitory control: Evidence from a developmental negative priming study. *Child Development, 87*(6), 1825–1840.

Alshamsi, A., Pianesi, F., Lepri, B., Pentland, A., and Rahwan, I. (2015). Beyond contagion: Reality mining reveals complex patterns of social influence. *PLoS ONE, 10*(8).

Amiraux, V. (2013). The 'illegal covering' saga: What's next? Sociological perspectives. *Social Identities, 19*(6), 794–806.

Amit, E., Hoeflin, C., Hamzah, N., and Fedorenko, E. (2017). An asymmetrical relationship between verbal and visual thinking: Converging evidence from behavior and fMRI. *Neuroimage, 152*, 619–627.

Andrés-Roqueta, C., Adrian, J. E., Clemente, R. A., and Katsos, N. (2013). Which are the best predictors of theory of mind delay in children with specific language impairment? *International Journal of Language and Communication Disorders, 48*(6), 726–737.

Ankony, R. (2011). A new strategy for America's war on terrorism. *Patrolling Magazine* (Winter), 56–57.

Anon. (2011). The Professor of Signs: 1. In K. Briggs (Ed.) *Folk Tales of Britain* (Vol. 1: Narratives, pp.254–256). London: Folio Society.

Anzieu, D. (1990). *The Psychic Envelope*. London: Karnac.

Ardizzi, M., Umiltà, M. A., Evangelista, V., Di Liscia, A., Ravera, R., and Gallese, V. (2016). Less empathic and more reactive: The different impact of childhood maltreatment on facial mimicry and vagal regulation. *PLoS ONE, 11*(9).

Arlet, M., Jubin, R., Masataka, N., and Lemasson, A. (2015). Grooming-at-a-distance by exchanging calls in non-human primates. *Biology Letters, 11*(10).

Armoudian, M. (2015). Constructing 'the others' during conflict: How journalism's norms and structures temper extreme portrayals. *International Journal of Press/Politics, 20*(3), 360–381.

Artelli, M. J., Deckro, R. F., Zalewski, D. J., Leach, S. E., and Perry, M. B. (2010). A control theory model of deployed soldiers' morale. *International Journal of Operational Research, 7*(1), 31–53.

Asbrock, F., and Fritsche, I. (2013). Authoritarian reactions to terrorist threat: Who is being threatened, the Me or the We? *International Journal of Psychology, 48*(1), 35–49.

Assink, M., van der Put, C. E., Hoeve, M., de Vries, S. L. A., Stams, G. J. J. M., and Oort, F. J. (2015). Risk factors for persistent delinquent behavior among juveniles: A meta-analytic review. *Clinical Psychology Review, 42*, 47–61.

Auerbach, E. (1974/1946). *Mimesis*. Princeton, NJ: Princeton University Press.

Austin, J. L., and Urmson, J. O. (1962). *How to do Things with Words: The William James Lectures Delivered at Harvard University in 1955*. London: Clarendon Press.

Avenanti, A., Candidi, M., and Urgesi, C. (2013). Vicarious motor activation during action perception: Beyond correlational evidence. *Frontiers in Human Neuroscience, 7*, 185.

Ayduk, O., and Kross, E. (2010). From a distance: Implications of spontaneous self-distancing for adaptive self-reflection. *Journal of Personality and Social Psychology, 98*(5), 809–829.

Azzam, T. I., Beaulieu, D. A., and Bugental, D. B. (2007). Anxiety and hostility to an 'outsider', as moderated by low perceived power. *Emotion, 7*(3), 660–667.

Badets, A., Koch, I., and Philipp, A. M. (2016). A review of ideomotor approaches to perception, cognition, action, and language: Advancing a cultural recycling hypothesis. *Psychological Research, 80*(1), 1–15.

Balconi, M., and Canavesio, Y. (2013). High-frequency rTMS improves facial mimicry and detection responses in an empathic emotional task. *Neuroscience, 236*, 12–20.

Banatvala, J. (2016). Thomas Dover: Doctor, privateer, and rescuer of Robinson Crusoe. *BMJ, 355*.

Banissy, M. J., and Ward, J. (2007). Mirror-touch synesthesia is linked with empathy. *Nature Neuroscience, 10*(7), 815–816.

Banks, J., and Bowman, N. D. (2016). Avatars are (sometimes) people too: Linguistic indicators of parasocial and social ties in player–avatar relationships. *New Media and Society, 18*(7), 1257–1276.

Bara, B. G., Ciaramidaro, A., Walter, H., and Adenzato, M. (2011). Intentional minds: A philosophical analysis of intention tested through fMRI experiments involving people with schizophrenia, people with autism, and healthy individuals. *Frontiers in Human Neuroscience, 5*, 7.

Baron-Cohen, S., Ashwin, E., Ashwin, C., Tavassoli, T., and Chakrabarti, B. (2009). Talent in autism: Hyper-systemizing, hyper-attention to detail and sensory hypersensitivity. *Philosophical Transactions of the Royal Society of London. Series B, Biological Sciences, 364*(1522), 1377–1383.

Baron-Cohen, S., Leslie, A., and Frith, U. (1985). Does the autistic child have a 'theory of mind'? *Cognition, 21*, 37–46.

Bartholomew, R. H. D. (2015). *A Colorful History of Popular Delusions*. Amherst, NY: Prometheus Books.

Bartlett, M. S., Littlewort, G. C., Frank, M. G., and Lee, K. (2014). Automatic decoding of facial movements reveals deceptive pain expressions. *Current Biology, 24*(7), 738–743.

Bartlett, P. (2012). Psychology, law, and murders of gay men: Responding to homosexual advances. *Law and Psychology, 9.*

Bartov, O. (2003). Seeking the Roots of Modern Genocide: On the Macro and Microhistory of Mass Murder. In R. Gellately, and B. Kiernan (Eds) *The Specter of Genocide: Mass Murder in Historical Perspective* (pp.75–96). Cambridge: Cambridge University Press.

Basabe, N., and Valencia, J. (2007). Culture of peace: Sociostructural dimensions, cultural values, and emotional climate. *Journal of Social Issues, 63*(2), 405–419.

Bastian, M., Lerique, S., Adam, V., Franklin, M. S., Schooler, J. W., and Sackur, J. (2017). Language facilitates introspection: Verbal mind-wandering has privileged access to consciousness. *Consciousness and Cognition, 49*, 86–97.

Bate, S., Bennetts, R., Parris, B. A., Bindemann, M., Udale, R., and Bussunt, A. (2015). Oxytocin increases bias, but not accuracy, in face recognition line-ups. *Social Cognitive and Affective Neuroscience, 10*(7), 1010–1014.

Batki, A., Baron-Cohen, S., Wheelwright, S., Connellan, J., and Ahluwalia, J. (2000). Is there an innate gaze module? Evidence from human neonates. *Infant Behavior and Development, 23*(2), 223–229.

Bauernfeind, A. L., de Sousa, A. A., Avasthi, T., Dobson, S. D., *et al.* (2013). A volumetric comparison of the insular cortex and its subregions in primates. *Journal of Human Evolution, 64*(4), 263–279.

Bauman, C. W., McGraw, A. P., Bartels, D. M., and Warren, C. (2014). Revisiting external validity: Concerns about trolley problems and other sacrificial dilemmas in moral psychology. *Social and Personality Psychology Compass, 8*(9), 536–554.

Baumeister, R. F. (1987). How the self became a problem: A psychological review of historical research. *Journal of Personality and Social Psychology, 52*(1), 163–176.

BBC News (2016). Islamic State militant 'executes own mother' in Raqqa. *BBC News.* Available at www.bbc.co.uk/news/world-middle-east-35260475, accessed on 23 August 2017.

Becchio, C., Pierno, A., Mari, M., Lusher, D., and Castiello, U. (2007). Motor contagion from gaze: The case of autism. *Brain, 130*(Pt 9), 2401–2411.

Becker, G. (1976). Altruism, egoism, and genetic fitness: Economics and sociobiology. *Journal of Economic Literature, 14*(3), 817–826.

Belk, R. (2016). Extended self and the digital world. *Current Opinion in Psychology, 10*, 50–54.

Benjamin, W. (1968). *Illuminations.* New York: Schocken Books, 1969.

Berdahl, A., Torney, C. J., Ioannou, C. C., Faria, J. J., and Couzin, I. D. (2013). Emergent sensing of complex environments by mobile animal groups. *Science, 339*(6119), 574–576.

Berry, J. W., Worthington, E. L., Jr., O'Connor, L. E., Parrott, L., 3rd, and Wade, N. G. (2005). Forgivingness, vengeful rumination, and affective traits. *Journal of Personality, 73*(1), 183–225.

Bershad, A. K., Weafer, J. J., Kirkpatrick, M. G., Wardle, M. C., Miller, M. A., and de Wit, H. (2016). Oxytocin receptor gene variation predicts subjective responses to MDMA. *Social Neuroscience, 11*(6), 592–599.

Bien, N., Roebroeck, A., Goebel, R., and Sack, A. T. (2009). The brain's intention to imitate: The neurobiology of intentional versus automatic imitation. *Cerebral Cortex, 19*(10), 2338–2351.

Bigelow, A. E., and Power, M. (2014). Effects of maternal responsiveness on infant responsiveness and behavior in the still-face task. *Infancy, 19*(6), 558–584.

Binmore, K. (2004). *Do Conventions Need to be Common Knowledge?* Available at http://else.econ.ucl.ac.uk/papers/uploaded/261.pdf, accessed on 23 August 2017.

Black, A., Jr. (1990). Jonestown – two faces of suicide: A Durkheimian analysis. *Suicide and Life-Threatening Behavior, 20*(4), 285–306.

Bleiker, R., Campbell, D., Hutchison, E., and Nicholson, X. (2013). The visual dehumanisation of refugees. *Australian Journal of Political Science, 48*(4), 398–416.

Bleske-Rechek, A., Nelson, L. A., Baker, J. P., Remiker, M. W., and Brandt, S. J. (2010). Evolution and the trolley problem: People save five over one unless the one is young, genetically related, or a romantic partner. *Journal of Social, Evolutionary, and Cultural Psychology, 4*(3), 115–127.

Blight, O., Renucci, M., Tirard, A., Orgeas, J., and Provost, E. (2010). A new colony structure of the invasive Argentine ant (Linepithema humile) in Southern Europe. *Biological Invasions, 12*(6), 1491–1497.

Boa, E. (2006). Global intimations: Cultural geography in Buddenbrooks, Tonio Kröger, and Der Tod in Venedig. *Oxford German Studies, 35*(1), 21–32.

Boccardi, M., Frisoni, G. B., Hare, R. D., Cavedo, E., *et al.* (2011). Cortex and amygdala morphology in psychopathy. *Psychiatry Research: Neuroimaging, 193*(2), 85–92.

Böckler, A., Hömke, P., and Sebanz, N. (2014). Invisible man: Exclusion from shared attention affects gaze behavior and self-reports. *Social Psychological and Personality Science, 5*(2), 140–148.

Böckler, A., Sharifi, M., Kanske, P., Dziobek, I., and Singer, T. (2017). Social decision making in narcissism: Reduced generosity and increased retaliation are driven by alterations in perspective-taking and anger. *Personality and Individual Differences, 104*, 1–7.

Böckler, A., van der Wel, R. P. R. D., and Welsh, T. N. (2014). Catching eyes: Effects of social and nonsocial cues on attention capture. *Psychological Science, 25*(3), 720–727.

Bohn, M., Call, J., and Tomasello, M. (2015). Communication about absent entities in great apes and human infants. *Cognition, 145*, 63–72.

Bonnefon, J.-F., Shariff, A., and Rahwan, I. (2016). The social dilemma of autonomous vehicles. *Science, 352*(6293), 1573.

Bonner, J. (2009). *The Social Amoebae: The Biology of Cellular Slime Molds*. Princeton, NJ: Princeton University Press.

Book, A., Visser, B. A., and Volk, A. A. (2015). Unpacking 'evil': Claiming the core of the Dark Triad. *Personality and Individual Differences, 73*, 29–38.

Boothby, E. J., Smith, L. K., Clark, M. S., and Bargh, J. A. (2016). Psychological distance moderates the amplification of shared experience. *Personality and Social Psychology Bulletin, 42*(10), 1431–1444.

Borch, C. (2012). *The Politics of Crowds: An Alternative History of Sociology*. Cambridge: Cambridge University Press.

Borch, C., and Knudsen, B. T. (2013). Postmodern crowds: Re-inventing crowd thinking. *Distinktion: Journal of Social Theory, 14*(2), 109–113.

Bos, P. A., Hofman, D., Hermans, E. J., Montoya, E. R., Baron-Cohen, S., and van Honk, J. (2016). Testosterone reduces functional connectivity during the 'Reading the Mind in the Eyes' test. *Psychoneuroendocrinology, 68*, 194–201.

Bos, P. A., Montoya, E. R., Hermans, E. J., Keysers, C., and van Honk, J. (2015). Oxytocin reduces neural activity in the pain circuitry when seeing pain in others. *Neuroimage, 113*, 217–224.

Bosch, O. J. (2013). Maternal aggression in rodents: Brain oxytocin and vasopressin mediate pup defence. *Philosophical Transactions of the Royal Society B: Biological Sciences, 368*(1631).

Boucher, O., Rouleau, I., Lassonde, M., Lepore, F., Bouthillier, A., and Nguyen, D. K. (2015). Social information processing following resection of the insular cortex. *Neuropsychologia, 71*, 1–10.

Bourdieu, P. (1994). *Raisons Pratique*. Paris: Seuil.

Bowlby, J. (1969). *Attachment and Loss*. London: Hogarth Press; Institute of Psycho-Analysis.

Braadbaart, L., de Grauw, H., Perrett, D. I., Waiter, G. D., and Williams, J. H. G. (2014). The shared neural basis of empathy and facial imitation accuracy. *Neuroimage, 84*, 367–375.

Braten, S. (Ed.) (1998). *Intersubjective Communication and Emotion in Early Infancy*. Cambridge: Cambridge University Press.

Brazelton, T. B., Tronick, E., Adamson, L., Als, H., and Wise, S. (1975). Early Mother–Infant Reciprocity. In M. O'Connor (Ed.) *Ciba Foundation Symposium, Volume 33* (pp.137–154). Amsterdam: Elsevier.

Brentano, F. (1973/1874). *Psychology from an Empirical Standpoint.* (Originally published as *Psychologie Vom Empirischen Standpunkt.*) London: Routledge.

Breslau, J., Setodji, C. M., and Vaughan, C. A. (2016). Is cohesion within military units associated with post-deployment behavioral and mental health outcomes? *Journal of Affective Disorders, 198,* 102–107.

Broad, K. D., Curley, J. P., and Keverne, E. B. (2006). Mother–infant bonding and the evolution of mammalian social relationships. *Philosophical Transactions of the Royal Society B: Biological Sciences, 361*(1476), 2199–2214.

Broom, M., Borries, C., and Koenig, A. (2004). Infanticide and infant defence by males: Modelling the conditions in primate multi-male groups. *Journal of Theoretical Biology, 231*(2), 261–270.

Brown, H. M., and Klein, P. D. (2011). Writing, Asperger syndrome and theory of mind. *Journal of Autism and Developmental Disorders, 41*(11), 1464–1474.

Bruner, J. (1976). Early Rule Structure: The Case of Peek-a-Boo. In R. Harre (Ed.) *Life Sentences* (pp.55–62). London: John Wiley.

Bruner, J. (1986). *Actual Minds, Possible Worlds.* Cambridge, MA: Harvard University Press.

Bruner, J., and Kalmar, D. (1998). Narrative and Metanarrative in the Construction of Self. In M. Ferrari and R. Sternberg (Eds) *Self-Awareness: Its Nature and Development* (pp.308–331). New York: Guilford Press.

Bryant, L., Coffey, A., Povinelli, D. J., and Pruett, Jr., J. R. (2013). Theory of mind experience sampling in typical adults. *Consciousness and Cognition, 22*(3), 697–707.

Bryant, R. A., Hung, L., Guastella, A. J., and Mitchell, P. B. (2012). Oxytocin as a moderator of hypnotizability. *Psychoneuroendocrinology, 37*(1), 162–166.

Buber, M. (1958). *I and Thou.* New York: Scribner and Sons.

Buber, M. (2003). *I and Thou: A New Translation, with a Prologue and Notes.* New York: Touchstone.

Bucchioni, G., Lelard, T., Ahmaidi, S., Godefroy, O., Krystkowiak, P., and Mouras, H. (2015). Do we feel the same empathy for loved and hated peers? *PLoS ONE, 10*(5).

Buchanan, T. W., Bagley, S. L., Stansfield, R. B., and Preston, S. D. (2012). The empathic, physiological resonance of stress. *Society for Neuroscience, 7*(2), 191–201.

Bumann, D., and Krause, J. (1993). Front individuals lead in shoals of three-spined sticklebacks (Gasterosteus aculeatus) and juvenile roach (Rutilus rutilus). *Behavior, 125*, 189–198.

Burgoon, J. K., and Hale, J. L. (1984). The fundamental topoi of relational communication. *Communication Monographs, 51*(3), 193–214.

Burke, B. L., Kosloff, S., and Landau, M. J. (2013). Death goes to the polls: A meta-analysis of mortality salience effects on political attitudes. *Political Psychology, 34*(2), 183–200.

Burklund, L. J., Eisenberger, N. I., and Lieberman, M. D. (2007). The face of rejection: Rejection sensitivity moderates dorsal anterior cingulate activity to disapproving facial expressions. *Social Neuroscience, 2*(3–4), 238–253.

Burnett-Zeigler, I., Pfeiffer, P., Zivin, K., Glass, J., *et al.* (2012). Psychotherapy utilization for acute depression within the veterans affairs health care system. *Psychological Services, 9*(4), 325–335.

Cacioppo, J. T., Cacioppo, S., Adler, A. B., Lester, P. B., *et al.* (2016). The cultural context of loneliness: Risk factors in active duty soldiers. *Journal of Social and Clinical Psychology, 35*(10), 865–882.

Caillois, R. (2001). *Man, Play, and Games*. Champaign, IL: University of Illinois Press.

Call, J., and Tomasello, M. (1999). A nonverbal false belief task: The performance of children and great apes. *Child Development, 70*(2), 381–395.

Calvo, M. G., Gutiérrez-García, A., Avero, P., and Lundqvist, D. (2013). Attentional mechanisms in judging genuine and fake smiles: Eye-movement patterns. *Emotion, 13*(4), 792–802.

Campbell, M. W., and de Waal, F. B. M. (2011). Ingroup-outgroup bias in contagious yawning by chimpanzees supports link to empathy. *PLoS ONE, 6*(4).

Campbell, R. (2006). Altruism in Auguste Comte and Ayn Rand. *The Journal of Ayn Rand Studies, 7*(2).

Campbell, S. B., Leezenbaum, N. B., Schmidt, E. N., Day, T. N., and Brownell, C. A. (2015). Concern for another's distress in toddlers at high and low genetic risk for autism spectrum disorder. *Journal of Autism and Developmental Disorders, 45*(11), 3594–3605.

Canetti, E. (1984). *Crowds and Power*. New York: Straus and Giroux.

Cannon-Bowers, J. A., and Salas, E. (1998). *Making Decisions Under Stress: Implications for Individual and Team Training*. Washington, DC: American Psychological Association.

Cao, Y., Contreras-Huerta, L. S., McFadyen, J., and Cunnington, R. (2015). Racial bias in neural response to others' pain is reduced with other-race contact. *Cortex, 70*, 68–78.

Capellini, R., Sacchi, S., Ricciardelli, P., and Actis-Grosso, R. (2016). Social threat and motor resonance: When a menacing outgroup delays motor response. *Frontiers in Psychology, 7,* 1697.

Carney, J., Wlodarski, R., and Dunbar, R. (2014). Inference or enaction? The impact of genre on the narrative processing of other minds. *PLoS ONE, 9*(12).

Carter, C. S. (2013). Oxytocin pathways and the evolution of human behavior. *Annual Review of Psychology, 65,* 17–39.

Caspar, E. A., Christensen, J. F., Cleeremans, A., and Haggard, P. (2016). Coercion changes the sense of agency in the human brain. *Current Biology, 26*(5), 585–592.

Castano, E., and Giner-Sorolla, R. (2006). Not quite human: Infrahumanization in response to collective responsibility for intergroup killing. *Journal of Personality and Social Psychology, 90*(5), 804–818.

Castelli, L., and Tomelleri, S. (2008). Contextual effects on prejudiced attitudes: When the presence of others leads to more egalitarian responses. *Journal of Experimental Social Psychology, 44*(3), 679–686.

Cauda, F., Geminiani, G. C., and Vercelli, A. (2014). Evolutionary appearance of von Economo's neurons in the mammalian cerebral cortex. *Frontiers in Human Neuroscience, 8,* 104.

Čehajić, S., Brown, R., and González, R. (2009). What do I care? Perceived ingroup responsibility and dehumanization as predictors of empathy felt for the victim group. *Group Processes and Intergroup Relations, 12*(6), 715–729.

Cela-Conde, C. J., Garcia-Prieto, J., Ramasco, J. J., Mirasso, C. R., et al. (2013). Dynamics of brain networks in the aesthetic appreciation. *Proceedings of the National Academy of Sciences, 110 Suppl 2,* 10454–10461.

Çelik, A. B., Bilali, R., and Iqbal, Y. (2016). Patterns of 'othering' in Turkey: A study of ethnic, ideological, and sectarian polarisation. *South European Society and Politics, 22*(2), 217–238.

Chabon, M. (2012). What to make of Finnegans Wake? *The New York Review of Books,* 1–5.

Chakraborty, T., Srinivasan, S., Ganguly, N., Mukherjee, A., and Bhowmick, S. (2016). Permanence and community structure in complex networks. *ACM Transactions on Knowledge Discovery from Data, 11*(2).

Chartrand, T. L., and Lakin, J. L. (2013). The antecedents and consequences of human behavioral mimicry. *Annual Review of Psychology, 64,* 285–308.

Chatard, A., Selimbegović, L., Konan, P. N., Arndt, J., et al. (2011). Terror management in times of war: Mortality salience effects on self-esteem and governmental and army support. *Journal of Peace Research, 48*(2), 225–234.

Chatel-Goldman, J., Congedo, M., Jutten, C., and Schwartz, J.-L. (2014). Touch increases autonomic coupling between romantic partners. *Frontiers in Behavioral Neuroscience, 8*, 95.

Chatel-Goldman, J., Schwartz, J.-L., Jutten, C., and Congedo, M. (2013). Nonlocal mind from the perspective of social cognition. *Frontiers in Human Neuroscience, 7*, 107.

Cheetham, M., Pedroni, A., Antley, A., Slater, M., and Jäncke, L. (2009). Virtual Milgram: Empathic concern or personal distress? Evidence from functional MRI and dispositional measures. *Frontiers in Human Neuroscience, 3*, 29.

Cheng, X., Li, X., and Hu, Y. (2015). Synchronous brain activity during cooperative exchange depends on gender of partner: A fNIRS-based hyperscanning study. *Human Brain Mapping, 36*(6), 2039–2048.

Chevalier, N., Dauvier, B., and Blaye, A. (2017). From prioritizing objects to prioritizing cues: A developmental shift for cognitive control. *Developmental Science*. doi:10.1111/desc.12534.

Chiarella, S. S., and Poulin-Dubois, D. (2015). 'Aren't you supposed to be sad?' Infants do not treat a stoic person as an unreliable emoter. *Infant Behavior and Development, 38*, 57–66.

Chisholm, J. D., Chapman, C. S., Amm, M., Bischof, W. F., Smilek, D., and Kingstone, A. (2014). A cognitive ethology study of first- and third-person perspectives. *PLoS ONE, 9*(3).

Chivers, T. (2014). Born to kill? How to spot a psychopath. *The Telegraph*, 6 April.

Christov-Moore, L., Simpson, E. A., Coudé, G., Grigaityte, K., Iacoboni, M., and Ferrari, P. F. (2014). Empathy: Gender effects in brain and behavior. *Neuroscience and Biobehavioral Reviews, 46*(P4), 604–627.

Christov-Moore, L., Sugiyama, T., Grigaityte, K., and Iacoboni, M. (2016). Increasing generosity by disrupting prefrontal cortex. *Social Neuroscience, 12*(2), 174–181.

Chung, Y. S., Barch, D., and Strube, M. (2014). A meta-analysis of mentalizing impairments in adults with schizophrenia and autism spectrum disorder. *Schizophrenia Bulletin, 40*(3), 602–616.

Chwe, M. (2001). *Rational Ritual*. Princeton: Princeton University Press.

Cialdini, R. B., Schaller, M., Houlihan, D., and Arps, K. (1987). Empathy-based helping: Is it selflessly or selfishly motivated? *Journal of Personality and Social Psychology, 52*(4), 749–758.

Cicirelli, V. G. (2002). Fear of death in older adults: Predictions from terror management theory. *Journals of Gerontology, Series B, Psychological Sciences and Social Sciences, 57*(4), P358–P366.

Cikara, M. (2015). Intergroup Schadenfreude: Motivating participation in collective violence. *Current Opinion in Behavioral Sciences, 3*, 12–17.

Cikara, M., Bruneau, E., Van Bavel, J. J., and Saxe, R. (2014). Their pain gives us pleasure: How intergroup dynamics shape empathic failures and counter-empathic responses. *Journal of Experimental Social Psychology, 55*, 110–125.

Cikara, M., Bruneau, E. G., and Saxe, R. R. (2011). Us and them: Intergroup failures of empathy. *Current Directions in Psychological Science, 20*(3), 149–153.

Cimpian, A. (2016). The privileged status of category representations in early development. *Child Development Perspectives, 10*(2), 99–104.

Clair, R. P., Rastogi, R., Blatchley, E. R., Clawson, R. A., Erdmann, C., and Lee, S. (2016). Extended narrative empathy: Poly-narratives and the practice of open defecation. *Communication Theory, 26*(4), 469–488.

Clancy, P. M. (1999). The socialization of affect in Japanese mother–child conversation. *Journal of Pragmatics, 31*(11), 1397–1421.

Cleckley, H. (2011/1957). *The Caricature of Love: A Discussion of Social, Psychiatric, and Literary Manifestations of Pathologic Sexuality*. Otto, NC: Red Pill Press.

Cocking, C. (2013). Crowd flight in response to police dispersal techniques: A momentary lapse of reason? *Journal of Investigative Psychology and Offender Profiling, 10*(2), 219–236.

Cocking, C., Drury, J., and Reicher, S. (2009). The psychology of crowd behaviour in emergency evacuations: Results from two interview studies and implications for the Fire and Rescue Services. *The Irish Journal of Psychology, 30*(1–2), 59–73.

Coeckelbergh, M. (2016). Is it wrong to kick a robot? Towards a relational and critical robot ethics and beyond. *Frontiers in Artificial Intelligence and Applications, 290*, 7–8.

Cohen, E., Ivenshitz, M., Amor-Baroukh, V., Greenberger, V., and Segal, M. (2008). Determinants of spontaneous activity in networks of cultured hippocampus. *Brain Research, 1235*, 21–30.

Cohen, F., and Solomon, S. (2011). The politics of mortal terror. *Current Directions in Psychological Science, 20*(5), 316–320.

Cohen, S. (1973). *Folk Devils and Moral Panics*. St Albans: Paladin.

Cohen-Almagor, R. (2017). Jihad online: How do terrorists use the internet? *Advances in Intelligent Systems and Computing, 503*, 55–66.

Coleman, S. (2007). *Popular Delusions: How Social Conformity Molds Society and Politics*. Amherst, NY: Cambria Press.

Colgan, J. D., and Weeks, J. L. P. (2015). Revolution, personalist dictatorships, and international conflict. *International Organization, 69*(1), 163–194.

Colle, L., Baron-Cohen, S., Wheelwright, S., and van der Lely, H. K. J. (2008). Narrative discourse in adults with high-functioning autism or Asperger syndrome. *Journal of Autism and Developmental Disorders, 38*(1), 28–40.

Collet, C., Di Rienzo, F., El Hoyek, N., and Guillot, A. (2013). Autonomic nervous system correlates in movement observation and motor imagery. *Frontiers in Human Neuroscience, 7,* 415.

Colonnesi, C., Zijlstra, B. J. H., van der Zande, A., and Bögels, S. M. (2012). Coordination of gaze, facial expressions and vocalizations of early infant communication with mother and father. *Infant Behavior and Development, 35*(3), 523–532.

Comte, A. (1973/1851). *Containing the General View of Positivism and Introductory Principles: Volume 1* (Trans.: Bridges, J. H.). New York: Burt Franklin.

Constable, G. W. A., Rogers, T., McKane, A. J., and Tarnita, C. E. (2016). Demographic noise can reverse the direction of deterministic selection. *Proceedings of the National Academy of Sciences, 113*(32), E4745–E4754.

Cooley, C. (1902). *Human Nature and the Social Order.* New York: Scribner's.

Coppola, M., and Brentari, D. (2014). From iconic handshapes to grammatical contrasts: Longitudinal evidence from a child homesigner. *Frontiers in Psychology, 5,* 830.

Corballis, M. C. (2015). What's left in language? Beyond the classical model. *Annals of the New York Academy of Sciences, 1359*(1), 14–29.

Corballis, M. C. (2017). Language evolution: A changing perspective. *Trends in Cognitive Sciences, 21*(4), 229–236.

Cowan, D. G., Vanman, E. J., and Nielsen, M. (2014). Motivated empathy: The mechanics of the empathic gaze. *Cognition and Emotion, 28*(8), 1522–1530.

Crawley, D., and Suarez, R. (2016). Empathy, social dominance orientation, mortality salience, and perceptions of a criminal defendant. *SAGE Open, 6*(1).

Creed, R. S., Denny-Brown, J. C., Eccles, J., Liddell, E., and Sherrington, C. (1938). *Reflex Activity of the Spinal Cord.* Oxford: Clarendon Press.

Crespi, B. J., and Yanega, D. (1995). The definition of eusociality. *Behavioral Ecology, 6*(1), 109–115.

Croft, D. P., Johnstone, R. A., Ellis, S., Nattrass, S., *et al.* (2017). Reproductive conflict and the evolution of menopause in killer whales. *Current Biology, 27*(2), 298–304.

Crone, D. L., and Laham, S. M. (2017). Utilitarian preferences or action preferences? De-confounding action and moral code in sacrificial dilemmas. *Personality and Individual Differences, 104,* 476–481.

Cross, H., and Harlow, H. (1965). Prolonged and progressive effects of partial isolation on the behaviour of macaque monkeys. *Journal of Experimental Research in Personality, 1*, 39–49.

Cross, K. A., and Iacoboni, M. (2014). Neural systems for preparatory control of imitation. *Philosophical Transactions of the Royal Society B: Biological Sciences, 369*(1644). doi:10.1098/rstb.2013.0176

Croy, I., Bojanowski, V., and Hummel, T. (2013). Men without a sense of smell exhibit a strongly reduced number of sexual relationships, women exhibit reduced partnership security: A reanalysis of previously published data. *Biological Psychology, 92*(2), 292–294.

Cummins, F. (2014). Voice, (inter-)subjectivity, and real time recurrent interaction. *Frontiers in Psychology, 5*, 760.

Cunningham, S. J., Vergunst, F., Macrae, C. N., and Turk, D. J. (2013). Exploring early self-referential memory effects through ownership. *British Journal of Developmental Psychology, 31*(3), 289–301.

Cwir, D., Carr, P. B., Walton, G. M., and Spencer, S. J. (2011). Your heart makes my heart move: Cues of social connectedness cause shared emotions and physiological states among strangers. *Journal of Experimental Social Psychology, 47*(3), 661–664.

Czarna, A. Z., Wróbel, M., Dufner, M., and Zeigler-Hill, V. (2015). Narcissism and emotional contagion: Do narcissists 'catch' the emotions of others? *Social Psychological and Personality Science, 6*(3), 318–324.

Dalsklev, M., and Kunst, J. R. (2015). The effect of disgust-eliciting media portrayals on outgroup dehumanization and support of deportation in a Norwegian sample. *International Journal of Intercultural Relations, 47*, 28–40.

Darwin, C. (1989/1874). *The Voyage of the Beagle*. Harmondsworth: Penguin Classics.

Dastur, F. (2008). Phenomenology and pathology of hatred. *Confrontations Psychiatriques, 47*, 8–19.

Daum, M. M., Gampe, A., Wronski, C., and Attig, M. (2016). Effects of movement distance, duration, velocity, and type on action prediction in 12-month-olds. *Infant Behavior and Development, 43*, 75–84.

Dawkins, R. (1976). *The Selfish Gene*. Oxford: Oxford University Press.

De Coster, L., Verschuere, B., Goubert, L., Tsakiris, M., and Brass, M. (2013). I suffer more from your pain when you act like me: Being imitated enhances affective responses to seeing someone else in pain. *Cognitive, Affective and Behavioral Neuroscience, 13*(3), 519–532.

De Dreu, C. K. W., Greer, L. L., Van Kleef, G. A., Shalvi, S., and Handgraaf, M. J. J. (2011). Oxytocin promotes human ethnocentrism. *Proceedings of the National Academy of Sciences, 108*(4), 1262–1266.

de Oliveira-Souza, R., Hare, R. D., Bramati, I. E., Garrido, G. J., *et al.* (2008). Psychopathy as a disorder of the moral brain: Fronto-temporo-limbic grey matter reductions demonstrated by voxel-based morphometry. *Neuroimage, 40*(3), 1202–1213.

De Villiers, J. G., and De Villiers, P. A. (2014). The role of language in theory of mind development. *Topics in Language Disorders, 34*(4), 313–328.

de Waal, F. B. M. (2012). The antiquity of empathy. *Science, 336*(6083), 874–876.

de Waal, F. B. M., and Preston, S. D. (2017). Mammalian empathy: Behavioural manifestations and neural basis. *Nature Reviews Neuroscience* (advance online publication). doi:10.1038/nrn.2017.72

Decety, J. (2014). The neuroevolution of empathy and caring for others: Why it matters for morality. *Research and Perspectives in Neurosciences, 21*, 127–151.

Decety, J. (2015). The neural pathways, development and functions of empathy. *Current Opinion in Behavioral Sciences, 3*, 1–6.

Decety, J., and Lamm, C. (2007). The role of the right temporoparietal junction in social interaction: How low-level computational processes contribute to meta-cognition. *The Neuroscientist, 13*(6), 580–593.

Decety, J., and Moriguchi, Y. (2007). The empathic brain and its dysfunction in psychiatric populations: Implications for intervention across different clinical conditions. *BioPsychoSocial Medicine, 1*, 22.

Deffa, O. J. (2016). The impact of homogeneity on intra-group cohesion: A macro-level comparison of minority communities in a Western diaspora. *Journal of Multilingual and Multicultural Development, 37*(4), 343–356.

Deigh, J. (2014). Psychopathic Resentment. In T. Schramme (Ed.) *Being Amoral: Psychopathy and Moral Incapacity* (pp.209–226). Cambridge, MA: MIT Press.

Dein, S., and Littlewood, R. (2005). Apocalyptic suicide: From a pathological to an escathological interpretation. *International Journal of Social Psychiatry, 51*(3), 198–210.

DeLay, S. (2016). The toiling lily: Narrative life, responsibility, and the ontological ground of self-deception. *Phenomenology and the Cognitive Sciences, 15*(1), 103–116.

Derrida, J. (1988/1972). Signature Event Context. In G. Graf (Ed.) *Limited Inc* (pp.1–24). Evanston, IL: Northwestern University Press.

Di Paolo, E. A., and De Jaegher, H. (2012). The interactive brain hypothesis. *Frontiers in Human Neuroscience, 6*, 163.

Diener, E., Lusk, R., DeFour, D., and Flax, R. (1980). Deindividuation: Effects of group size, density, number of observers, and group member similarity on self-consciousness and disinhibited behavior. *Journal of Personality and Social Psychology, 39*(3), 449–459.

Dixon, T. (2008). *The Invention of Altruism: Making Moral Meanings in Victorian Britain.* Oxford: Oxford University Press.

Dodell-Feder, D., Lincoln, S. H., Coulson, J. P., and Hooker, C. I. (2013). Using fiction to assess mental state understanding: A new task for assessing theory of mind in adults. *PLoS ONE, 8*(11).

Doherty, M. J. (2006). The development of mentalistic gaze understanding. *Infant and Child Development, 15*(2), 179–186.

Doi, H., and Shinohara, K. (2012). Electrophysiological responses in mothers to their own and unfamiliar child's gaze information. *Brain and Cognition, 80*(2), 266–276.

Doom, J. R., Vanzomeren-Dohm, A. A., and Simpson, J. A. (2016). Early unpredictability predicts increased adolescent externalizing behaviors and substance use: A life history perspective. *Development and Psychopathology, 28*(4), 1505–1516.

Doucet, S., Soussignan, R., Sagot, P., and Schaal, B. (2009). The secretion of Areolar (Montgomery's) glands from lactating women elicits selective, unconditional responses in neonates. *PLoS ONE, 4*(10).

Du Preez, J., Sundin, J., Wessely, S., and Fear, N. T. (2011). Unit cohesion and mental health in the UK armed forces. *Occupational Medicine, 62*(1), 47–53.

Dubas, J. S., Heijkoop, M., and van Aken, M. A. G. (2009). A preliminary investigation of parent-progeny olfactory recognition and parental investment. *Human Nature, 20*(1), 80–92.

Duffy, K. A., and Chartrand, T. L. (2015). Mimicry: Causes and consequences. *Current Opinion in Behavioral Sciences, 3*, 112–116.

Duke, A. A., and Bègue, L. (2015). The drunk utilitarian: Blood alcohol concentration predicts utilitarian responses in moral dilemmas. *Cognition, 134*, 121–127.

Dullstein, M. (2013). Direct perception and simulation: Stein's account of empathy. *Review of Philosophy and Psychology, 4*(2), 333–350.

Dumas, G., Nadel, J., Soussignan, R., Martinerie, J., and Garnero, L. (2010). Inter-brain synchronization during social interaction. *PLoS ONE, 5*(8).

Dumont, B., Boissy, A., Achard, C., Sibbald, A. M., and Erhard, H. W. (2005). Consistency of animal order in spontaneous group movements allows the measurement of leadership in a group of grazing heifers. *Applied Animal Behaviour Science, 95*(1–2), 55–66.

Dunbar, R. I., Baron, R., Frangou, A., Pearce, E., *et al.* (2012). Social laughter is correlated with an elevated pain threshold. *Proceedings. Biological Sciences/The Royal Society, 279*(1731), 1161–1167.

Dunbar, R. I. M. (2004). Gossip in evolutionary perspective. *Review of General Psychology, 8*(2), 100–110.

Durkheim, E. (1915/1912). *The Elementary Forms of Religious Life.* London: George Allen and Unwin.

Durkheim, E. (1970). *Suicide: A Study in Sociology* (Trans.: Simpson, G.). London: Routledge and Kegan Paul.

Durkheim, E. (1984). *The Division of Labour in Society.* London: Macmillan.

Dutton, K., and McNab, A. (2014). *The Good Psychopath's Guide to Success.* London: Transworld Publishers.

Dutton, K., McNab, A., and Murray, R. (2016). *Sorted! The Good Psychopath's Guide to Bossing Your Life.* London: Penguin.

Echterhoff, G., Higgins, E. T., and Levine, J. M. (2009). Shared reality: Experiencing commonality with others' inner states about the world. *Perspectives on Psychological Science, 4*(5), 496–521.

Eckmann, J. P., Jacobi, S., Marom, S., Moses, E., and Zbinden, C. (2008). Leader neurons in population bursts of 2D living neural networks. *New Journal of Physics, 10.*

Edele, A., Dziobek, I., and Keller, M. (2013). Explaining altruistic sharing in the dictator game: The role of affective empathy, cognitive empathy, and justice sensitivity. *Learning and Individual Differences, 24*, 96–102.

Einwohner, R. L. (2014). Authorities and uncertainties: Applying lessons from the study of Jewish resistance during the Holocaust to the Milgram legacy. *Journal of Social Issues, 70*(3), 531–543.

Eisenberg, N., Fabes, R., and Spinrad, T. L. (2006). Prosocial Development. In W. Damon, and R. Lerner (Eds) *Handbook of Child Psychology* (6th ed.) (pp.646–718). Chichester: Wiley.

Eisenberger, N. I. (2012). The pain of social disconnection: Examining the shared neural underpinnings of physical and social pain. *Nature Reviews, Neuroscience, 13*(6), 421–434.

Eliastam, J. (2016). Interrupting separateness, disrupting comfort: An autoethnographic account of lived religion, ubuntu and spatial justice. *HTS Teologiese Studies/Theological Studies, 72*(1).

Eres, R., and Molenberghs, P. (2013). The influence of group membership on the neural correlates involved in empathy. *Frontiers in Human Neuroscience*, April.

Eres, R., Decety, J., Louis, W. R., and Molenberghs, P. (2015). Individual differences in local gray matter density are associated with differences in affective and cognitive empathy. *Neuroimage, 117*, 305–310.

Eriksson, A. (2015). *Punishing the Other: The Social Production of Immorality Revisited*. Abingdon: Routledge.

Ernst, U. R., Van Hiel, M. B., Depuydt, G., Boerjan, B., De Loof, A., and Schoofs, L. (2015). Epigenetics and locust life phase transitions. *Journal of Experimental Biology, 218*(1), 88–99.

Eskine, K. J., Kacinik, N. A., and Prinz, J. J. (2011). A bad taste in the mouth. *Psychological Science, 22*(3), 295–299.

Fairbairn, C. E., Sayette, M. A., Aalen, O. O., and Frigessi, A. (2015). Alcohol and emotional contagion: An examination of the spreading of smiles in male and female drinking groups. *Clinical Psychological Science, 3*(5), 686–701.

Faivre, N., Berthet, V., and Kouider, S. (2012). Nonconscious influences from emotional faces: A comparison of visual crowding, masking, and continuous flash suppression. *Frontiers in Psychology, 3*, 129.

Fanti, K. A., Kyranides, M. N., and Panayiotou, G. (2017). Facial reactions to violent and comedy films: Association with callous–unemotional traits and impulsive aggression. *Cognition and Emotion, 31*(2), 209–224.

Farrington, D. P. (1989). Early predictors of adolescent aggression and adult violence. *Violence and Victims, 4*(2), 79–100.

Farroni, T., Massaccesi, S., Menon, E., and Johnson, M. H. (2007). Direct gaze modulates face recognition in young infants. *Cognition, 102*(3), 396–404.

Fatfouta, R., Gerlach, T. M., Schröder-Abé, M., and Merkl, A. (2015). Narcissism and lack of interpersonal forgiveness: The mediating role of state anger, state rumination, and state empathy. *Personality and Individual Differences, 75*, 36–40.

Fawcett, C., and Tunçgenç, B. (2017). Infants' use of movement synchrony to infer social affiliation in others. *Journal of Experimental Child Psychology, 160*, 127–136.

Federico, C. M., Ekstrom, P., Tagar, M. R., and Williams, A. L. (2016). Epistemic motivation and the structure of moral intuition: Dispositional need for closure as a predictor of individualizing and binding morality. *European Journal of Personality, 30*(3), 227–239.

Fehr, E., and Camerer, C. F. (2007). Social neuroeconomics: The neural circuitry of social preferences. *Trends in Cognitive Sciences, 11*(10), 419–427.

Feldman, R., Magori-Cohen, R., Galili, G., Singer, M., and Louzoun, Y. (2011). Mother and infant coordinate heart rhythms through episodes of interaction synchrony. *Infant Behavior and Development, 34*(4), 569–577.

Feng, C., Li, Z., Feng, X., Wang, L., Tian, T., and Luo, Y. J. (2016). Social hierarchy modulates neural responses of empathy for pain. *Social Cognitive and Affective Neuroscience, 11*(3), 485–495.

Fernández, C. (2013). Mindful storytellers: Emerging pragmatics and theory of mind development. *First Language, 33*(1), 20–46.

Fessler, D. M. T., and Holbrook, C. (2014). Marching into battle: Synchronized walking diminishes the conceptualized formidability of an antagonist in men. *Biology Letters, 10*(8).

Festinger, L., Pepitone, A., and Newcomb, T. (1952). Some consequences of de-individuation in a group. *The Journal of Abnormal and Social Psychology, 47*(S2), 382–389.

Fields, L. (1996). Psychopathy, other-regarding moral beliefs, and responsibility. *Philosophy, Psychiatry, and Psychology, 3*(4), 261–277.

Figueiredo, B., Pacheco, A., Costa, R., Conde, A., and Teixeira, C. (2010). Mother's anxiety and depression during the third pregnancy trimester and neonate's mother versus stranger's face/voice visual preference. *Early Human Development, 86*(8), 479–485.

Finis, J., Enticott, P. G., Pollok, B., Munchau, A., Schnitzler, A., and Fitzgerald, P. B. (2013). Repetitive transcranial magnetic stimulation of the supplementary motor area induces echophenomena. *Cortex, 49*(7), 1978–1982.

Fischer, A. H., Becker, D., and Veenstra, L. (2012). Emotional mimicry in social context: The case of disgust and pride. *Frontiers in Psychology, 3*, 475.

Fisher, W. (1987). *Human Communication as Narration: Toward a Philosophy of Reason, Value, and Action.* Columbia: University of South Carolina Press.

Fisher, W. R. (1984). Narration as a human communication paradigm: The case of public moral argument. *Communication Monographs, 51*(1), 1–22.

Fiske, A. P. (1992). The four elementary forms of sociality: Framework for a unified theory of social relations. *Psychological Review, 99*(4), 689–723.

Fitch, W. T., and Braccini, S. N. (2013). Primate laterality and the biology and evolution of human handedness: A review and synthesis. *Annals of the New York Academy of Sciences, 1288*, 70–85.

Flannery, D. J., Modzeleski, W., and Kretschmar, J. M. (2013). Violence and school shootings. *Current Psychiatry Reports, 15*(1).

Flinders, M. (2012). Debating demonization: In defence of politics, politicians and political science. *Contemporary Politics, 18*(3), 355–366.

Flinders, M., and Wood, M. (2015). From folk devils to folk heroes: Rethinking the theory of moral panics. *Deviant Behavior, 36*(8), 640–656.

Florian, V., Mikulincer, M., and Hirschberger, G. (2001). An existentialist view on mortality salience effects: Personal hardiness, death-thought accessibility, and cultural worldview defence. *British Journal of Social Psychology, 40*(3), 437–453.

Foot, P. (1967). The problem of abortion and the doctrine of the double effect in virtues and vices. *Oxford Review, 5*, 1–7.

Foroni, F., and Semin, G. (2011). When does mimicry affect evaluative judgment? *Emotion, 11*(3), 687–690.

Forster, E. M. (1909). The machine stops. *Oxford and Cambridge Review.*

Forster, E. M. (1910). *Howards End.* London: Hodder and Stoughton.

Foster, K. R., and Ratnieks, F. L. W. (2005). A new eusocial vertebrate? *Trends in Ecology and Evolution, 20*(7), 363–364.

Franchak, J. M., Heeger, D. J., Hasson, U., and Adolph, K. E. (2016). Free viewing gaze behavior in infants and adults. *Infancy, 21*(3), 262–287.

Frankopan, P. (2015). *The Silk Roads.* London: Bloomsbury.

Frederick, R. (2015). News feature: The search for what sets humans apart. *Proceedings of the National Academy of Sciences of the United States of America, 112*(2), 299–301.

Freud, S. (1913). *The Interpretation of Dreams.* New York: The Macmillan Company.

Freud, S. (1922). *Group Psychology and the Analysis of the Ego.* London: Hogarth Press.

Freud, S. (1955/1912). *Totem and Taboo, Volume 13.* London: Hogarth Press.

Freud, S. (1992/1900). *The Interpretation of Dreams.* London: Penguin.

Fridland, E., and Moore, R. (2015). Imitation reconsidered. *Philosophical Psychology, 28*(6), 856–880.

Friedman, R. S., and Arndt, J. (2005). Reexploring the connection between terror management theory and dissonance theory. *Personality and Social Psychology Bulletin, 31*(9), 1217–1225.

Frischen, A., Bayliss, A. P., and Tipper, S. P. (2007). Gaze cueing of attention: Visual attention, social cognition, and individual differences. *Psychological Bulletin, 133*, 694–724.

Frith, C. D., and Frith, U. (2011). Mechanisms of social cognition. *Annual Review of Psychology, 63*(1), 287–313.

Froese, T., and Fuchs, T. (2012). The extended body: A case study in the neurophenomenology of social interaction. *Phenomenology and the Cognitive Sciences, 11*(2), 205–235.

Fusaroli, R., Gangopadhyay, N., and Tylén, K. (2014). The dialogically extended mind: Language as skilful intersubjective engagement. *Cognitive Systems Research, 29–30*(1), 31–39.

Fussell, S. R., and Krauss, R. M. (1991). Accuracy and bias in estimates of others' knowledge. *European Journal of Social Psychology, 21*(5), 445–454.

Gaca, K. L. (2011). Girls, Women, and the Significance of Sexual Violence in Ancient Warfare. In E. D. Heineman (Ed.) *Sexual Violence in Conflict Zones: From the Ancient World to the Era of Human Rights* (pp.73–88). Philadelphia, PA: University of Pennsylvania Press.

Galinsky, A. D., Rucker, D. D., and Magee, J. C. (2016). Power and perspective-taking: A critical examination. *Journal of Experimental Social Psychology, 67*, 91–92.

Gallagher, S. (2014). In your face: Transcendence in embodied interaction. *Frontiers in Human Neuroscience, 8*, 495.

Gallagher, S., and Varga, S. (2015). Social cognition and psychopathology: A critical overview. *World Psychiatry, 14*(1), 5–14.

Gallese, V. (2007). Before and below 'theory of mind': Embodied simulation and the neural correlates of social cognition. *Philosophical Transactions of the Royal Society B: Biological Sciences, 362*(1480), 659–669.

Galton, F. (1907). Vox populi. *Nature, 75*(1949), 450.

Gamannossi, B. A., and Pinto, G. (2014). Theory of mind and language of mind in narratives: Developmental trends from kindergarten to primary school. *First Language, 34*(3), 262–272.

Gangopadhyay, N., and Miyahara, K. (2015). Perception and the problem of access to other minds. *Philosophical Psychology, 28*(5), 695–714.

Gauchou, H. L., Rensink, R. A., and Fels, S. (2012). Expression of nonconscious knowledge via ideomotor actions. *Consciousness and Cognition, 21*(2), 976–982.

Gellately, R. (2001). *Backing Hitler: Consent and Coercion in Nazi Germany.* Oxford: Oxford University Press.

Georgescu, A. L., Kuzmanovic, B., Santos, N. S., Tepest, R., *et al.* (2014). Perceiving nonverbal behavior: Neural correlates of processing movement fluency and contingency in dyadic interactions. *Human Brain Mapping, 35*(4), 1362–1378.

Georgescu, A. L., Kuzmanovic, B., Schilbach, L., Tepest, R., *et al.* (2013). Neural correlates of 'social gaze' processing in high-functioning autism under systematic variation of gaze duration. *NeuroImage: Clinical, 3*, 340–351.

Giannitelli, M., Xavier, J., François, A., Bodeau, N., *et al.* (2015). Facial, vocal and cross-modal emotion processing in early-onset schizophrenia spectrum disorders. *Schizophrenia Research, 168*(1–2), 252–259.

Gibson, T., and Hare, C. (2016). Moral epistemology and ideological conflict in American political behavior. *Social Science Quarterly, 97*(5), 1157–1173.

Gigone, D. H. R. (1993). The common knowledge effect: Information sharing and group judgment. *Journal of Personality and Social Psychology, 65*(5), 959–974.

Gilbert, C. D., and Li, W. (2013). Top-down influences on visual processing. *Nature Reviews Neuroscience, 14*(5), 350–363.

Gilead, M., Katzir, M., Eyal, T., and Liberman, N. (2016). Neural correlates of processing 'self-conscious' vs. 'basic' emotions. *Neuropsychologia, 81*, 207–218.

Giner-Sorolla, R., Leidner, B., and Castano, E. (2011). Dehumanization, Demonization, and Morality Shifting. In M. A. Hogg, and D. L. Blaylock (Eds) *Extremism and the Psychology of Uncertainty* (pp.165–182). Chichester: Wiley-Blackwell.

Ginsburg, H. J., Pollman, V. A., and Wauson, M. S. (1977). An ethological analysis of nonverbal inhibitors of aggressive behavior in male elementary school children. *Developmental Psychology, 13*(4), 417–418.

Gladwell, M. (2000). *The Tipping Point: How Little Things Can Make a Big Difference.* London: Little, Brown.

Gleditsch, N. P., Pinker, S., Thayer, B. A., Levy, J. S., and Thompson, W. R. (2013). The forum: The decline of war. *International Studies Review, 15*(3), 396–419.

Gleichgerrcht, E., Torralva, T., Rattazzi, A., Marenco, V., Roca, M., and Manes, F. (2012). Selective impairment of cognitive empathy for moral judgment in adults with high functioning autism. *Social Cognitive and Affective Neuroscience, 8*(7), 780–788.

Glenn, A. L., Kurzban, R., and Raine, A. (2011). Evolutionary theory and psychopathy. *Aggression and Violent Behavior, 16*, 371–380.

Glover, V. (2007). The effects of maternal anxiety or stress during pregnancy on the fetus and the long-term development of the child. *Nutrition and Health, 19*(1–2), 61–62.

Godman, M. (2013). Why we do things together: The social motivation for joint action. *Philosophical Psychology, 26*(4), 588–603.

Goepner, E. (2016). Measuring the effectiveness of America's war on terror. *Parameters, 46*(1), 107–120.

Gold, D. (2015). The politics of emotion: A case study of the Israeli-Palestinian conflict. *Israel Studies Review, 30*(2), 113–129.

Goldie, P. (2012). *The Mess Inside: Narrative, Emotion, and the Mind.* Oxford: Oxford University Press.

Golding, W. (1954). *Lord of the Flies.* London: Faber and Faber.

Goller, A. I., Richards, K., Novak, S., and Ward, J. (2013). Mirror-touch synaesthesia in the phantom limbs of amputees. *Cortex, 49*(1), 243–251.

Gonzalez-Liencres, C., Shamay-Tsoory, S. G., and Brüne, M. (2013). Towards a neuroscience of empathy: Ontogeny, phylogeny, brain mechanisms, context and psychopathology. *Neuroscience and Biobehavioral Reviews, 37*(8), 1537–1548.

González-Pardo, A., Palero, F., and Camacho, D. (2014). Micro and macro lemmings simulations based on ants colonies. *Lecture Notes in Computer Science (including subseries Lecture Notes in Artificial Intelligence and Lecture Notes in Bioinformatics), 8602,* 337–348.

Goode, E., and Nachman, B.-Y. (2009). *Moral Panics.* Chichester: Wiley-Blackwell.

Gordin, S. (2003). *The Purple Cow.* New York: Portfolio.

Gredebäck, G., Fikke, L., and Melinder, A. (2010). The development of joint visual attention: A longitudinal study of gaze following during interactions with mothers and strangers. *Developmental Science, 13*(6), 839–848.

Greene, J. D., Nystrom, L. E., Engell, A. D., Darley, J. M., and Cohen, J. D. (2004). The neural bases of cognitive conflict and control in moral judgment. *Neuron, 44*(2), 389–400.

Gregory, R., Cheng, H., Rupp, H. A., Sengelaub, D. R., and Heiman, J. R. (2015). Oxytocin increases VTA activation to infant and sexual stimuli in nulliparous and postpartum women. *Hormones and Behavior, 69,* 82–88.

Guibourdenche, J., Fournier, T., Malassine, A., and Evain-Brion, D. (2009). Development and hormonal functions of the human placenta. *Folia Histochem Cytobiol, 47*(5), S35–40.

Gutsell, J. N., and Inzlicht, M. (2010). Empathy constrained: Prejudice predicts reduced mental simulation of actions during observation of outgroups. *Journal of Experimental Social Psychology, 46*(5), 841–845.

Gvirsman, S. D., Huesmann, L. R., Dubow, E. F., Landau, S. F., Boxer, P., and Shikaki, K. (2016). The longitudinal effects of chronic mediated exposure to political violence on ideological beliefs about political conflicts among youths. *Political Communication, 33*(1), 98–117.

Haas, B. W., Filkowski, M. M., Cochran, R. N., Denison, L., *et al.* (2016). Epigenetic modification of OXT and human sociability. *Proceedings of the National Academy of Sciences, 113*(27), E3816–E3823.

Hacker, P. M. S. (2013). *The Intellectual Powers.* Oxford: Wiley Blackwell.

Halpern, J. (1987). Using reasoning about knowledge to analyse distributed systems. *Annual Review of Computer Science, 2,* 37–68.

Ham, M. I., Bettencourt, L. M., McDaniel, F. D., and Gross, G. W. (2008). Spontaneous coordinated activity in cultured networks: Analysis of multiple ignition sites, primary circuits, and burst phase delay distributions. *Journal of Computational Neuroscience, 24*(3), 346–357.

Hamilton, A. F. D. C. (2015). The neurocognitive mechanisms of imitation. *Current Opinion in Behavioral Sciences, 3,* 63–67.

Hamlin, J. K. (2014). The Origins of Human Morality: Complex Socio-Moral Evaluations by Preverbal Infants. In J. Decety, and Y. Christen (Eds) *New Frontiers in Social Neuroscience* (pp.165–188). Cham: Springer International Publishing.

Happé, F., and Conway, J. R. (2016). Recent progress in understanding skills and impairments in social cognition. *Current Opinion in Pediatrics, 28*(6), 736–742.

Hare, R. D., and Neumann, C. S. (2008). Psychopathy as a clinical and empirical construct. *Annual Review of Clinical Psychology, 4*, 217–246.

Hari, R., Bourguignon, M., Piitulainen, H., Smeds, E., De Tiège, X., and Jousmäki, V. (2014). Human primary motor cortex is both activated and stabilized during observation of other person's phasic motor actions. *Philosophical Transactions of the Royal Society B: Biological Sciences, 369*(1644).

Harper, S. (2014). Framing the Philpotts: Anti-welfarism and the British newspaper reporting of the Derby house fire verdict. *International Journal of Media and Cultural Politics, 10*(1), 83–98.

Hashikawa, K., Hashikawa, Y., Falkner, A., and Lin, D. (2016). The neural circuits of mating and fighting in male mice. *Current Opinion in Neurobiology, 38*, 27–37.

Haslam, N., Kashima, Y., Loughnan, S., Shi, J., and Suitner, C. (2008). Subhuman, inhuman, and superhuman: Contrasting humans with nonhumans in three cultures. *Social Cognition, 26*(2), 248–258.

Haslam, N., and Loughnan, S. (2014). Dehumanization and infrahumanization. *Annual Review of Psychology, 65*(1), 399–423.

Hatfield, E., Cacioppo, J., and Rapson, R. (1994). *Emotional Contagion.* Cambridge: Cambridge University Press.

Hayasaki, E. (2015). This doctor knows exactly how you feel. *Pacific Standard.* Available at https://psmag.com/social-justice/is-mirror-touch-synesthesia-a-superpower-or-a-curse, accessed on 24 August 2017.

Hecht, E. E., Patterson, R., and Barbey, A. K. (2012). What can other animals tell us about human social cognition? An evolutionary perspective on reflective and reflexive processing. *Frontiers in Human Neuroscience, 6*, 224.

Heerey, E. A., Keltner, D., and Capps, L. M. (2003). Making sense of self-conscious emotion: Linking theory of mind and emotion in children with autism. *Emotion, 3*(4), 394–400.

Heidegger, M. (1962/1927). *Being and Time.* New York: Harper and Row.

Hein, G., Engelmann, J. B., Vollberg, M. C., and Tobler, P. N. (2015). How learning shapes the empathic brain. *Proceedings of the National Academy of Sciences of the United States of America, 113*(1), 80–85.

Hellmann, J. K., Reddon, A. R., Ligocki, I. Y., O'Connor, C. M., *et al.* (2015). Group response to social perturbation: Impacts of isotocin and the social landscape. *Animal Behaviour, 105*, 55–62.

Henderson, D. K. (1939). *Psychopathic States*. New York: WW Norton and Co.

Hennig, H. (2014). Synchronization in human musical rhythms and mutually interacting complex systems. *Proceedings of the National Academy of Sciences of the United States of America, 111*(36), 12974–12979.

Henricks, T. (2016). Reason and rationalization: A theory of modern play. *American Journal of Play, 8*(3), 287–325.

Herodotus. (2003). *Histories*. Harmondsworth: Penguin.

Herschbach, M. (2015). Direct social perception and dual process theories of mindreading. *Consciousness and Cognition, 36*, 483–497.

Heyes, C. (2014). False belief in infancy: A fresh look. *Developmental Science, 17*(5), 647–659.

Hillier, B., and Hanson, J. E. (1984). *The Social Logic of Space*. Cambridge: Cambridge University Press.

Hirsh, J. B., and Kang, S. K. (2016). Mechanisms of identity conflict: Uncertainty, anxiety, and the behavioral inhibition system. *Personality and Social Psychology Review, 20*(3), 223–244.

Hobson, R. P. (2002). *The Cradle of Thought*. London: Macmillan.

Hodson, G., and Costello, K. (2007). Interpersonal disgust, ideological orientations, and dehumanization as predictors of intergroup attitudes. *Psychological Science, 18*(8), 691–698.

Hoehl, S., and Striano, T. (2010). The development of emotional face and eye gaze processing. *Developmental Science, 13*(6), 813–825.

Hofman, D., Bos, P. A., Schutter, D. J. L. G., and van Honk, J. (2012). Fairness modulates non-conscious facial mimicry in women. *Proceedings of the Royal Society B: Biological Sciences, 279*(1742), 3535–3539.

Holbrook, C., Izuma, K., Deblieck, C., Fessler, D. M. T., and Iacoboni, M. (2016). Neuromodulation of group prejudice and religious belief. *Social Cognitive and Affective Neuroscience, 11*(3), 387–394.

Holland, E., Wolf, E. B., Looser, C., and Cuddy, A. (2017). Visual attention to powerful postures: People avert their gaze from nonverbal dominance displays. *Journal of Experimental Social Psychology, 68*, 60–67.

Hollingshead, R. (1970/1851). Introduction. In A. Schopenhauer (Ed.) *Essays and Aphorisms*. London: Penguin Classics.

Hopkins, N., Reicher, S. D., Khan, S. S., Tewari, S., Srinivasan, N., and Stevenson, C. (2016). Explaining effervescence: Investigating the relationship between shared social identity and positive experience in crowds. *Cognition and Emotion, 30*(1), 20–32.

Hoyle, F. (1959). *The Black Cloud.* London: Penguin Classics.

Hrdy, S. B. (2016). Variable postpartum responsiveness among humans and other primates with 'cooperative breeding': A comparative and evolutionary perspective. *Hormones and Behavior, 77,* 272–283.

Huebner, B. (2014). *Macrocognition.* New York: Oxford University Press.

Hume, D. (1978). *A Treatise of Human Nature, Second Volume.* Oxford: Clarendon Press.

Hume, D. (1999). *An Enquiry Concerning Human Understanding and Concerning the Principles of Morals.* Oxford: Oxford University Press.

Hume, D., and Flew, A. (1988). *An Enquiry Concerning Human Understanding.* La Salle, IL: Open Court.

Husserl, E. (1970). *The Crisis of European Sciences and Transcendental Phenomenology: An Introduction to Phenomenological Philosophy* (Trans. with an introduction: Carr, D.). Evanston: Northwestern University Press.

Hutcherson, C. A., Montaser-Kouhsari, L., Woodward, J., and Rangel, A. (2015). Emotional and utilitarian appraisals of moral dilemmas are encoded in separate areas and integrated in ventromedial prefrontal cortex. *Journal of Neuroscience, 35*(36), 12593–12605.

Hyatt, C. S., and Black, S. J. (2004). *The Psychopath's Notebook: In Four Parts.* Tempe, AZ: Falcon Press.

Hysek, C. M., Schmid, Y., Simmler, L. D., Domes, G., *et al.* (2014). MDMA enhances emotional empathy and prosocial behavior. *Social Cognitive and Affective Neuroscience, 9*(11), 1645–1652.

Iatridis, T. (2013). Occupational status differences in attributions of uniquely human emotions. *British Journal of Social Psychology, 52*(3), 431–449.

Ihl, C., and Bowyer, R. T. (2011). Leadership in mixed-sex groups of muskoxen during the snow-free season. *Journal of Mammalogy, 92*(4), 819–827.

Immordino-Yang, M. H., Yang, X.-F., and Damasio, H. (2014). Correlations between social-emotional feelings and anterior insula activity are independent from visceral states but influenced by culture. *Frontiers in Human Neuroscience, 8,* 728.

Inagaki, T. K., and Eisenberger, N. I. (2012). Neural correlates of giving support to a loved one. *Psychosomatic Medicine, 74*(1), 3–7.

Ivie, R. L., and Giner, O. (2015). *Hunt the Devil.* Tuscaloosa, AL: University of Alabama Press.

Jablonka, E., Ginsburg, S., and Dor, D. (2012). The co-evolution of language and emotions. *Philosophical Transactions of the Royal Society B: Biological Sciences, 367*(1599), 2152–2159.

Jackson, F. (1982). Epiphenomenal qualia. *Philosophical Quarterly, 32,* 127–136.

Jacobs, A., Sueur, C., Deneubourg, J. L., and Petit, O. (2011). Social network influences decision making during collective movements in brown lemurs (Eulemur fulvus fulvus). *International Journal of Primatology, 32*(3), 721–736.

Jalava, J. G. S., and Maraun, M. (2015). *The Myth of the Born Criminal: Psychopathy, Neurobiology, and the Creation of the Modern Degenerate.* Buffalo, NY: University of Toronto Press.

Jankowiak-Siuda, K., Rymarczyk, K., Żurawski, Ł., Jednoróg, K., and Marchewka, A. (2015). Physical attractiveness and sex as modulatory factors of empathic brain responses to pain. *Frontiers in Behavioral Neuroscience, 9,* 236.

Jankowski, K. F., and Takahashi, H. (2014). Cognitive neuroscience of social emotions and implications for psychopathology: Examining embarrassment, guilt, envy, and schadenfreude. *Psychiatry and Clinical Neurosciences, 68*(5), 319–336.

Jetten, J., and Hornsey, M. J. (2014). Deviance and dissent in groups. *Annual Review of Psychology, 65*(1), 461–485.

Jeurissen, D., Sack, A. T., Roebroeck, A., Russ, B. E., and Pascual-Leone, A. (2014). TMS affects moral judgment, showing the role of DLPFC and TPJ in cognitive and emotional processing. *Frontiers in Neuroscience, 8,* 18.

Jiang, J., Dai, B., Peng, D., Zhu, C., Liu, L., and Lu, C. (2012). Neural synchronization during face-to-face communication. *The Journal of Neuroscience, 32*(45), 16064–16069.

Joffé, G. (2016). Global jihad and foreign fighters. *Small Wars and Insurgencies, 27*(5), 800–816.

Jolliffe, D., and Farrington, D. P. (2011). Is low empathy related to bullying after controlling for individual and social background variables? *Journal of Adolescence, 34*(1), 59–71.

Jonas, E., and Fritsche, I. (2013). Destined to die but not to wage war: How existential threat can contribute to escalation or de-escalation of violent intergroup conflict. *American Psychologist, 68*(7), 543–558.

Jonas, E., Greenberg, J., and Frey, D. (2003). Connecting terror management and dissonance theory: Evidence that mortality salience increases the preference for supporting information after decisions. *Personality and Social Psychology Bulletin, 29*(9), 1181–1189.

Jonason, P. K., and Krause, L. (2013). The emotional deficits associated with the Dark Triad traits: Cognitive empathy, affective empathy, and alexithymia. *Personality and Individual Differences, 55*(5), 532–537.

Jonason, P. K., Webster, G. D., Schmitt, D. P., Li, N. P., and Crysel, L. (2012). The antihero in popular culture: Life history theory and the dark triad personality traits. *Review of General Psychology, 16*(2), 192–199.

Jure, R., Pogonza, R., and Rapin, I. (2016). Autism spectrum disorders (ASD) in blind children: Very high prevalence, potentially better outlook. *Journal of Autism and Developmental Disorders, 46*(3), 749–759.

Kagan, J., and Snidman, N. (1999). Early childhood predictors of adult anxiety disorders. *Biological Psychiatry, 46*(11), 1536–1541.

Kaiser, J., Davey, G. C. L., Parkhouse, T., Meeres, J., and Scott, R. B. (2016). Emotional facial activation induced by unconsciously perceived dynamic facial expressions. *International Journal of Psychophysiology, 110*, 207–211.

Kao, A. B., and Couzin, I. D. (2014). Decision accuracy in complex environments is often maximized by small group sizes. *Proceedings of the Royal Society B: Biological Sciences, 281*(1784), 20133305.

Kaplan, J. T., Gimbel, S. I., and Harris, S. (2016). Neural correlates of maintaining one's political beliefs in the face of counterevidence. *Scientific Reports, 6*, 39589.

Kastenmüller, A., Greitemeyer, T., Hindocha, N., Tattersall, A. J., and Fischer, P. (2013). Disaster threat and justice sensitivity: A terror management perspective. *Journal of Applied Social Psychology, 43*(10), 2100–2106.

Keith, A. (1948). *A New Theory of Human Evolution.* London: Watts and Co.

Keller, A., and Malaspina, D. (2013). Hidden consequences of olfactory dysfunction: A patient report series. *BMC Ear, Nose and Throat Disorders, 13*(1), 8.

Kendon, A. (1967). Some functions of gaze direction in social interaction. *Acta Psychologica, 32*, 1–25.

Kent, P., Awadia, A., Zhao, L., Ensan, D., *et al.* (2016). Effects of intranasal and peripheral oxytocin or gastrin-releasing peptide administration on social interaction and corticosterone levels in rats. *Psychoneuroendocrinology, 64*, 123–130.

Ketelaars, M. P., Jansonius, K., Cuperus, J., and Verhoeven, L. (2016). Narrative competence in children with pragmatic language impairment: A longitudinal study. *International Journal of Language and Communication Disorders, 51*(2), 162–173.

Khalid, S., Deska, J. C., and Hugenberg, K. (2016). The eyes are the windows to the mind: Direct eye gaze triggers the ascription of others' minds. *Personality and Social Psychology Bulletin, 42*(12), 1666–1677.

Kiehl, K. A. (2014). *The Psychopath Whisperer: Inside the Minds of Those Without a Conscience.* London: Oneworld.

Kiehl, K. A., and Hoffman, M. B. (2011). The criminal psychopath: History, neuroscience, treatment, and economics. *Jurimetrics, 51,* 355–397.

Kiernan, B. (2008). *The Pol Pot Regime.* New Haven, CT: Yale University Press.

Kim, S., Fonagy, P., Koos, O., Dorsett, K., and Strathearn, L. (2014). Maternal oxytocin response predicts mother-to-infant gaze. *Brain Research, 1580,* 133–142.

Kim-Cohen, J., Arseneault, L., Caspi, A., Tomas, M. P., Taylor, A., and Moffitt, T. E. (2005). Validity of DSM-IV conduct disorder in 4½–5-year-old children: A longitudinal epidemiological study. *American Journal of Psychiatry, 162*(6), 1108–1117.

Kirkpatrick, M. G., Lee, R., Wardle, M. C., Jacob, S., and de Wit, H. (2014). Effects of MDMA and intranasal oxytocin on social and emotional processing. *Neuropsychopharmacology, 39*(7), 1654–1663.

Kiryukhin, D. (2016). Russia and Ukraine: The clash of conservative projects. *European Politics and Society, 17*(4), 438–452.

Kisilevsky, B. S., Hains, S. M., Lee, K., Xie, X., *et al.* (2003). Effects of experience on fetal voice recognition. *Psychological Science, 14*(3), 220–224.

Kissi, E. (2003). Genocide in Cambodia and Ethiopia. In R. Gellately, and B. Kiernan (Eds) *The Specter of Genocide: Mass Murder in Historical Perspective* (pp.307–324). Cambridge: Cambridge University Press.

Klin, A. (2000). Attributing social meaning to ambiguous visual stimuli in higher-functioning autism and Asperger syndrome: The Social Attribution Task. *Journal of Child Psychology and Psychiatry and Allied Disciplines, 41*(7), 831–846.

Knecht, T. (1999). Amok und pseudo-amok/Amok and quasi-amok. *Schweizer Archiv fuer Neurologie und Psychiatrie, 150*(3), 142–148.

Knoll, J. L. I., and Hatters-Friedman, S. (2015). The homicide-suicide phenomenon: Findings of psychological autopsies. *Journal of Forensic Sciences, 60*(5), 1253–1257.

Koch, J. (1888). *Kurzgefasster Leitfaden der Psychiatrie (Short Textbook of Psychiatry).* Berlin.

Koenigs, M., Young, L., Adolphs, R., Tranel, D., *et al.* (2007). Damage to the prefrontal cortex increases utilitarian moral judgements. *Nature, 446*(7138), 908–911.

Kokkinaki, T., and Vitalaki, E. (2013). Exploring spontaneous imitation in infancy: A three generation inter-familial study. *Europe's Journal of Psychology, 9*(2), 259–275.

Konvalinka, I., Bauer, M., Stahlhut, C., Hansen, L. K., Roepstorff, A., and Frith, C. D. (2014). Frontal alpha oscillations distinguish leaders from followers: Multivariate decoding of mutually interacting brains. _Neuroimage, 94_, 79–88.

Koomen, W., and Van Der Pligt, J. (2016). _The Psychology of Radicalization and Terrorism_. London: Routledge.

Krall, S. C., Rottschy, C., Oberwelland, E., Bzdok, D., _et al._ (2015). The role of the right temporoparietal junction in attention and social interaction as revealed by ALE meta-analysis. _Brain Structure and Function, 220_(2), 587–604.

Krebs, D. L. (2012). The Evolution of a Sense of Morality. In E. Slingerland, and M. Collard (Eds) _Creating Consilience: Integrating the Sciences and the Humanities_ (pp.299–317). New York: Oxford University Press.

Kret, M. E., Fischer, A. H., and De Dreu, C. K. W. (2015). Pupil mimicry correlates with trust in in-group partners with dilating pupils. _Psychological Science, 26_(9), 1401–1410.

Kret, M. E., Stekelenburg, J. J., Roelofs, K., and de Gelder, B. (2013). Perception of face and body expressions using electromyography, pupillometry and gaze measures. _Frontiers in Psychology, 4_, 28.

Krueger, J. (2011). Extended cognition and the space of social interaction. _Consciousness and Cognition, 20_(3), 643–657.

Krueger, J. (2013). Merleau-Ponty on shared emotions and the joint ownership thesis. _Continental Philosophy Review, 46_(4), 509–531.

Kruglanski, A. W., Pierro, A., Mannetti, L., and De Grada, E. (2006). Groups as epistemic providers: Need for closure and the unfolding of group-centrism. _Psychological Review, 113_(1), 84–100.

Künecke, J., Hildebrandt, A., Recio, G., Sommer, W., and Wilhelm, O. (2014). Facial EMG responses to emotional expressions are related to emotion perception ability. _PLoS ONE, 9_(1).

Laidlaw, K. E. W., Rothwell, A., and Kingstone, A. (2016). Camouflaged attention: Covert attention is critical to social communication in natural settings. _Evolution and Human Behavior_. doi:10.1016/j.evolhumbehav.2016.04.004

Laing, R. D., Phillipson, H., and Lee, A. R. (1966). _Interpersonal Perception: A Theory and a Method of Research_. London: Tavistock Publications; New York: Springer Publishing.

Lamm, C., Decety, J., and Singer, T. (2011). Meta-analytic evidence for common and distinct neural networks associated with directly experienced pain and empathy for pain. _Neuroimage, 54_(3), 2492–2502.

Landau, M. J., Solomon, S., Greenberg, J., Cohen, F., *et al.* (2004). Deliver us from evil: The effects of mortality salience and reminders of 9/11 on support for President George W. Bush. *Personality and Social Psychology Bulletin, 30*(9), 1136–1150.

Lara-Carrasco, J., Simard, V., Saint-Onge, K., Lamoureux-Tremblay, V., and Nielsen, T. (2013). Maternal representations in the dreams of pregnant women: A prospective comparative study. *Frontiers in Psychology, 4*, 551.

Launay, J., Pearce, E., Wlodarski, R., van Duijn, M., Carney, J., and Dunbar, R. I. M. (2015). Higher-order mentalising and executive functioning. *Personality and Individual Differences, 86*, 6–14.

Lavine, H., Lodge, M., and Freitas, K. (2005). Threat, authoritarianism, and selective exposure to information. *Political Psychology, 26*(2), 219–244.

Le Bon, G. (1930/1896). *The Crowd: A Study of the Popular Mind.* London: Ernest Benn.

Lee, T. W., Josephs, O., Dolan, R. J., and Critchley, H. D. (2006). Imitating expressions: Emotion-specific neural substrates in facial mimicry. *Social Cognitive and Affective Neuroscience, 1*(2), 122–135.

Leidner, B., Castano, E., Zaiser, E., and Giner-Sorolla, R. (2010). Ingroup glorification, moral disengagement, and justice in the context of collective violence. *Personality and Social Psychology Bulletin, 36*(8), 1115–1129.

Lemogne, C., Smadja, J., Zerdazi, E. H., Soudry, Y., *et al.* (2015). Congenital anosmia and emotion recognition: A case-control study. *Neuropsychologia, 72*, 52–58.

Lerner, M. J., and Clayton, S. (2011). *Justice and Self-Interest: Two Fundamental Motives.* New York: Cambridge University Press.

Lessing, D. (1989). *The Fifth Child.* London: Paladin.

Lessing, D. (2000). *Ben, in the World.* London: Flamingo.

Lewis, D. (2002). *Convention: A Philosophical Study.* Chichester: Wiley.

Li, J., Zhao, Y., Li, R., Broster, L. S., Zhou, C., and Yang, S. (2015). Association of oxytocin receptor gene (OXTR) rs53576 polymorphism with sociality: A meta-analysis. *PLoS ONE, 10*(6).

Li, M., Leidner, B., and Castano, E. (2014). Toward a comprehensive taxonomy of dehumanization: Integrating two senses of humanness, mind perception theory, and stereotype content model. *TPM – Testing, Psychometrics, Methodology in Applied Psychology, 21*(3), 285–300.

Liang, J. G., and Sandmann, L. R. (2015). Leadership for community engagement: A distributed leadership perspective. *Journal of Higher Education Outreach and Engagement, 19*(1), 35–64.

Liao, X., Rong, S., and Queller, D. C. (2015). Relatedness, conflict, and the evolution of eusociality. *PLoS Biol, 13*(3).

Lichtenfeld, S., Buechner, V. L., Maier, M. A., and Fernández-Capo, M. (2015). Forgive and forget: Differences between decisional and emotional forgiveness. *PLoS ONE, 10*(5).

Lickel, B., Kushlev, K., Savalei, V., Matta, S., and Schmader, T. (2014). Shame and the motivation to change the self. *Emotion, 14*(6), 1049–1061.

Lieberman, J. D., Arndt, J., Personius, J., and Cook, A. (2001). Vicarious annihilation: The effect of mortality salience on perceptions of hate crimes. *Law and Human Behavior, 25*(6), 547–566.

Lieven, E., and Stoll, S. (2013). Early communicative development in two cultures: A comparison of the communicative environments of children from two cultures. *Human Development, 56*(3), 178–206.

Likowski, K., Muhlberger, A., Seibt, B., Pauli, P., and Weyers, P. (2011). Processes underlying congruent and incongruent facial reactions to emotional facial expressions. *Emotion, 11*(3), 457–467.

Likowski, K. U., Muhlberger, A., Gerdes, A. B., Wieser, M. J., Pauli, P., and Weyers, P. (2012). Facial mimicry and the mirror neuron system: Simultaneous acquisition of facial electromyography and functional magnetic resonance imaging. *Frontiers in Human Neuroscience, 6*, 214.

Lim, A., and Okuno, H. G. (2015). A recipe for empathy: Integrating the mirror system, insula, somatosensory cortex and motherese. *International Journal of Social Robotics, 7*(1), 35–49.

Lim, D., and DeSteno, D. (2016). Suffering and compassion: The links among adverse life experiences, empathy, compassion, and prosocial behavior. *Emotion, 16*(2), 175–182.

Lin, J., and Lucas, T. A. (2015). A particle swarm optimization model of emergency airplane evacuations with emotion. *Networks and Heterogeneous Media, 10*(3), 631–646.

Lindenberger, U., Li, S. C., Gruber, W., and Müller, V. (2009). Brains swinging in concert: Cortical phase synchronization while playing guitar. *BMC Neuroscience, 10*(22), 1–12.

Liu, T., and Pelowski, M. (2014). A new research trend in social neuroscience: Towards an interactive-brain neuroscience. *PsyCh Journal, 3*(3), 177–188.

Liu, Y., Lin, W., Xu, P., Zhang, D., and Luo, Y. (2015). Neural basis of disgust perception in racial prejudice. *Human Brain Mapping, 36*(12), 5275–5286.

Livius, T. (1919). *Livy: Books I and II with an English Translation.* Cambridge, MA: Harvard University Press.

Locard, H. (2004). *Pol Pot's Little Red Book: The Sayings of Angkar.* Chiang Mai: Silkworm Books.

Low, K. E. Y. (2013). Olfactive frames of remembering: Theorizing self, senses and society. *Sociological Review, 61*(4), 688–708.

Low, S., and Espelage, D. (2013). Differentiating cyber bullying perpetration from non-physical bullying: Commonalities across race, individual, and family predictors. *Psychology of Violence, 3*(1), 39–52.

Lu, Y. (2014). The a priori value and feeling in Max Scheler and Wang Yangming. *Asian Philosophy, 24*(3), 197–211.

Lübke, K. T., and Pause, B. M. (2015). Always follow your nose: The functional significance of social chemosignals in human reproduction and survival. *Hormones and Behavior, 68*, 134–144.

Luo, S., Shi, Z., Yang, X., Wang, X., and Han, S. (2014). Reminders of mortality decrease midcingulate activity in response to others' suffering. *Social Cognitive and Affective Neuroscience, 9*(4), 477–486.

Lymer, J. (2014). Infant imitation and the self: A response to Welsh. *Philosophical Psychology, 27*(2), 235–257.

Lynn, S. K., Hoge, E. A., Fischer, L. E., Barrett, L. F., and Simon, N. M. (2014). Gender differences in oxytocin-associated disruption of decision bias during emotion perception. *Psychiatry Research, 219*(1), 198–203.

MacCarron, P., and Dunbar, R. I. M. (2016). Identifying natural grouping structure in gelada baboons: A network approach. *Animal Behaviour, 114*, 119–128.

Mackay, C. (1852). *Extraordinary Popular Delusions and the Madness of Crowds.* London: Office of the National Illustrated Library.

MacLean, E. L., Krupenye, C., and Hare, B. (2014). Dogs (Canis familiaris) account for body orientation but not visual barriers when responding to pointing gestures. *Journal of Comparative Psychology, 128*(3), 285–297.

MacSweeney, M., Capek, C. M., Campbell, R., and Woll, B. (2008). The signing brain: The neurobiology of sign language. *Trends in Cognitive Sciences, 12*(11), 432–440.

Mahmut, M. K., and Stevenson, R. J. (2016). Investigating left- and right-nostril olfactory abilities with respect to psychopathy. *Chemosensory Perception, 9*(3), 131–140.

Mai, X., Zhang, W., Hu, X., Zhen, Z., *et al.* (2016). Using tDCS to explore the role of the right temporo-parietal junction in theory of mind and cognitive empathy. *Frontiers in Psychology, 7*, 380.

Maister, L., Banissy, M. J., and Tsakiris, M. (2013). Mirror-touch synaesthesia changes representations of self-identity. *Neuropsychologia, 51*(5), 802–808.

Malka, A., Osborne, D., Soto, C. J., Greaves, L. M., Sibley, C. G., and Lelkes, Y. (2016). Binding moral foundations and the narrowing of ideological conflict to the traditional morality domain. *Personality and Social Psychology Bulletin, 42*(9), 1243–1257.

Malory, T. (1920). *Le Morte d'Arthur*. London: Philip Lee Warner.

Mampe, B., Friederici, A. D., Christophe, A., and Wermke, K. (2009). Newborns' cry melody is shaped by their native language. *Current Biology, 19*(23), 1994–1997.

Mancke, F., and Herpertz, S. C. (2014). Antisocial personality disorder. *Psychiatrie, 11*(2), 113–121.

Manini, B., Cardone, D., Ebisch, S., Bafunno, D., Aureli, T., and Merla, A. (2013). Mom feels what her child feels: Thermal signatures of vicarious autonomic response while watching children in a stressful situation. *Frontiers in Human Neuroscience, 7*. doi:10.3389/fnhum.2013.00299

Mannes, A. E., Soll, J. B., and Larrick, R. P. (2014). The wisdom of select crowds. *Journal of Personality and Social Psychology, 107*(2), 276–299.

Mansfield, C. D., Pasupathi, M., and McLean, K. C. (2015). Is narrating growth in stories of personal transgressions associated with increased well-being, self-compassion, and forgiveness of others? *Journal of Research in Personality, 58*, 69–83.

Marissen, M., Deen, M., and Franken, I. (2011). Disturbed emotion recognition in patients with narcissistic personality disorder. *Psychiatry Research, 198*(2), 269–273.

Markus, H. R., and Lin, L. R. (1999). Conflict Ways: Cultural Diversity in the Meanings and Practices of Conflict. In D. Prentice, and D. Miller (Eds) *Cultural Divides: Understanding and Overcoming Group Conflict* (pp.302–333). New York: Russell Sage.

Martin, G. (2015). Stop the boats! Moral panic in Australia over asylum seekers. *Continuum, 29*(3), 304–322.

Martin, G. B., and Clark, R. D. (1982). Distress crying in neonates: Species and peer specificity. *Developmental Psychology, 18*(1), 3–9.

Martin, L. J., Hathaway, G., Isbester, K., Mirali, S., *et al.* (2014). Reducing social stress elicits emotional contagion of pain in mouse and human strangers. *Current Biology, 25*(3), 326–332.

Martin, W. (2010). The origin of mitochondria. *Nature Education, 3*(9), 58.

Martínez, R., Rodriguez-Bailon, R., Moya, M., and Vaes, J. (2017). How do different humanness measures relate? Confronting the attribution of secondary emotions, human uniqueness, and human nature traits. *Journal of Social Psychology, 157*(2), 165–180.

Masicampo, E. J., and Baumeister, R. F. (2013). Conscious thought does not guide moment-to-moment actions – it serves social and cultural functions. *Frontiers in Psychology, 4,* 478.

Masten, A. S., and Narayan, A. J. (2011). Child development in the context of disaster, war, and terrorism: Pathways of risk and resilience. *Annual Review of Psychology, 63*(1), 227–257.

Masur, E. F., and Olson, J. (2008). Mothers' and infants' responses to their partners' spontaneous action and vocal/verbal imitation. *Infant Behavior and Development, 31*(4), 704–715.

Matsumoto, D., Hwang, H. C., and Frank, M. G. (2017). Emotion and aggressive intergroup cognitions: The ANCODI hypothesis. *Aggressive Behavior, 43*(1), 93–107.

Mayer, F. S., Duval, S., Holtz, R., and Bowman, C. (1985). Self-focus, helping request salience, felt responsibility, and helping behavior. *Personality and Social Psychology Bulletin, 11*(2), 133–144.

Mayne, R., Jones, J., Gale, E., and Adamatzky, A. (2017). On coupled oscillator dynamics and incident behaviour patterns in slime mould Physarum polycephalum: Emergence of wave packets, global streaming clock frequencies and anticipation of periodic stimuli. *International Journal of Parallel, Emergent and Distributed Systems, 32*(1), 95–118.

McAlister, A. L., and Wilczak, B. (2015). Moral Disengagement in 'War Fever': How Can We Resist? In M. Galluccio (Ed.) *Handbook of International Negotiation: Interpersonal, Intercultural, and Diplomatic Perspectives* (pp.33–43). Cham: Springer.

McBurney, D. H., Shoup, M. L., and Streeter, S. A. (2006). Olfactory comfort: Smelling a partner's clothing during periods of separation. *Journal of Applied Social Psychology, 36*(9), 2325–2335.

McDougall, W. (1920). *The Group Mind.* New York: G. P. Putnam's and Sons.

McGuigan, N., and Robertson, S. (2015). The influence of peers on the tendency of 3- and 4-year-old children to over-imitate. *Journal of Experimental Child Psychology, 136,* 42–54.

McKay, F. H., Thomas, S. L., and Warwick Blood, R. (2011). 'Any one of these boat people could be a terrorist for all we know!' Media representations and public perceptions of 'boat people' arrivals in Australia. *Journalism, 12*(5), 607–626.

Meares, R. (1983). Keats and the 'impersonal' therapist: A note on empathy and the therapeutic screen. *Psychiatry: Journal for the Study of Interpersonal Processes, 46*(1), 73–82.

Meloy, J. R. (2001). *The Mark of Cain: Psychoanalytic Insight and the Psychopath.* Hillsdale, NJ: Analytic Press.

Meltzoff, A., and Moore, M. (1977). Imitation of facial and manual gestures by human neonates. *Science, 198*(4312), 74–78.

Mercier, H., and Sperber, D. (2011). Why do humans reason? Arguments for an argumentative theory. *Behavioral and Brain Sciences, 34*(2), 57–111.

Mercier, H., and Sperber, D. (2017). *The Enigma of Reason.* Cambridge, MA: Harvard University Press.

Merleau-Ponty, M. (1962/1945). *Phenomenology of Perception.* London: Routledge.

Mesulam, M. M. (1998). From sensation to cognition. *Brain, 121*(6), 1013–1052.

Milgram, S. (1963). Behavioral study of obedience. *Journal of Abnormal and Social Psychology, 67*, 371–378.

Milgram, S. (1965). Some conditions of obedience and disobedience to authority. *Human Relations, 18*(1), 57–76.

Milinski, M., Croy, I., Hummel, T., and Boehm, T. (2013). Major histocompatibility complex peptide ligands as olfactory cues in human body odour assessment. *Proceedings of the Royal Society of London B: Biological Sciences, 280*(1755).

Miller, R., and Cushman, F. (2013). Aversive for me, wrong for you: First-person behavioral aversions underlie the moral condemnation of harm. *Social and Personality Psychology Compass, 7*(10), 707–718.

Miller, R. M., Hannikainen, I. A., and Cushman, F. A. (2014). Bad actions or bad outcomes? Differentiating affective contributions to the moral condemnation of harm. *Emotion, 14*(3), 573–587.

Miller, S. E., and Marcovitch, S. (2015). Examining executive function in the second year of life: Coherence, stability, and relations to joint attention and language. *Developmental Psychology, 51*(1), 101–114.

Miranda, D., and Kim, J. (2015). Peer contagion, lenient legal-ethical position, and music piracy intentions in emerging adults: Mindfulness as a protective factor. *Musicae Scientiae, 19*(1), 3–22.

Moller, A. C., and Deci, E. L. (2010). Interpersonal control, dehumanization, and violence: A self-determination theory perspective. *Group Processes and Intergroup Relations, 13*(1), 41–53.

Montag, C., Gallinat, J., and Heinz, A. (2008). Theodor Lipps and the concept of empathy: 1851–1914. *American Journal of Psychiatry, 165*(10), 1261.

Montague, D. P., and Walker-Andrews, A. S. (2001). Peekaboo: A new look at infants' perception of emotion expressions. *Developmental Psychology, 37*(6), 826–838.

Moore, R. (2015). Meaning and ostension in great ape gestural communication. *Animal Cognition, 19*(1), 223–231.

Morelli, S. A., Rameson, L. T., and Lieberman, M. D. (2014). The neural components of empathy: Predicting daily prosocial behavior. *Social Cognitive and Affective Neuroscience, 9*(1), 39–47.

Morin, A. (2011). Self-awareness part 2: Neuroanatomy and importance of inner speech. *Social and Personality Psychology Compass, 5*(12), 1004–1017.

Morin, A., El-Sayed, E., and Racy, F. (2015). Self-Awareness, Inner Speech, and Theory of Mind in Typical and ASD Individuals: A Critical Review. In E. Sherwood (Ed.) *Theory of Mind: Development in Children, Brain Mechanisms and Social Implications* (pp.43–113). Hauppauge, NY: Nova Science Publishers.

Mosek-Eilon, V., Hirschberger, G., Kanat-Maymon, Y., and Feldman, R. (2013). Infant reminders alter sympathetic reactivity and reduce couple hostility at the transition to parenthood. *Developmental Psychology, 49*(7), 1385–1395.

Mosquera-Doñate, G., and Boguñá, M. (2015). Follow the leader: Herding behavior in heterogeneous populations. *Physical Review E: Statistical, Nonlinear, and Soft Matter Physics, 91*(5).

Muir, K., Madill, A., and Brown, C. (2016). Individual differences in emotional processing and autobiographical memory: Interoceptive awareness and alexithymia in the fading affect bias. *Cognition and Emotion*, 1–13. doi:10.108 0/02699931.2016.1225005

Muldoon, O. T., and Downes, C. (2007). Social identification and post-traumatic stress symptoms in post-conflict Northern Ireland. *British Journal of Psychiatry, 191*(2), 146–149.

Müller, V., Sänger, J., and Lindenberger, U. (2013). Intra- and inter-brain synchronization during musical improvisation on the guitar. *PLoS ONE, 8*(9).

Müller-Pinzler, L., Gazzola, V., Keysers, C., Sommer, J., *et al.* (2015). Neural pathways of embarrassment and their modulation by social anxiety. *Neuroimage, 119*, 252–261.

Müller-Pinzler, L., Rademacher, L., Paulus, F. M., and Krach, S. (2016). When your friends make you cringe: Social closeness modulates vicarious embarrassment-related neural activity. *Social Cognitive and Affective Neuroscience, 11*(3), 466–475.

Nagy, E. (2011). The newborn infant: A missing stage in developmental psychology. *Infant and Child Development, 20*(1), 3–19.

Nail, P. R., McGregor, I., Drinkwater, A. E., Steele, G. M., and Thompson, A. W. (2009). Threat causes liberals to think like conservatives. *Journal of Experimental Social Psychology, 45*(4), 901–907.

Nakajima, M., Görlich, A., and Heintz, N. (2015). Oxytocin modulates female sociosexual behavior through a specific class of prefrontal cortical interneurons. *Cell, 159*(2), 295–305.

Nakrani, S., and Tovey, C. (2007). From honeybees to internet servers: Biomimicry for distributed management of internet hosting centers. *Bioinspiration and Biomimetics, 2*(4), S182–197.

Nateghian, S., Dastgiri, S. S., and Mullet, E. (2015). Dispositional forgiveness and PTSD among Iranian veterans of the 1980–1988 war. *Journal of Loss and Trauma, 20*(2), 123–130.

Neath, K., Nilsen, E. S., Gittsovich, K., and Itier, R. J. (2013). Attention orienting by gaze and facial expressions across development. *Emotion, 13*(3), 397–408.

Neumann, C. S., Hare, R. D., and Pardini, D. A. (2015). Antisociality and the construct of psychopathy: Data from across the globe. *Journal of Personality, 83*(6), 678–692.

Neumann, D., Zupan, B., Malec, J. F., and Hammond, F. (2014). Relationships between alexithymia, affect recognition, and empathy after traumatic brain injury. *Journal of Head Trauma Rehabilitation, 29*(1), E18–E27.

Newell, B. R., and Shanks, D. R. (2014). Unconscious influences on decision making: A critical review. *Behavioral and Brain Sciences, 37*(1), 1–19.

Niedźwiecka, A., and Tomalski, P. (2015). Gaze-cueing effect depends on facial expression of emotion in 9- to 12-month-old infants. *Frontiers in Psychology, 6*, 122.

Nietzsche, F. (2001/1882). *The Gay Science*. Cambridge: Cambridge University Press.

Nisbett, R. E., Caputo, C., Legant, P., and Maracek, J. (1973). Behaviour as seen by the actor and as seen by the observer. *Journal of Personality and Social Psychology, 27*(2), 154–164.

Nisbett, R. E., and Masuda, T. (2003). Culture and point of view. *Proceedings of the National Academy of Sciences, 100*(19), 11163–11170.

Nomikou, I., Leonardi, G., Rohlfing, K. J., and Raczaszek-Leonardi, J. (2016). Constructing interaction: The development of gaze dynamics. *Infant and Child Development, 25*(3), 277–295.

Norenzayan, A. (2016). Theodiversity. *Annual Review of Psychology, 67*(1), 465–488.

Norscia, I., Demuru, E., and Palagi, E. (2016). She more than he: Gender bias supports the empathic nature of yawn contagion in Homo sapiens. *Royal Society Open Science, 3*(2).

Novelli, D., Drury, J., Reicher, S., and Stott, C. (2013). Crowdedness mediates the effect of social identification on positive emotion in a crowd: A survey of two crowd events. *PLoS ONE, 8*(11).

Nowak, M. (2011). The complicated history of Einfühlung. *Argument, 1*, 301–326.

Nowak, M. A., Tarnita, C. E., and Wilson, E. O. (2010). The evolution of eusociality. *Nature, 466*(7310), 1057–1062.

Nowak, R., Keller, M., Val-Laillet, D., and Lévy, F. (2007). Perinatal visceral events and brain mechanisms involved in the development of mother–young bonding in sheep. *Hormones and Behavior, 52*(1), 92–98.

Nowrasteh, A. (2016). Terrorism and immigration: A risk analysis. *Policy Analysis, 798*. Available at www.cato.org/publications/policy-analysis/terrorism-immigration-risk-analysis, accessed on 25 August 2017.

Nummenmaa, L., Tuominen, L., Dunbar, R., Hirvonen, J., *et al.* (2016). Social touch modulates endogenous μ-opioid system activity in humans. *Neuroimage, 138*, 242–247.

O'Connor, C. M., Marsh-Rollo, S. E., Aubin-Horth, N., and Balshine, S. (2016). Species-specific patterns of nonapeptide brain gene expression relative to pair-bonding behavior in grouping and non-grouping cichlids. *Hormones and Behavior, 80*, 30–38.

Oaten, M., Stevenson, R. J., and Case, T. I. (2009). Disgust as a disease-avoidance mechanism. *Psychological Bulletin, 135*(2), 303–321.

Obladen, M. (2016). Despising the weak: Long shadows of infant murder in Nazi Germany. *Archives of Disease in Childhood: Fetal and Neonatal Edition, 101*(3), F190–F194.

Ogden, T. (1984). Instinct, phantasy, and psychological deep structure: A reinterpretation of aspects of the work of Melanie Klein. *Contemporary Psychoanalysis, 20*, 500–525.

Okimoto, T. G., Wenzel, M., and Hornsey, M. J. (2015). Apologies demanded yet devalued: Normative dilution in the age of apology. *Journal of Experimental Social Psychology, 60*, 133–136.

Olson, K. R., Dunham, Y., Dweck, C. S., Spelke, E. S., and Banaji, M. R. (2008). Judgments of the lucky across development and culture. *Journal of Personality and Social Psychology, 94*(5), 757–776.

Ondobaka, S., and Bekkering, H. (2013) Conceptual and perceptuo-motor action control and action recognition. *Cortex, 49*(10), 2966–2967.

Oostenbroek, J., and Over, H. (2015). Young children contrast their behavior to that of out-group members. *Journal of Experimental Child Psychology, 139*(11), 234–241.

Osang, T., and Weber, S. (2017). Immigration policies, labor complementarities, population size and cultural frictions: Theory and evidence. *International Journal of Economic Theory, 13*(1), 95–111.

Otsuka, Y., Ichikawa, H., Clifford, C. W. G., Kanazawa, S., and Yamaguchi, M. K. (2016). Wollaston's effect in infants: Do infants integrate eye and head information in gaze perception? *Journal of Vision, 16*(3), 4.

Overpeck, M. D., Brenner, R. A., Trumble, A. C., Trifiletti, L. B., and Berendes, H. W. (1998). Risk factors for infant homicide in the United States. *New England Journal of Medicine, 339*(17), 1211–1216.

Páez, D., Rimé, B., Basabe, N., Wlodarczyk, A., and Zumeta, L. (2015). Psychosocial effects of perceived emotional synchrony in collective gatherings. *Journal of Personality and Social Psychology, 108*(5), 711–729.

Palombit, R. A. (2015). Infanticide as sexual conflict: Coevolution of male strategies and female counterstrategies. *Cold Spring Harbor Perspectives in Biology, 7*(6), 1–31.

Paluck, E. L. (2009). Reducing intergroup prejudice and conflict using the media: A field experiment in Rwanda. *Journal of Personality and Social Psychology, 96*(3), 574–587.

Panahi, O. (2016). Could there be a solution to the trolley problem? *Philosophy Now.* Available at https://philosophynow.org/issues/116/Could_There_Be_A_Solution_To_The_Trolley_Problem, accessed on 2 November 2017.

Parma, V., Bulgheroni, M., Tirindelli, R., and Castiello, U. (2013). Body odors promote automatic imitation in autism. *Biological Psychiatry, 74*(3), 220–226.

Paulus, F. M. (Ed.) (2015). *Psychology of Group Influence* (2nd ed.). New York: Psychology Press.

Paulus, F. M., Müller-Pinzler, L., Jansen, A., Gazzola, V., and Krach, S. (2015). Mentalizing and the role of the posterior superior temporal sulcus in sharing others' embarrassment. *Cerebral Cortex, 25*(8), 2065–2075.

Pearce, E., Launay, J., and Dunbar, R. I. M. (2015). The ice-breaker effect: Singing mediates fast social bonding. *Royal Society Open Science, 2*(10), 150221.

Peirce, C. S., Marquand, A., Ladd-Franklin, C., Mitchell, O. H., Gilman, B. I., and University, J. H. (1883). *Studies in Logic.* London: Little, Brown.

Perea García, J. O., Ehlers, K. R., and Tylén, K. (2017). Bodily constraints contributing to multimodal referentiality in humans: The contribution of a de-pigmented sclera to proto-declaratives. *Language and Communication, 54,* 73–81.

Perez, E. C., Elie, J. E., Boucaud, I. C. A., Soulage, C. O., *et al.* (2015). Physiological resonance between mates through calls as possible evidence of empathic processes in songbirds. *Hormones and Behavior, 75*, 130–141.

Perez-Osorio, J., Müller, H. J., Wiese, E., and Wykowska, A. (2015). Gaze following is modulated by expectations regarding others' action goals. *PLoS ONE, 10*(11).

Peters, K., and Kashima, Y. (2015). A multimodal theory of affect diffusion. *Psychological Bulletin, 141*(5), 966–992.

Pfaff, D. (2015). *The Altruistic Brain.* New York: Oxford University Press.

Pfaff, D., Martin, E. M., and Kow, L.-M. (2007). Generalized brain arousal mechanisms contributing to libido. *Neuropsychoanalysis, 9*(2), 173–181.

Philippi, C. L., Feinstein, J. S., Khalsa, S. S., Damasio, A., *et al.* (2012). Preserved self-awareness following extensive bilateral brain damage to the insula, anterior cingulate, and medial prefrontal cortices. *PLoS ONE, 7*(8).

Pierno, A. C., Becchio, C., Wall, M. B., Smith, A. T., Turella, L., and Castiello, U. (2006). When gaze turns into grasp. *Journal of Cognitive Neuroscience, 18*(12), 2130–2137.

Pillot, M. H., Gautrais, J., Gouello, J., Michelena, P., Sibbald, A., and Bon, R. (2010). Moving together: Incidental leaders and naïve followers. *Behavioural Processes, 83*(3), 235–241.

Pinel, E., Long, A., Landau, M., Alexander, K., and Pysszczynksi, T. (2006). Seeing I to I: A pathway to interpersonal connectedness. *Journal of Personality and Social Psychology, 90*(2), 243–257.

Pinker, S. (2011). *The Better Angels of Our Nature.* New York: Viking Press.

Pinto, G., Tarchi, C., Accorti Gamannossi, B., and Bigozzi, L. (2016). Mental state talk in children's face-to-face and telephone narratives. *Journal of Applied Developmental Psychology, 44*, 21–27.

Pond, R. S., DeWall, C. N., Lambert, N. M., Deckman, T., Bonser, I. M., and Fincham, F. D. (2012). Repulsed by violence: Disgust sensitivity buffers trait, behavioral, and daily aggression. *Journal of Personality and Social Psychology, 102*(1), 175–188.

Population Reference Bureau (2015). *2015 World Population Data Sheet.* Available at www.prb.org/Publications/Datasheets/2015/2015-world-population-data-sheet.aspx, accessed on 16 August 2017.

Poria, S., Cambria, E., Winterstein, G., and Huang, G. B. (2014). Sentic patterns: Dependency-based rules for concept-level sentiment analysis. *Knowledge-Based Systems, 69*, 45–63.

Porter, M. A., Coltheart, M., and Langdon, R. (2008). Theory of mind in Williams syndrome assessed using a nonverbal task. *Journal of Autism and Developmental Disorders, 38*(5), 806–814.

Powell, J., Lewis, P. A., Roberts, N., García-Fiñana, M., and Dunbar, R. I. M. (2012). Orbital prefrontal cortex volume predicts social network size: An imaging study of individual differences in humans. *Proceedings of the Royal Society of London B: Biological Sciences, 279*(1736), 2157–2162.

Prati, F., Crisp, R. J., Meleady, R., and Rubini, M. (2016). Humanizing outgroups through multiple categorization: The roles of individuation and threat. *Personality and Social Psychology Bulletin, 42*(4), 526–539.

Prati, F., Crisp, R. J., and Rubini, M. (2015). Counter-stereotypes reduce emotional intergroup bias by eliciting surprise in the face of unexpected category combinations. *Journal of Experimental Social Psychology, 61*, 31–43.

Premack, D., and Woodruff, G. (1978). Does the chimpanzee have a theory of mind? *Behavioral and Brain Science, 1*, 515–526.

Preston, L., Shumsky, E., and Goldberg, A. (2002). From an Empathic Stance to an Empathic Dance: Empathy as a Bidirectional Negotiation. In A. Goldberg (Ed.) *Progress in Self Psychology* (pp.47–61). Hillsdale, NJ: The Analytic Press.

Preston, S. D. (2013). The origins of altruism in offspring care. *Psychological Bulletin, 139*(6), 1305–1341.

Preston, S. D., de Waal, F. B. M., and Post, S. G. (2002). The Communication of Emotions and the Possibility of Empathy in Animals. In S. Post, L. G. Underwood, J. P. Schloss, and W. B. Hurlburt (Eds) *Altruism and Altruistic Love: Science, Philosophy, and Religion in Dialogue* (pp.284–308). Oxford: Oxford University Press.

Prichard, J. (1835). *Moral Insanity*. London: Sherwood, Gilbert and Piper.

Prinsen, J., Bernaerts, S., Wang, Y., de Beukelaar, T. T., *et al.* (2017). Direct eye contact enhances mirroring of others' movements: A transcranial magnetic stimulation study. *Neuropsychologia, 95*, 111–118.

Propp, V. (1968). *Morphology of the Folktale* (2nd ed.). Austin, TX: University of Texas Press.

Pyszczynski, T., Solomon, S., and Greenberg, J. (2002). *In the Wake of 9/11: The Psychology of Terror*. Washington: American Psychological Society.

Rakhlin, N., Kornilov, S. A., Reich, J., Babyonyshev, M., Koposov, R. A., and Grigorenko, E. L. (2011). The relationship between syntactic development and theory of mind: Evidence from a small-population study of a developmental language disorder. *Journal of Neurolinguistics, 24*(4), 476–496.

Rands, S. A., Cowlishaw, G., Pettifor, R. A., Rowcliffe, J. M., and Johnstone, R. A. (2003). Spontaneous emergence of leaders and followers in foraging pairs. *Nature, 423*(6938), 432–434.

Rankin, A. M., and Philip, P. J. (1963). An epidemic of laughing in the Bukoba district of Tanganyika. *Central African Medical Journal, 9*, 167–170.

Raz, G., Jacob, Y., Gonen, T., Winetraub, Y., *et al.* (2014). Cry for her or cry with her: Context-dependent dissociation of two modes of cinematic empathy reflected in network cohesion dynamics. *Social Cognitive and Affective Neuroscience, 9*(1), 30–38.

Reagans, R. M. B. (2016). Network structure and knowledge transfer: The effects of cohesion and range. *Administrative Science Quarterly, 48*(2), 240–267.

Redcay, E., Dodell-Feder, D., Pearrow, M. J., Mavros, P. L., *et al.* (2010). Live face-to-face interaction during fMRI: A new tool for social cognitive neuroscience. *Neuroimage, 50*(4), 1639–1647.

Reddy, V. (2008). *How Infants Know Minds.* Cambridge, MA; London: Harvard University Press.

Reeck, M. (2015). The making of a saint for all seasons: The saintly body, the ecumenical tradition of North India, and the hagiographical account of Haji Waris Ali Shah's life. *Religions of South Asia, 9*(3), 290–304.

Reed, M. (2015). Social network influence on consistent choice. *Journal of Choice Modelling, 17*, 28–38.

Reffay, M., Petitjean, L., Coscoy, S., Grasland-Mongrain, E., *et al.* (2011). Orientation and polarity in collectively migrating cell structures: Statics and dynamics. *Biophysical Journal, 100*(11), 2566–2575.

Reicher, S. D., Haslam, S. A., and Miller, A. G. (2014). What makes a person a perpetrator? The intellectual, moral, and methodological arguments for revisiting Milgram's research on the influence of authority. *Journal of Social Issues, 70*(3), 393–408.

Reicher, S. D., Spears, R., and Postmes, T. (1995). A social identity model of deindividuation phenomena. *European Review of Social Psychology, 6*(1), 161–198.

Reicherts, P., Wieser, M. J., Gerdes, A. B., Likowski, K. U., *et al.* (2012). Electrocortical evidence for preferential processing of dynamic pain expressions compared to other emotional expressions. *Pain, 153*(9), 1959–1964.

Reid, C. R., and Latty, T. (2016). Collective behaviour and swarm intelligence in slime moulds. *FEMS Microbiology Reviews, 40*(6), 798–806.

Renata Aron, N. (2017) 'This 1967 classroom experiment proved how easy it was for Americans to become Nazis.' *Timeline*, 25 January. Available at https://timeline.com/this-1967-classroom-experiment-proved-how-easy-it-was-for-americans-to-become-nazis-ab63cedaf7dd#.f5g0925ev, accessed on 15 August 2017.

Renger, D., Mommert, A., Renger, S., and Simon, B. (2016). When less equal is less human: Intragroup (dis)respect and the experience of being human. *Journal of Social Psychology, 156*(5), 553–563.

Rennung, M., and Göritz, A. S. (2015). Facing sorrow as a group unites. Facing sorrow in a group divides. *PLoS ONE, 10*(9).

Reynolds, C. (1987). Flocks, herds and schools: A distributed behavioral model. *Computer Graphics, 21*(4), 25–34.

Richman, S. B., Dewall, C. N., Pond, R. S., Jr., Lambert, N. M., and Fincham, F. D. (2014). Disgusted by vengeance: Disgust sensitivity predicts lower vengeance. *Journal of Social and Clinical Psychology, 33*(9), 831–846.

Rickman, J. (1957). *Selected Contributions to Psycho-Analysis.* London: Hogarth Press; reprinted (2003) with a new preface. London: Karnac Books.

Ricks, D., and Wing, L. (1975). Language, communication, and the use of symbols in normal and autistic children. *Journal of Autism & Childhood Schizophrenia, 5*, 191–221.

Riehl, C. (2016). Infanticide and within-clutch competition select for reproductive synchrony in a cooperative bird. *Evolution, 70*(8), 1760–1769.

Riem, M. M. E., Bakermans-Kranenburg, M. J., Voorthuis, A., and van Ijzendoorn, M. H. (2014). Oxytocin effects on mind-reading are moderated by experiences of maternal love withdrawal: An fMRI study. *Progress in Neuro-Psychopharmacology and Biological Psychiatry, 51*, 105–112.

Riggins, T., Geng, F., Blankenship, S. L., and Redcay, E. (2016). Hippocampal functional connectivity and episodic memory in early childhood. *Developmental Cognitive Neuroscience, 19*, 58–69.

Riva, P., Brambilla, M., and Vaes, J. (2016). Bad guys suffer less (social pain): Moral status influences judgements of others' social suffering. *British Journal of Social Psychology, 55*(1), 88–108.

Rochat, P. (2001). *The Infant's World.* Cambridge, MA; London: Harvard University Press.

Rombough, A., and Iarocci, G. (2013). Orienting in response to gaze and the social use of gaze among children with autism spectrum disorder. *Journal of Autism and Developmental Disorders, 43*(7), 1584–1596.

Ronson, J. (2012). *The Psychopath Test.* London: Picador.

Rosenbaum, S., Hirwa, J. P., Silk, J. B., and Stoinski, T. S. (2016). Relationships between adult male and maturing mountain gorillas (Gorilla beringei beringei) persist across developmental stages and social upheaval. *Ethology, 122*(2), 134–150.

Rosenberg, L. (2015). *Human Swarming and the Future of Collective Intelligence.* Available at www.singularityweblog.com/human-swarming-and-the-future-of-collective-intelligence, accessed on 25 August 2017.

Rosenthal, S. B., Twomey, C. R., Hartnett, A. T., Wu, H. S., and Couzin, I. D. (2015). Revealing the hidden networks of interaction in mobile animal groups allows prediction of complex behavioral contagion. *Proceedings of the National Academy of Sciences, 112*(15), 4690–4695.

Ross, J., Anderson, J. R., and Campbell, R. N. (2011). Situational changes in self-awareness influence 3- and 4-year-olds' self-regulation. *Journal of Experimental Child Psychology, 108*(1), 126–138.

Roth, L., Kaffenberger, T., Herwig, U., and Brühl, A. B. (2014). Brain activation associated with pride and shame. *Neuropsychobiology, 69*(2), 95–106.

Rothgerber, H. (1997). External intergroup threat as an antecedent to perceptions of in-group and out-group homogeneity. *Journal of Personality and Social Psychology, 73*(6), 1206–1212.

Rotter, M. (2011). Embitterment and Personality Disorder. In M. Linden, and A. Maercker (Eds) *Embitterment: Societal, Psychological, and Clinical Perspectives* (pp.177–186). Leipzig: Springer-Verlag Wien.

Roy, L. (1997). Consciousness according to Schleiermacher. *The Journal of Religion, 77*(2), 217–232.

Royzman, E. B., Goodwin, G. P., and Leeman, R. F. (2011). When sentimental rules collide: 'Norms with feelings' in the dilemmatic context. *Cognition, 121*(1), 101–114.

Rubio-Fernández, P. (2016). The director task: A test of Theory-of-Mind use or selective attention? *Psychonomic Bulletin and Review*, 1–8. doi:10.3758/s13423-016-1190-7

Ruckmann, J., Bodden, M., Jansen, A., Kircher, T., Dodel, R., and Rief, W. (2015). How pain empathy depends on ingroup/outgroup decisions: A functional magnet resonance imaging study. *Psychiatry Research, 234*(1), 57–65.

Rueda, P., Fernández-Berrocal, P., and Baron-Cohen, S. (2015). Dissociation between cognitive and affective empathy in youth with Asperger syndrome. *European Journal of Developmental Psychology, 12*(1), 85–98.

Rychlowska, M., Cañadas, E., Wood, A., Krumhuber, E. G., Fischer, A., and Niedenthal, P. M. (2014). Blocking mimicry makes true and false smiles look the same. *PLoS ONE, 9*(3).

Saeri, A. K., Iyer, A., and Louis, W. R. (2015). Right-wing authoritarianism and social dominance orientation predict outsiders' responses to an external group conflict: Implications for identification, anger, and collective action. *Analyses of Social Issues and Public Policy, 15*(1), 303–332.

Sagi, A., and Hoffman, M. L. (1976). Empathic distress in the newborn. *Developmental Psychology, 12*(2), 175–176.

Sah, W. H. (2013). *The Development of Coherence in Narratives: Causal Relations.* Paper presented at the 27th Pacific Asia Conference on Language, Information, and Computation, PACLIC 27.

Sampson, T. (2012). *Virality: Contagion Theory in the Age of Networks.* Minneapolis: University of Minnesota Press.

Sandel, A. A., Reddy, R. B., and Mitani, J. C. (2016). Adolescent male chimpanzees do not form a dominance hierarchy with their peers. *Primates*, 1–11. doi:10.1007/s10329-016-0553-z

Sanderson, G. (2004). Existentialism, globalisation and the cultural other. *International Education Journal, 4*(4), 1–20.

Sänger, J., Müller, V., and Lindenberger, U. (2012). Intra- and interbrain synchronization and network properties when playing guitar in duets. *Frontiers in Human Neuroscience, 3*, 312.

Sänger, J., Müller, V., and Lindenberger, U. (2013). Directionality in hyperbrain networks discriminates between leaders and followers in guitar duets. *Frontiers in Human Neuroscience, 7*, 234.

Santamaría-García, H., Burgaleta, M., and Sebastián-Gallés, N. (2015). Neuroanatomical markers of social hierarchy recognition in humans: A combined ERP/MRI study. *The Journal of Neuroscience, 35*(30), 10843.

Santiesteban, I., Bird, G., Tew, O., Cioffi, M. C., and Banissy, M. J. (2015). Mirror-touch synaesthesia: Difficulties inhibiting the other. *Cortex, 71*, 116–121.

Sarlo, M., Lotto, L., Rumiati, R., and Palomba, D. (2014). If it makes you feel bad, don't do it! Egoistic rather than altruistic empathy modulates neural and behavioral responses in moral dilemmas. *Physiology and Behavior, 130*, 127–134.

Sartre, J.-P. (1969). *Being and Nothingness*. London: Routledge.

Sartre, J.-P. (2003/1943). *Being and Nothingness: An Essay on Phenomenological Ontology*. London: Routledge.

Sartre, J.-P. (2004/1960). *Critique of Dialectical Reason: Volumes 1 and 2*. London: Verso.

Sato, W., Fujimura, T., Kochiyama, T., and Suzuki, N. (2013). Relationships among facial mimicry, emotional experience, and emotion recognition. *PLoS ONE, 8*(3).

Saux, M. S. (2007). Immigration and terrorism. A constructed connection: The Spanish case. *European Journal on Criminal Policy and Research, 13*(1–2), 57–72.

Schaal, B., Marlier, L., and Soussignan, R. (2000). Human foetuses learn odours from their pregnant mother's diet. *Chemical Senses, 25*(6), 729–737.

Schafer, R. (1976). *A New Language for Psycho-Analysis*. New Haven, CT: Yale University Press.

Scheff, T. (2007). Runaway Nationalism. In J. R. Tracy, and J. Tangney (Eds) *The Self-Conscious Emotions* (pp.426–439). New York: Guilford Press.

Scheff, T. J. (1999). Collective Emotions in Warfare. In L. Kurtz (Ed.) *Encyclopedia of Violence, Peace, and Conflict* (pp.319–329). Cambridge, MA: Academic Press.

Scheidel, W. (2017). *The Great Leveler: Violence and the History of Inequality from the Stone Age to the Twenty-First Century*. Princeton, NJ: Princeton University Press.

Scheinin, M. (2010). Resisting Panic: Lessons about the Role of Human Rights during the Long Decade after 9/11. In C. Gearty, and C. Douzinas (Eds), *The Cambridge Companion to Human Rights Law* (pp.293–306). Cambridge: Cambridge University Press.

Scheler, M. (1954). *The Nature of Sympathy*. Hamden, CT: Archon.

Schiermer, B. (2013). Aura, cult value, and the postmodern crowd: A Durkheimian reading of Walter Benjamin's artwork essay. *Distinktion: Journal of Social Theory, 14*(2), 191–210.

Schilbach, L. (2015). Eye to eye, face to face and brain to brain: Novel approaches to study the behavioral dynamics and neural mechanisms of social interactions. *Current Opinion in Behavioral Sciences, 3*, 130–135.

Schimel, J., Wohl, M. J. A., and Williams, T. (2006). Terror management and trait empathy: Evidence that mortality salience promotes reactions of forgiveness among people with high (vs. low) trait empathy. *Motivation and Emotion, 30*(3), 214–224.

Schindler, S., Reinhard, M. A., and Stahlberg, D. (2013). Tit for tat in the face of death: The effect of mortality salience on reciprocal behavior. *Journal of Experimental Social Psychology, 49*(1), 87–92.

Schleiermacher, F., and Crouter, R. (1988). *On Religion: Speeches to Its Cultured Despisers. Introduction, Translation, and Notes*. Cambridge: Cambridge University Press.

Schouten, A. P., van den Hooff, B., and Feldberg, F. (2016). Virtual team work: Group decision making in 3D virtual environments. *Communication Research, 43*(2), 180–210.

Schutz, A. (1966). The Problem of Transcendental Intersubjectivity in Husserl. In *Collected Papers, Volume 3* (pp.51–83). The Hague: Martinus Nijhoff.

Schutz, A. (1967). *The Phenomenology of the Social World*. Evanston, IL: Northwestern University Press.

Seara-Cardoso, A., Sebastian, C. L., Viding, E., and Roiser, J. P. (2015). Affective resonance in response to others' emotional faces varies with affective ratings and psychopathic traits in amygdala and anterior insula. *Social Neuroscience 11*(2), 140–152.

Seigel, J. (2005). *The Idea of the Self*. Cambridge: Cambridge University Press.

Seiryte, A., and Rusconi, E. (2015). The Empathy Quotient (EQ) predicts perceived strength of bodily illusions and illusion-related sensations of pain. *Personality and Individual Differences, 77*, 112–117.

Seitschek, T. (2012). Religion and Reliefs. In H. Birx (Ed.) *21st Century Anthropology: A Reference Handbook*. London: Sage.

Sellaro, R., Guroglu, B., Nitsche, M. A., van den Wildenberg, V. *et al.* (2015). Increasing the role of belief information in moral judgments by stimulating the right temporoparietal junction. *Neuropsychologia, 77*, 400–408.

Senju, A. (2013). Atypical development of spontaneous social cognition in autism spectrum disorders. *Brain and Development, 35*(2), 96–101.

Senju, A., and Johnson, M. H. (2009). The eye contact effect: Mechanisms and development. *Trends in Cognitive Sciences, 13*(3), 127–134.

Senzaki, S., Masuda, T., and Ishii, K. (2014). When is perception top-down and when is it not? Culture, narrative, and attention. *Cognitive Science, 38*(7), 1493–1506.

Shamay-Tsoory, S. G. (2014). Dynamic functional integration of distinct neural empathy systems. *Social Cognitive and Affective Neuroscience, 9*(1), 1–2.

Shang, Y., and Ye, Y. (2017). Leader-follower fixed-time group consensus control of multiagent systems under directed topology. *Complexity, 2017*. doi:10.1155/2017/3465076

Shariatmadari, D. (2015). Swarms, floods and marauders: The toxic metaphors of the migration debate. *The Guardian*, 10 August.

Sheng, F., Liu, Q., Li, H., Fang, F., and Han, S. (2014). Task modulations of racial bias in neural responses to others' suffering. *Neuroimage, 88*, 263–270.

Shenhav, A., and Mendes, W. B. (2014). Aiming for the stomach and hitting the heart: Dissociable triggers and sources for disgust reactions. *Emotion, 14*(2), 301–309.

Sherif, M., Hogg, M., and Abrams, D. (2001). Superordinate Goals in the Reduction of Intergroup Conflict. In M. A. Hogg, and D. Abrams (Eds) *Intergroup Relations: Essential Readings. Key Readings in Social Psychology* (pp.64–70). Philadelphia, PA: Psychology Press.

Shteynberg, G. (2015). Shared attention at the origin: On the psychological power of descriptive norms. *Journal of Cross-Cultural Psychology, 46*(10), 1245–1251.

Shteynberg, G., and Apfelbaum, E. P. (2013). The power of shared experience: Simultaneous observation with similar others facilitates social learning. *Social Psychological and Personality Science, 4*(6), 738–744.

Shteynberg, G., Bramlett, J. M., Fles, E. H., and Cameron, J. (2016). The broadcast of shared attention and its impact on political persuasion. *Journal of Personality and Social Psychology, 111*(5), 665–673.

Shteynberg, G., Hirsh, J. B., Galinsky, A. D., and Knight, A. P. (2014). Shared attention increases mood infusion. *Journal of Experimental Psychology: General, 143*(1), 123–130.

Shuto, T. (1985). Empathy and altruism in children: Exploratory study on measuring emotional empathy. *Japanese Journal of Educational Psychology, 33*(3), 226–231.

Sidanius, J., and Pratto, F. (2012). Social Dominance Theory. In P. A. M. Van Lange, A. Kruglanski, and E. Higgins (Eds) *Handbook of Theories of Social Psychology* (Vol. 2). Los Angeles: Sage.

Sidis, B. (1903). *The Psychology of Suggestion: A Research into the Subconscious Nature of Man and Society.* New York: D. Appleton and Company.

Siller, M., Swanson, M. R., Serlin, G., and Teachworth, A. G. (2014). Internal state language in the storybook narratives of children with and without autism spectrum disorder: Investigating relations to theory of mind abilities. *Research in Autism Spectrum Disorders, 8*(5), 589–596.

Simpson, E. A., Murray, L., Paukner, A., and Ferrari, P. F. (2014). The mirror neuron system as revealed through neonatal imitation: Presence from birth, predictive power and evidence of plasticity. *Philosophical Transactions of the Royal Society of London B: Biological Sciences, 369*(1644).

Simpson, S. J., and Sword, G. A. (2008). Locusts. *Current Biology, 18*(9), R364–R366.

Sinnott-Armstrong, W. (2014). Do Psychopaths Refute Internalism? In T. Schramme (Ed.) *Being Amoral: Psychopathy and Moral Incapacity.* Cambridge, MA: MIT Press.

Skerry, A. E., and Spelke, E. S. (2014). Preverbal infants identify emotional reactions that are incongruent with goal outcomes. *Cognition, 130*(2), 204–216.

Skitka, L. J., and Morgan, G. S. (2014). The social and political implications of moral conviction. *Political Psychology, 35*(S1), 95–110.

Skjelsbæk, I. (2012). *The Political Psychology of War Rape.* Abingdon: Routledge.

Skuse, D. H., Lori, A., Cubells, J. F., Lee, I., *et al.* (2014). Common polymorphism in the oxytocin receptor gene (OXTR) is associated with human social recognition skills. *Proceedings of the National Academy of Sciences of the United States of America, 111*(5), 1987–1992.

Slaby, J., and Stephan, A. (2008). Affective intentionality and self-consciousness. *Social Cognition, Emotion, and Self-Consciousness, 17*(2), 506–513.

Sloman, S. F. P. (2017). *The Knowledge Illusion: Why We Never Think Alone.* New York: Riverhead.

Slote, M. (2013). Egoism and emotion. *Philosophia (United States), 41*(2), 313–335.

Smeets, M. A. M., and Dijksterhuis, G. B. (2014). Smelly primes: When olfactory primes do or do not work. *Frontiers in Psychology, 5*, 96.

Smiley, C., and Fakunle, D. (2016). From 'brute' to 'thug': The demonization and criminalization of unarmed Black male victims in America. *Journal of Human Behavior in the Social Environment, 26*(3–4), 350–366.

Smith, A. (1805). *An Inquiry into the Nature and Causes of the Wealth of Nations... New edition... Embellished with an elegant head of the author.* Glasgow: R. Chapman.

Smith, A. (1982/1723). *Lectures on Jurisprudence* (Eds) R. L. Meek, D. D. Raphael, and P. G. Stein. Indianapolis: Liberty Fund.

Smith, A. (2002/1785). *The Theory of Moral Sentiments (Cambridge Texts in the History of Philosophy).* Cambridge: Cambridge University Press.

Smith, A., Haakonssen, K., Ameriks, K., and Clarke, D. (2002). *The Theory of Moral Sentiments.* Cambridge: Cambridge University Press.

Smith, A. D. (2015). Ethnosymbolism. In J. Stone, R. M. Dennis, P. S. Rizova, A. D. Smith, and X. Hou (Eds) *The Wiley Blackwell Encyclopedia of Race, Ethnicity and Nationalism.* Chichester: John Wiley and Sons.

Smith, K. E., Porges, E. C., Norman, G. J., Connelly, J. J., and Decety, J. (2014). Oxytocin receptor gene variation predicts empathic concern and autonomic arousal while perceiving harm to others. *Social Neuroscience, 9*(1), 1–9.

Soames, S. (2016). Propositions as cognitive acts. *Synthese*, 1–15. doi:10.1007/s11229-016-1168-z

Sofianidis, G., Elliott, M. T., Wing, A. M., and Hatzitaki, V. (2014). Can dancers suppress the haptically mediated interpersonal entrainment during rhythmic sway? *Acta Psychologica, 150*, 106–113.

Sofsky, W. (1997/1993). *The Order of Terror (Die Ordnung des Terrors)* (Trans.: W. Templer). Princeton, NJ: Princeton University Press.

Solera, F., Calderara, S., and Cucchiara, R. (2014). *Learning to Identify Leaders in Crowd.* Paper presented at the IEEE Computer Society Conference on Computer Vision and Pattern Recognition Workshops.

Solomon, S., Greenberg, J., and Pyszczynski, T. (2000). Pride and prejudice: Fear of death and social behavior. *Current Directions in Psychological Science, 9*(6), 200–204.

Sommer, M., Hajak, G., Dohnel, K., Schwerdtner, J., Meinhardt, J., and Muller, J. L. (2006). Integration of emotion and cognition in patients with psychopathy. *Progress in Brain Research, 156*, 457–466.

Sommer, M., Meinhardt, J., Rothmayr, C., Döhnel, K., *et al.* (2014). Me or you? Neural correlates of moral reasoning in everyday conflict situations in adolescents and adults. *Social Neuroscience, 9*(5), 452–470.

Sommer, V. (2006). The Holy Wars about Infanticide. Which Side Are You On? And Why? In C. P. van Schaik, and C. J. Hanson (Eds) *Infanticide by Males and its Implications* (pp.9–26). Cambridge: Cambridge University Press.

Sommerville, J. A., Schmidt, M. F. H., Yun, J. E., and Burns, M. (2013). The development of fairness expectations and prosocial behavior in the second year of life. *Infancy, 18*(1), 40–66.

Sonnby-Borgstrom, M. (2002). Automatic mimicry reactions as related to differences in emotional empathy. *Scandinavian Journal of Psychology, 43*(5), 433–443.

Soussignan, R., Chadwick, M., Philip, L., Conty, L., Dezecache, G., and Grèzes, J. (2013). Self-relevance appraisal of gaze direction and dynamic facial expressions: Effects on facial electromyographic and autonomic reactions. *Emotion, 13*(2), 330–337.

Sowden, S., and Catmur, C. (2013). The role of the right temporoparietal junction in the control of imitation. *Cerebral Cortex, 25*(4), 1107–1113.

Spanoudis, G. (2016). Theory of mind and specific language impairment in school-age children. *Journal of Communication Disorders, 61*, 83–96.

Spence, D. P. (1993). The hermeneutic turn: Soft science or loyal opposition? *Psychoanalytic Dialogues, 3*(1), 1–10.

Spence, N. (1984). *Narrative Truth and Historical Truth*. New York: WW Norton and Co.

Sperber, D. A. N. (1997). Intuitive and reflective beliefs. *Mind and Language, 12*(1), 67–83.

Sperber, D. A. N., Clément, F., Heintz, C., Mascaro, O., *et al.* (2010). Epistemic vigilance. *Mind and Language, 25*(4), 359–393.

Sripokangkul, S. (2015). Inferior to non-humans, lower than animals, and worse than demons: The demonization of Red Shirts in Thailand. *Asian Social Science, 11*(24), 331–342.

St Jacques, P. L., and Schacter, D. L. (2013). Modifying memory: Selectively enhancing and updating personal memories for a museum tour by reactivating them. *Psychological Science, 24*(4), 537–543.

Stefanovics, E. A., He, H., Cavalcanti, M., Neto, H., *et al.* (2016). Witchcraft and biopsychosocial causes of mental illness: Attitudes and beliefs about mental illness among health professionals in five countries. *The Journal of Nervous and Mental Disease, 204*(3), 169–174.

Stein, E. (1989). *The Collected Works of Edith Stein*. New York: Springer.

Stein, J. (2016). Valuing life as necessary for moral status. *Neuroethics, 9*(1), 45–51.

Stein, T., Senju, A., Peelen, M. V., and Sterzer, P. (2011). Eye contact facilitates awareness of faces during interocular suppression. *Cognition, 119*(2), 307–311.

Stevenson, M., Soto, J., and Adams, R. (2012). More than meets the eye: The role of self-identity in decoding complex emotional states. *Emotion, 12*, 882–886.

Stillman, T. F., Baumeister, R. F., and Mele, A. R. (2011). Free will in everyday life: Autobiographical accounts of free and unfree actions. *Philosophical Psychology,* *24*(3), 381–394.

Strachan, E. (2014). *The Illustrated History of the First World War.* Oxford: Oxford University Press.

Strachan, J. W. A., and Tipper, S. P. (2017). Examining the durability of incidentally learned trust from gaze cues. *Quarterly Journal of Experimental Psychology,* *70*(10), 2060–2075.

Strandburg-Peshkin, A., Farine, D. R., Couzin, I. D., and Crofoot, M. C. (2015). Shared decision-making drives collective movement in wild baboons. *Science,* *348*(6241), 1358–1361.

Straton, D. (1990). Catharsis reconsidered. *Australian and New Zealand Journal of Psychiatry, 24*(4), 543–551.

Stuart, S. A. J. (2013). The union of two nervous systems: Neurophenomenology, enkinaesthesia, and the Alexander technique. *Constructivist Foundations, 8*(3), 314–323.

Sturm, V. E., Yokoyama, J. S., Seeley, W. W., Kramer, J. H., Miller, B. L., and Rankin, K. P. (2013). Heightened emotional contagion in mild cognitive impairment and Alzheimer's disease is associated with temporal lobe degeneration. *Proceedings of the National Academy of Sciences of the United States of America,* *110*(24), 9944–9949.

Sullivan, A. C., Ong, A. C. H., La Macchia, S. T., and Louis, W. R. (2016). The impact of unpunished hate crimes: When derogating the victim extends into derogating the group. *Social Justice Research, 29*(3), 310–330.

Sullivan, R. M., Wilson, D. A., Ravel, N., and Mouly, A. M. (2015). Olfactory memory networks: From emotional learning to social behaviors. *Frontiers in Behavioral Neuroscience, 9*, 36.

Sun, Z., Yu, W., Zhou, J., and Shen, M. (2017). Perceiving crowd attention: Gaze following in human crowds with conflicting cues. *Attention, Perception, and Psychophysics, 79*(4), 1039–1049.

Sundararajan, L., and Raina, M. K. (2016). Mind and creativity: Insights from rasa theory with special focus on sahṛdaya (the appreciative critic). *Theory and Psychology, 26*(6), 159–165.

Surowiecki, J. (2004). *The Wisdom of Crowds: Why the Many Are Smarter Than the Few and How Collective Wisdom Shapes Business, Economies, Societies, and Nations* (1st ed.). New York: Doubleday.

Sutton, M. (2015). The British moral panic creation is bust. *Best Thinking Science.* Available at www.bestthinking.com/articles/science/social_sciences/ sociology/the-british-moral-panic-creation-myth-is-bust, accessed on 25 August 2017.

Swiderska, A., Krumhuber, E. G., and Kappas, A. (2013). *When Humans Become Objects: Out-Group Effects in Real and Artificial Faces.* Paper presented at the Proceedings of the 2013 Humaine Association Conference on Affective Computing and Intelligent Interaction, ACII 2013.

Tajfel, H. (1982). Social psychology of intergroup relations. *Annual Review of Psychology, 33*(1), 1–39.

Tamietto, M., Castelli, L., Vighetti, S., Perozzo, P., *et al.* (2009). Unseen facial and bodily expressions trigger fast emotional reactions. *Proceedings of the National Academy of Sciences, 106*(42), 17661–17666.

Tantam, D. (1984). A prophet in the group. *Group Analysis, 17*(1), 44–53.

Tantam, D. (2003). The flavour of emotions. *Psychology and Psychotherapy, 76*(1), 23–45.

Tantam, D. (2009). *Can the World Afford Autistic Spectrum Disorder? Nonverbal Communication, Asperger Syndrome and the Interbrain.* London: Jessica Kingsley Publishers.

Tantam, D., and Whittaker, J. (1992). Personality disorder and self-wounding. *British Journal of Psychiatry, 161*(4), 451–464.

Tarde, G. (1903/1890). *The Laws of Imitation* (Trans.: Clews, E.). New York: Henry Holt and Co.

Taylor, G., Slade, P., and Herbert, J. S. (2014). Infant face interest is associated with voice information and maternal psychological health. *Infant Behavior and Development, 37*(4), 597–605.

Taylor, L. K., Merrilees, C. E., Goeke-Morey, M. C., Shirlow, P., and Cummings, E. M. (2016). Trajectories of adolescent aggression and family cohesion: The potential to perpetuate or ameliorate political conflict. *Journal of Clinical Child and Adolescent Psychology, 45*(2), 114–128.

Taylor, P. J., Leese, M., Williams, D., Butwell, M., Daly, R., and Larkin, E. (1998). Mental disorder and violence: A special (high security) hospital study. *British Journal of Psychiatry, 172*, 218–226.

Tero, A., Takagi, S., Saigusa, T., Ito, K., *et al.* (2010). Rules for biologically inspired adaptive network design. *Science, 327*(5964), 439–442.

Tewari, S., Khan, S., Hopkins, N., Srinivasan, N., and Reicher, S. (2012). Participation in mass gatherings can benefit well-being: Longitudinal and control data from a north Indian Hindu pilgrimage event. *PLoS ONE, 7*(10).

Theidon, K. (2015). Hidden in plain sight. *Current Anthropology, 56*, S191–S200.

Thigpen, C., and Cleckley, H. (1992/1954). *The Three Faces of Eve, Revised Edition.* New York City: McGraw Hill Education

Thomas, K. A., DeScioli, P., De Freitas, J., and Pinker, S. (2016). Recursive mentalizing and common knowledge in the bystander effect. *Journal of Experimental Psychology: General, 145*(5), 1–9.

Thomas, K. A., DeScioli, P., Haque, O. S., and Pinker, S. (2014). The psychology of coordination and common knowledge. *J Pers Soc Psychol, 107*(4), 657–676.

Thompson, J. (1976). Killing, letting die, and the trolley problem. *The Monist, 59*(2), 204–217.

Tillas, A. (2015). Language as grist to the mill of cognition. *Cognitive Processing, 16*(3), 219–243.

Titchener, E. (2014/1909). Introspection and empathy. *Dialogues in Philosophy, Mental and Neuro Sciences, 7*, 25–30.

Todd, A. R., and Simpson, A. J. (2016). Anxiety impairs spontaneous perspective calculation: Evidence from a level-1 visual perspective-taking task. *Cognition, 156*, 88–94.

Tollenaar, M. S., Chatzimanoli, M., van der Wee, N. J. A., and Putman, P. (2013). Enhanced orienting of attention in response to emotional gaze cues after oxytocin administration in healthy young men. *Psychoneuroendocrinology, 38*(9), 1797–1802.

Toulmin, S. (1958). *The Uses of Argument*. Cambridge: Cambridge University Press.

Tracy, J. L., Randles, D., and Steckler, C. M. (2015). The nonverbal communication of emotions. *Current Opinion in Behavioral Sciences, 3*, 25–30.

Trevarthen, C. (2005). Stepping Away from the Mirror: Pride and Shame in Adventures of Companionship Reflections on the Nature and Emotional Needs of Infant Intersubjectivity. In C. Carter, L. Ahnert, K. Grossman, S. Hrdy, *et al.* (Eds) *Attachment and Bonding: A New Synthesis. Dahlem Workshop Report 92* (pp.55–84). Cambridge, MA: MIT Press.

Trevarthen, C., and Aitken, K. J. (2001). Infant intersubjectivity: Research, theory, and clinical applications. *Journal of Child Psychology and Psychiatry and Allied Disciplines, 42*(1), 3–48.

Trigg, D. (2013). The body of the other: Intercorporeality and the phenomenology of agoraphobia. *Continental Philosophy Review, 46*(3), 413–429.

Trotter, W. (1909). *The Instinct of the Herd in Peace and War*. London: Ernest Benn Ltd.

Tucci, K., González-Avella, J. C., and Cosenza, M. G. (2016). Rise of an alternative majority against opinion leaders. *Physica A: Statistical Mechanics and its Applications, 446*, 75–81.

Tuller, H. M., Bryan, C. J., Heyman, G. D., and Christenfeld, N. J. S. (2015). Seeing the other side: Perspective taking and the moderation of extremity. *Journal of Experimental Social Psychology, 59*, 18–23.

Turner, J. H., and Maryanski, A. (2012). The biology and neurology of group processes. *Advances in Group Processes, 29,* 1–37.

Tylén, K., Allen, M., Hunter, B. K., and Roepstorff, A. (2012). Interaction versus observation: Distinctive modes of social cognition in human brain and behavior? A combined fMRI and eye-tracking study. *Frontiers in Human Neuroscience, 6,* 331.

Tyrlik, M., Konecny, S., and Kukla, L. (2013). Predictors of pregnancy-related emotions. *Journal of Clinical Medicine Research, 5*(2), 112–120.

Ueda, R. (1969). Peek-a-boo: An entry into the world of the autistic child. *Journal of Special Education, 3*(3), 309–312.

Ünal, E., and Papafragou, A. (2016). Interactions between language and mental representations. *Language Learning, 66*(3), 554–580.

Underwood, M. K. (2004). Glares of contempt, eye rolls of disgust and turning away to exclude: Non-verbal forms of social aggression among girls. *Feminism and Psychology, 14*(3), 371–375.

Uvnas-Moberg, K. (1996). Neuroendocrinology of the mother–child interaction. *Trends in Endocrinology and Metabolism, 7*(4), 126–131.

Valdesolo, P., and DeSteno, D. (2011). Synchrony and the social tuning of compassion. *Emotion, 11*(2), 262–266.

Valdesolo, P., Ouyang, J., and DeSteno, D. (2010). The rhythm of joint action: Synchrony promotes cooperative ability. *Journal of Experimental Social Psychology, 46*(4), 693–695.

van Baaren, R., Janssen, L., Chartrand, T. L., and Dijksterhuis, A. (2009). Where is the love? The social aspects of mimicry. *Philosophical Transactions of the Royal Society B: Biological Sciences, 364*(1528), 2381–2389.

van Bakel, H. J., Maas, A. J., Vreeswijk, C. M., and Vingerhoets, A. J. (2013). Pictorial representation of attachment: Measuring the parent–fetus relationship in expectant mothers and fathers. *BMC Pregnancy and Childbirth, 13,* 138.

Van de Vondervoort, J. W., and Hamlin, J. K. (2016). Evidence for intuitive morality: Preverbal infants make sociomoral evaluations. *Child Development Perspectives, 10*(3), 143–148.

Van Deurzen, E. (2009). *Everyday Mysteries: Existential Dimensions of Psychotherapy* (2nd ed.). London: Routledge.

Van Deurzen, E. (2015). *Paradox and Passion in Psychotherapy: An Existential Approach to Therapy and Counselling* (2nd ed.). Chichester: Wiley.

Van Dillen, L. F., Enter, D., Peters, L. P. M., van Dijk, W. W., and Rotteveel, M. (2017). Moral fixations: The role of moral integrity and social anxiety in the selective avoidance of social threat. *Biological Psychology, 122,* 51–58.

Van Hiel, A., Hautman, L., Cornelis, I., and De Clercq, B. (2007). Football hooliganism: Comparing self-awareness and social identity theory explanations. *Journal of Community and Applied Social Psychology, 17*(3), 169–186.

Van Lange, P. A. M. (2008). Does empathy trigger only altruistic motivation? How about selflessness or justice? *Emotion, 8*(6), 766–774.

Van Langen, M. A. M., Wissink, I. B., Van Vugt, E. S., Van der Stouwe, T., and Stams, G. J. J. M. (2014). The relation between empathy and offending: A meta-analysis. *Aggression and Violent Behavior, 19*(2), 179–189.

van Zonneveld, L., Platje, E., de Sonneville, L. M. J., van Goozen, S. H. M., and Swaab, H. (2017). Affective empathy, cognitive empathy and social attention in children at high risk of criminal behaviour. *Journal of Child Psychology and Psychiatry and Allied Disciplines.* doi:10.1111/jcpp.12724

Vander Heyden, K. M., Huizinga, M., Raijmakers, M. E. J., and Jolles, J. (2017). Children's representations of another person's spatial perspective: Different strategies for different viewpoints? *Journal of Experimental Child Psychology, 153,* 57–73.

Vandevoorde, J., and Le Borgne, P. (2015). Dissociation and violent behavior: A review. *Evolution Psychiatrique, 80*(1), 187–208.

Vautier, E. (2009). Playing the 'race card': White anxieties and the expression and repression of popular racisms in the 1997 UK election. *Patterns of Prejudice, 43*(2), 122–141.

Vazansky, A. (2013). Army in Anguish. In T. Maulucci, Jr and D. Junker (Eds) *GIs in Germany: The Social, Economic, Cultural, and Political History of the American Military Presence* (pp.273–295). Cambridge: Cambridge University Press.

Veening, J. G., and Olivier, B. (2013). Intranasal administration of oxytocin: Behavioral and clinical effects, a review. *Neuroscience and Biobehavioral Reviews, 37*(8), 1445–1465.

Verissimo, D. S. (2012). On the threshold of the visible world: The notion of body schema in Merleau-Ponty's courses at the Sorbonne. *Psicologia USP, 23*(2), 367–394.

Vernot, B., Tucci, S., Kelso, J., Schraiber, J. G., *et al.* (2016). Excavating Neandertal and Denisovan DNA from the genomes of Melanesian individuals. *Science, 352*(6282), 235–239.

Vico, G. (1968/1744). *The New Science of Giambattista Vico* (2nd ed.) (Trans.: Bergin, T. G., and Fisch, M. H.). Ithaca, NY: Cornell University Press.

Vollm, B. A., Taylor, A. N., Richardson, P., Corcoran, R., *et al.* (2006). Neuronal correlates of theory of mind and empathy: A functional magnetic resonance imaging study in a nonverbal task. *Neuroimage, 29*(1), 90–98.

Voorthuis, A., Riem, M. M. E., Van Ijzendoorn, M. H., and Bakermans-Kranenburg, M. J. (2014). Reading the mind in the infant eyes: Paradoxical effects of oxytocin on neural activity and emotion recognition in watching pictures of infant faces. *Brain Research, 1580*, 151–159.

Vygotsky, L. (1966). *Thought and Language.* Cambridge, MA: Harvard University Press.

Vygotsky, L. (1971). *The Psychology of Art.* Cambridge, MA: Harvard University Press.

Wagner, J. B., Hirsch, S. B., Vogel-Farley, V. K., Redcay, E., and Nelson, C. A. (2012). Eye-tracking, autonomic, and electrophysiological correlates of emotional face processing in adolescents with autism spectrum disorder. *Journal of Autism and Developmental Disorders, 3*(1), 188–199.

Wall, I. R. (2016). The law of crowds. *Legal Studies, 36*(3), 395–414.

Wallrabenstein, I., Gerber, J., Rasche, S., Croy, I., *et al.* (2015). The smelling of Hedione results in sex-differentiated human brain activity. *Neuroimage, 113*, 365–373.

Walt, S. M. (1992). Revolution and war. *World Politics, 44*(3), 321–368.

Wang, Y., and Hamilton, A. F. (2012). Social top-down response modulation (STORM): A model of the control of mimicry in social interaction. *Frontiers in Human Neuroscience, 6*, 153.

Ward, J., and Banissy, M. J. (2015). Explaining mirror-touch synesthesia. *Cognitive Neuroscience.* doi:10.1080/17588928.2015.1042444

Watanabe, T., Takezawa, M., Nakawake, Y., Kunimatsu, A., *et al.* (2014). Two distinct neural mechanisms underlying indirect reciprocity. *Proceedings of the National Academy of Sciences of the United States of America, 111*(11), 3990–3995.

Waters, S. F., West, T. V., and Mendes, W. B. (2014). Stress contagion. *Psychological Science, 25*(4), 934–942.

Watson, A. (2011). Morale. In J. Winter (Ed.) *The Cambridge History of the First World War. Volume II: The State* (pp.174–195). Cambridge: Cambridge University Press.

Watson-Jones, R. E., and Legare, C. H. (2016). The social functions of group rituals. *Current Directions in Psychological Science, 25*(1), 42–46.

Webster, R. J., and Saucier, D. A. (2015). Demons are everywhere: The effects of belief in pure evil, demonization, and retribution on punishing criminal perpetrators. *Personality and Individual Differences, 74*, 72–77.

Wegner, D. M. (2002). *The Illusion of Conscious Will.* Cambridge, MA: MIT Press.

Weisfeld, G. E., and Weisfeld, M. B. (2014). Does a humorous element characterize embarrassment? *Humor, 27*(1), 65–85.

Weisel, O., and Böhm, R. (2015). 'Ingroup love' and 'outgroup hate' in intergroup conflict between natural groups. *Journal of Experimental Social Psychology, 60*, 110–120.

Weisel, O., and Zultan, R. (2016). Social motives in intergroup conflict: Group identity and perceived target of threat. *European Economic Review, 90*, 122–133.

Welch, M. (2003). Ironies of social control and the criminalization of immigrants. *Crime, Law and Social Change, 39*(4), 319–337.

Wesson, D. W. (2013). Sniffing behavior communicates social hierarchy. *Current Biology, 23*(7), 575–580.

Whissell, T. (1991). Phonoemotional profiling: A description of the emotional flavour of English texts on the basis of the phonemes employed in them. *Perceptual and Motor Skills, 91*(2), 617–648.

Whiten, A. (2013). Humans are not alone in computing how others see the world. *Animal Behaviour, 86*(2), 213–221.

Whitlock, F. A. (1982). A note on moral insanity and psychopathic disorders. *The Psychiatrist, 6*(4), 57–59.

Wiik, K. L., Loman, M. M., Van Ryzin, M. J., Armstrong, J. M., *et al.* (2011). Behavioral and emotional symptoms of post-institutionalized children in middle childhood. *Journal of Child Psychology and Psychiatry, 52*(1), 56–63.

Williams, H. (2016). Explicating the key notions of copresence and verification in relation to Husserl's use of the term direct to describe empathy. *Human Studies*, 1–18. doi:10.1007/s10746-016-9414-4

Wilson, E. O. (2014). *The Social Conquest of Earth.* New York: Liveright Publishing Co.

Wilson, J. R., and Scheutz, M. (2015). A model of empathy to shape trolley problem moral judgements. http://dx.doi.org/10.1109/ACII.2015.7344559

Wiltermuth, S. (2012). Synchrony and destructive obedience. *Social Influence, 7*(2), 78–89.

Wimmer, H., and Perner, J. (1983). Beliefs about beliefs: Representation and constraining function of wrong beliefs in young children's understanding of deception. *Cognition, 13*(1), 103–128.

Winnicott, D. W. (1957). *The Child, the Family, and the Outside World.* London: Penguin.

Wittgenstein, L. (1922). *Tractatus Logico-Philosophicus.* London: Kegan-Paul.

Wittgenstein, L. (1958). *Philosophical Investigations.* Oxford: Basil Blackwell.

Wittgenstein, L., Anscombe, G. E. M., and Wittgenstein, L. S. W. (1953). *Philosophical Investigations (Philosophische Untersuchungen)* (Trans.: Anscombe, G. E. M.). Oxford: Basil Blackwell.

Wlodarski, R. (2015). The relationship between cognitive and affective empathy and human mating strategies. *Evolutionary Psychological Science, 1*(4), 232–240.

Woodford, J. (2003). *Lemming Suicide Myth Disney Film Faked Bogus Behavior.* Available at www.adfg.alaska.gov/index.cfm?adfg=wildlifenews.view_article&articles_id=56, accessed on 25 August 2017.

Woollard, F. (2008). Doing and allowing, threats and sequences. *Pacific Philosophical Quarterly, 89*(2), 261–277.

WWF (2017). *Chimpanzees.* Available at http://wwf.panda.org/what_we_do/endangered_species/great_apes/chimpanzees, accessed on 16 August 2017.

Xavier, J., Magnat, J., Sherman, A., Gauthier, S., Cohen, D., and Chaby, L. (2017). A developmental and clinical perspective of rhythmic interpersonal coordination: From mimicry toward the interconnection of minds. *Journal of Physiology – Paris.* doi:10.1016/j.jphysparis.2017.06.001

Xiao, N. G., Wu, R., Quinn, P. C., Liu, S., *et al.* (2017). Infants rely more on gaze cues from own-race than other-race adults for learning under uncertainty. *Child Development.* doi:10.1111/cdev.12798

Yalom, I. D. (1975). *The Theory and Practice of Group Psychotherapy* (1st ed.). New York: Basic Books.

Yamamuro, K., Ota, T., Iida, J., Nakanishi, Y., *et al.* (2015). Prefrontal dysfunction in pediatric Tourette's disorder as measured by near-infrared spectroscopy. *BMC Psychiatry, 15*(1), 1.

Yanagizawa-Drott, D. (2014). Propaganda and conflict: Evidence from the Rwandan genocide. *The Quarterly Journal of Economics, 129*(4), 1947–1994.

Yang, S. (2013). Emotion, experiential memory and selfhood. *Organon F, 20*(1), 18–36.

Yang, X., and Marchetti, M. C. (2015). Hydrodynamics of turning flocks. *Physical Review Letters, 115*(25), 258101.

Yang, Y., Liu, X. X., Fang, Y., and Hong, Y. Y. (2014). Unresolved World War II animosity dampens empathy toward 2011 Japanese earthquake and tsunami. *Journal of Cross-Cultural Psychology, 45*(2), 171–191.

Yeo, J. H. (2013). A phenomenological reading of Zhuzi. *Philosophy East and West, 63*(2), 251–274.

Yokouchi, K., Fukushima, N., Kakegawa, A., Kawagishi, K., Fukuyama, T., and Moriizumi, T. (2007). Functional role of lingual nerve in breastfeeding. *International Journal of Developmental Neuroscience, 25*(2), 115–119.

Yokoyama, T., Sakai, H., Noguchi, Y., and Kita, S. (2014). Perception of direct gaze does not require focus of attention. *Scientific Reports, 4*, 3858.

Yu, C., Fidan, B., Shames, I., Sandeep, S., and Anderson, B. D. O. (2015). *Collision Free Coordination of Autonomous Multiagent Systems.* Paper presented at the 2007 European Control Conference, ECC 2007.

Yuill, N., Hinske, S., Williams, S. E., and Leith, G. (2014). How getting noticed helps getting on: Successful attention capture doubles children's cooperative play. *Frontiers in Psychology, 5*, 418.

Zahavi, D. (2014). Empathy and other-directed intentionality. *Topoi, 33*(1), 129–142.

Zahavi, D. (2016). Second-person engagement, self-alienation, and group-identification. *Topoi*, 1–10. doi:10.1007/s11245-016-9444-6

Zak, P. J., and Barraza, J. A. (2013). The neurobiology of collective action. *Frontiers in Neuroscience*, 7 November. doi:10.3389/fnins.2013.00211

Zakrzewska, A., and Bader, D. A. (2016). Tracking local communities in streaming graphs with a dynamic algorithm. *Social Network Analysis and Mining, 6*(1).

Zara, G., and Farrington, D. P. (2016). *Criminal Recidivism: Explanation, Prediction and Prevention.* Abingdon: Routledge.

Zhang, J. Q., Huang, Z. G., Wu, Z. X., Su, R., and Lai, Y. C. (2016). Controlling herding in minority game systems. *Scientific Reports, 6.* doi:10.1038/srep20925

Zhang, X., Chan, F. T. S., Adamatzky, A., Mahadevan, S., *et al.* (2017). An intelligent physarum solver for supply chain network design under profit maximization and oligopolistic competition. *International Journal of Production Research, 55*(1), 244–263.

Zhang, Y. (2016). Functional diversity and group creativity: The role of group longevity. *Journal of Applied Behavioral Science, 52*(1), 97–123.

Zheng, H., Kendrick, K. M., and Yu, R. (2016). Fear or greed? Oxytocin regulates inter-individual conflict by enhancing fear in men. *Hormones and Behavior, 85*, 12–18.

Zheng, X., Fehr, R., Tai, K., Narayanan, J., and Gelfand, M. J. (2014). The unburdening effects of forgiveness: Effects on slant perception and jumping height. *Social Psychological and Personality Science, 5*, 1–8.

Zink, C. F., Kempf, L., Hakimi, S., Rainey, C. A., Stein, J. L., and Meyer-Lindenberg, A. (2011). Vasopressin modulates social recognition-related activity in the left temporoparietal junction in humans. *Translational Psychiatry, 1*(4), e3.

Zisook, S., Byrd, D., Kuck, J., and Jeste, D. V. (1995). Command hallucinations in outpatients with schizophrenia. *Journal of Clinical Psychiatry, 56*(10), 462–465.

Zlatev, J. (Ed.) (2008). *The Shared Mind: Perspectives on Intersubjectivity.* Amsterdam and Philadelphia: John Benjamins.

Zlatev, J. (2014). Human uniqueness, bodily mimesis and the evolution of language. *Humana Mente Journal of Philosophical Studies, 27*, 197–219.

Zlatev, J., Racine, T., Sinha, C., and Itkonen, E. (2008). Intersubjectivity: What Makes Us Human. In J. Zlatev (Ed.) *The Shared Mind: Perspectives on Intersubjectivity* (pp.1–13). Amsterdam and Philadelphia: John Benjamins.

Zumeta, L. N., Oriol, X., Telletxea, S., Amutio, A., and Basabe, N. (2015). Collective efficacy in sports and physical activities: Perceived emotional synchrony and shared flow. *Frontiers in Psychology, 6,* 1960.

Subject Index

affective empathy 34, 78
allomothering 126–7
altruism
    altruistic suicide 90–2
    as a brain function 92
    development of 91
    economic 93
    as 'giving over to the other' 93–4
    overview of 90–3
always-on nature of interbrain 79
appeasement 222–3
argument 170, 177, 197
attachment
    bonds 49–50
    theory 58–9
attention, shared 76–8
autism, narrative and 156

babies *see* infancy
bees 101
blind justice 147–8
blindsight 52
bodies
    features supporting gaze reflexes 72
    seen as inviolate 48–9

bottom-up theories of nonverbal
    communication 46–57
'boundary' metaphor 137
brain
    insular network 55, 61–2
    mind-brain dualism 18–9, 46–7
    orbitofrontal cortex 37–8
    split brains 48
Brutus (Roman ruler) 142–5
bunching 171
Bush, George W. 255–6
bystander effect 213
Byzantine army game 205–6

Cambodia (Khmer Rouge) 216–21
catharsis 102
children
    maltreated 68
    'savagery' of 124
    see also infancy
chimpanzees
    conflict in 135
    tool use 158
cognitive empathy 41–2, 78

cohesion 113–6
  family 103
collaboration 213–4
collectives, singular names for 100
common knowledge
  changes social behaviour 208
  collaboration and 213–4
  gaining 209–10
  game theory and 204–6
  and the interbrain 210–2
  the internet and 303
  and links with leaders 228–34
  popular delusions and 206–7
  transmission of 207–9, 231–2, 303
  and war 262, 273–5
communication
  of information 180–1
  orbitofrontal cortex and 37–8
  see also nonverbal communication
complementarity 63
compliance 221–4
Comrade Duch 219, 221
confirmation bias 28
conflict
  in ancient Rome 142–8
  conflict theory view of 134–5
  consensus social theory view of 134
  as evolutionary stage 135
  internal 137–8
  unconscious 83, 194–5
  see also war
connectedness
  feelings 183–8
  intersubjectivity 22, 30–1, 129–30
  and mirroring 25–6
  neuronal synchronization 20–1, 23
  nonverbal communication and 33–5
  'wishful' intuition of 28–9
consciousness, human 32
consensus social theory 134
contagion
  of arousal 23
  emotional 33–4, 74–6

laughter epidemic 85–6
  Le Bon's model 100
  yawning 113
cooperation 202–6
coordination 202–6
'cringe' 191–2
crowds
  characteristics of 96
  deindividuation when in 95–9, 123
  Elaborated Social Identity Model
    (ESIM) 98
  enjoyment of participation in 102–3
  evacuation of 112
  flock behaviour 101
  'giving in' to 95
  gregarious/solitary switch when in
    111, 120
  legal proscription of 101
  'mobs' 106–7
  nonverbal communication within 98
  out-group creation 103
  'primal horde' (Freud) 111–2
  'psychopathology' of 99–102
  religion and 121–4
  singular names for 100
  swarms 105–6, 111–2, 114–6, 276–7

danger signals 47
death, fear of 264
death instinct 195–6
deceit 162–3
decision-making, by groups 200–2
degenerationism 286–7, 288, 290
dehumanization 240–3
deindividuation 95–9, 123
demonization 239–40, 294–5
disconnection
  causes of 235–6
  through negativity 236–7
disgust
  displacement of 190
  link with nausea 55, 61–2
  negative emotions and feeling 237

displacement 189–90
dissociation 287
dogs, itch scratching 51
dreams, Freud on 188–9
driverless cars 152–4

echomimia 64
economic altruism 93
effervescent moods 122
Elaborated Social Identity Model
    (ESIM) 98
embarrassment 191–2
emotional contagion 33–4, 74–6
emotions
    connection through narrative 187–8
    induced by narrative 188–91
    self-conscious 213–5
'emotors' 185
empathy
    Adam Smith on 211–2
    affective 34, 78
    cognitive 41–2, 78
    current focus on 251–2
    definition of 24
    testosterone and 226–7
enfacement illusion 73
equality
    in spontaneous groups 109–12
    taken as self-evident 108
eusociality 233
evacuation of crowds 112
'executive self' 83, 84
extended cognition theories 129
extended minds 163, 202
eye contact 68, 70, 241

facial expressions, memory of 99
facial imitation 70–1
facial mimicry 64–6
facial responsiveness 88
fairness rule 141
false-belief test 155–6
family cohesion 103
fanaticism 94

favouritism, in-group 119–20
'feedforward' process 36
Finnegans Wake (Joyce) 172–4
flock behaviour 101
foetus-mother communication 50
free-loading 137

game theory 204–6
gaze
    eye contact 68, 70, 241
    mutual 69–70
    reflexes 67–70
    responses to 65–6
gramarye (Scott) 167–8
gregarious/solitary switch 111, 120
grooming behaviour 104–5
'group-think' 202
groups
    connection with the leader 225–30
    decision-making by 200–2
    equality in 109–12
    expulsion from 236–7

hate 238
historical truth 175–9
honey algorithm 101
Howards End (Forster) 172–4
Humean sympathy 57–60

I-it relationship 21
identification 58
imagination 79, 98
imitation, facial 70–1
imprinting 50
in-groups
    favouritism 119–20
    grooming behaviour 104–5
    honour and duty to 244–7
    origins of concept 90
    swarm-like features of 120–1
    threat and 117–8
    threats to leader of 246–8
    U.S. as (after twin towers attack) 259
individualism 43

inequality 166–7
infancy
  memories of 87
  nonverbal communication in 50,
    87–9
infanticide 60, 126
information
  communication of 180–1
  see also common knowledge
insular network 55, 61–2
intention
  attribution of 35–6
  tendency to exaggerate 51
intentionality 171
interaction theory 128–9
interbrain
  always-on nature of 79
  definition of 18
  use of the term 66
internal conflict 137–8
internal narrative 45
internet connections 301–5
intersubjectivity 22, 30–1, 129–30
intuition
  and science 17–8
  of the universe 30
Jonestown massacre 223–4

Keats, John 47
knowledge see common knowledge;
    information

labelling theory 291
laughter, epidemic of 85–6
leaders
  charismatic 230–1
  common knowledge links with
    228–34
  Comrade Duch 219, 221
  connection with group 225–30
  establishment of 124–5
  George W. Bush 255–6
  and in- and out-groups 246–8
  obedience to 221–4

Pol Pot 217–8
  Reverend Jones 223–4
  temporary 226
lemmings' 'suicide' 116
Lucretia, rape of 142–3
ludus 140

marching 20–1
MDMA 61, 118
memory, of very early experiences 87
mental connections, vs. interbrain
    connections 78–9
mimicry 63–6
  infant-carer 26, 71
  see also imitation
mind
  concept of 179–80
  see also theory of mind
mind-brain dualism 18–9, 46–7
mirror neurons 72–4, 75
mirror-touch synaesthesia 73
mirroring
  connectedness and 25–6
  deliberate and involuntary 26–7
'mobs' 106–7
monsters/monstrosities
  creation of 285–9
  dangerous, severely abnormal
    personality disorder (DSPD)
    296–8
  medical explanations of 286–9
  othering of 281, 296, 299
  psychopaths 289–96
Montaigne 160
moral convictions 230–1
moral dilemma (trolley problem)
    148–54
moral panic 265–6, 277–83
mortality salience 257, 262
'murder-suicides' 223
music 172–4
musicians' neuronal synchronization 23
mutual gaze 69–70

narcissistic personality disorder 295
narrative
    autism and 156
    and develop of the self 159–61
    emotional connection through
        187–8
    inducing emotions 188–91
    internal 45
    shared 174–5
    theory of mind and 40–1
    truth (vs. historical truth) 175–9
nausea-disgust link 55, 61–2
neuroeconomics 93
non-awareness 47–52
nonverbal communication
    bottom-up theories of 46–57
    connectedness and 33–5
    innate 62–80
    top-down theories of 34–8
    within crowds 98

oaths 231
obedience 221–4
oral story-telling 43
orbitofrontal cortex 37–8
other people
    connections with 164–6
    existence of 162–3, 183–4
othering 281, 296, 299
Ouija phenomenon 115
out-groups
    creation of 103
    social dominance theory 109
oxytocin
    and attachment behaviour 117–8
    link with suggestibility 94

paidia 140
pain, compassionate response to others'
        56–7, 60
panic, moral 265–6, 277–83
path creation 107
person-to-person contact 98

perspective taking 181–3
play 139–41
Pol Pot 217–8
'positivism', as term for scorn 91
post-traumatic stress disorder 85
'precocial' development 50
predictability 182–3, 184
Prisoners' Dilemma Game 93
'professor of signs' story 196–8
promiscuity, empathy and 84
psychopaths
    modern conception of 290–1
    original use of term 289
    overview of 292–6
pygmy chimpanzees 135

quale 31–2

rape of Lucretia 142–3
reasoning 170
reciprocal gaze 26
religion
    and crowds 121–4
    dual perceptions of the world in 194
    effervescent moods 122
    experience of oneness with God
        29–30
revolutions 216, 258, 265
Roman rule 142–8

scratch reflex 51
self
    'executive' 83, 84
    narrative and development of the
        159–61
self-awareness
    and consciousness 32
    and theory of mind 44–5
self-conscious emotions 213–5
self-control, violence and 136
separateness, bodily 49–51
shared attention 76–8
shared narrative 174–5

Sharia law 148

signals *see* danger signals

similarity, nonverbal connection using 63

simulation theory 128

smell
  connection through 46–7
  male-female attraction 53
  parenting behaviour and 53–4
  'trace of' 67

social dominance theory 109

social phase 192

sociality 233–4

solipsism 162–3, 183–4

sophists 191

speech 158–9
  see also narrative

Spielrein, Sabina 195–6

split brains 48

'still face' experiment 88

story-telling
  oral 43
  recognizable grammar in 197–8

Strange Stories Test 155

stranger anxiety 139

submission 220

suicide
  altruistic 90–2
  Jonestown massacre 223–4
  lemmings 116
  'murder-suicides' 223

swarms 105–6, 111–2, 114–6, 120–1, 276–7

sympathy, Humean 57–60

synaesthesia, mirror-touch 73

synchronous movement 20–1

terminology 44, 71

terror
  factors which lead to 264–7
  The Terror 216, 258
  see also terrorism

terror management theory 264

terrorism
  connections of terrorists 275–85
  democratization of 284–5
  lone terrorists 283–4
  moral terror (panic) 265–6, 277–83
  new narrative on 256–9
  purpose of 275
  Vlad the impaler 278–81

theory of mind
  false-belief test 155–6
  and narrative speech development 40–1
  opposition with interbrain 138–41
  original studies on 154–7
  overview of 38–43
  Sally-Anne marble test 39–40
  and self-awareness 44–5
  simulation theory 128
  Strange Stories Test 155
  'theory theory' 128

thinking, language's role in 83

threat 117–8, 246–8

Titus Livius 142–8

Tokyo subway system 108

top-down processes 34–8

transcendence 123–4

trolley problem 148–54

truth, narrative vs. historical 175–9

Turing test 163

unconscious conflict 83, 194–5

UNUM software 115

violence
  motives for 135–6
  self-control and 136
  see also conflict; war

visual perspective taking 38

Vlad the impaler 278–81

war
  causes of 260–3
  championship approach to
      prevention of 274
  common knowledge and 262, 273–5
  declared after twin towers attack
      254, 256

effect of 272–3
ending of 267–8
explanations for 255
interbrain in 269–72
moral importance of 263
non-combatant casualties 261–2
revolutions 216, 258, 265

Author Index

Note: A page number followed by n indicates that the reference is in the chapter endnotes.

Aaltola, E. 34 *n*17, 75
Ab Wahab, M. N. 101 *n*11
AbdulSabur, N. Y. 161
Abell, F. 36 *n*20
Abrahams, N. 148 *n*25
Abrams, D. 121
Adams, D. B. 222 *n*7
Adams, R. 119 *n*28
Adolphs, R. 69
Aguirre, M. 198
Ainley, V. 48 *n*31
Aïte, A. 187
Aitken, K. J. 130
Alshamsi, A. 34
Amiraux, V. 265 *n*20
Amit, E. 83
Anderson, J. R. 98
Andrés-Roqueta, C. 40
Ankony, R. 258
Anscombe, G. E. M. 172
Anzieu, D. 137
Apfelbaum, E. P. 77 *n*85

Ardizzi, M. 68
Arlet, M. 105
Armoudian, M. 243 *n*28
Arndt, J. 273
Aron, R. 125
Artelli, M. J. 256
Asbrock, F. 264 *n*16
Assink, M. 293
Atyabi, A. 101 *n*11
Auerbach, E. 160
Austin, J. L. 180
Avenanti, A. 72 *n*73
Ayduk, O. 85
Azzam, T. I. 139 *n*10

Bader, D. A. 236
Badets, A. 66
Balconi, M. 65
Banatvala, J. 260
Banissy, M. J. 73, 73 *n*75
Banks, J. 234
Bara, B. G. 159
Barbey, A. K. 33 *n*14
Barch, D. 156
Baron-Cohen, S. 39, 39 *n*25, 42, 155
Barraza, J. A. 118

Bartholomew, R. H. D. 206
Bartlett, M. S. 56 n37, 282
Bartlett, P. 292
Bartov, O. 251
Basabe, N. 134 n2
Bastian, M. 83
Bate, S. 118
Batki, A. 68
Bauernfeind, A. L. 55 n34
Bauman, C. W. 151
Baumeister, R. F. 83, 84
Bayliss, A. P. 69
BBC News 148 n24
Beaulieu, D. A. 139 n10
Becchio, C. 70
Becker, D. 56 n36
Becker, G. 127
Bègue, L. 151
Bekkering, H. 69
Belk, R. 135 n3, 302 n52
Benjamin, W. 190
Berdahl, A. 229 n10
Berry, J. W. 238
Bershad, A. K. 118
Berthet, V. 65
Bien, N. 64
Bigelow, A. E. 88
Bilali, R. 103
Binmore, K. 205
Black, A. 224
Black, S. J. 298 n51
Blaye, A. 139 n9
Bleiker, R. 243 n29
Bleske-Rechek, A. 151, 153 n31
Blight, O. 110 n21, 119 n29
Boa, E. 265
Boccardi, M. 293 n46
Böckler, A. 70, 295
Boguñá, M. 124
Böhm, R. 120, 240 n22
Bohn, M. 158
Bojanowski, V. 67

Bonnefon, J.-F. 153
Bonner, J. 49
Book, A. 295
Boothby, E. J. 209 n10
Borch, C. 97, 224, 225
Borries, C. 60, 126
Bos, P. A. 60 n50, 227, 303
Bosch, O. J. 118
Boucher, O. 54
Bourdieu, P. 269
Bowlby, J. 50, 59
Bowman, N. D. 234
Bowyer, R. T. 125
Braadbaart, L. 75
Braccini, S. N. 158
Brambilla, M. 242
Braten, S. 66
Brazelton, T. B. 89
Brentano, F. 44 n28, 171 n1
Brentari, D. 172
Breslau, J. 263 n12
Briggs, K. 196
Broad, K. D. 54
Broom, M. 60, 126
Brown, C. 85
Brown, H. M. 40
Brown, R. 243 n27
Brüne, M. 261
Bruneau, E. G. 243 n30
Bruner, J. 140 n11, 157 n33, 161
Bryant, L. 94
Bryant, R. A. 118
Buber, M. 21, 192, 193 n10
Bucchioni, G. 237
Buchanan, T. W. 226
Bugental, D. B. 139 n10
Bumann, D. 225
Burgaleta, M. 213
Burgoon, J. K. 222 n6
Burke, B. L. 272 n36
Burklund, L. J. 236
Burnett-Zeigler, I. 77 n81

Cacioppo, J. 74, 263 *n*13
Caillois, R. 140 *n*13
Calderara, S. 223
Call, J. 155, 158
Calvo, M. G. 162
Camacho, D. 236
Camerer, C. F. 93
Campbell, M. W. 120
Campbell, R. 91, 98
Campbell, S. B. 87
Canavesio, Y. 65
Candidi, M. 72 *n*73
Canetti, E. 58, 100, 109 *n*19
Cannon-Bowers, J. A. 202 *n*3
Cao, Y. 60 *n*46
Capellini, R. 245 *n*31
Capps, L. M. 191
Carney, J. 44
Carter, C. S. 118
Case, T. I. 137
Caspar, E. A. 221
Castano, E. 121, 191, 230 *n*18, 242
    *n*24, 243 *n*27, 251 *n*2
Castelli, L. 110 *n*20
Catmur, C. 150
Cauda, F. 64
Cehajic, S. 243 *n*27
Cela-Conde, C. J. 65
Çelik, A. B. 103
Chabon, M. 172
Chakraborty, T 236
Chartrand, T. L. 26, 63, 64, 71 *n*70, 73
Chatard, A. 273 *n*37
Chatel-Goldman, J. 64, 66
Cheetham, M. 221, 222 *n*4
Cheng, X. 23, 66
Chevalier, N. 139 *n*9
Chiarella, S. S. 87
Chisholm, J. D. 193
Chivers, T. 293
Christov-Moore, L. 90, 156
Chung, Y. S. 156
Chwe, M. 210 *n*11

Cialdini, R. B. 91
Cicirelli, V. G. 264 *n*15
Cikara, M. 120, 243 *n*30
Cimpian, A. 171
Clair, R. P. 170
Clancy, P. M. 191 *n*8
Clark, R. D. 62 *n*62
Clayton, S. 272
Cleckley, H. 290 *n*44
Cocking, C. 102 *n*14, 112
Coeckelbergh, M. 241
Cohen, E. 125
Cohen, F. 256 *n*7
Cohen, S. 278
Cohen-Almagor, R. 275 *n*38
Coleman, S. 207 *n*6, 215 *n*12
Colgan, J. D. 265 *n*17
Colle, L. 156
Collet, C. 23
Colonnesi, C. 68
Coltheart, M. 155
Comte, A. 91, 93
Constable, G. W. A. 126
Conway, J. R. 156
Cooley, C. 25
Coppola, M. 172
Corballis, M. C. 174
Cosenza, M. G. 124
Costello, K. 242 *n*25
Couzin, I. D. 115, 202 *n*2
Cowan, D. G. 70
Crawley, D. 271 *n*27
Creed, R. S. 51
Crespi, B. J. 233
Crisp, R. J. 243
Croft, D. P. 233
Crone, D. L. 149
Cross, H. 59
Cross, K. A. 134 *n*1
Crouter, R. 30
Croy, I. 7
Cucchiara, R. 223
Cummins, F. 63 *n*63

Cunningham, S. J. 87
Curley, J. P. 54
Cushman, F. 150, 152 *n*30
Cwir, D. 22
Czarna, A. Z. 295

Dalsklev, M. 243 *n*29
Damasio, H. 62 *n*60
Darwin, C. 64
Dastgiri, S. S. 238
Dastur, F. 271
Daum, M. M. 138 *n*5
Dauvier, B. 139 *n*9
Dawkins, R. 207
De Coster, L. 71 *n*69
De Dreu, C. K. W. 70, 118 *n*26
De Jaegher, H. 66
de Oliveira-Souza, R. 293 *n*45
De Villiers, J. G. 41, 156
De Villiers, P. A. 41, 156
de Waal, F. B. M. 66, 74 *n*78, 93 *n*6,
    120
Decety, J. 24, 34 *n*18, 57 *n*41, 60 *n*45,
    60 *n*47, 74 *n*76, 75
Deci, E. L. 241 *n*23
Deen, M. 295
Deffa, O. J. 165 *n*38
Deigh, J. 303 *n*54
Dein, S. 223
DeLay, S. 162
Demuru, E. 113
Derrida, J. 174
Deska, J. C. 66
DeSteno, D. 20*n*2, 20*n*3, 237
Di Paolo, E. A. 66
Diener, E. 96
Dijksterhuis, G. B. 62 *n*55
Dixon, T. 91
Dodell-Feder, D. 155
Doherty, M. J. 69
Doi, H. 68
Doom, J. R. 182
Dor, D. 162 *n*35

Doucet, S. 54
Downes, C. 282
Drury, J. 112
Du Preez, J. 263
Dubas, J. S. 53
Duffy, K. A. 26, 63, 64, 72
Duke, A. A. 151
Dullstein, M. 34 *n*16, 75
Dumas, G. 23, 66
Dumont, B. 125
Dunbar, R. 38, 44, 63 *n*63, 103 *n*15,
    105, 165 *n*39
Durkheim, E. 90, 122 *n*32, 127, 166
    *n*40
Dutton, K. 298 *n*51
Dziobek, I. 92

Echterhoff, G. 66
Eckmann, J. P. 125
Edele, A. 92
Ehlers, K. R. 72
Einwohner, R. L. 247
Eisenberg, N. 89, 92
Eisenberger, N. I. 104, 105, 236
El-Sayed, E. 159
Eliastam, J. 232
Eres, R. 57 *n*40, 261
Eriksson, A. 283 *n*39
Ernst, U. R. 111
Eskine, K. J. 61 *n*52
Espelage, D. 67

Fabes, R. 89, 92
Fairbairn, C. E. 30
Faivre, N. 65
Fakunle, D. 239
Fanti, K. A. 237
Farrington, D. P. 252 *n*3, 293, 294
Farroni, T. 68
Fatfouta, R 238
Fawcett, C. 25 *n*6
Federico, C. M. 230 *n*11
Fehr, E. 93

Feldberg, F. 103

Feldman, R. 68

Fels, S. 115

Feng, C. 225

Fernández, C. 40, 40 *n*26

Fernández-Berrocal, P. 42

Fessler, D. M. T. 20 *n*1

Festinger, L. 96

Fields, L. 298

Fikke, L. 69

Finis, J. 64

Fischer, A. H. 56 *n*36, 70

Fisher, W. 170, 176

Fiske, A. P. 66, 233

Fitch, W. T. 158

Flannery, D. J. 288 *n*43

Flew, A. 29 *n*9

Flinders, M. 239 *n*20, 243

Florian, V. 273

Foot, P. 149 *n*26

Foroni, F. 75

Forster, E. M. 173, 305 *n*55

Foster, K. R. 233

Franchak, J. M. 138 *n*7, 139 *n*8

Frank, M. G. 237

Franken, I. 295

Frankopan, P. 104 *n*16, 261

Frederick, R. 158

Freitas, K. 273

Freud, S. 52, 102, 111, 112, 188 *n*6, 224

Frey, D. 273

Fridland, E. 25 *n*7

Friedman, R. S. 273

Frischen, A. 69, 77 *n*80

Frith, C. D. 69 *n*66

Frith, U. 36 *n*20, 39 *n*25, 69 *n*66

Froese, T. 66

Fuchs, T. 66

Fusaroli, R. 164 *n*37

Fussell, S. R. 206 *n*5

Gaca, K. L. 292

Galinsky, A. D. 187

Gallagher, S. 128 *n*37, 194

Gallese, V. 66

Gallinat, J. 24

Galton, F. 201

Gamannossi, B. A. 41

Gangopadhyay, N. 163, 164 *n*37

Gauchou, H. L. 115

Gellately, R. 220

Geminiani, G. C. 64

Georgescu, A. L. 68

Giannitelli, M. 64

Gibson, T. 267 *n*24

Gigone, D. H. R. 208

Gilbert, C. D. 36

Gilead, M. 214

Gimbel, S. I. 245 *n*34

Giner, O. 239

Giner-Sorolla, R. 121, 191, 239 *n*18, 243 *n*27

Ginsburg, H. J. 222 *n*5

Ginsburg, S. 162 *n*35

Gladwell, M. 207 *n*7

Gleditsch, N. P. 254 *n*4

Gleichgerrcht, E. 151 *n*29

Glenn, A. L. 293 *n*46

Glover, V. 50

Godman, M. 103

Goepner, E. 256 *n*8

Gold, D. 261

Goldberg, A. 74 *n*78

Goldie, P. 170, 185

Golding, W. 124 *n*36

Goller, A. I. 73

González, R. 124, 243 *n*27

González-Avella, J. C. 124

Gonzalez-Liencres, C. 261

González-Pardo, A. 236

Goode, E. 278

Goodwin, G. P. 165

Gordin, S. 207

Göritz, A. S. 103

Görlich, A. 117

Gredebäck, G. 69

Greenberg, J. 258, 260, 264 *n*16, 273
Greene, J. D. 150
Gregory, R. 54
Guibourdenche, J. 50
Gutsell, J. N. 104
Gvirsman, S. D. 267

Haas, B. W. 118
Hacker, P. M. S. 44
Hale, J. L. 222 *n*6
Halpern, J. 205
Ham, M. I. 125
Hamilton, A. F. 73, 166
Hamlin, J. K. 87
Hannikainen, I. A. 152 *n*30
Hanson, J. E. 232
Happé, F. 36 *n*20, 156
Hare, B. 182
Hare, C. 267 *n*24
Hare, R. D. 293, 293 *n*47, 294 *n*48
Hari, R. 73
Harlow, H. 59
Harper, S. 244
Harris, S. 245 *n*34
Hashikawa, K. 255 *n*6
Haslam, N. 104, 222 *n*3, 242, 242 *n*24
Haslam, S. A. 222 *n*3
Hatfield, E. 74
Hatters-Friedman, S. 223 *n*8
Hayasaki, E. 73
Hecht, E. E. 33 *n*14
Heerey, E. A. 191
Heidegger, M. 30
Heijkoop, M. 53
Hein, G. 121 *n*30
Heintz, N. 117
Heinz, A. 24
Hellmann, J. K. 225
Henderson, D. K. 289
Hennig, H. 23, 71 *n*71
Henricks, T. 140
Herbert, J. S. 139 *n*8
Herodotus 164

Herpertz, S. C. 104
Herschbach, M. 66
Heyes, C. 89
Higgins, E. T. 66
Hillier, B. 232
Hirschberger, G. 273
Hirsh, J. B. 137
Hobson, R. P. 130
Hodson, G. 242 *n*25
Hoehl, S. 69
Hoffman, M. B. 294
Hoffman, M. L. 62 *n*61
Hofman, D. 88
Hogg, M. 121
Holbrook, C. 20*n*1, 267
Holland, E. 225
Hollingshead, R. 194 *n*12
Hömke, P. 70
Hopkins, N. 122
Hornsey, M. J. 238, 241
Hoyle, F. 163
Hrdy, S. B. 126
Huebner, B. 163 *n*36
Hugenberg, K. 66
Hume, D. 29 *n*9, 57–60
Hummel, T. 67
Husserl, E. 30, 74, 79 *n*87
Hutcherson, C. A. 61 *n*53
Hwang, H. C. 237
Hyatt, C. S. 298 *n*51
Hysek, C. M. 61

Iacoboni, M. 134 *n*1
Iarocci, G. 34
Iatridis, T. 242
Ihl, C. 125
Immordino-Yang, M. H. 62 *n*60
Inagaki, T. K. 105
Inzlicht, M. 104
Iqbal, Y. 103
Ishii, K. 36
Ivie, R. L. 239
Iyer, A. 266 *n*22

Jablonka, E. 162 *n*35
Jackson, F. 31, 31 *n*12
Jacobs, A. 125
Jalava, J. G. S. 299
Jankowiak-Siuda, K. 60 *n*48
Jankowski, K. F. 56 *n*35
Jetten, J. 241
Jeurissen, D. 150
Jiang, J. 23
Joffé, G. 260 *n*10
Johnson, M. H. 155
Jolliffe, D. 252 *n*3
Jonas, E. 272 *n*31, 273
Jonason, P. K. 295
Jure, R. 156

Kacinik, N. A. 61 *n*52
Kagan, J. 59
Kaiser, J. 65
Kalmar, D. 161
Kang, S. K. 137
Kao, A. B. 202 *n*2
Kaplan, J. T. 245 *n*34
Kappas, A. 242 *n*26
Kashima, Y. 33 *n*15
Kastenmüller, A. 272 *n*33
Keith, A. 90
Keller, A. 53
Keller, M. 92
Keltner, D. 191
Kendon, A. 69
Kendrick, K. M. 118
Kent, P. 104
Ketelaars, M. P. 156
Keverne, E. B. 54
Khalid, S. 66
Kiehl, K. A. 294, 298 *n*51
Kiernan, B. 217
Kim, J. 165
Kim, S. 68
Kim-Cohen, J. 293
Kingstone, A. 69
Kirkpatrick, M. G. 61

Kiryukhin, D. 261
Kisilevsky, B. S. 50
Kissi, E. 218
Klein, P. D. 40
Klin, A. 36 *n*20
Knecht, T. 287 *n*41
Knoll, J. L. I. 223 *n*8
Knudsen, B. T. 225
Koch, I. 66
Koch, J. 289
Koenig, A. 60, 126
Koenigs, M. 150
Kokkinaki, T. 25 *n*8
Konecny, S. 49
Konvalinka, I. 72
Koomen, W. 266
Kosloff, S. 272 *n*36
Kouider, S. 65
Kow, L.-M. 189
Krall, S. C. 150
Krause, J. 225
Krause, L. 295
Krauss, R. M. 206 *n*5
Krebs, D. L. 165
Kret, M. E. 62, 65, 70, 118
Kretschmar, J. M. 288 *n*43
Kross, E. 85
Krueger, J. 66, 89, 129 *n*38
Kruglanski, A. W. 245 *n*32
Krumhuber, E. G. 242 *n*26
Krupenye, C. 182
Kukla, L. 49
Künecke, J. 65
Kunst, J. R. 243 *n*29
Kurzban, R. 293 *n*46
Kyranides, M. N. 237

Laham, S. M. 149
Laidlaw, K. E. W. 69
Laing, R. D. 179
Lakin, J. L. 71 *n*70
Lamm, C. 34 *n*18, 74 *n*76, 75
Landau, M. J. 258

Langdon, R. 155

Lara-Carrasco, J. 50

Larrick, R. P. 206

Latty, T. 235, 235 *n*14

Launay, J. 29, 63 *n*63

Lavine, H. 273

Le Bon, G. 74 *n*77, 96, 96 *n*8, 96 *n*9,
100, 105, 224, 226

Le Borgne, P. 287 *n*42

Lee, A. R. 179

Lee, T. W. 75

Leeman, R. F. 165

Legare, C. H. 123 *n*35

Leidner, B. 121, 191, 238 *n*18, 242 *n*24,
243

Lemogne, C. 55, 77 *n*82

Lerner, M. J. 272

Leslie, A. 39 *n*25

Lessing, D. 296 *n*49, 296 *n*50

Levine, J. M. 66

Lewis, D. 205

Li, J. 118

Li, W. 36

Li, X. 23

Liang, J. G. 125

Liao, X. 233

Lichtenfeld, S. 238

Lickel, B. 178 *n*2

Lieberman, J. D. 267

Lieberman, M. D. 72 *n*74, 236

Lieven, E. 138

Likowski, K. 65, 84 *n*2

Lim, A. 88

Lim, D. 237

Lin, J. 112

Lin, L. R. 138

Lindenberger, U. 23

Littlewood, R. 223

Liu, T. 23

Liu, Y. 243 *n*30

Livius, T. 142 *n*14, 143 *n*15, 144 *n*16,
17, 145 *n*18, 146 *n*19, 20, 21, 22,
147 *n*23

Locard, H. 218, 220 *n*1

Lodge, M. 273

Lorenz, K. 50, 58, 59

Loughnan, S. 104, 222 *n*3, 242 *n*24

Louis, W. R. 266 *n*22

Low, K. E. Y. 46 *n*29

Low, S. 67

Lu, Y. 49

Lübke, K. T. 46, 53, 55 *n*33

Lucas, T. A. 112

Luo, S. 272 *n*30

Lymer, J. 71

Lynn, S. K. 225

McAlister, A. L. 266 *n*21, 267

McBurney, D. H. 67

MacCarron, P. 103 *n*15

McDougall, W. 224

McGuigan, N. 139

Mackay, C. 206

McKay, F. H. 278

MacLean, E. L. 182

McLean, K. C. 238

McNab, A. 298 *n*51

MacSweeney, M. 35 *n*19

Madill, A. 85

Magee, J. C. 187

Mahmut, M. K. 55

Mai, X. 150

Maister, L. 48 *n*31, 73

Malaspina, D. 53

Malka, A. 271 *n*28, 295

Malory, T. 268 *n*25, 269, 270 *n*26

Mampe, B. 26

Mancke, F. 104

Manini, B. 58, 59

Mannes, A. E. 206

Mansfield, C. D. 238

Maraun, M. 299

Marchetti, M. C. 158

Marcovitch, S. 83

Marissen, M. 295

Markus, H. R. 138

Marlier, L. 50, 62 *n*56
Martin, E. M. 189
Martin, G. 62 *n*62, 278
Martin, L. J. 226
Martin, W. 49
Martínez, R. 242
Maryanski, A. 129
Masicampo, E. J. 84
Masten, A. S. 104
Masuda, T. 36, 43 *n*27
Masur, E. F. 26
Matsumoto, D. 237
Mayer, F. S. 97
Mayne, R. 235
Meares, R. 47
Mele, A. R. 83
Melinder, A. 69
Meloy, J. R. 298 *n*51
Meltzoff, A. 71
Mendes, W. B. 56 *n*38, 226
Mercier, H. 170
Merleau-Ponty, M. 30, 66, 78, 89
Mesulam, M. M. 38 *n*22
Midgley, M. 148
Mikulincer, M. 273
Milgram, S. 221, 222 *n*2
Milinski, M. 53
Miller, A. G. 222 *n*3
Miller, R. 150, 152 *n*30, 190 *n*7
Miller, S. E. 83
Miranda, D. 165
Mitani, J. C. 166
Miyahara, K. 163
Modzeleski, W. 288 *n*43
Molenberghs, P. 261
Moller, A. C. 241 *n*23
Montag, C. 24
Montague, D. P. 140 *n*aa
Moore, M. 71
Moore, R. 25 *n*7, 159
Morelli, S. A. 72 *n*74
Morgan, G. S. 230 *n*11
Moriguchi, Y. 60 *n*45

Morin, A. 159, 159 *n*34
Mosek-Eilon, V. 34
Mosquera-Doñate, G. 124
Muir, K. 85
Muldoon, O. T. 282
Müller, V. 23, 66
Müller-Pinzler, L. 62 *n*59, 191
Mullet, E. 238

Nachman, B.-Y. 278
Nagy, E. 26
Nail, P. R. 245 *n*32
Nakajima, M. 117
Nakrani, S. 101 *n*11
Narayan, A. J. 104
Nateghian, S. 238
Neath, K. 69
Nefti-Meziani, S. 101 *n*11
Neumann, C. S. 293, 293 *n*47, 294 *n*48
Neumann, D. 40
Newcomb, T. 96
Newell, B. R. 51 *n*32
Niedzwiecka, A. 69
Nielsen, M. 70
Nietzsche, F. 91
Nisbett, R. E. 43 *n*27, 160
Nomikou, I. 138 *n*5
Norenzayan, A. 240
Norscia, I. 113
Novelli, D. 110
Nowak, M. 24, 233
Nowak, R. 54
Nowrasteh, A. 257 *n*9
Nummenmaa, L. 105

Oaten, M. 137
Obladen, M. 60
O'Connor, C. M. 225
Ogden, T. 130
Okimoto, T. G. 238
Okuno, H. G. 88
Olivier, B. 118
Olson, J. 26

Olson, K. R. 272
Ondobaka, S. 69
Oostenbroek, J. 139 *n*10
Osang, T. 282
Otsuka, Y. 138 *n*6
Ouyang, J. 20 *n*3
Over, H. 139 *n*10
Overpeck, M. D. 126

Páez, D. 122, 122 *n*33
Palagi, E. 113
Palero, F. 236
Palombit, R. A. 126
Paluck, E. L. 208
Panahi, O. 149 *n*28
Panayiotou, G. 237
Papafragou, A. 83
Pardini, D. A. 293 *n*47
Parma, V. 67 *n*64
Pasupathi, M. 238
Patterson, R. 33 *n*14
Paulus, F. M. 113, 192 *n*9
Pause, B. M. 46, 53, 55 *n*33
Pearce, E. 63 *n*63
Peirce, C. S. 52
Pelowski, M. 23
Pepitone, A. 96
Perea García, J. O. 72
Perez, E. C. 69, 226, 233
Perez-Osorio, J. 69
Perner, J. 39 *n*24
Peters, K. 33 *n*15
Pfaff, D. 92, 189
Philip, P. J. 86 *n*1, 86 *n*3
Philipp, A. M. 66
Philippi, C. L. 32 *n*13
Phillipson, H. 179
Pierno, A. C. 70
Pillot, M. H. 125
Pinel, E. 22, 23
Pinker, S. 135–6
Pinto, G. 41, 233
Pobric 150

Pogonza, R. 156
Pollman, V. A. 222 *n*5
Pond, R. S. 236 *n*15
Population Reference Bureau 158
Poria, S. 62 *n*58
Porter, M. A. 155
Post, S. G. 74 *n*78
Postmes, T. 95
Poulin-Dubois, D. 87
Powell, J. 38 *n*21, 165 *n*39
Power, M. 88
Prati, F. 243
Pratto, F. 109 *n*18
Premack, D. 39 *n*23, 154 *n*32, 155
Preston, L. 74 *n*78
Preston, S. D. 66, 74 *n*78, 225
Prichard, J. 289
Prinsen, J. 26
Prinz, J. J. 61 *n*52
Propp, V. 198
Proust, M. 61, 82
Pyszczynski, T. 258, 260, 264 *n*16

Queller, D. C. 233

Racy, F. 159
Rahwan, I. 153
Raina, M. K. 198
Raine, A. 293 *n*46
Rakhlin, N. 40
Rameson, L. T. 72 *n*74
Rand, A. 91
Randles, D. 34, 74
Rands, S. A. 125
Rankin, A. M. 86 *n*1, 86 *n*3
Rapin, I. 156
Rapson, R. 74
Ratnieks, F. L. W. 233
Raz, G. 60 *n*49
Reagans, R. M. B. 209 *n*8
Redcay, E. 63, 78
Reddy, R. B. 166
Reddy, V. 130

Reeck, M. 228
Reed, M. 267 *n*23
Reffay, M. 125
Reicher, S. 95, 97, 98, 112, 222 *n*3
Reicherts, P. 65
Reid, C. R. 235, 235 *n*14
Reinhard, M. A. 272 *n*32
Renata Aron, N. 125
Renger, D. 242, 244
Rennung, M. 103
Rensink, R. A. 115
Reynolds, C. 100
Richman, S. B. 237
Rickman, J. 130
Ricks, C. 47 *n*30
Riehl, C. 60
Riem, M. M. E. 118, 118 *n*25, 120
Riggins, T. 87
Riva, P. 242
Robertson, S. 139
Rochat, P. 130
Rogers, C. 44
Rombough, A. 34
Rong, S. 233
Ronson, J. 298 *n*51
Rosenbaum, S. 126
Rosenberg, L. 114 *n*23, 115
Rosenthal, S. B. 112
Ross, J. 98
Roth, L. 56 *n*35
Rothgerber, H. 114
Rothwell, A. 69
Rotter, M. 272 *n*35
Roy, L. 29
Royzman, E. B. 165
Rubini, M. 243
Rubio-Fernández, P. 182
Rucker, D. D. 187
Ruckmann, J. 120
Rueda, P. 42
Rusconi, E. 73
Rychlowska, M. 63, 162

Saeri, A. K. 266 *n*22
Sagi, A. 62 *n*61
Sah, W. H. 176
St Jacques, P. L. 87
Salas, E. 202 *n*3
Sampson, T. 79
Sandel, A. A. 166
Sanderson, G. 265 *n*18
Sandmann, L. R. 125
Sänger, J. 23
Santamaría-García, H. 213
Santiesteban, I. 73
Sarlo, M. 151
Sartre, J.-P. 91, 94, 96 *n*7
Sato, W. 65, 75
Saucier, D. A. 239 *n*21
Saux, M. S. 278
Saxe, R. R. 243 *n*30
Schaal, B. 50, 62 *n*56
Schacter, D. L. 87
Schafer, R. 44
Scheff, T. 228 *n*9, 261
Scheidel, W. 99, 258
Scheinin, M. 278
Scheler, M. 24, 78
Scheutz, M. 151
Schiermer, B. 190
Schilbach, L. 70 *n*68
Schimel, J. 272 *n*34
Schindler, S. 272 *n*32
Schleiermacher, F. 29, 30
Schouten, A. P. 103
Schutz, A. 22, 192
Scruton, R. 43
Seara-Cardoso, A. 57 *n*39
Sebanz, N. 70
Sebastián-Gallés, N. 214
Seigel, J. 160
Seiryte, A. 73
Seitschek, T. 121
Sellaro, R. 150
Semin, G. 75
Senju, A. 70 *n*67, 155

Senzaki, S. 36

Setodji, C. M. 263 *n*12

Shamay-Tsoory, S. G. 78 *n*86, 261

Shang, Y. 235 *n*13

Shanks, D. R. 51 *n*32

Shariatmadari, D. 116 *n*24

Shariff, A. 153

Sheng, F. 121 *n*31

Shenhav, A. 56 *n*38

Sherif, M. 121

Sherrington, C. 51

Shinohara, K. 68

Shoup, M. L. 67

Shteynberg, G. 77 *n*84, 77 *n*85, 209, 209 *n*9

Shumsky, E. 74 *n*78

Shuto, T. 91

Sidanius, J. 109 *n*18

Sidis, B. 102 *n*12

Siller, M. 41

Simpson, A. J. 187

Simpson, E. A. 26, 72 *n*72

Simpson, J. A. 182

Simpson, S. J. 111

Singer, T. 74 *n*76

Sinnott-Armstrong, W. 303 *n*53

Skerry, A. E. 87

Skitka, L. J. 230 *n*11

Skjelsbæk, I. 271 *n*29

Skuse, D. H. 118

Slaby, J. 159

Slade, P. 139 *n*8

Sloman, S. F. P. 170, 273

Slote, M. 92 *n*4

Smeets, M. A. M. 62 *n*55

Smiley, C. 239

Smith, A. 29 *n*10, 93, 177, 204, 211

Smith, K. E. 61 *n*51, 228

Snidman, N. 59

Soames, S. 174

Sofianidis, G. 72

Sofsky, W. 113

Solera, F. 223

Soll, J. B. 206

Solomon, S. 256 *n*7, 258, 264, 264 *n*16

Sommer, M. 60, 126, 165

Sommerville, J. A. 93 *n*5

Sonnby-Borgstrom, M. 65

Soto, J. 119 *n*28

Soussignan, R. 50, 62 *n*56, 70

Sowden, S. 150

Spanoudis, G. 156

Spears, R. 95

Spelke, E. S. 87

Spence, D. P. 175

Spence, N. 175

Sperber, D. 170, 230

Spinrad, T. L. 89, 92

Sripokangkul, S. 239

Stahlberg, D. 272 *n*32

Steckler, C. M. 34, 74

Stefanovics, E. A. 239 *n*19

Stein, E. 24, 30, 34, 74, 75

Stein, J. 60

Stein, T. 62, 70

Stephan, A. 159

Stevenson, M. 55, 119 *n*28

Stevenson, R. J. 83, 137

Stillman, T. F. 83

Stoll, S. 138

Strachan, E. 263 *n*14

Strachan, J. W. A. 106

Strandburg-Peshkin, A. 110, 112 *n*22

Straton, D. 103

Streeter, S. A. 67

Striano, T. 69

Strube, M. 156

Stuart, S. A. J. 66

Sturm, V. E. 64

Suarez, R. 271 *n*27

Sullivan, A. C. 272

Sullivan, R. M. 87

Sun, Z. 106

Sundararajan, L. 198

Surowiecki, J. 200 *n*1, 202 *n*4

Sutton, M. 266

Swiderska, A. 242 *n*26
Sword, G. A. 111

Tajfel, H. 119 *n*27
Takahashi, H. 56 *n*35
Tamietto, M. 76 *n*79
Tantam, D. 61 *n*54, 66, 67, 68 *n*65, 98,
    128, 164, 185 *n*5, 284 *n*40, 304
Tarde, G. 79, 97
Tarnita, C. E. 233
Taylor, G. 139 *n*8
Taylor, L. K. 103
Taylor, P. J. 288
Tero, A. 108
Tewari, S. 122 *n*34
Theidon, K. 126
Thigpen, C. 290 *n*44
Thomas, K. A. 212
Thomas, S. L. 278
Thompson, J. 149 *n*27
Tillas, A. 172
Tinbergen, N. 50, 58
Tipper, S. P. 69, 106
Titchener, E. 24
Todd, A. R. 187
Tollenaar, M. S. 225
Tomalski, P. 69
Tomasello, M. 155, 158
Tomelleri, S. 110 *n*20
Toulmin, S. 177
Tovey, C. 101 *n*11
Tracy, J. L. 34, 74
Trevarthen, C. 130
Trigg, D. 66
Trotter, W. 106 *n*17, 131 *n*39
Tsakiris, M. 48 *n*31, 73
Tucci, K. 124
Tuller, H. M. 238 *n*17
Tunçgenç, B. 25 *n*6
Turner, J. H. 129
Tylén, K. 72, 78, 164 *n*37
Tyrlik, M. 49

Ueda, R. 140 *n*12
Ünal, E. 83
Underwood, M. K. 237 *n*16
United Nations 250 *n*1
Urgesi, C. 72 *n*73
Urmson, J. O. 180
Uvnas-Moberg, K. 54

Vaes, J. 242
Valdesolo, P. 20 *n*2, 20 *n*3
Valencia, J. 134 *n*2
van Aken, M. A. G. 53
van Baaren, R. 25 *n*5
van Bakel, H. J. 50
Van de Vondervoort, J. W. 87
van den Hooff, B. 103
Van Der Pligt, J. 266
Van Deurzen, E. 78, 194 *n*11
Van Dillen, L. F. 240
Van Hiel, A. 98
Van Lange, P. A. M. 91
Van Langen, M. A. M. 252 *n*3
van Zonneveld, L. 294
Vander Heyden, K. M. 178 *n*3
Vandevoorde, J. 287 *n*42
Vanman, E. J. 70
Vanzomeren-Dohm, A. A. 182
Varga, S. 128 *n*37
Vaughan, C. A. 263 *n*12
Vautier, E. 265 *n*19
Vazansky, A. 262 *n*11
Veening, J. G. 118
Veenstra, L. 56 *n*36
Vercelli, A. 64
Verissimo, D. S. 66
Vernot, B. 255 *n*5
Vico, G. 205
Visser, B. A. 295
Vitalaki, E. 25 *n*8
Volk, A. A. 295
Vollm, B. A. 155
Voorthuis, A. 68, 119
Vygotsky, L. 158

Wagner, J. B. 70
Walker-Andrews, A. S. 140 *n*11
Wall, I. R. 226
Wallrabenstein, I. 53
Walt, S. M. 265 *n*17
Wang, Y. 166
Ward, J. 73 *n*75
Warwick Blood, R. 278
Watanabe, T. 93
Waters, S. F. 226
Watson-Jones, R. E. 123 *n*35
Wauson, M. S. 222 *n*5
Weber, S. 140, 282
Webster, R. J. 239 *n*21
Weeks, J. L. P. 265 *n*17
Wegner, D. M. 95
Weisel, O. 120, 240 *n*22, 245 *n*33
Weisfeld, G. E. 213
Weisfeld, M. B. 213
Welch, M. 278
Wenzel, M. 238
Wesson, D. W. 225
West, T. V. 226
Whissell, T. 62 *n*57
Whiten, A. 182 *n*4
Whitlock, F. A. 289
Whittaker, J. 68 *n*65
Wiik, K. L. 26
Wilczak, B. 266 *n*21, 267
Williams, H. 30
Williams, T. 272 *n*34
Wilson, E. O. 233, 234 *n*12
Wilson, J. R. 151
Wiltermuth, S. 20 *n*4
Wimmer, H. 39 *n*24
Wing, L. 47 *n*30
Winnicott, D. W. 89, 197
Wittgenstein, L. 21, 172
Wlodarski, R. 44, 84
Wohl, M. J. A. 272 *n*34

Wojtyla, K. 43
Wood, M. 239 *n*20, 243
Woodford, J. 116
Woodruff, G. 39 *n*23, 154 *n*32, 155
Woollard, F. 149
WWF 158

Xavier, J. 65
Xiao, N. G. 119

Yalom, I. D. 58
Yamamuro, K. 64
Yanagizawa-Drott, D. 208
Yanega, D. 233
Yang, S. 161
Yang, X. 62 *n*60, 158
Yang, Y. 103
Ye, Y. 235 *n*13
Yeo, J. H. 66
Yokouchi, K. 54
Yokoyama, T. 62, 70
Yu, C. 101 *n*10, 202
Yu, R. 118
Yuill, N. 77 *n*83

Zahavi, D. 24, 30, 31 *n*11, 66
Zak, P. J. 118
Zakrzewska, A. 236
Zara, G. 293
Zhang, J. Q. 100
Zhang, X. 235
Zhang, Y. 114
Zheng, H. 118
Zheng, X. 238
Zink, C. F. 118
Zisook, S. 288
Zlatev, J. 26, 44, 130
Zultan, R. 245 *n*33
Zumeta, L. N. 102 *n*13

Digby Tantam is Emeritus Professor of Psychiatry at the University of Sheffield, a Visiting Professor in the Department of Psychology at Middlesex University, and a Director of the Septimus group of companies. He is a practising psychiatrist and teacher in London. Digby is the author of *Can the World Afford Autistic Spectrum Disorder?*, *Autism Spectrum Disorders Through the Life Span* (both published by Jessica Kingsley), *Emotional Wellbeing and Mental Health* (Sage), and an editor or author of 11 other books, including the *Wiley World Handbook of Existential Therapy* (forthcoming: with Emmy van Deurzen; Simon du Plock; Erik Craig; Alfried Laengle; and Kirk Schneider).